Foundations of Linguistics

by
Franklin C. Southworth
and
Chander J. Daswani

THE FREE PRESS
A Division of Macmillan Publishing Co., Inc.
NEW YORK

Collier Macmillan Publishers
LONDON

Copyright © 1974 by The Free Press
A Division of Macmillan Publishing Co., Inc.

The Free Press
A Division of Macmillan Publishing Co., Inc.
866 Third Avenue, New York, N.Y. 10022

Collier–Macmillan Canada Ltd.

Library of Congress Catalog Card Number: 73-9137

Printed in the United States of America

printing number

1   2   3   4   5   6   7   8   9   10

Library of Congress Cataloging in Publication Data

Southworth, Franklin C
    Foundations of linguistics.

    Bibliography: p.
    1. Linguistics.   I. Daswani, Chander J., joint
author. II. Title.
P121.S65   410   73-9137
ISBN 0-02-930300-1

Contents

Part III: Meaning 171

Part IV: Sociolinguistics 231

Part V: Historical–Comparative Linguistics 275

Part VI: Applied Linguistics 319

Preface

This book is intended to appeal to the range of student interest represented in the typical introductory linguistics course. Students in such courses include those who are contemplating a career in linguistics or in related fields (such as anthropology or language teaching), as well as those motivated by a general interest in the workings of language and its relationship to other human activities. Because the book is intended for such a wide audience, we have tried to present a fairly broad spectrum of views which would be representative of contemporary linguists, rather than a single self-consistent system such as an individual teacher might prefer to present, or which some other textbooks in the field have presented.

Accordingly, we have presented some views which might be identified with structural linguistics, some associated with transformational–generative linguistics, and others derived from sociolinguistics and anthropological linguistics. We have tried to show the way in which these different views are related. Nevertheless, the differences among them might appear as inconsistencies without a word of warning. Specifically:

(1) In Part I, Chapter 3 presents a structuralist view of phonology, which can be contrasted with that of Chapter 6, derived from recent work in transformational–generative theory. We view these two approaches as each having a certain value, though in different spheres. The first has been primarily concerned with questions of transcription, and is therefore relevant to various practical applications of linguistics (see for example Ch. 8). The second approach has grown out of theoretical questions of linguistic structure, particularly the relationship between phonological rules and other types of grammatical rules. The practical implications of this work are not yet

particularly apparent, though workers in this field feel that important theoretical advances have been made in recent years.

(2) Part II presents a somewhat traditional, structuralist picture of grammar (Chapters 10–12), as background for understanding the trans-formational–generative picture of Chapter 13. Again, the two approaches differ in their relative importance for practical and theoretical work. Chapter 17, at the end of Part III, is a continuation of the presentation of Part II, indicating the ways in which contemporary grammatical theory is attempting to deal with semantics within the context of grammatical structure. We can distinguish the following four stages of development in the mainstream of grammatical theory: (1) the dominance of the structuralist approach (Chs. 10–12); (2) the first phase (pre-1964) of the transformational gen-erative approach (Ch. 12.2–13.8); (3) the second (post-1964) phase of this approach (Ch. 13.9–13.12); (4) later approaches, notably that of generative semantics and case grammar (Ch. 17). Chapters 10–13 and 17 are written so that they can be read consecutively. The reader should be forewarned, however, that the ground rules have changed in each of these phases, and there is a need to be alert for these changes. For example, the requirement of the later TG theory that transformations do not change meanings (see 13.10) has necessitated changes in the formulation of a number of trans-formations, such as those presented in 13.7.

(3) Part III combines some traditional approaches to the study of meaning (Ch. 14) with some viewpoints derived from anthropological linguistics (Chs. 15–16), in addition to the formal linguistic approach of Chapter 17.

Parts I–III represent the core of a course in linguistics. Parts IV–VI are intended to provide brief introductions to three related fields: sociolinguistics, historical–comparative linguistics, and applied linguistics, with suggested supplementary readings for each. Taken all together, the book contains more than enough material for a one-semester introductory course, and thus gives the instructor a choice of coverage. With the supplementary readings, the book could be used as the basis for a two-semester course covering these ancillary fields along with the basic material on descriptive linguistics.

ACKNOWLEDGMENTS

The authors wish to acknowledge the substantial help given by Professors Joseph Williams and Sarah Thomason, who both read a preliminary version of the text and offered many valuable suggestions. (The authors take respon-sibility for the presentation of their suggestions, as well as for any possible errors of interpretation or fact.) We also wish to thank Mr. H. C. Narang, who prepared the Index.

Chapter 1

LANGUAGE
AS AN OBJECT OF STUDY

tyala təhan lagli ahe (Marathi)
Er hat Durst (German)
avanukku taaham (Tamil)
kayatibe nísa (Zapotec)
haʔtaːthɛs (Seneca)

1.1 SOME QUESTIONS ABOUT LANGUAGE

For the majority of people in the world, the above sentences are gibberish.
Yet all of these happen to be different ways of conveying a message corresponding to the English sentence 'He is thirsty'. Even a superficial
examination indicates them to be very different from each other: apart from
the differences in sounds, they also differ in the number of separate words.
A more detailed analysis indicates even greater differences: the Marathi
sentence means literally "to-him (tyala) thirst (təhan) attached (lagli)
is (ahe)"; the German means "He has thirst"; the Tamil sentence
means "to-him thirst", and where the context makes it clear, could

1

be simply expressed as *taaham* 'thirst'; in Zapotec, the sentence means "he-is-dying (kayati-be 'dying–he') water"; and the single Seneca word can be analyzed as h-aʔta:-thɛ-s "(as for) me–inside part–be dry–action in progress".

There is no human society which does not possess a language. Thus, language is, first of all, a defining characteristic of society. Beyond this, it is our most highly developed system of communication and symbolization, intimately linked with thinking and intelligence. Anyone can state this without knowing very much about how language works, or how it functions in society. In order to understand how important it really is, we must ask more detailed questions, and seek the answers by observation, inference, and scientific reasoning. Most of the really interesting questions about language are still unanswered. Some questions, such as those regarding the origin of language and its early diffusion, can only be speculated about (see 23.4).

Scholars who are concerned with the observation of language in its various manifestations have amassed great quantities of detailed information about the formal properties of language. They have formulated rules which govern how we combine sounds and other linguistic elements, how these elements relate to the situations in which they are used, and to the phenomena to which they refer.

In other words, linguists have discovered a great deal about the what and the how of various languages. As they amass more and more information, we learn more about how to approach some of the *why* questions of language, and why they have remained so long unanswered. For example, of the six possible orderings of the elements subject–verb–object which could theoretically occur, why are only three (VSO, SVO, SOV) found in any significant proportion as dominant orders among the world's languages? Seeking the answer to such a question could lead us to look for correlations in cognitive processes, stages of language learning, social behavior, structural constraints within the language, and perhaps elsewhere. We do not know in advance whether the answer to such a question is likely to be trivial, or perhaps a significant generalization about language behavior.

Questions about the *why* of language can often be answered on several different levels. For example, if we ask why a particular word is used in a particular way, or why it has a particular meaning, the most obvious and superficial answer is that the word was used this way by speakers of a preceding generation (sometimes with slight differences), by the generation preceding that one, etc. Thus, English speakers nowadays use the word *bread* because the word has come down to them from Old English *brēad* with various changes in pronunciation. (Why does pronunciation change? This is one of the big unanswered questions, though linguists have some ideas about it; see Ch. 22.) Similarly, French speakers call their cultural equivalent of bread *pain*, Spanish speakers call it *pan*, Italian speakers call it *pane*, etc., because of divergent changes from an original Latin *panis*. In some cases the inquiry ends there, because historical sources do not furnish any more interesting information. In other cases, the search may reveal the motivation for a particular usage: for example, when we trace the history of English *book* and *write*, we find a single Old English word *bōc* which meant both 'book' and 'beech' (tree) and we find that *write* is related to earlier words meaning 'scratch' or 'tear', leading to the supposition that the ancestors of our books were pieces of beech wood with (probably Runic) characters scratched on them. It can be surmised that, as writing became more common, the word *write* gradually lost the meaning 'scratch', etc., and as books came to be made of other materials, the words *book* and *beech* came to be differentiated from each other.

1.2 THE RELEVANCE OF THE STUDY OF LANGUAGE

A fundamental distinction needs to be made between the study of LANGUAGE and the study of A LANGUAGE. The primary task of a LANGUAGE STUDENT is to acquire certain practical skills, which will permit him to perform such activities as conversing, reading, eavesdropping, or interpreting literature. The STUDENT OF LANGUAGE, on the other hand, is often more concerned with general properties of language structure, and how they are exemplified in a particular language, than with the acquisition of skills. Of course, the language learner is often motivated by general curiosity about "the way language works", and the student of language may also want to learn to use a language.

But it is clear that a language can be studied from different points of view and for different purposes, even though many students may be motivated to some extent by both of these goals. The closest parallel to this distinction can perhaps be found in the study of mathematics: most students of this subject are concerned with its use as a tool, which they need in scientific research or some practical sphere of work. A few are interested in it for its own sake. The latter are likely to become teachers of mathematics, and to make theoretical contributions which are of interest primarily to other mathematicians. Of course, it is possible for a person to combine this type of interest with others, and disciplines like mathematical logic and mathematical physics have arisen in response to this sharing of concerns among different fields. This parallel also holds for the student of language, who may be in addition a social anthropologist, a language teacher, a lexicographer, a psychologist, a logician, or various other things.

A specialist in the study of language, in the sense just described, is known as a LINGUIST, and his field of study is called LINGUISTICS. (The popular use of the term *linguist* in the meaning "person skilled in a number of languages" will be avoided here—though of course an individual can be a linguist in both senses.) The relationship between this field of study and others is perhaps most obvious in the case of language teaching, though we must point out that while some are both linguists and language teachers, many language teachers are not linguists and vice versa. A language teacher usually has some practical knowledge of the language being taught, as well as some professional interest in it (for example, as a student of its literature). He will generally make use of some sort of teaching materials such as teaching manuals, tapes, and films, usually prepared by others.

If he is a linguist, he may prepare such materials himself, either basing them on his own research and observations of the language, or on an already-existing DESCRIPTIVE GRAMMAR of the language, and possibly also a CON-TRASTIVE GRAMMAR (which compares the structures of two languages and provides information relevant to teachers about the problems most likely to be encountered by speakers of one language when learning the other). The person who writes such a grammar needs to know not only the language, but also ways to observe, analyze, and present information about linguistic usage; as will be seen from the following chapters, such techniques are often very indirectly related to the particular uses which the student has in mind when undertaking the study of a new language.

Linguistic study is also important to other spheres of activity, though not as directly or obviously as to language teaching. In some cases, the theoretical findings of linguistics (for example, the existence of properties such as those discussed in 1.6) are of interest to scholars in other fields. The fields of cultural anthropology and sociology have been traditionally very close to linguistics, and a considerable exchange of ideas and cross-fertilization has taken place over the years. For the anthropologist, the study of language is not only important as a technique for acquiring language skills for communication in a new society where he may want to work, but is also part of the methodology of analyzing social behavior, of which language is an important part. Archaeologists and students of prehistory use linguistics not only to decipher and interpret ancient texts, but also to construct theories (via the method of linguistic reconstruction, see 23.2) about the movement of prehistoric populations.

Several other fields can be mentioned which overlap in their subject-matter or theoretical orientations, and which have some potentiality for mutually beneficial collaboration with linguistics; for example, literature, literary history, and literary criticism; psychology and psychiatry; philosophy and logic; communications and communication engineering; language planning and educational language policy (see Ch. 25); language "development" (creation of new technical terms, new scripts, etc., for previously "undeveloped" languages). Because of such overlaps, people working in these fields sometimes study the methods of linguistics, and occasionally consult linguists about particular problems within their own disciplines.

1.3 THE FIELD OF LINGUISTICS

Though relatively small among academic disciplines, linguistics is large enough to accomodate quite a variety of approaches, and a number of competing notions as to what can properly be called "linguistics." Probably most linguists would agree that the central task of their field is to discover and describe the regularities in language behavior, though this task would be performed in very different ways by linguists committed to different theoretical biases.

In later chapters, we will discuss in detail some of the different approaches being used by linguists. As background for this, we may mention here a fundamental controversy which concerns the basic subject matter of linguistics. Until recently many linguists have accepted the view of Ferdinand de Saussure, a Swiss linguist who has perhaps the clearest right to the title "father of modern linguistics."

Saussure distinguished between *la langue* (the LANGUAGE SYSTEM shared by all speakers of a language) and *la parole* (the ACT OF SPEECH); he considered the former to be the true subject of linguistics, which is concerned with structural relations, and the second to be the subject-matter of ancillary fields like phonetics, which is concerned with the measurement of observed phenomena. He compared *la langue* to a symphony, which he believed to exist independently of the manner in which it is performed, and independently of any mistakes which might be committed at a particular performance. Though clearly recognizing the close relationship between langue and parole, Saussure claimed that:

> Language (*la langue*) exists collectively (*dans la collectivité*) in the form of a set of impressions deposited in each brain, rather like a dictionary of which all the copies, identical to each other, might be distributed among individuals. It is thus something which is in each person, and is at the same time common to all and lying outside the control of those who possess it. (1949, p. 38)

Many linguists have accepted the notion that *la langue* is the proper subject of linguistic study, and that it is deposited more or less in the same form in each individual. They have therefore assumed that the ABSTRACT

STRUCTURE of language can be sought more or less indifferently from any speaker. This structure is viewed as existing independently from any interferences deriving from *la parole* such as might be caused by memory lapses, interruptions, changes of mind in the middle of a sentence, overflows of emotion, and the like. This has inevitably led them to concentrate on specimens of language out of normal social context—ideal samples (as it were) of the ideal language system. This approach has been extremely successful up to the present, and though some may have felt that the study of *la parole* was being neglected, it is only recently that there has been any great outcry about this. (This question is discussed further in 20.1; see also 18.1, last paragraph.)

Although they disagree about such principles, linguists (as opposed to anthropologists, philologists, historians, literary scholars, etc.) share the belief that the object of their study is *the language itself*, and their purpose is to examine and describe its nature and its internal relationships. It is not to use linguistic facts for the purpose of explaining some other phenomenon, such as mental processes or social behavior. Thus the linguist is primarily a writer of rules, which account for his (and others') observations. Ideally, the linguist's rules are presented as descriptive grammars, which account for the way a language is used in a SPEECH COMMUNITY (any group of people who communicate with each other by means of a language). Ideally, these descriptions are used by specialists in other fields (see 1.2) who can apply the findings to their own problems. As it happens, neither of these ideal statements corresponds to the prevalent reality, for a number of reasons. First of all, there is widespread disagreement among linguists on a comprehensive theory which would permit the writing of definitive overall grammars of the type mentioned; this disagreement includes methods of data collection, sampling procedures, methods of analysis, criteria of evidence, methods of presentation, and assumptions about the nature of verbal behavior. Thus, it is much more common for linguists to deal with isolated parts of language structure in the form of short articles, and to frequently reformulate their conclusions. Often such articles are written primarily in order to prove a theoretical point. Incidentally, though linguists have been very critical of traditional grammarians because they have insensitively imposed the categories of Latin grammar on all languages, whether appropriate or not, it is also true that these scholars produced a substantial number of usable (if imperfect) linguistic descriptions, many of which have not yet been replaced by more up-to-date versions.

Another major reason why linguists have failed to achieve complete agreement about their discipline is that they cannot agree on what is in fact relevant to their study. Thus non-linguists find much that linguists write to be unreadable, to be concerned with superficial aspects of speech which appear irrelevant to the way people really communicate. Perhaps some of these defects will be repaired by future linguists. For the sake of a little perspective, we may note briefly some of the things which an "ideal grammar" would have to contain if it were to satisfy all of its potential users. It would contain not only the rules of pronunciation and grammar, but the total vocabulary as used by all groups within the speech community. It would include all local variants and all socially differentiated dialect forms (see 18.3). It would list complete details of the phonetic measurements of all sounds in all positions (e.g, at the beginnings and ends of words), in all styles of speech. Some users might demand frequency counts of sounds and words (useful for the development of shorthand systems and typewriter keyboards), as well as frequencies of combinations of sounds (needed for studies of perception), etc. For any one language, even that of a small speech community, such a grammar would be a lifetime job for several linguists. This indicates what present-day linguists are demanding of themselves, and explains why so much of the task remains to be done.

1.4   TYPES OF LINGUISTIC STUDY

It is customary to distinguish two major divisions of linguistic study, known as DESCRIPTIVE (or SYNCHRONIC) LINGUISTICS, and HISTORICAL (or DIACHRONIC) LINGUISTICS. This distinction owes its first clear formulation to Saussure (see 1.3), who was a strong proponent of the study of a language as a coherent system with its own internal logic and relationships. The main emphasis in Saussure's day was on the study of historical development of language, and many scholars of that period viewed a language as simply the aggregate end-point of a variety of unconnected historical processes. Saussure's insistence on the systematic structural properties of language led to the creation of the field of STRUCTURAL LINGUISTICS.

Synchronic and diachronic linguistics are interdependent fields, for they share a number of assumptions and methods, as well as a division into three principal segments known as PHONOLOGY (the study of sounds), GRAMMAR (the study of forms and their combinations), and SEMANTICS (the study of meaning). Each of these is also a subfield which can be examined from either a diachronic or synchronic viewpoint, thus giving rise to descriptive phonology (Chs. 3–6), descriptive grammar (Chs. 9–13), descriptive semantics (Chs. 14, 17), historical phonology (21.2–3), historical grammar (21.4), and historical semantics (21.5). (The terms *descriptive grammar* and *historical grammar* are also used in the sense of the overall synchronic and diachronic study of a language, respectively.)

Other types of linguistic study which may be mentioned in this brief

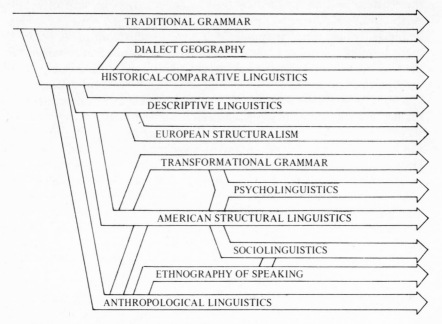

Figure 1.1. Development of principal trends in Western linguistics.

overview, and which are described elsewhere in this book, are: DIALECT GEOGRAPHY (18.2), TRANSFORMATIONAL-GENERATIVE LINGUISTICS (Chs. 13, 17), SOCIOLINGUISTICS (Ch. 20), ANTHROPOLOGICAL LINGUISTICS, and its most recent form, the ETHNOGRAPHY OF SPEAKING (18.1). The historical relationships among these are depicted in a rough way in the accompanying diagram; each of the branchings represents one or more individuals who were trained in the earlier field (represented as the source of the branch), and who created a new field or subfield by extensive innovations in methodology and scope of their work.

1.5   STATUS OF LINGUISTICS AS A SCIENCE

Considering that modern linguistics traces its ancestry both to traditional grammar (cultivated primarily by students of classical languages) and to anthropology, it is not surprising that some linguists consider themselves social scientists, whereas others would place their field among the humanities. Some features of both appear in the work of most linguists. At the same time, many linguists have clearly tried to create a more empirical base for their field, so that statements made by linguists could be verified as rigorously as scientists verify their statements, and would not simply reflect the impressions, whims, and tastes of those who make them. This drive has not, however, been strong enough to prevent bias in data selection and presentation, or in the selection of problems for study, because of assumptions about the nature of language which are often based on philosophical positions, rather than on the linguistic data alone. On the other hand, there has been general agreement (at least in principle) on two empirical points. The first is that linguistic study is DESCRIPTIVE, rather than PRESCRIPTIVE. Linguists have insisted on this point largely because they are reacting against some of the work of traditional grammarians, as seen particularly in the school grammars of European languages of the nineteenth and early twentieth centuries.

The modern linguist claims that his concern is with reporting actual usage, whereas the traditional grammarian emphasized "proper" usage, usually restricted to the formal written variety of the language. Some of the best-known traditional grammarians, such as Jespersen and Kruisinga, based their work on observation of actual usage, and did not indulge in normative judgments. It has also been pointed out that the traditional grammars often tolerated ordinary conversational usage. By and large, however, the grammarian's purpose was and is to legislate a relatively restricted norm, which is almost always that of the educated elite. (Elitism is not unknown in modern linguistics; see Ch. 19.)

The tendency to legislate was often linked with the assumption that there is a single basic logic which underlies all grammatical systems. This logic was often thought to appear in its purest form in the classical languages of Europe, Greek and Latin. Modern linguists, on the other hand, would insist that the description of a language should be congruent with the structure observed, and not based on the categories of some other language, some external logic. Thus, we would require that the description be INTERNALLY MOTIVATED.

The classic example of failure to observe this principle is the application of the inflectional systems of Latin to languages like English, which lack most of the Latin categories. If, for example, we set out to describe the English verb in such terms, we would end up with the following list of six forms in the present tense:

Singular	First person (I)	*love*	(Latin: amo
	Second person (you)	*love*	amas
	Third person (he/she)	*loves*	amat
Plural	First person (we)	*love*	amāmus
	Second person (you)	*love*	amātis
	Third person (they)	*love*	amant)

(Since English has only two forms—*love* and *loves*—for most verbs, the full apparatus of Latin grammar is not needed.) Traditional grammarians argue that, since the Latin categories are "logical," and since they fit most languages (i.e., most languages do not have *more* than six forms), there is no reason not to base the description on the Latin system. Though this may have been an argument at a time when one could expect the users of a grammar to know Latin, this is no longer valid. Further, the requirement of congruence means that we expect our grammatical description to correspond to the way in which native speakers use the language, which includes how they learn it, what kinds of mistakes they make, how they generalize constructions, etc. It is hardly possible to do this if we assume in advance that only certain principles of linguistic organization are permissible. (These remarks, which are rather abstract and without detailed examples, can be understood more clearly on the basis of the discussion in Parts II and III.)

1.6 SOME PROPERTIES OF LANGUAGE

When a person says, 'I'm thirsty', he is producing a series of sound waves in the atmosphere, which are related to a sensation which is of some significance to him and to any person who hears and understands him. In other words, he is converting *meaning* into *sound*. The person who understands him, does so by reversing the process and converting the sounds he hears into meaning. (Of course this is done instantaneously and unconsciously, and often may be assisted by non-verbal cues such as gestures.) This is, in essence, the most common function of language, though it also has other functions (see 14.9, 18.1). This activity is made possible by several properties, which are found in all languages, and which we can call SEMANTICITY, CONVENTIONALITY, and DUALITY. By SEMANTICITY we mean simply the fact that there is a constant relationship between certain parts of the linguistic signal (such as the word *thirsty*, or *thirst*) and certain observable or describable phenomena in the real world (such as the sensation in one's insides which we know requires liquid to be satisfied). This relationship between word and sensation is not, however, innate in man, but is CONVENTIONAL: that is, there is no reason other than the existence of a tradition for English speakers to use the word *thirsty* for this sensation, or for French speakers to say *soif* 'thirst', Tamil speakers to say *taaham*, etc. The grammatical differences in these cases are also conventional or arbitrary; that is, there is no natural reason for the fact that English uses an adjective, German a noun, and Seneca a verb to refer to the sensation of thirst.

An additional feature, of great importance in the structure of human language, is the DUAL ORGANIZATION of every linguistic utterance. The number of distinctive sound units or PHONEMES used in any language is rather small, generally under fifty. These sound units have no meaning in themselves, but can be combined into thousands and thousands of distinct meaningful linguistic units known as MORPHEMES—such as *bin, pin; bet, pet; beer, peer;* etc. Each of these pairs of words is distinguished by the same difference in sound, though the sounds represented by *b* and *p* do not mean anything in isolation. It seems obvious that speech as we know it could not exist without this dual organization. If each meaningful unit had to be totally distinct in sound from all others, then we would either have to be content with a very small vocabulary, or else we would have to learn to distinguish thousands of different sounds. Even assuming we could do this, communication would be possible only over very short distances, and would be made impossible by any extraneous noises.

The features of conventionality and semanticity also appear in the communication systems of non-human creatures, but the organization of human language is much more complex and flexible, because of the feature of duality as well as two other features: PRODUCTIVITY, and DISPLACEMENT. Productivity refers to the capacity of human speakers to combine meaningful elements into new meaningful utterances which they have never heard before, but which are immediately understandable to hearers who know the language (see 9.1 for some examples). Displacement refers to the possibility of talking about something which is not present in the immediate environment (such as events which occurred in the past), or which is non-existent (such as a unicorn) or hypothetical. Man is almost unique in having this capacity, which makes him the only animal able to lie. (Honey-bees are able to transmit information about distant sources of food to other bees, but they are not known to lie about them.)

All human languages have three interrelated organizational systems: a PHONOLOGICAL system, a GRAMMATICAL system, and a SEMANTIC system. Therefore, every language must have a set of sounds, a set of grammatical elements, a set of grammatical rules which determine the possible combinations of the elements, and a set of meanings which are expressible. It is the business of the linguist to describe all of these. In the process of doing so, linguists have discovered certain units of description which appear to be useable for all languages, such as:

the DISTINCTIVE FEATURE (the minimal distinctive difference in sound, such as the feature which distinguishes *pin* from *bin* in English— see Ch. 6);

the PHONEME (the smallest unit of sound structure; thus, English *shin* contains three phonemes: /š/, /i/, /n/—see Ch. 3);

the MORPHEME (the minimal unit of grammatical structure: thus, *thirsty* contains two morphemes, *thirst* and *-y*—see 11.1);

the SEMANTIC COMPONENT (the minimal feature of meaning, such as the feature FEMALE which distinguishes *girl* from *boy*—see 16.2).

Linguists have also recognized (or, in some cases, adapted from traditional grammar) certain organizing principles of language structure, such as:

the principle of HIERARCHICAL STRUCTURE, which makes possible the analysis of utterances of different degrees of complexity in terms of the same basic parts (see 10.1);

the distinction between DEEP STRUCTURE and SURFACE STRUCTURE, and the existence of TRANSFORMATIONAL RELATIONSHIPS between them.

This last point, which is discussed in Chapter 13, can be illustrated briefly by the following examples:

1   His refusal slightly surprised me.
2   Her insistence finally annoyed me.
3   Their dog really bit me.

Each of these sentences consists of a subject (*his refusal, her insistence, their dog*), an adverb (*slightly, finally, really*), a transitive verb form (*surprised, annoyed, bit*), and an object (*me*). In spite of this superficial similarity, sentence 3 is clearly different from 1 and 2. We can explain this difference by noting that sentences 1 and 2 can be paraphrased by sentences of a more complex type (such as *He refused and that surprised me slightly*, or *The fact that he refused surprised me slightly*, etc.), whereas this cannot be done with sentence 3. In this case, we could say that the resemblance between sentence 3 and the others is merely in the surface structure, whereas in the deep structure sentences like 1 and 2 are equivalent to complex sentences formed from two or more simple sentences.

1.7   ORGANIZATION OF THIS BOOK

The first three parts of this book treat the basic component parts of descriptive linguistics: phonology (I), grammar (II), and semantics (III). Part IV deals with sociolinguistics, a relatively new approach to linguistics (some might consider it a separate branch); Part V is devoted to historical linguistics and its uses; Part VI discusses two major areas (language teaching and language planning) in which linguistic principles are being applied to practical problems by linguists and others. The organization reflects in general the order in which the authors think the book should logically be read, but we have tried to present each section in a way which would make it possible to take the sections in other orders, if desired.

NOTES

1.1 Seneca: Chafe 1967; Zapotec: Pickett 1960
   English *write, read*: Strang 1970, p. 395
   Word order in the world's languages: Greenberg 1963, pp. 58–90
1.6. Properties of language: Hockett 1960

SUGGESTED SUPPLEMENTARY READING

The field of linguistics and its history: Lyons 1968, Ch. 1 (overview of the history of linguistics in the west); Carroll 1953 (general description of the current state of linguistics in the United States); Joos 1966 (see especially editor's introduction and comments); Hall 1951 (development of linguistics in the United States, 1925–50); Greenberg 1968, Chs. 2–3 (the anthropological viewpoint); Dingwall 1971 (survey of some current approaches)

Linguistics and related fields: Saporta 1961; Mandelbaum 1951; Sebeok 1960; Brown 1970

Properties of language: Hockett 1960 (discussion of "design features" of language in relation to human and animal communication and the origin of speech); Greenberg 1963 (universal features of language—see especially articles by Hockett, Greenberg, Jakobson, Casagrande, Osgood)

Languages of the world: Meillet and Cohen 1952

Contrastive Grammar: Stockwell and Bowen 1965; Stockwell, Bowen, and Martin 1965 (Spanish); Agard and Di Pietro 1965 *a–b* (English and Italian)

FOLLOW-UP

(In this section, following each chapter, can be found a variety of items including questions to check your understanding of the chapter, items for individual study or class discussion, and suggestions for projects which can be carried out individually or in teams.)

1   Write brief definitions of the following terms used in this chapter: phonology, grammar, semantics.

2   Explain the distinction between the following pairs of terms: student of language—student of a language; descriptive (synchronic) linguistics—

historical (diachronic) linguistics; language system (*la langue*)—speech (*la parole*); descriptive grammar—prescriptive grammar.

3 Try to find examples to illustrate the following "design features" of language (see Hockett 1960): semanticity, conventionality, displacement, productivity, duality. According to Hockett, the first of these is present in gibbon calls, in the dancing of bees to indicate the location of a food source, and possibly in the songs of some birds. Arbitrariness is present in gibbon calls. Displacement and productivity characterize both gibbon calls and bee dancing, but duality of patterning exists only in human language. What do these facts indicate about the uniqueness of human language?

4 Suggestions for discussion:
   What is the relationship (if any) between linguistics and anthropology? sociology? psychology?
   What are the tasks of linguistics?
   (Discussing these questions at the beginning of a course may help to clarify areas of uncertainty, and may guide students in formulating more specific questions and seeking their answers.)

PART I

CHANNELS OF COMMUNICATION

Chapter 2

INTRODUCTION

2.1 KINDS OF CHANNELS

In studying any form of communication, some attention must be given at the outset to the nature of the channels through which messages are transmitted. In human language, most messages can be transmitted through different channels and still remain the same. For example, an English message such as "Wednesday mostly cloudy, high in the 70's" could be transmitted by various means: in writing, over the telephone, over the radio, or by word of mouth. In each case, the transmission is accomplished by different means: either by marks on paper, or by electrical impulses traveling over a wire, by radio waves in the atmosphere, or (in the case of normal speech) by sound waves moving from the speaker to the hearer. The message in each case is, in some sense, the same—since we would regard the written and spoken messages, for example, as having the same grammatical form, containing the same words, and conveying the same meaning. In this sense, then, the study of channels can be separated from the study of other aspects of linguistic structure, such as grammar (Part II) or semantics (Part III).

Ordinary human communication involves mainly the AUDITORY channel, in which messages are produced (or ENCODED) by the human vocal apparatus, and received (or DECODED) by the human ear. Apart from writing, the VISUAL channel is used for the transmission of gestures, facial expressions, and other signals which often accompany spoken language. (One should not confuse CHANNELS with MEDIA, i.e., the various systems for transmitting messages through a particular channel—for example, written, pictorial, and gestural media all use the visual channel.) One can also speak of a tactile channel, as for example in communication between a mother and an infant. In certain situations, one channel may be used to the exclusion of others: the visual channel is used exclusively in written communication, or in sign language as used by the deaf; the Braille writing system used by the blind makes use of the tactile channel; in using the telephone, we are restricted to the auditory channel, and cannot supplement with gestures (though many people do gesture in spite of this). The visual channel also has the common function of storing messages (in written form), though nowadays auditory messages can also be stored on records or tapes by means of recording devices. In most face-to-face communication situations, however, the auditory and visual channels function together in ways which often make it difficult to separate them (see Ch. 7).

The auditory channel itself can be subdivided into a number of different parts which function to some extent independently of one another. The following examples show (in written form) pairs of sentences which contrast with each other in different ways, by making use of different aspects of the auditory channel:

1   *a.* Come on!
     b. Come in!
2   *a.* He's out.
     b. He's out?
3   *a.* I SAW him.
     b. I saw HIM.

In example (1), the written difference between *on* and *in* (or between *o* and *i*) corresponds to a difference in the position of the speaker's vocal organs, primarily the position of his tongue and the degree of openness of his mouth (details below in Chapter 4); such differences are known technically as differences in SEGMENTAL PHONEMES. Example (2) shows, as well as possible within the limits of English punctuation, the difference in INTONATION which signals the distinction between a statement (with falling intonation) and a question (with rising intonation). Example (3) illustrates the well-known phenomenon of STRESS in English; the stress on SAW in 3*a* identifies what the speaker did (e.g., *saw* as opposed to *heard*), whereas the stress on *him* in

3b indicates the person seen. (Segmental phonemes are discussed in Chapter 3, and their physiological properties in Chapter 4; stress and intonation are treated in Chapter 5.)

Many other features could be mentioned. Differences in loudness, pitch, and speed (including drawled or clipped speech) tell us a great deal about a person's emotional state. Voice qualities not only tell us the sex and approximate age of the speaker, but also may enable us to identify individuals. Disturbances such as stuttering and hiccuping also may indicate something about the speaker's emotional state, as do certain sound effects such as a sobbing or raspy voice, or "vocal gestures" such as a Bronx cheer, a laugh, or a sigh. Permanent defects, such as cleft palate or missing teeth, also produce a response in the hearer, even though this may not be under the speaker's control; the same is true of temporary ailments such as a cold or sore throat. Dialect and foreign "accents" may or may not be under the speaker's control, but nevertheless have a communicative value. Some of these signals may appear to have no function in communication, but all are significant to the extent that they tell the hearer something about the speaker; in addition, most of these can be controlled to some extent by speakers, even if only in artificial situations (such as on the stage, where much use is made of many of these to represent particular emotions or situations). A complete study of human vocal communication would include all the above, and more. Linguists have concentrated on only a few of these different modes of communication; some others have been studied by psychologists, psychiatrists, or by linguists working in collaboration with others. This book will focus on those areas which are fairly well explored, though Chapter 7 presents a discussion of some of the areas which remain to be investigated.

2.2 REPRESENTING PRONUNCIATION

It should be obvious to any person who has studied a foreign language that there is a practical need for an accurate scheme to describe pronunciation. The languages that we study usually have some sort of writing system already, either one that is fairly close to the spoken form (such as the systems used for German, Spanish, Russian, or Hindi) or one that is less close (such as that used for English or Urdu). A few people, mainly anthropologists, missionaries, and linguists, have been obliged to deal with the problems of unwritten languages, and have had to develop general principles to guide them in working out new writing systems. It is largely from the work of such people that the original motivation arose to study techniques for describing and representing pronunciation. These techniques are now available for those who are interested in studying the role of pronunciation differences in human communication. This chapter and the following ones will present the general principles involved in setting up an accurate way of representing the pronunciation of a particular language.

The person who begins the study of a foreign language is faced with the problem of having to produce unfamiliar sounds. A system that would represent each different sound with a different symbol would help him identify and imitate those sounds. Such a system should indicate as many differences in sound as necessary. The problem is: what does necessary mean? It is clear that any differences which are significant to the native must be noted. As speakers of English we would not accept, for example, a system which failed to note the distinction between *beet* and *bit*, or between *tie* and *die*. On the other hand, there are many differences which are audible to a trained phonetician which we as natives would feel are not worth noting. For example, a little observation will show us that the initial consonants of *cool* and *keel*, though similar, differ in the place at which the tongue touches the roof of the mouth, as well as in the degree of rounding and protrusion of the lips. Similarly, one can observe a difference between the *t* sound in *cart*, and that in *bathtub* (i.e., the *t* of *tub* as it is pronounced in *bathtub*), though as English speakers we would not hesitate to say that these are the same sound. Further examples could be adduced, but they would only illustrate the point that there are a lot of differences which we do not notice, and which do not seem worth bothering with.

Now, consider the case of a speaker of French, who does not in his language distinguish between the vowels *bit* and *beet*, and who thus would find it difficult to make that distinction in English. To him, this may seem like a rather subtle distinction, primarily because it is not in his linguistic experience. Since this distinction is an obvious one to English speakers, the Frenchman's reaction may seem strange to us. In order to get an idea of how he feels, we can put ourselves in his position and look at one of the distinctions which exists in French, but is lacking in English. This can be illustrated by the following two sentences:

Donnez-moi deux thés.   'Give me two teas'
Donnez-moi deux taies.   'Give me two pillow-cases'

The difference in the final vowel sound is the only thing which distinguishes these two sentences from each other when spoken. (The two sounds are similar, though in the first the position of the tongue in the mouth would be higher than in the second. The first is similar to the vowel sound of English *day*, the second closer to the vowel of *dead*.) Most English speakers, in the initial stage of learning French, will render both of these sounds with the vowel sound of English *day*, thus making the two sentences identical. And yet, this distinction is as important to the Frenchman as the difference between *beet* and *bit* is to us. The English speaker fails to make the distinction because he has no comparable difference in his native speech (at least, not at the end of a word). The term MINIMAL PAIR is used for minimally different pairs of words such as *beet–bit* or *thé–taie*.

2.3 IDENTIFYING CONTRASTS

In studying a new language, we need to identify the critical distinctions in sound, that is, those which are significant to the native speaker. To a certain extent, a native speaker can help us, but we must interpret his information cautiously. Suppose we are investigating English, and we are told that the following is a minimal pair:

> Have you seen the prince?
> Have you seen the prints?

If, as newcomers to English, we are unable to hear this difference, we have several choices. We can keep trying to hear it, with the danger that we may end up convincing ourselves that the native must be right, and imagining that we hear something that is not there. This is in fact what sometimes happens in a teacher–student situation, when the student's insecurity prevents him from questioning the teacher's judgment; the teacher, on his part, may be misled by differences in spelling, and may compound the problem by using an artificial pronunciation.

Alternatively, we can simply decide that the native is wrong, and that he is deceiving himself. This is equally dangerous, since it means we rely completely on our own ears and reject the native's judgment. A better alternative than either of these is to check one native against another, in order to see whether the distinction which one claims to make is heard by the other. In the case of *prince* and *prints*, we might make this test by asking native A to say the two sentences in a predetermined but random order, and asking native B to write what he hears. In languages which have no writing systems, B could identify the members of the minimal pair by some other means, such as description or paraphrase. If speaker B can identify the word to the satisfaction of speaker A, then clearly there is a relevant distinction, and the newcomer must try to learn what it is. If, on the other hand, speaker B is unable to make the distinction, there are several possible explanations. If no speaker can be found who can identify the difference, then it is likely that A is deceiving himself, and we would look for some explanation for this. In the case given here, an obvious explanation would be the difference in spelling. Speakers of English have been known to insist that such pairs as *grey* and *gray*, *pour* and *pore*, *horse* and *hoarse* are distinct from each other—purely on the basis of spelling. (Actually, the last two are distinct for some Americans, but even those who do *not* distinguish them are occasionally confused by the difference in spelling.) In one case, an experienced linguist was obliged to admit that he had been misled into believing that words such as *latter* and *ladder* were distinct in his own speech. When challenged by one of his students, he submitted to being tested against himself by means of a tape recorder, using sentences such as:

A man had a ladder and a scaffold. He put the ladder [or latter] against the house.

When it turned out that he was unable to identify more than fifty percent of the sentences correctly, he was obliged to admit that the distinction was not there. Another explanation for such self-deception is the fact that certain distinctions which are present in careful or formal speech (for example, in lecture style) tend to disappear in more relaxed, informal speech. This is the case with *latter* and *ladder* for many Americans, and also for many other distinctions. Most educated Americans can distinguish the following pair of sentences, but most would normally not do so:

I want to see everyone except John.
I want to see everyone accept John.

The reason for insisting on an empirical test of minimal pairs is that most people are not aware of such variations in style, or the inconsistent ways in which speech and writing are often related.

On the other hand, it may turn out that speaker A is right, even if speaker B is not able to identify a distinction. This will often be true if A and B speak different dialects, and can only be verified by finding a speaker who has the same dialect as A. If, for example, A is a New Yorker, he may insist that the following written sentence has two pronunciations which are distinct in meaning: We eat what we can. In one reading, this means 'We eat what we are able', and in the other it means 'We eat what we put in cans'. Other Americans have been observed to scoff at the statement that these are different, but many New Yorkers are able to hear the distinction with 100 percent accuracy. Similarly, in the speech of many Americans, *merry* rhymes with *Mary*; these speakers are likely to have difficulty in recognizing the distinction when it occurs in the speech of others. Other familiar differences are that between *which* and *witch*, *where* and *wear* (apparently fast disappearing in the speech of most Americans), and that between *you* and *Hugh* which distinguishes sentences such as the following:

What did *you* think of it?
What did *Hugh* think of it?

The notion of SIGNIFICANT DISTINCTIONS, or CONTRASTS, in pronunciation requires some further clarification. While it is true that English speakers can hear the difference between *bit* and *beet* under good acoustic conditions (just as French speakers can hear the difference between *thé* and *taie*), it does not often happen that two sentences are distinguished from each other only by this single difference. It is true that one might say *Give me a bit* or *Give me a beet*, but normally the surrounding circumstances would make it clear which one was being asked for, even if the acoustic conditions were so bad that one could not hear the difference. This is amply demonstrated by the foreign speaker's ability to make himself understood most of the time, in spite of ignoring certain important distinctions. Thus, in general, there are very few cases where we have to rely solely on such minimal items of pronunciation in order to know what has been said. Nevertheless, there are certain circumstances in which we are called upon to observe these distinctions. Consider, for example, the problem of a hostess meeting a number of unknown people, whom she must then introduce to others. She must be able to distinguish between Mr. Peel and Mr. Beal, or between Mrs. Ditter and Mrs. Dieter, Miss Harper and Miss Hopper, purely on the basis of what she hears, in order to be able to pass the information on to some other person. As native speakers of English, we are all able to do this, given the appropriate conditions—that is, if there is not too much noise or general confusion taking place at the same time. The fact that we sometimes fail, and have to ask for a name to be spelled, is an indication of the importance of context, since if we do not hear a person's name properly, there is no context to help us. (Where dialect differences are involved, of course, spelling the name may have the function of facilitating the "translation" from one dialect to another.)

We will ask of our writing system not only that it represent such potential differences, but also that it be able to represent them consistently. Roughly, this means that we should be able to represent those sounds which sound the same with the same symbols, and those sounds which sound different with different symbols. Many spelling systems fail to meet this criterion. For example, the English word written *read* will rhyme with *reed* in a sentence such as "Did you read today's newspaper?" and with *red* in a sentence such as "I read a new book yesterday." The linguist requires that those forms which sound the same, such as *pour* and *pore*, should be written the same; those which sound different, such as *read* (present) and *read* (past), should have distinct spellings—though these principles can be suspended under certain circumstances (see Ch. 8).

SUGGESTED SUPPLEMENTARY READING

Gudschinsky 1967

FOLLOW-UP

1   Define the following terms used in this chapter: channel (of communication), medium (of communication), phoneme, minimal pair.

2   In the auditory channel, there is an intimate relationship between information load (the amount of information put into the channel) and channel noise (any disturbance which reduces the amount of information reaching the hearer, including extraneous sounds, foreign "accents," etc.). Can you think of situations in which one can "get the message" without having to hear everything said by a speaker? Can you think of the opposite kind of situation, where every sound is important?

3   What channels do the deaf-and-dumb use for communicating? What channels do the blind use? Are other channels possible? To what extent do people with unimpaired sight and hearing use any of these channels?

Chapter 3

PHONEMES AND
THEIR REPRESENTATIONS

This chapter will propose a system for writing the sounds of English designed to remedy the defects mentioned in the previous chapter, and to fulfil the requirements of a scientific writing system. In order to illustrate further the principles involved, it will also be useful to look briefly at two other languages which are quite different from English. For this purpose two languages of India, Tamil and Hindi-Urdu, have been chosen (see 3.6).

3.1 ENGLISH CONSONANTS

Native speakers of English the world over differ very little in the number of distinct consonant sounds they produce. (Vowels show a great deal of variation; see 3.5). The following set of twenty-one symbols can be used to represent those English consonants which occur most commonly at the beginnings of words; three aditional items are discussed below.

25

Symbol	*Examples* (in standard spelling)
/p/	*p*in, *p*at, *p*ie, *p*ill, *p*en, *p*ot, *p*eer
/t/	*t*in, *t*oo, *t*ie, *t*ill, *t*en, *t*ot, *t*ear
/c/	*ch*in, *ch*at, *ch*ew, *ch*ill, *ch*eer
/k/	*k*in, *c*at, *c*oo, *k*ill, *K*en, *c*ot
/b/	*b*in, *b*at, *b*oo, *b*uy, *b*ill, *B*en, *b*eer
/d/	*d*in, *d*o, *d*ie, *d*ill, *d*en, *d*ot, *d*eer
/j/	*g*in, *J*ew, *J*ill, *j*ay, *j*eer
/g/	*g*at, *g*oo, *g*uy, *g*ill, *g*ay, *g*ot, *g*ear
/m/	*m*at, *m*oo, *m*y, *m*ill, *m*ay, *m*ere
/n/	g*n*at, *n*ew, *n*igh, *n*il, *n*eigh, *n*ot, *n*ear
/f/	*f*in, *f*at, *f*ie, *f*ill, *f*ink, *f*en, *F*ay, *f*ear
/θ/	*th*in, *th*igh, *th*ink, *th*aw
/s/	*s*in, *s*at, *s*ue, *s*igh, *s*ill, *s*ay, *s*ot, *s*ear
/š/	*sh*in, *sh*oe, *sh*y, *sh*ill, *sh*ay, *sh*ot, *sh*ear
/v/	*v*at, *v*ie, *v*eal, *v*eer
/z/	*z*oo, *z*inc, *z*eal, *Z*en
/r/	*r*at, *r*ue, *r*ye, *r*ill, *r*ay, *r*ot, *r*ear
/l/	*L*ynn, *L*ou, *l*ie, *L*il, *l*ay, *l*ot, *l*eer
/y/	*y*ou, *y*en, *y*aw, *y*ear, *y*acht
/w/	*w*in, *w*oo, *Y*, *w*ill, *w*ay, *w*eir
/h/	*h*at, *wh*o, *h*igh, *h*ill, *h*en, *h*ay, *h*ot, *h*ere

Notes on the symbols:

1 The order in which the symbols are presented here is based on the phonetic characteristics of the phonemes. This will be made clear in Chapter 4.

2 The symbol /c/ is used where normal English spelling uses *ch*. Actually, there is no serious objection to using *ch*, but some linguists prefer a single symbol for economy's sake, and because the combination *c + h* is misleading from the point of view of pronunciation. The use of the letter *c* for this sound is also traditional in writing certain other languages, such as Italian.

3 /š/ and /θ/ (the latter borrowed from Greek) replace the usual *sh* and *th*, respectively. As in the case of /c/, a single symbol is preferred; there is no basis for treating these as consisting of more than one sound.

4 Note that /g/ represents *only* the initial sound of *get*, *got*, etc.; the initial sound of *gin* is represented by /j/.

The method of arriving at this list is that discussed in Chapter 2: by comparing minimally different messages (such as *It's a pill, It's a bill,* etc.), one arrives at an irreducible list of sounds which require distinct representations. The words given as examples provide minimal pairs for each contrasting pair of consonant sounds. This irreducible list of contrasting sounds can be called the PHONEMIC INVENTORY of the language, and each of them is known as a PHONEME. (The slant lines /.../ have traditionally been used to denote phonemes.)

3.2 MEDIAL CONSONANTS

The same set of contrasts can be demonstrated in other positions in English words; for example, all occur in the middle of words preceding a stressed vowel, and all but /h/ occur as well at the ends of words, as in the following examples:

/p/ apart, lip
/t/ atone, bit
/c/ achieve, much
/k/ akin, kick

/b/ above, stab
/d/ redeem, bid
/j/ rejoice, sage
/g/ ago, big

/m/ omit, slam
/n/ enough, pin

/f/ before, off
/θ/ rethink, lath
/s/ receive, pass
/š/ ashamed, mash

/v/ reveal, love
/z/ result, keys

/r/ serene, more (no example at end of words in "*r*-less" dialects)
/l/ alone, pool
/y/ coyote, boy
/w/ aware, now
/h/ ahoy (no example at end of word)

3.3 MARGINAL CONSONANTS

There are three additional consonant phonemes in English which have not yet been discussed, either because they could not be satisfactorily illustrated at the beginnings of words, or because they involve low-frequency contrasts. All of the contrasts already shown are readily understood and accepted by English speakers, but the three remaining ones are often less easily grasped; and therefore they are singled out for special treatment here.

It is likely that most speakers of English are unaware that the sound written *th* in the words *thigh, thin, ether,* etc. is different from that in *thy, then, either;* but when this is pointed out, it is usually easily recognized. The contrast between /θ/ (as in *thin*) and /ð/ (as in *thou*) is difficult to demonstrate because both are rather rare sounds, in the sense that the number of words in which they occur is small (although in frequency of occurrence, /ð/ is actually very high because it appears in the words *the, that, this, then, they,* etc.). Minimal pairs can be found to contrast /ð/ with /θ/, for example:

/θ/: Give them ether.
/ð/: Give them either.

This pair, of course, only works for those who say *either* with the vowel of *eat;* it is not a minimal pair for those who pronounce *either* with the vowel of *eye.* For all the other initial consonants, the words *that, thy, then,* and *they* provide minimal pairs with the words given in 3.1.

Another phoneme which presents a similar problem is the final consonant of *beige* and *rouge,* written /ž/ (parallel with /š/). This same consonant also occurs in words like *vision, delusion, collision.* It is rare initially, though those who have the word *genre* /žanrə/ in their vocabulary do use it. It is also a relatively new phoneme, and thus it is difficult to find minimal pairs to contrast it with certain other phonemes. The following pairs have been proposed to contrast it with /š/: *illusion–Aleutian, delusion–dilution, glazier–glacier, azure–Asher, confusion–Confucian.* Near pairs, such as *vision–fission, closure–kosher, evasion–ovation, treasure–thresher,* are plentiful enough to show that there is contrast in terms of general position.

The third case to be mentioned here involves the sound represented as *ng* in words like *thing, things, singer;* this sound also does not occur initially in English. Apart from this it presents difficulty because, although many English speakers distinguish between the sound in *singer* and that in *finger,* many others do not. For those who distinguish these, we can write /ŋ/ for the sound in *thing* and *singer,* but /ŋg/ for the sound of *finger, linger, stronger;* /ŋk/ would be used in *think, bank,* etc. Many speakers in the vicinity of New

York pronounce *singer* and *finger* so that they differ only in the initial consonant, and both rhyme with the usual pronunciation of *finger* in other areas (i.e., both sound to others as though they are said with /ŋg/). Since /ŋ/ does not occur initially, and /ŋg/ does not occur finally, the only place where there is potential contrast between these two is medially between vowels, and even in this position no minimal pairs have been reported. Therefore it is easy to see how, for practical purposes, English gets along very well without a separate symbol for this phoneme.

3.4 SUMMARY OF CONSONANT PHONEMES

The following chart shows the twenty-four consonant phonemes of English, arranged according to phonetic categories to be discussed in the next chapter:

p	t	c	k
b	d	j	g
m	n		ŋ
f	θ		
v	ð		
	s	š	
	z	ž	
w	r	y	h
	l		

3.5 ENGLISH VOWELS

Since the dialects of English vary greatly in how many vowels they have and in how they are pronounced, it is difficult to describe them accurately within a single system. Most varieties of American English which have been studied distinguish at least the following fourteen stressed vowel sounds (vowels in unstressed position are discussed in Chapter 5):

1   beet, seat, peat, keel, keen
2   bit, sit, pit, kill, bill, kin
3   bait, sate, pate, kale, bail, cane
4   bet, set, pet, bell, Ken
5   bat, sat, pat, Cal, can
6   but, putt, dull

7 boot, suit, cool, Boule, Kuhn
8 soot, put, bull
9 boat, coal, bowl, cone
10 bought, sought, call, ball, law
11 sot, pot, con
12 bite, sight, bile, kine
13 bout, pout, cowl
14 coil, boil, coin

The examples given provide minimal pairs for each of the contrasts illustrated here. Even for those speakers who do not have the same vowel in their pronunciation of all the words in each row, there are still fourteen different vowel sounds (in most cases): for example, some speakers do not distinguish *kin* from *Ken*, but still distinguish *bit* and *bet*. For many Americans, the vowel of *sot* (number 11) is the same as the first vowel of *father*, though for others they are different.

The list below shows a system for representing the vowel phonemes of American English. There are various other systems in use which are equivalent to this one. There are various theoretical reasons for the choice of a transcription system, which we need not go into here.

The examples given in parentheses at the end of each line show the "received pronunciation" (RP), the traditionally elite variety of British English, as analyzed by Daniel Jones. The most important differences between U.S. and British vowels which show up on the chart involve: (*a*) item 5, which includes words like *grass, path, staff* with U.S. /æ/ and RP /a/, and (*b*) items 10–11, which in RP are distinguished by the length of the vowel (short /ɔ/ in *top, lot, sock*, long /ɔː/ in *caught, law, all*). Other differences

English Vowels

1.	/i/	– *beat*	=	/bit/ (RP biːt)
2.	/ɪ/	– *bit*	=	/bɪt/ (bit)
3.	/e/	– *bait*	=	/bet/ (beit)
4.	/ɛ/	– *bet*	=	/bɛt/ (bet)
5.	/æ/	– *bat*	=	/bæt/ (bæt)
6.	/ʌ/	– *but*	=	/bʌt/ (bʌt)
7.	/u/	– *boot*	=	/but/ (buːt)
8.	/ʊ/	– *book*	=	/bʊk/ (buk)
9.	/o/	– *boat*	=	/bot/ (bout)
10.	/ɔ/	– *bought*	=	/bɔt/ (bɔːt)
11.	/a/	– *pot*	=	/pat/ (pɔt); also /pɔt/ (like #10) in some U.S. dialects
12.	/ay/	– *bite*	=	/bayt/ (bait)
13.	/aw/	– *bout*	=	/bawt/ (baut)
14.	/oy/	– *boil*	=	/boyl/ (bɔil)

occur in words which have /r/ following the vowel, such as *fur, beer, far, poor*, since in RP and certain eastern U.S. dialects (the "*r*-less" varieties) the consonantal closure of the /r/ has been replaced by a prolongation of the vowel, sometimes with a change in quality. Thus *fur* = /fʌr/ or /fəː/, *far* = /far/ or /faː/, etc.

3.6 SOME CONTRASTING EXAMPLES

The following examples illustrate the working of the principles of analysis shown above, making use of data from two languages which are quite different from English. The first example is from a rural variety of Tamil (spoken in South India). In this language, a sound *t* (similar to the first sound of French *tasse* or Spanish *taza*) is found at the beginning of words—e.g., *taːlu* 'tongue', *tale* 'head', and also occurs doubled in such words as *atte* 'father's sister', *pattu* 'ten'.[1] It is not found without the doubling between vowels, though a similar sound, which we can write with the symbol *ð* (like the *th* in English *other*), is found in words like *kaðe* 'story', *saːðam* 'cooked rice' (high-caste term). After *n* another similar sound, *d* (as in French *doux*, Spanish *dolce*) is found—e.g., *inda* 'this', *sonda* '(one's) own'. Though these three sounds would be clearly distinguishable to a linguist with a background of English, he would be unable to find any minimal pairs to show a contrast between any two of them. In fact, careful examination of the distribution of *t, d,* and *ð* in this variety of Tamil shows the following facts:

1   no word begins with *d* or *ð*
2   single *t* or *d* are never found between vowels
3   *d* or *ð* are never doubled
4   *t* or *ð* never occur after *n*

This appears then to be a set of complementary sounds appearing in different surroundings, and thus we would be justified in considering them to be different versions of the same thing. Earlier linguists coined the term COM-PLEMENTARY DISTRIBUTION to refer to such situations as this, and proposed a general principle that complementary sounds that resembled each other sufficiently could be regarded as members of the same structural element known as a PHONEME. This conclusion is possible only if we can specify the exact pronunciation of the phoneme according to the PHONOLOGICAL ENVIRONMENT, by rules such as the following:

1 The colon represents vowel length (see 4.6). The double *tt* is similar to that in English *cattail* or Italian *fatto* 'done'.

Tamil /t/ is pronounced as: [ð] between vowels;
[d] after /n/;
[t] elsewhere.

(Traditionally, phonemes are written between slant lines. Square brackets are used whenever necessary to designate ALLOPHONES, the individual positionally-determined sounds such as Tamil [ð d t]. A phoneme is a class of sounds, and is therefore an abstract entity which cannot be pronounced. An allophone is a particular, phonetically describable sound which is a member of the phoneme and manifests it in a particular environment.)

This phonemic principle makes it possible to use PHONEMIC WRITINGS which use a single symbol for each phoneme, ignoring allophonic or sub-phonemic differences. Thus we can use the symbol /t/ in representing all the above words: /ta:lu/ (phonetically [t]); /atte/ (phonetically [tt]); /kate/ (phonetically [ð]); /inta/ (phonetically [d]); etc. It should not surprise us to learn that the Tamil writing system uses a single symbol for all three of these sounds, and that Tamilians experience no difficulty as a result.

In fact, the Tamil speaker deals with this /t/ in much the same way as the English speaker deals with his own phoneme /t/. Unless it is called to our attention, most of us are not aware that the /t/ in *train* is pronounced differently than the /t/ of *bathtub*. (This can be checked by pronouncing *bathtub*, holding the *t* of *tub* exactly where it is at the back of the upper teeth, and then saying *train*.) The allophone of /t/ in (*bath*)*tub* is DENTAL (with the tongue touching the teeth), while the allophone occurring in *train* is ALVEOLAR (with the tongue against the gum-ridge behind the teeth). By considering these two allophones to be members of the same phoneme, the linguist accounts for the fact that objectively different sounds are in-distinguishable within the PHONOLOGICAL SYSTEM of the language.

In Hindi-Urdu (a language of North India), there occur sounds similar to these allophones of English /t/—but in this case, they are in contrast, and thus must be considered as distinct phonemes; this is shown by the following minimal pairs:

/vo gata hɛ/   'He sings' (unaspirated dental [t̪])
/vo gatʰa hɛ/   'That's a *gatha* (verse)' (aspirated dental [t̪ʰ])
/vo ata hɛ/   'He comes' (unaspirated dental [t̪])
/vo aṭa hɛ/   'That's *ata* (whole-grain flour)' (unaspirated retroflex [ṭ])
/ye satʰ lana/   'Take these along' (aspirated dental [t̪ʰ])
/ye saṭʰ lana/   'Take these sixty' (aspirated retroflex [ṭʰ])

Thus, Hindi-Urdu has four phonemes /t tʰ ṭ ṭʰ/ corresponding to a single English phoneme, and both of the writing systems used to represent this language observe this four-way distinction. Broadly speaking, most traditional writing systems in fact adhere to this phonemic principle, and ignore subphonemic differences.

3.7   FREE VARIATION AND FREE ALTERNATION

In some cases, we may notice variations in the pronunciation of the same word, even when spoken by the same person at different times. For example, in the northeastern United States, some speakers show fluctuation in the vowel sound of such words as *bad* or *man*. In some cases, it is a low front vowel, moderately long, which can be represented phonetically as [æ] (see 4.5). In other cases, the sound begins as a mid-front vowel (similar to that of *bet* or *bait*), and glides toward the mid-central position (that of the vowel in *but*). Speakers differ in their range of variation, but many speakers produce audibly different versions of this vowel. The same type of variation can be found in other languages. For example, if an English speaker hears a Tamilian pronounce the word for 'son' several times, he will get the impression that there are two distinct pronunciations: *magan* (with a *g* sound like that in *nugget*), and *mahan* (with an *h*-sound like that of *ahead*).

Where such variation occurs, it is always possible that we are dealing with FREE VARIATION, or differences that play no role in distinguishing word meanings. As long as there are no minimal pairs that are distinguished by the difference in question, it would be regarded as a SUB-PHONEMIC difference, and the two sounds would be treated as allophones of the same phoneme. This is the case for Tamil *g* ∼ *h* (the symbol ∼ is often used to indicate free variation), and is true for the variations in the vowel of *bad* and *man* in American English, at least for many speakers. These speakers would then be said to have a single phoneme /æ/, which has different allophones ([æ], [ɛːə], [eːə], etc.) in free variation. (On the other hand, such variation may relate to differences in social background or in social situation, which are discussed in Ch. 18.)

There are other cases of variation which at first appear similar to these just mentioned, but on closer inspection turn out to be different. For example, some Americans pronounce the first vowel of the word *either* like the first vowel of *even*, and some pronounce it like the first vowel in *ivory*. Some pronounce *leisure* to rhyme with *pleasure*, and others make it rhyme with *seizure*. *Lever* sometimes rhymes with *fever*, and sometimes with *never*. But these cases differ in two ways from those discussed above. First, not all words with the sound in question show this variation, even when the surrounding sounds are similar. Thus, while *lever* varies, *never and fever* do not.

In the case of /æ/, those speakers who show variation in the words *bad* and *man* generally show identical variation in *mad, sad, had, fad, glad,* . . . and in *ban, can, fan, pan, ran,* . . . Secondly, in this second set of cases we can find minimal pairs which are distinguished by the sounds in question. For example, the two vowels of *either* serve to distinguish *fever* and *fiver*; the two sounds of *leisure* distinguish *geese* from *guess*. In such cases, speakers readily recognize the differences, and sometimes even attach meaningful differences to them. (For example, many Americans find the pronunciation of *either* with /ay/ to be elegant-sounding, while others consider it affected.) This type of variation between distinct phonemes in particular words is sometimes known as FREE ALTERNATION.

3.8 PHONETICS AND PHONEMICS

The overall study of pronunciation is known in linguistics as PHONOLOGY. The discussion in this chapter is based on a somewhat traditional approach to phonology, which derives in large part from practical work with hitherto unwritten languages. This approach is still of great importance to teachers of language, for anthropologists investigating new languages, for language planners devising new writing systems or improving old ones, etc. A newer approach, described in Chapter 6, has replaced traditional phonology in theoretical linguistic work, but has not supplanted it in these practical domains.

Traditional phonology distinguishes between a PHONETIC LEVEL and a PHONEMIC LEVEL, for reasons which are primarily practical. In approaching a new language which has no writing system, the linguist needs to be able to describe sounds and have some means for representing them. On the PHONETIC LEVEL, all distinctions audible to the linguist are relevant. He needs to have terms for describing how they are produced, and the ways in which they differ from each other. If he is describing a language like Tamil, he will write *h* when he hears *h*, and *g* when he hears *g*. If speakers seem to be making some distinction which he is not able to hear, he will do his best to find out what it is and devise a way to represent it. (Chapter 4 contains a detailed discussion of phonetics, and provides the basis for practical training in phonetic transcription.)

Whereas on the phonetic level the linguist confronts the sounds of a language directly, on the PHONEMIC LEVEL he provides a description of them which deals with the way in which they are used. Thus, the distinction between dental [t̪] and retroflex [ṭ] is relevant on the phonetic level in both Hindi-Urdu and English, but on the phonemic level it is only relevant to

Hindi-Urdu, not to English. However, it is only after identifying the phonetic differences and studying the ways in which they operate in the language (whether they contrast, or are complementary, or are in free variation) that the linguist can provide a phonemic analysis and a method of phonemic transcription. Thus the two levels respond to different needs, and have different functions: the phonetic level is relevant to the linguist's analysis, and is largely irrelevant to speakers of the language, while the phonemic level provides both the linguist and the users of the lanugage with a means for representing it.

NOTES

3.5. RP: Jones 1956
/æ/ in U.S. English: Labov 1966

SUGGESTED SUPPLEMENTARY READING

Phonemes of English: Trager and Smith 1951; Jones 1956
Phonemics: Pike 1947; Bloch and Trager 1942

FOLLOW-UP

1 Define: phonemic inventory, complementary distribution, (phonological) environment, allophone, phonemic writing, phonological system, free variation, sub-phonemic (difference), (study of) phonology.

2 Explain the distinctions: phonetic level—phonemic level; phonetic writing—phonemic writing.

3 Using the transcription system introduced in this chapter, transcribe the following words in your own English: bat, pitch, drunk, blame, lodge, shoes, math, said, aye, cello, indict, yacht, baked, judge, beau, eight, of, off, gnat, though, ghost, half, yolk, should, move, stove, love, choir, psalm, myrrh, corps, scene, question, itch, eighth, myth.

4 Convert the following phonemic writings into ordinary English spelling (in some cases, there may be more than one possible spelling): /bit, tek,

stret, tɔk, laws, lʊk, fon, rɛd, rid, et, sayt, wet, mit, cɛk, strɛc, brɪj, no, saw, haws, hawz, noyzi, bɔsi, skawər, sut, kræk/.

5   Regional varieties of English differ considerably in their vowel systems. Try to determine the vowel inventory of your own speech. (Note that you may have a difference in the number of contrasts in your speech, depending on how carefully you are speaking. Try to note this difference.) The following sets of words may help you to find how many contrasting vowel sounds you have:

 a. bit, beet, bet, bait, bat, but, bottle, put, boot, boat, bought, bite, bout, caught, cot.

 b. din, dean, den, Dane, Dan, dun, don, dune, dawn, dine, down, coin, tone.

 c. Mary, merry, marry, Murray; Harry, hairy, hurry; fairy, ferry, furry; mirror, nearer; error, fairer.

 d. (In the following words, if you pronounce the /r/, how many different vowels or vowel combinations are found before /r/? If you do not pronounce the /r/, how many different vowel or vowel combinations occur before the word-final consonant?) bid, bead, beard, bed, paid, bared, bad, bud, bird, pod, bard, good, mood, moored, bawd, abode, bored, road, bide, loud.

 e. (In the following words, if you pronounce the /r/, how many vowel sounds occur before /r/? If you do not pronounce the /r/, how many different vowel sounds occur in word-final position?) beer, bier, bare, burr, bar, boor, bore, boar, buyer, liar, bower, lawyer, foyer.

 f. bill, peel, bell, bail, pal, dull, doll, bull, pool, bowl, ball, bile, boil, bowel.

Generally speaking, the number of contrasts before consonants like /t/ or /d/ is greatest. Therefore, a useful way to check on your phonemic inventory and distribution is to list the distinct phonemes occurring before /t/ or /d/ down the left-hand side of a page, then make columns for other positions, as follows:

Phoneme	before /t/	before /d/	before /r#/	before /rd/	before /l/	before /n#/	etc.
ɪ	bit	bid	(etc.)				
i	beat	bead					
(etc.)							

6   If you know a language other than English, try to establish its phonemic inventory by finding minimal pairs for all phonemic contrasts, in the same way as suggested in no. 5.

Chapter 4
ARTICULATORY PHONETICS

4.1 PHONETICS AND ARTICULATION

The examples given in 3.6 show that distinctions in pronunciation which are significant in one language are often not relevant in another. Obviously, an individual's ability to perceive the distinctions which exist in his native speech, and which he has been "tuned in" to since early childhood, will be greater than his ability to recognize new distinctions which are not functional in his own speech. Therefore, those who wish to study the ways in which different languages (and different varieties of the same language) make different uses of the possibilities of pronunciation require training to sharpen their awareness of phonetic differences. Part of this training is the study of the mechanisms of human sound production, known as ARTICULATORY PHONETICS.

A description of a particular articulatory mechanism is an adequate and convenient way for talking about the sounds produced by the mechanism; by specifying the positions of the relevant organs of articulation in the production of a certain sound, we specify approximately the quality of that sound (even though we do not describe the sound directly). With practice, trained phoneticians also find it possible to describe a new sound in terms of its articulation; usually, this involves trying first to imitate the sound, and then describing the positions of one's tongue, lips, etc., while doing so. Thus, for practical work of this kind, it is necessary to develop some sense of one's articulatory organs and what they are doing. This is a major reason why a written presentation like this book is totally inadequate to give an idea of what articulatory phonetics is all about; to thoroughly understand it, it is necessary also to hear, imitate, and introspect about a variety of sounds, both familiar and unfamiliar. Thus the discussion here cannot substitute for a live presentation.

Even a single speech sound is a complex event. Suppose we want to describe the articulation of the sound of English /n/, as in the word *any*. We would have to specify at least the following details:

1   the speaker is pumping air from the lungs out through the nasal passage, which is opened by means of lowering the VELUM (see 4.3)
2   the lips are open, but the mouth is sealed air-tight by the tongue, which is placed against the roof of the mouth just behind the upper teeth
3   the vocal cords are vibrating, so as to produce a humming sound

Having specified this much, we have described a type of sound which includes those represented by the letter *n* in most western writing systems. The set of sounds so described includes a number of audibly different varieties, since we have not said anything about loudness, pitch, or length of the sound; we have not specified the type of onset (abrupt or gradual), the amount of breathiness, or the positions of other organs (such as the back of the tongue) which could affect the sound quality, and which would be phonemically distinctive in some languages. In short, we have described not one sound, but a class of sounds; we can be more precise if necessary, and this chapter involves a discussion of the various ways in which this can be done.

4.2   ANALYSIS OF THE STREAM OF SPEECH

Production of human speech sounds involves various organs of the body, such as the lungs, larynx, throat, nose, tongue, teeth and lips. All the organs that participate in the production of speech sounds have other important functions, mostly related to respiration and eating. Speech sounds are a product of four processes, each involving one or more of the organs listed above. The lungs provide the AIR-STREAM which carries sound (air-streams that do not involve the lungs are discussed below). The VOCAL CORDS, which are situated in the larynx, provide PHONATION as the air-stream rushes through the GLOTTIS (the space between the vocal cords). This is responsible for the distinction, among other things, between VOICED and VOICELESS sounds. The position of the VELUM controls the passage of the air through the nose and makes for the distinction between ORAL and NASAL sounds. Finally, the tongue, the teeth and the lips further modify the air-stream to produce the distinctions among different consonant sounds, and between consonant and vowel sounds.

The "stream of speech" resulting from this process is continuous, but is analyzable into successive stretches of maximal RESONANCE, separated by CONSTRICTIONS of greater or lesser degree. In the word *perceptible*, for example, there are four points of maximum resonance corresponding to the parts of the word spelled with *er*, *e*, *i*, *le*; the remainder, those parts of the word corresponding to the letters *p*, *c*, *pt*, *b*, are points of minimal resonance produced by partial or complete CLOSURE. (The [s] sound represented by the letter *c* involves partial closure with resultant friction, while the others involve complete, though very brief, closure.) This alternation of resonance and constriction makes it possible to analyze speech into successive SYL-LABLES, each containing a resonant NUCLEUS and optionally other sounds. The four syllables of *per-cep-ti-ble* all have, in addition to the nucleus, a constriction which functions as the syllable ONSET; and the second syllable, *-cep-*, has in addition a constriction serving as its CODA. Syllables appear to correspond to a fundamental physiological unit in speech production known as a CHEST-PULSE, since there is evidence that the air-stream from the lungs is released intermittently rather than with a steady pressure. (Although the lungs are the usual source for the air-stream, alternative mechanisms are described in 4.4).

Clearly, sounds which function as syllable nuclei must be those in which resonance predominates, whereas those that function as MARGINAL sounds (i.e., either onsets or codas) are those involving constriction as a primary characteristic. The terms VOCOID and CONTOID are used, respectively, to denote these two types of speech sounds. While the distinction between vocoids and contoids is related to the familiar distinction between VOWELS and CONSONANTS, it is not identical. First, of course, it should be clear that the discussion here relates to sounds rather than letters. Secondly, it must be pointed out that resonance is a relative matter: vowel sounds like /i/ (e.g., in *lazy* /lézi/) have greater resonance than sounds like the /n/ in *didn't*, the /s/ of *psst* /pst/, the /l/ of *subtle* /sə́tl/, or the /θ/ of width /wɪtθ/, but these sounds are in turn more resonant than the *t* of *too* or the *b* of *bee*. Furthermore, these sounds of intermediate resonance can also function as syllable nuclei from the phonetic point of view, since for example the /n/ of *didn't* and the /l/ of *subtle* are more resonant than the surrounding sounds. This question is discussed further in Chapter 6; for the purposes of this chapter, the distinction made between contoids and vocoids will serve.

4.3   CONTOID ARTICULATIONS

One of the most important ways in which speech sounds differ from each other is in their MANNER OF ARTICULATION, that is the type of action involved in their production. For example, there are various points in the speech tract where the air can be stopped by blocking the passage completely. The vocal cords can be closed, producing a GLOTTAL STOP (similar to a cough or the sound heard between the two vowels in *Oh-oh*! or an emphatically pronounced *Out*!). The tongue can be used to block the passage of air through the mouth at various points: for example, touching the back of the teeth (to produce a sound like the /t/ or /d/ of French, Italian, or Hindi-Urdu), or touching the

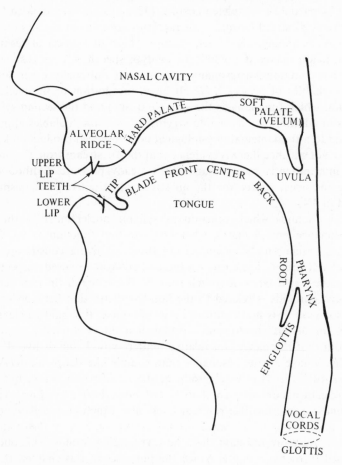

Figure 4-1. The articulatory organs.

soft palate (see Figure 4-1) to produce a sound like English /k/ or /g/. If the lips are closed momentarily to block the air passage, the resulting sound is known as a BILABIAL STOP—for example, English /p/ or /b/.

Thus, STOPS (also known as OCCLUSIVES) form a category of sounds distinguished from others by their manner of articulation. In the case of a bilabial stop, for example, the air flow will be completely stopped only if the nasal passage is also closed; if the lips are closed and the nasal passage is opened, then a sound of the type [m] is produced, known as a bilabial NASAL. (The opening and closing of the nasal passage is effected by a valve-like action at the VELIC, where the NASAL PASSAGE opens into the back of the mouth or ORAL PASSAGE.) If, instead of making a complete closure, a partial closure is made so that the air stream is impeded but not completely cut off, a hissing sound may be heard, as in the most common allophones of English /f/ or /s/. Sounds produced in this way are known as FRICATIVES or SPIRANTS.

All sounds which can be continued are known as CONTINUANTS. Apart from nasals and fricatives, this category includes LATERALS (sounds like English /l/ in which the air escapes around the sides of the tongue) and TRILLS (produced by a vibrating mechanism) such as the sound written *rr* in Spanish *perro* 'dog'. A sound similar to a trill, but consisting of a single very brief closure, is known as a FLAP—for example, the familiar /r/ sound of Spanish, Italian, southern French, Russian, Hindi-Urdu.

It should be kept in mind that we are not describing phonemes here, but phones (sounds). When a phoneme, such as English /s/, is offered as an example of a particular sound, we are referring to the most common allophones of the phoneme, since the phoneme itself (as noted above) is not pronounceable. (Strictly speaking, only phones occur in speech. Thus, if the phrase *kick the stick* is pronounced, a sequence of nine phones occurs which can be transcribed [kˡ-ɪ-k-ð̵-ə-s-t-ɪ-k]. The third and ninth phones are—under normal circumstances—identical, or at least indistinguishable by ear, and therefore are instances of the same allophone.)

The categories *stop, nasal, spirant* (or *fricative*), *trill, flap*, and *lateral* are all distinguished from each other by their manner of articulation. A second major type of difference is according to PLACE OF ARTICULATION, i.e., the particular point in the speech tract where the activity takes place. In discussing place of articulation, it is convenient to distinguish between ACTIVE ARTIC-ULATORS (organs capable of movement) and PASSIVE ARTICULATORS or POINTS OF ARTICULATION (those points where the active articulators make contact). The major active articulators are the LIPS, the TONGUE, and the UVULA. The tongue, being extremely mobile, can be divided into three more or less separate articulators which function in slightly different ways: the TIP or APEX, the FRONT or BLADE, and the BACK or DORSUM. The major passive articulators are: LIPS, TEETH, the ALVEOLAR RIDGE (a bony ridge located just behind the upper teeth), the PALATE (the hard part of the roof of the mouth), the VELUM or SOFT PALATE, and the back wall of the throat. (There is no point, of course, in insisting too strictly on the distinction between active and passive articulators, since in some cases—e.g., when both lips, or both vocal cords, articulate against each other—it is useless to try to distinguish which is which.) By referring to both the active and passive articulators, it is possible to specify such types of sounds as the following: LABIO–DENTAL (lower lip and upper teeth), BILABIAL (both lips), APICO–DENTAL (apex of tongue against upper teeth), LAMINO-PALATAL (blade of tongue against palate), DORSO–VELAR (back of tongue against soft palate), etc.

The accompanying table shows the major types of articulation discussed so far, and gives the symbols used for them in the International Phonetic Alphabet (IPA), with a few alternative symbols used commonly by American linguists (in parentheses). Note that the table distinguishes between VOICED and VOICELESS sounds, and that most stops and fricatives exist in both varieties. In singing or humming, the vibration which produces the tone is the work of the vocal cords; in speech, this vibrating action is constantly turning on and off. If one listens carefully to oneself in pronouncing a word like *dazed* (/dezd/), one can hear this humming sound continue throughout almost the whole word. In a word like *taste* (/test/), on the other hand, the humming is heard during the articulation of the vowel, but is turned off for the /st/ at the end. (The difference is more audible if one holds one's hands over one's ears at the same time.) Sounds accompanied by this vibrating action of the vocal cords are known as VOICED sounds, and those without it are known as VOICELESS. English / b d j g m n ŋ v ð z ž r l /, for example, are normally voiced, whereas / p t c k f θ s š / are voiceless. Since this distinction is often found in stops and fricatives of European languages, there exist symbols for both types in most cases, as Figure 4-2 shows. Nasals, trills, flaps, and laterals are most commonly voiced, though Welsh is famous for its voiceless *l*.

Following are miscellaneous remarks on the various sounds illustrated in the table, and the ways of symbolizing them: (1) Dental [t] and [d] are commonly heard in French and Spanish, whereas the apical stops of English and German are usually apico–alveolar. (2) The RETROFLEX stops are produced by curling the tip of the tongue back so that the underside of the tongue actually contacts the roof of the mouth; strictly speaking, *retroflex* refers to the shape of the tongue and not to a point of articulation, since retroflection is possible at various points of articulation, from alveolar to velar. A phonemic distinction between dental vs. retroflex is common to most of the major languages of India, and one variety of Tamil actually has distinct dental, alveolar, and retroflex stops.

(3) Combinations like [tʃ], [dʒ] are often used to represent stops that are AFFRICATED, i.e., consisting of a stop followed by a brief fricative-like sound, as in *chin, gin*. Some linguists consider these to be a separate articulatory

| | | Labial | | Apical | | | Laminal or Dorsal | | | |
		Bilabial	Labio–dental	Dental	Alveolar	Retroflex	Palatal	Velar	Uvular	Glottal
Stops (plosives)	Voiceless	p		t		t (ṭ)	c	k	q	ʔ
	Voiced	b		d		ḍ (ḑ)	ɟ	g	G	
Fricatives (spirants)	Voiceless	ɸ	f	θ	s	ṣ (ṣ)	ʃ (š)	x		h
	Voiced	β	v	ð	z	ẓ (ẓ)	ʒ (ž)	ɣ		ɦ
Nasals		m			n	ɳ (ṇ)	ɲ (ñ)	ŋ		
Trills					r				R	
Flaps					ɾ	ɽ (ɽ)			R	
Laterals					l	ɭ (ḷ)	ʎ			

Figure 4-2. Basic consonant sounds. (The symbols are those of the International Phonetic Alphabet, with additional symbols used by American linguists given in parentheses.)

type, called AFFRICATES. Other types of affricated stops also occur, such as [pᶠ], [tˢ] (as in German *Pfeffer*, *Zahn*), and even [kˣ] (heard in some dialects of Swiss German). (4) The difference between dorso–palatal and dorso–velar [k] was illustrated in Chapter 2, with the two allophones of English /k/ respectively in /kil/ *keel* and /kul/ *cool*. A phonemic contrast between dorso–velar [k], [g] and dorso–uvular [q], [G] is found in Arabic.

(5) The GLOTTAL STOP, mentioned above, is produced by closing the GLOTTIS (the aperture formed by the vocal cords); it is the sound heard as the beginning of a cough, or of a grunt of pain or effort (as when lifting or throwing). In some varieties of New England or Scottish English, the same sound is often heard as a substitute for the *t* in *bottle*, *rattle*, etc. Since the vocal cords are responsible also for voicing, it follows that the glottal stop cannot be voiced.

(6) Among the spirants, the symbols [f] and [v] usually represent the labio–dental sounds which are common in the well-known European languages. The bilabial [ɸ] can be reproduced by a person blowing out a match, though as a speech sound the lips would normally be less protruded, and the force of articulation somewhat less. Labio–dental stops are also possible, but

not common. (7) Many Americans produce [s] and [z] as lamino–alveolars (with the tongue tip behind the lower teeth). (8) The symbol [x] represents the type of sound heard in German *doch, ach* ("Achlaut"), or Scottish *loch*. Its voiced counterpart, [ɣ], is often heard as the French or German "*uvular r*", except in cases where this is a uvular trill (see 11 below).

(9) The sound represented by [h] is produced by friction resulting from partial closure of the vocal cords, with no vibration; often additional tension in the throat muscles adds to the friction. The "*voiced h*", [ɦ], is produced by very lax vibration of the vocal cords, accompanied by throat friction. This is heard between vowels in English, for example in such words as *aha* or *oho*, especially when pronounced with dramatic emphasis. English [h] is often a frictionless, voiceless vocoid, especially in initial position (see 4.6 Vowel modifications).

(10) Nasals are possible in all positions except the glottal. A labio–dental nasal commonly occurs in English words like *sunfish* and *infield* in rapid speech, though this is presumably to be treated as an allophone of /n/. The palatal nasal [ɲ] is familiar from French (*bagne, vigne*) and Spanish (*cañón, piñón*). The retroflex nasal occurs as distinct from the dental in many languages of India. (11) The trill [r] is the alveolar trill of Spanish, Russian, etc.; the [R] represents the uvular trill found particularly in northern French. Many speakers of this variety of French will have the single flap [R'], the full trill [R], and the dorso–velar fricative [ɣ] as allophones of a single /r/ phoneme. The uvular trill [R] is particularly clearly audible in recordings by certain popular French singers. (12) The palatal lateral [ʎ] is heard in some varieties of Spanish, in such words as *calle, ellos*, though many varieties of new world Spanish have [y] in these cases. Russian contains a true palatal [ʎ], e.g. in [stáʎ] стапь 'steel'.

(13) A type of sound which might also have been included here is that known as SEMI-VOWELS, e.g., like the first sound in English *way* and *yacht*. Semi-vowels function as consonants in syllable structure, but phonetically they are nonsyllabic vocoids, and are therefore discussed below in 4.5.

(14) The reader should not assume that the blanks in the table imply that the missing articulations are impossible. All are possible, and when they occur, symbols are readily found to represent them. The table includes only those sounds which occur commonly enough to have standard symbols.

4.4 CONTOID MODIFICATIONS

The basic articulatory types described above can be modified in various ways. Where two articulations occur simultaneously, we can usually distinguish a PRIMARY and a SECONDARY articulation: thus, for example, the initial consonant of Russian [pʸatʸ] пять 'five' is primarily a voiceless bilabial stop, with a secondary narrowing in the lamino–palatal region. Such a narrowing, known as PALATALIZATION, is accomplished by raising the tongue close to the palate so that a narrow channel is formed between them. The sound produced is acoustically similar to a consonant plus *y*, as in English *pew* /pyu/, Hindi-Urdu /pyar/ 'affection', but the palatalized /pʸ/ is different in that the palatalization is simultaneous with the labial closure. Palatalization can affect any consonant except one whose primary articulation is palatal; it can be symbolized, as here, with a raised *y*.

Other common types of secondary articulations are LABIALIZATION (rounding and/or protrusion of the lips), indicated by a small *w* as in [kʷ] (representing the labialized [k] of English *cool*, for example); VELARIZATION (raising of the back of the tongue) indicated by a small *x*, as in Russian [lˣ] in [stalˣ] стап 'stood'; GLOTTALIZATION (simultaneous closure of the glottis), represented by [ʔ], e.g. [pʔ]. Glottalized stops are distinct from plain stops in certain languages of South and Central America; voiceless stops are glottalized in some varieties of American English, especially in word-final position (e.g., [blækʔ kæt] *black cat*, [ðætʔ wən] *that one*).

Other types of modifications have to do with manner of articulation. Affrication and voicing have already been mentioned above. Another very common modification is ASPIRATION (see 3.6). Aspiration affects mainly stops, though aspirated nasals, trills, and laterals are also possible. An aspirated stop is distinguished from a simple (or UNASPIRATED) one by the fact that the former is followed by audible air friction (like a short [h] sound); if a vowel follows such a stop, this [h] sound intervenes between the stop and the vowel, whereas a vowel following a simple stop lacks this intervening breathy quality. The voiceless stops / p t k / of English are usually aspirated at the beginning of a syllable when followed by a stressed vowel (as in *pin, tin, kin, impinge, until, akin*). They are unaspirated in certain other positions, for example after /s/ (even when a stressed vowel follows—e.g., *spill, still, skill*) or at the end of a word (as in *nip, nit, nick*). The voiceless stops of Spanish, French, Italian, and Russian are unaspirated in all positions.

Hindi-Urdu has a contrast between aspirated and unaspirated stops at five points of articulation (see the appendix to this chapter); it also has aspirated voiced stops, which are phonetically [bɦ dɦ ɖɦ ɟɦ gɦ] (with voiced [ɦ]). English stops and affricates show another type of modification: / p t c k / are produced with more muscular effort than / b d j g /; the former are said to be TENSE as opposed to the latter, which are LAX. Actually, this distinction between tense and lax is as important in English as the distinction between voiced and voiceless, since in some positions (especially in rapid speech) the voicing of the "voiced" stops is inaudible. This is different from the situation in French or Hindi-Urdu, for example, where the voiced stops are almost always fully voiced.

In the discussion so far, it has been assumed that we were dealing with sounds produced by air being pushed outward by pressure from the lungs. The reverse procedure is also possible, with the air being sucked into the mouth or nose by one of several mechanisms. This process is known as IMPLOSION, and sounds produced in this way are IMPLOSIVES. Sindhi, a language of north India, has a set of implosive voiced stops which contrast with plain stops. In producing an implosive [b], for example, the Sindhi speaker creates a partial vacuum between the lips and the glottis by closing both and then moving the larynx downward; the two closures are then released more or less simultaneously. A following vowel can be produced by outward-flowing air. Implosion is indicated by [>], and outward pressure by [<], thus: [b>], [b<]. In most cases, of course, it is not necessary to indicate pressure except when there is a contrast. The CLICKS of certain African languages are related to implosives, but they normally use a dorso–velar instead of a glottal closure. The sound written *tsk-tsk* or *tch-tch* in English is usually an apico–dental click; the clucking sound used to start a horse is most commonly a UNILATERAL (released on one side) lamino–palatal click; a kiss is a bilabial affricated click. Apart from the few languages in which implosives and clicks have phonemic status, they appear mainly as paralinguistic signals of the types illustrated here.

4.5 VOCOID ARTICULATIONS

As noted above, vocoids are sounds which are characterized by a maximum of resonance and a minimum of constriction of the vocal organs. The characteristic resonances of different vowels, which serve to distinguish them from each other, are primarily the result of the placement of the tongue. This extremely mobile organ can move horizontally (forward or back) as well as vertically, and is capable of being bunched up so as to create resonance cavities of different sizes in front and in back of it, even though its total volume does not change.

Though the shape of the tongue is unique for each vowel, its different positions can be described in terms of (*a*) TONGUE HEIGHT (the raising of the highest part of the tongue) and (*b*) TONGUE POSITION (the location of the highest part in the front-to-back dimension). For example: in pronouncing the /i/ of French *si* 'yes', or Hindi-Urdu *bhi* 'also', the tongue is bunched close to the alveolar ridge, producing a high front vowel; the sound of French *ou* 'where', or Hindi-Urdu *tu* 'thou', requires the tongue to be bunched close to the back of the soft palate, and thus would be classified as a high back sound; the vowel of English *bat* is a low front sound; and so on.

These examples also illustrate another important distinguishing charac-

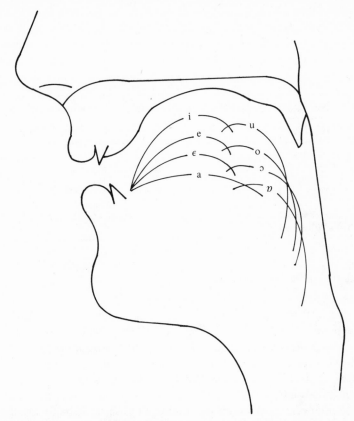

Figure 4-3. Vocoid articulations (showing height and position of the tongue: see 4.5).

teristic of vowel sounds, namely the conformation of the lips: ROUNDED in the case of French *ou*, UNROUNDED (or SPREAD) in the case of *si*. In English, Hindi-Urdu, Spanish, and many other languages, front vowels are typically unrounded and back vowels are normally rounded. Other languages, such as French or German, have rounding as a minimal distinguishing feature of pairs of vowels: compare French *vie* 'life' (high front unrounded) and *vue* 'view' (high front rounded), *fait* 'done' (mid front unrounded) and *feu* 'fire' (mid front rounded). Back unrounded vowels also occur, though they are rare in the world's languages: for example, [ɯ] in Russian [tɯ] 'thou'.

Figure 4-4 shows the IPA symbols for the most common vowels. The symbols [ɪ ɨ ʊ] are commonly used by American linguists, but are not in general use. Typical specimens of the most common vowel sounds are as follows: [i]–French *vie*, [y]–French *vue*, [e]–French *été* 'summer' or Hindi-

		Front		Central		Back				
		Unrounded	Rounded	Unrounded	Rounded	Unrounded	Rounded			
Tongue Position (IPA)	Close	i	y (ü)	ɨ	ʉ	ɯ	u	High		Tongue Position (U.S.)
	Half-close	e	ɸ			ɤ	o	Mid	(upper)	
	Half-open	ɛ	œ (ö)	ə		ʌ	ɔ		(lower)	
	Open	æ		ɐ				Low	(upper)	
		a				ɑ	ɒ		(lower)	
Semi-vowels		j (y)	ɥ				w	Semi-vowels		
		Front		Central		Back				

Figure 4-4. Basic vowel sounds.

Urdu /the/ 'they were', [ɸ]–French *fameuse* 'famous', [ɛ]–English *red*, [œ]–German *hören* 'hear', [æ]–English *bat*, [a]–French *patte*, [ə]–the unstressed vowel at the end of English *sofa* or at the beginning of *above*, [u]–French *ou*, [o]–French *eau* 'water' or Hindi-Urdu /cəlo/ 'go!', [ɔ]–French *or* 'gold' or Hindi-Urdu /ɔrət/ 'woman', [ɑ]–Russian /rat/ 'happy', [ɒ]–Russian /tot/ 'that'.

The high central vowel [ɨ] is found in English, principally in unstressed position, in words such as *horses* [horsɨz], decide [dɨsayd], etc. Some speakers of English also have [ɨ] occasionally in stressed position in a few words, e.g., *children* [cɨldrɨn], *sister* [sɨstər], *this* [ðɨs] and *just* (as in *He just left*) [jɨs] or [jɨst], usually distinct from *gist* [jɪst] and from *just* [jʌst] (as in *a just man*). This vowel (known as "BARRED I") actually constitutes a distinct phoneme in the speech of many Americans, but was not discussed in Chapter 3 because of its rareness in stressed position. Its role in determining the placement of stress is discussed in 5.2.

In case the reader is confused about the relationships between this set of symbols and the set adopted for representing the phonemes of English in Chapter 3, it should be made clear that the adoption of symbols for either purpose is done according to what is most convenient. Since a phoneme must be defined in terms of its allophones, it does not matter much which symbol is used for a phoneme as long as we describe properly what that symbol is used for. Thus, for example, the English phoneme for which we use the symbol /ə/ has two main allophones, one mid-central (phonetic symbol [ə]) and one mid-back (phonetic symbol [ʌ]). The choice of a symbol to represent the phoneme has no direct relationship to the use of the phonetic symbols. In general, the symbol for a phoneme will be chosen so as to be as close as possible to the phonetic symbols used for its most common allophone, but there is no necessary connection between the phonetic and phonemic symbols.

4.6 VOWEL MODIFICATIONS

Modifications of vowel sounds include the following main types:

1 nasalization
2 degree of tension (especially of tongue and lips)
3 duration or length
4 diphthongization

NASALIZED vowels are produced by opening the nasal passage, so that air flows through the mouth and nose simultaneously. The most common symbol of nasalization is the tilde [~] placed over the vowel. Many languages have phonemic nasalization: thus, French *beau* [bo] and *bon* [bõ], Hindi-Urdu [hɛ] 'is' and [hɛ̃] 'are', are distinguished solely by the nasalization of the vowel. Differences in TENSION are not uncommon, though are less often independently distinctive than other features of vowels. French [e] in *thé* is produced with more muscular tension in the tongue than the [ɛ] in *taie*, but tongue height also accounts for part of the difference. The first members of the English pairs [i ɪ], [e ɛ], [u ʊ], and [o ɔ] are more tense than the second members; in this case also, tongue height (and for some speakers, diphthongization) also plays a part.

VOWEL LENGTH is important in many languages, though often accompanied by differences in quality (e.g., tongue height). Classical Latin is said to have had five pairs of vowels, each distinguished by length (viz., / a ā e ē i ī o ō u ū /), but it is likely that there were also differences in height, and perhaps also in tension. Symbols for length, apart from the traditional macron [¯], are [ă] (short), [a] (normal), [a·] (slightly longer than normal), [aː] (long), [aːː] (extra long), etc.

Some varieties of English have contrasts in length. For example, some speakers will distinguish the words *have* (as in *I have it*) from *halve* (as in *You should halve it*), primarily by the greater length of the latter. The difference between *merry* and *Mary*, for some speakers who distinguish them, is primarily in the length of the vowel (the second being longer). For those who distinguish *real* from *reel*, the first is often pronounced with a lengthened

/ɪ/ (as distinct from the normal /ɪ/ of *rill*). Other common examples are *mirror* (with normal /ɪ/) vs. *merer* (with lengthened /ɪ/), *terrible* (with normal /ɛ/) vs. *tearable* (with lengthened /ɛ/) *bomb* (with normal /a/) vs. *balm* (with lengthened /a/), *can* 'be able' (with normal /æ/) vs. *can* 'put in cans' (with lengthened /æ/).

The last two often have differences in tongue height or position, in addition to the length difference. These contrasts have not been adequately described as yet, since there is a great deal of regional variation in the use of the length contrast, and furthermore a great deal of apparently free variation. Any of the symbols suggested here for length can be used for indicating these contrasts in transcribing English. Some linguists have proposed the symbol /h/ for this purpose, and thus would write the words with lengthened vowels as follows: /hæhv/ *halve*, /mɛhri/ *Mary*, /rɪhl/ *real*, /mɪhrər/ *merer*, /tɛhrɪbl/ *tearable*, /bahm/ *balm*, /kæhn/ *can*.

Some vowel sounds, particularly short ones, are uniform in quality throughout their duration, whereas in other cases, the tongue and/or other organs move during the production of the vowel, producing DIPHTHONGIZA-TION. For example, the sound of English *ow* as in *cow* starts out with [a] and ends up with something in the neighborhood of [u]. We often have the impression that such sounds consist of a sequence of two distinct sounds, although instrumental observation indicates that there is no point at which one stops and the other begins, since the transition is gradual. Phonemically, such sounds are often represented as vowel sequences. Usually, one of the vowels is more prominent than the other because of length, stress, or tension. Thus, in the case of *ow*, the [a] is much longer than the [u]. This can be represented [a ːu], where the [u] denotes an extremely short sound; in fact, it is so short that it is difficult to determine exactly what its quality is, and it can be considered as indicating the direction toward which the sound is gliding rather than its actual ending point.

English /aw/ /ay/ and /oy/ are diphthongs, and in many people's speech / i e o u / (as in *beet*, *bait*, *boat*, *boot*) are also diphthongized. Failure to realize this is one of the reasons why many English speakers (British as well as American) diphthongize the vowels of other languages (such as French, German, Italian, or Spanish) which are *not* normally diphthongized. This is one of the most noticeable characteristics of an American accent, in fact; as it happens, in most other languages the distinction is not phonemic, so that there is not likely to be any misunderstanding as a result, but merely a foreign sound.

The initial sounds of *way* and *yacht* are also non-syllabic vocoids, and are similar to those just mentioned. These SEMI-VOWELS are often represented by the symbols [w] and [y] (European linguists prefer [j] for the latter). When there is any need to specify the height of non-syllabic vocoids, symbols of the type [i̯ e̯ u̯ o̯] can be used.

The "AMERICAN R" is produced with the tongue retracted and raised in such a way as to partially close the oral passage, but leaving a small opening in the center of the palate. It is normally frictionless. It can be regarded as a semi-vowel (symbol:[ɹ]) when preceded or followed by a vowel, as in *rat* [ɹæt], *throw* [θɹou̯], *car* [kaːɹ]. In other cases it functions as a vowel (symbol: [ɚ]): *bird* [bɚːd], *fur* [fɚː], etc. (Speakers of "*r*-less" dialects have [bɜːd], [fɜː], or [bɪːd], [fɪː], in these cases.)

As noted above, the phoneme /h/ in English occurs most commonly as a non-syllabic, voiceless vocoid. In initial position, it has the characteristics of the following vowel. Thus, the usual pronunciation of English *hat, hate* could be phonetically transcribed as [æ̥ æ t], [ɛ̥ ɛ e̥ t] (where the subscript circle indicates DEVOICING).

4.7   ACOUSTIC PHONETICS

As opposed to the study of the ways in which sounds are produced, ACOUSTIC PHONETICS is the direct study of the physical properties of speech sounds. This is a highly technical study which depends on very sophisticated measuring instruments; the main instrument used is the SOUND SPECTROGRAPH, which produces a frequency profile of a sound showing the amount of energy present at each frequency. These pictures of sound, known as SPECTRO-GRAMS, show that certain sounds (including all vowels or vocoids, and also other continuant sounds such as [m] or [l]) have most of their energy concentrated at particular characteristic frequencies, which show up as prominent streaks (known as FORMANTS) on the spectrogram. Such sounds can be called VOCALIC, as compared with the remaining sounds which are characterized by more diffuse or random acoustic energy. An additional finding of acoustic phonetics is that the frequency of vowel formants correlates well with the relative size of the two resonating cavities produced by the tongue (4.17). Acoustic phonetics has also been important in developing the theory of distinctive features (6.2).

APPENDIX TO CHAPTER 4

Consonant phonemes of French, German, Spanish, Russian, and Hindi-Urdu. (The following brief descriptions may be instructive to readers familiar with one or more of these languages. In many cases, there are other possible ways of phonemicizing, but for the sake of brevity a single alternative has been arbitrarily chosen here. Though readers may not agree with the phonemic solutions proposed here, they may at least serve to stimulate discussion.)

French

Stops	$\left\{\begin{array}{l}\text{p}\\\text{b}\end{array}\right.$	t d		k g
Nasals	m	n	ɲ	
Fricatives	$\left\{\begin{array}{l}\text{f}\\\text{v}\end{array}\right.$	s z	ʃ ʒ	r
Lateral	l			

Semi-vowels: /y/ (front unrounded)
              /ɥ/ (front rounded)
              /w/ (back rounded)

Notes

1. / k g r / are velar, though /r/ is an apical trill in some varieties (see 4.3, note 11).
2. / ɲ ʃ ʒ / are lamino–palatal, though /ɲ/ has an allophone [ŋ] in some positions.

Examples

/pa/	*pas*	'step'
/ba/	*bas*	'low'
/te/	*thé*	'tea'
/de/	*dé*	'die'
/kɛ/	*quai*	'quai'
/gɛ/	*gai*	'gay'
/mõ/	*mon*	'my'
/nõ/	*non*	'no', /ano/ *anneau* 'ring'
/aɲo/	*agneau*	'lamb'
/fɛ̃/	*fin*	'end'
/vɛ̃/	*vin*	'wine'
/asi/	*assis*	'seated'
/azi/	*Asie*	'Asia'
/aʃe/	*haché*	'chopped'
/aʒe/	*âgé*	'aged'
/ru/	*roux*	'rust'
/lu/	*loup*	'wolf'
/yɛr/	*hier*	'yesterday'
/ɥit/	*huit*	'eight'
/wi/	*oui*	'yes'

German

Stops	{ p { b	t d		k g	ʔ
Nasals	m	n		ŋ	
Fricatives	{ f { v	s z	ʃ (ʒ)	x r	
Lateral	l				
Semi-vowels			y	h	

Notes

1. The affricated stops [pᶠ], [tˢ], and [tˢ̌] (as in /pféfer/ *Pfeffer* "pepper', /tsúŋe/ *Zunge* 'tongue', /kvetš/ *Quetsch* 'prune') can be considered as single phonemes or as sequences of /p/ + /f/, /t/ + /s/, /t/ + /š/ (as here).
2. /x/ has the allophone [ç] (palatal) after a front vowel, as in /íx/ *Ich* 'I', /bléx/ *Blech* 'tin', and the allophone [x] after a non-front vowel, as in /ax/ *ach* (exclamation), /kox/ *Koch* 'cook'.
3. /r/ is a velar fricative in some dialects, and an alveolar flap or trill in others.
4. /ž/ is used in French words such as /etá:že/ *Etage* 'story' by some speakers.
5. The glottal stop /ʔ/ marks grammatical boundaries in such words as /geʔöfnet/ *geöffnet* 'opened', /beʔáiligen/ *beeiligen* 'hurry up'.

Examples

/páin/	*Pein*	'pain'
/báin/	*Bein*	'leg'
/táix/	*Teich*	'pond'
/dáix/	*Deich*	'dike'
/káil/	*Keil*	'wedge'
/gáil/	*geil*	'fat'
/máin/	*mein*	'my'
/náin/	*nein*	'no', /zin/ *Sinn* 'sense'
/zíŋ/	*sing*	'sing'
/fáin/	*fein*	'fine'
/váin/	*Wein*	'wine'
/hásen/	*hassen*	'hate'
/há:zen/	*Hasen*	'hares'
/táše/	*Tasche*	'pocket'
/záxe/	*Sache*	'thing'
/ráin/	*rein*	'pure'

/láin/	*Lein*	'flax'
/yá/	*ja*	'yes'
/háil/	*heil*	'healthy'

Spanish

Stops	p	t	c	k
	b	d		g
Nasals	m	n	ɲ	
Fricatives	f	s (θ)		x
Lateral		l	(ʎ)	
Trill-flap		r		
Semi-vowels	w		y	

Notes

1. /b d g/ have fricative allophones [ß ð ɣ] in intervocalic position; otherwise they are stops.
2. /θ/ is a distinct phoneme only in the Castilian dialect. Other speakers substitute /s/.
3. /ʎ/ is a distinct phoneme in certain dialects. Other speakers use /y/.
4. /r/ is pronounced as a trill in initial position, and as a flap otherwise; the intervocalic trill in words like /pérro/ *perro* 'dog' is considered a double /r/.
5. /s/ has the voiced allophone [z] before voiced sounds, as in /es bwéno/ [ezbwéno] *es bueno* 'is good', /mísmo/ [mízmo] *mismo* 'same'. Note that there is no contrasting phoneme /z/. In some parts of Spain and Latin America, final /s/ is a weakly aspirated [h].
6. /n/ has the allophone [ŋ] before velar consonants or /w/, as in /sínko/ [síŋko] *cinco* 'five', /sín xóta/ [síŋ xóta] *sin jota* 'without *j*', /un wébo/ [uŋ wéßo] *un huevo* 'an egg'.

Examples

/pán/	*pan*	'bread'
/bán/	*van*	'they go'
/tán/	*tan*	'so'
/dán/	*dan*	'they give'
/céke/	*cheque*	'check'
/díka/	*dica*	'said'
/díga/	*diga*	'would say'
/kómo/	*como*	'like'
/bwéno/	*bueno*	'good'

/swéɲo/	sueño	'sleep'
/fín/	fin	'end'
/sín/	sin	'without'
(/θínko/	cinko	'five'—see note 2)
/káxa/	caja	'cage'
/léy/	ley	'law'
(/káʎe/	calle	'street'—see note 3)
/rópa/	ropa	'clothing'
/wébo/	huevo	'egg'
/yélo/	hielo	'ice'

Russian

Stops	⎧p,	pʸ	t,	tʸ	c	č	k
	⎩b,	bʸ	d,	dʸ			g
Nasals	m,	mʸ	n,	nʸ			
Fricatives	⎰f,	fʸ	s,	sʸ	s	šč	x
	⎱v,	vʸ	z,	zʸ	z	žj	
Laterals			l,	lʸ			
Semi-vowels						y	(h)

Notes

1. All labial and apical consonants (columns 1 and 2) occur in two varieties: plain (unmarked) and palatalized (indicated by [ʸ]). Plain consonants are velarized in many circumstances. The laminal consonants are either plain (column 3) or palatalized (column 4). The velars (column 5) have plain or palatalized allophones depending on the following vowel. Palatalized consonants could also be considered as clusters of a plain consonant plus /y/, except that there are contrasts such as: /sʸéstʸ/ 'sit down' (with palatalized /sʸ/), /syéstʸ/ 'eat up' (with plain /s/ followed by /y/).
2. /c/ is pronounced like [ts] as in English *cats*, sometimes as a voiced [dz] as in English *cads*; /č/ is correspondingly pronounced as [tš] or [dž]. /š/ is like the *sh* of *shoe*, and /šč/ is a long palatalized counterpart; /ž/ and /žj/ are the corresponding voiced sounds.
3. /h/ is a distinct phoneme for some speakers, but only used in a few words or phrases.
4. The allophones of vowels differ depending on whether the preceding consonants are plain or palatalized: thus, for example, /i/ in /bítʸ/ 'to be' is an unrounded back [ɯ], whereas in /bʸítʸ/ 'to fight' it is a front [i]. Russian actually uses different symbols for these two vowels.

The Russian spelling system does not have separate signs for palatalized and plain consonants on the whole: the difference is indicated by different vowel letters, or when no vowel follows, by the sign ь called /mʸáxkay znák/ 'soft sign', which shows that the preceding consonant is palatalized.

5. As in German, no Russian word can end in a voiced stop or fricative. Thus there are some changes of form in certain words, depending on the presence or absence of vowel endings, e.g., /zdaróf/ 'well, healthy' (masc.) vs. /zdaróva/ (fem.), /rát/ 'happy' (masc.) vs. /ráda/ (fem.).

6. Russian has no [ŋ], either as a phoneme or as an allophone of /n/: the /n/ of a word like /bank/ 'bánk' is always dental.

Examples

/pót/	под	'under'
/pʸót/	пьёт	'drank', /pʸítʸ/ пить 'to drink'
/bóx/	бог	'God', /bítʸ/ быть 'to be'
/bʸót/	бьёт	'fought', /bʸítʸ/ бить 'to fight'
/tót/	тот	'that' /tí/ ты 'thou'
/tʸótʸa/	тётя	'aunt', /tʸíxiy/ тихий 'quiet'
/dá/	да	'yes', /díšit/ дышит 'breathes'
/dʸádʸa/	дядя	'uncle', /dʸétʸi/ дети 'children'
/céliy/	целый	'whole'
/čáy/	чай	'tea'
/kák/	как	'how'
/gót/	год	'year'
/xólm/	холм	'hill'
/másla/	масло	'butter', /mí/ мы 'we'
/mʸása/	мясо	'meat', /mʸír/ мир 'peace'
/nós/	нос	'nose'
/nʸós/	нёс	'carried', /nʸét/ нет 'no'
/fákt/	факт	'fact'
/fʸíga/	фига	'fig'
/vót/	вот	'here...is', /ví/ вы 'you'
/vʸít/	вид	'view'
/sín/	сын	'son'
/sʸínʸiy/	синий	'blue'
/zá/	за	'behind'
/zʸími/	зимы	'winters'
/šítʸ/	шить	'to sew'
/žítʸ/	жить	'to live'
/ščí/	щи	'cabbage soup'
/žjót/	жёт	'burns'
/rát/	рад	'happy', /ríba/ рыба 'fish'

/r^{y}át/	ряд	'line', /ríga/ рига 'Riga'
/lučši/	лучше	'better'
/l^{y}ud^{y}i/	люди	'people'
/ya/	я	'I'

Hindi-Urdu

Stops	p	t	ṭ	c	k	(ḳ)
	p^h	t^h	ṭ^h	c^h	k^h	
	b	d	ḍ	j	g	
	b^h	d^h	ḍ^h	j^h	g^h	
Nasals	m	n	(ṇ)			
Fricatives	(f)	s	(ṣ)	š	(x)	
		(z)			(ɤ)	
Flap		r				
Lateral		l				
Semi-vowels	w			y	h	

Notes

1. This table shows four classes of stops (voiceless unaspirated, voiceless aspirated, voiced unaspirated, voiced aspirated) at five points of articulation: bilabial, dental, retroflex, palatal, and velar. The aspirated stops have been considered by some linguists to consist of stop plus /h/, though the native writing system uses completely distinct symbols for all 20 stops.
2. Retroflex /ṇ/ and /ṣ/ have separate symbols in the Hindi writing system, but are replaced by dental /n/ and /s/ in the speech of most people. The distinction is written only in learned words of Sanskrit origin.
3. The fricatives / f x z ɤ / and the pharyngeal stop /ḳ/ are used only by some speakers, exclusively in words of Persian or Arabic origin, such as /fəḳir/ 'fakir', /xəbr/ 'news', /zəmin/ 'land', /bəɤær/ 'without'. Speakers who lack these phonemes substitute /p^h k^h j g k/ respectively, thus: /p^{h}əkir/, /k^{h}əbər/, /jəmin/, /bəgær/.

Examples

/pʊl/	'bridge'
/phul/	'flower'
/bat/	'thing'
/b^{h}at/	'cooked rice'
/sat/	'seven'
/sat^h/	'with'

/do/	'two'
/dʰo/	'wash'
/ṭik/	'teak'
/ṭʰik/	'O.K.'
/ḍak/	'mail'
/ḍʰai/	'two-and-one-half'
/cor/	'thief'
/cʰoḍ/	'let go'
/jun/	'June'
/jʰuṭʰ/	'lie'
/ka/	'of'
/kʰa/	'eat'
/gərəm/	'warm'
/gʰər/	'house'
/man/	'respect'
/nan/	'bread'
/saf/	'clean'
/šam/	'evening'
/rat/	'night'
/la/	'bring'
/vəhã/	'there'
/yəhã/	'here'
/hã/	'yes'

NOTES

Appendix

Spanish: Stockwell and Bowen 1965
Russian: Stilman et al. 1972
Hindi-Urdu: Southworth 1971, pp. 14–19

SUGGESTED SUPPLEMENTARY READING

Articulatory phonetics (general): Pike 1943, Heffner 1952, Malmberg 1963
English phonetics: Jones 1956
Acoustic phonetics: Joos 1948; Hockett 1955, ch. 5; Ladefoged 1962

FOLLOW-UP

1 Define: syllable, nucleus, vocoid, contoid, manner of articulation, point of articulation, articulatory phonetics, acoustic phonetics.

2 Explain the distinctions: voiced—voiceless; nasal—oral (vowel); stop—continuant.

3 Give examples of two different sounds each involving the following articulations: both lips, tongue tip and teeth, back of tongue and soft palate.

4 Name the organs of articulation (tongue, lips, teeth, etc.) implied by the following terms: labial, bilabial, labio–dental, apico–dental, apico–alveolar, dorso–velar.

5 Give examples of sounds which fit the following terms: voiceless stop, voiced nasal, voiceless fricative, voiced fricative, lateral, flap, trill.

6 Describe the vowel sounds in the following English words, in terms of (a) high–mid–low, (b) front–central–back, (c) rounded–unrounded: keep, moon, nut, back, law.

7 Give the appropriate symbols to represent the following articulations: high front unrounded vowel, mid back rounded vowel, mid front rounded vowel, apico–alveolar nasal consonant, voiced dorso–velar stop, voiceless apico–dental spirant.

Chapter 5

SUPRASEGMENTALS

5.1 TRANSITIONS

In English, and in some (not all) other languages, grammatical units such as words are separated from each other by audible signals, as illustrated by the following pairs of sentences:

1   *a.* Is there any mistake here?
     b. Is there any Miss Take here?
2   *a.* Get the night-rate.
     b. Get the nitrate.
3   *a.* Two fire engines were brought in to play.
     b. Two fire engines were brought into play.

Sentences 1*a* and 1*b* both contain a sequence of segmental phonemes / s t e k /, but the TRANSITIONS between the /s/ and the /t/ are different in the two cases. The type of transition found in 1*b*, with a somewhat lengthened /s/ in *Miss* (similar to the lengthening at the end of a sentence, as in *What's this?*) and an aspirated /t/ (similar to the aspiration at the beginning of a sentence, as in *Take it*), is known as an OPEN TRANSITION—as opposed to a CLOSE TRANSITION, such as that between /s/ and /t/ in *mistake*. A phonological unit known as a JUNCTURE is said to occur between /s/ and /t/ in such cases as 1*b*; this is also sometimes known as PLUS JUNCTURE, since it has traditionally been written with the symbol / + /. For most purposes, it can be written simply as a space.

Phonetically speaking, sounds preceding a juncture have the characteristics of sounds occurring at the end of an utterance, though perhaps less marked. Continuant sounds, especially vowels, in these positions tend to be more lax and more drawn-out than the same phonemes in other positions, and with a noticeable fading of volume toward the end. Thus, the /e/ in *say more* /se + mor/ is longer and laxer than the /e/ in *same ore* /sem + or/. The same phoneme at the end of an utterance, as in *I say* or *Go away*, would be still longer and laxer. In (some varieties of) English, pre-junctural stop allophones are CHECKED with glottalization, as in *that one* (with glottalized *t*). The same feature often occurs at the end of an utterance, as in *Get out* or *I won't*.

Correspondingly, sounds which follow a juncture have some of the characteristics of sounds occurring at the beginning of a sentence. For example, the /p/ in *this place*, other things being equal, will normally be pronounced with greater force than the /p/ in *displace*. In a stressed syllable at the beginning of a sentence, the additional force will be even more noticeable. In English and other Germanic languages, a glottal stop is often a feature of juncture before a vowel, especially if stressed. Thus, a distinct pronunciation of *some ore* will usually have a glottal stop before *ore*. Similarly in initial position in such utterances as *Alice did it*, *Oh no! I'm coming*, etc.

The use of space in standard English writing corresponds only partially with phonological juncture. There are many cases where we write spaces, where no juncture will be pronounced except in the most artificial speech. Thus, we do not normally distinguish between *a nice man* and *an ice man*, *alas* and *a lass*; in relaxed speech, *some more* sounds like *some ore*, *sent her* sounds like *center*, etc. Thus, in sentences like the following, only some of the written spaces correspond to phonological junctures:

/aysentər + ðəbʊks/	*I sent her the books*
/wərəl + rɛdi + tɪgo/	*We're all ready to go.*
/dont + gɪvɪt + tuɪm/	*Don't give it to him*
/kənayv + səmor + brɛdn + jæm/	*Can I have some more bread and jam?*

Conversely, there are a few cases where juncture is pronounced but space is not normally written: *unable* is often pronounced /ən + ebl/, as distinct from *enable* /ɪnebl/; *reform* is commonly /ri + form/ when it means "form again" (as in *The ice reformed*), as compared with /rɪform/ in *The criminal reformed*.

Juncture in certain other languages (German and Russian, for example) functions very much like that of English. French offers an example that is rather different, in that it has fewer internal junctures of the type shown here.

Though some languages may lack the type of juncture discussed here, all have transitional phenomena of other types. At major grammatical boundaries in a stretch of speech, there will usually be some sort of phonological boundary markers. Thus we can distinguish three different ways of saying *go* in the following examples:

> *Let's go home.*
> *When you go, tell me.*
> *Let's go.*

The vowel of *go* in the second sentence will normally be considerably longer than that in the first. We often have the impression that there is a pause between *go* and *tell* in such cases, but observation shows normally no actual cessation of speech. The main feature is the slowing down, with consequent lengthening of the vowel. In the third case, there is a similar though greater slowing, with a marked fade-out in volume. In this case also, though there may be a pause following such a sentence, it is not necessary to pause; one can say, for example, *I'm going to the movies. You want to come?* without any actual pause. These two types of major transition (or MACRO-JUNCTURE) are probably found in most languages, where they function to mark important grammatical boundaries. Various symbols are used to represent macrojunctures; in this book the usual symbols /,/ and /./ will be used.

Junctures, including both the macrojunctures and the MICROJUNCTURE /+/, can be considered distinct from segmental phonemes, in that their phonetic representations span a domain which may be larger than a single segment. Thus, though segmental phonemes are viewed as following one another like separate links in a chain, SUPRASEGMENTAL phonemes such as stress (5.2), pitch (5.3), and juncture are supposedly superimposed on this. While this view may not be strictly accurate, the distinction between segmental and suprasegmental is a convenient one. The two types of phonemes can be conceived of as separate systems which, however, function simultaneously in speech.

5.2 WORD STRESS

In English, STRESS and PITCH (or INTONATION) are closely linked together, and it is difficult to discuss them separately. This is true in most languages that have stress as a phonemic feature. (Presumably all languages have significant intonational differences, but many languages do not use stress in the same way that English does.) Differences in stress (also sometimes called ACCENT) can be illustrated by words such as the following, in which the vowel marked with /ˈ/ is more strongly stressed than any other in the word:

imitate	/ímɪtet/	– *imitation*	/ɪmɪtéšn/
feasible	/fízɪbl/	– *feasibility*	/fizɪbíłti/
hesitate	/hézɪtet/	– *hesitation*	/hɛzɪtéšn/
radiate	/rédiet/	– *radiation*	/rediéšn/
fascinate	/fǽsɪnet/	– *fascination*	/fæsɪnéšn/

The phenomenon that we call stress in cases of this kind is phonetically complex. It correlates to some extent with loudness, i.e., number of decibels, but not entirely; that is, speakers of English may agree that the first syllable of *imitate* is stressed, even in cases where instrumental measurement fails to establish this as the loudest syllable. Apparently, what we hear as stress involves other factors such as length, tension, and what we might call DISTINCTNESS of articulation: the unstressed vowels in the first syllables of the second column are all normally closer to the mid central [ə] than the corresponding stressed vowels in the first column. All of these features combine to produce vowels which are more PROMINENT than others in the same word. A few minimal pairs can be found to illustrate stress contrasts, though they are not common: *transfer* can be either /trǽnsfər/ (e.g., in *He got a transfer*) or /trænsfér/ (in *We're going to transfer him*), though many people use the first version in both cases; similarly, *pervert* can be /pə́rvərt/ or /pərvə́rt/. Many other cases, such as *contract* (/kántrækt/ or /kəntrǽkt/), are near-minimal pairs, but not completely minimal because of vowel changes. Languages that use stress in this way to differentiate words are said to have LEXICAL STRESS.

The words in the second column above were said to have an unstressed first syllable, though actually the first syllable in each of these cases has an audibly stronger stress than the syllable immediately following it. Thus, we can actually recognize three distinct DEGREES OF STRESS in a word like *imitation*, namely medium–weak–strong–weak, in that order. It happens, however, that the location of the MEDIUM and WEAK stresses is predictable, once we know the location of the strong or MAIN stress. As a general rule, every syllable that is two syllables removed from a strong stress within the same word will have medium stress; thus the first syllables of *feasibility*, *hesitation*, *radiation*, as well as the last syllables of *imitate*, *hesitate*, *radiate*, have medium stress. This rule applies only to a single PHONOLOGICAL WORD, that is a sequence of segmental phonemes not interrupted by juncture. The principal exception to the general rule is that, under most circumstances, the vowel /ɪ/ never bears the medium stress; thus in *unification* /yunɪfɪkéšn/, *immunization* (ɪmyɪnɪzéšn), *profitability* /prafɪtɪbílɪti/, *fossilization* /fasɪlɪzéšn/, *abra-cadabra* /æbrɪkɪdǽbrə/, it is the first and not the second syllable which has the medium stress. The remaining syllables have weak stress.

5.3 CONTOURS AND MACROSEGMENTS

A consideration of the role of stress in longer phrases can best be made in conjunction with a study of intonation. Consider the following ways of saying *no* (e.g., in answer to the question *You're not going, are you?*):

    a. No. (I can't.)
       [⟍]
    b. No? (Who says I'm not?)
       [⟋]
    c. No—(And so what?)
       [‿]

The line underneath the words indicates the rises and falls in pitch as the word is pronounced. In *a*, the pitch starts out at a high point and drops rapidly; the meaning of this is a simple statement of fact. In *b*, the pitch does approximately the opposite; in this particular case this indicates disagreement. The intonation in *c* rises gradually from low to mid; as compared with *a*, this would usually indicate some defensiveness, or perhaps simply indifference. In the last case, the distinctive part is not the rise, but the final mid pitch; the rise may be very slight, or even imperceptible, without changing the meaning. Following is a more obvious example of the contrast between *b* and *c*:

    What are you putting in my drink? Sugar?
    What are you putting in my drink, sugar?

(In the second case, *sugar* is used as a form of address.) These three different INTONATION CONTOURS must be recognized as minimal basic elements in the intonation system of English. It is possible to recognize more, but not fewer, than these.

These three basic contours can be represented provisionally as follows: /↓/ (falling, as in /no↓./); /↑/ (rising, as in /no↑./); /—/ (level, as in /no—./). These are shown here followed by /./ or TERMINAL JUNCTURE. The same basic contours also appear before /,/ juncture, as in:

If you don't like it, don't eat it.
/ɪfyɪ dónt láykɪt ↓ , dónt ítɪt ↓ ./
One, two, three, go.
/wɔ́n ↑ , tú ↑ , θrí ↑ , gó ↓ ./
(Are you going?) No, I'm not. (So what?)
        (nó—, aym nát ↓ ./

Normally, a MACROSEGMENT (a stretch of speech between two macro-junctures) will contain one and only one of these six intonation contours. The exact shape of the contour will depend on the length of the macrosegment, and of the placement of main stresses within it. Notice the differences in the following examples of /./:

/nó./ *No.*
[⌒]
/hiz nát./ *He's not.*
[— ⌒]
/hiz nát hír./ *He's not here.*
[— — ⌒]

In all these cases, the highest point of the pitch contour coincides with the beginning of the last stressed syllable. In the following examples of /?/, a similar situation can be seen:

/ján?/ *John?*
[⌒]
/ɪzɪt ján?/ *Is it John?*
[— ⌒]
/ɪzɪt ján smíθ?/ *Is it John Smith?*
[— — ⌒]

5.4 COMPOUND STRESS AND EMPHATIC STRESS

It should be observed that, although the last sentence above contains two main stress marks, actually the first one will be reduced to medium stress if the sentence is read with the pitch contour indicated here. As a general rule, within the same macrosegment, all syllables marked with /'/ except the last are lowered to medium stress in this way. There are two principal mechanisms which interfere with this rule: EMPHATIC STRESS and COMPOUND STRESS.

Emphatic stress is illustrated by the italicized word in the following sentences:

/hiz *nát* hír./ He's *not* here.
[— ⁀ —]
/ɪzɪt *ján* smíθ?/ Is it *John* Smith?
[—‿ ⁀]
/hiz nát *hír* ɪn ðə mórnɪŋ./ He's not *here* in the morning.
[——— ‾‾‾‾‾‾‾]

In such cases, as the contour lines show, the word (or syllable) with emphatic stress pre-empts the characteristic part of the contour (i.e., the rise or fall); at the same time, the following syllables marked with /´/ are spoken with LOWERED MAIN STRESS. It is possible for a single macro-segment to contain more than one contrastive stress, as in the following cases:

/*áy* wánt *kɔ́fi*, ɪnd *ší* wánts *tí*./ *I* want *coffee*, and *she* wants *tea*.
[‾ —— ‾‿ —— ‾ —— ⟍]
/*yú* gó *ráyt hóm*./ *You* go *right home*.
[‾ — ‾‾ ⟍]

COMPOUND STRESS has the result of lowering the second of two consecutive main stresses: in the following cases, the second stressed syllable will be spoken with lowered stress: *bank manager, skin disease, steam engine, horse whip, racing car, boxing match, fish fry, lighthouse keeper*. Since spaces are used to indicate microjunctures, the symbol /+/ can be used to mark those words affected by compound stress (although this is not a commonly accepted way of writing them). The same process can affect longer sequences, as in: *branch bank manager* /brǽnc+bǽnk+mǽnɪjər/, *life insurance company* /láyf+ɪnšɔ́rɪns+kɔ́mpɪni/, *racing car driver* /résɪŋ+kár+dráyvər/, *steam engine drivers' union* /stím+énjɪn+dráyvərz+yúnyən/. Such compounds are to be distinguished from CLOSE COMPOUNDS such as the following, which are not usually interrupted by microjuncture, and which have a main stress on the first member and a medium stress (unmarked) on the second: *lighthouse* /láythaws/, *blackbird* /blǽkbərd/, *blueberry* /blúbəri/, *forearm* /fórarm/, *someone* /sɔ́mwən/. Some compounds of this type, such as *hubcap, dustbin, stoplight, wristwatch*, can be spoken either as open or close compounds. Compounds of both these types are distinct from cases such as the following, with emphatic stress:

That's not a *green* bird, that's a *black* bird.
That's not a *red* berry, that's a *blue* berry.

The examples above show that certain classes of words are normally stressed in sentences (e.g., *John, wants, here, coffee, morning*) and certain ones are typically unstressed (e.g., *is, it, be, in, the*); these latter words can, however, bear the emphatic stress, as in:

Put it *in* the box.
John *is* here.
I said *the* Pennsylvania Railroad, not *a* Pennsylvania railroad.

5.5 CONCLUSIONS

Some discussions of English stress have distinguished four degrees of phonemic stress, which correspond to those labeled here as MAIN, LOWERED MAIN, MEDIUM, and WEAK, respectively. Since it seems possible to eliminate three of these in most cases by observing the conventions discussed above, we can speak of English as having a phonemic contrast between STRESSED syllables (marked /′/) and UNSTRESSED syllables (unmarked), as well as an EMPHATIC STRESS (marked by writing the affected word in italics) and a process of OPEN COMPOUNDING (written /＿＿′＿＿+＿＿′＿＿/). In addition, the following marks are used for INTONATION CONTOURS (see 5.3): / ↓ ↑ —.,/.

Note that there is a danger in using the sign /?/ to indicate a rising contour, since this symbol is normally used for all sentences which are grammatically questions, even though they do not all have rising intonation. For example, the normal intonation contour of a simple question such as *Where's my book?* would be /./, the same as in *There's my book.* The /?/ intonation, on the other hand, is the more normal one in a repeated question such as *What time did you say?* when the information is being asked for the second time. Both /?/ and /./ are common in "yes–no" questions such as *Is it ten o'clock yet?*

The suprasegmental phonemes of most other languages have been less studied than those of English, and thus there has not been much opportunity for comparative study in this field. It seems likely that all languages have contrasts involving the placement of stress in macrosegments (phrases or sentences), as well as intonation contrasts. In listening to certain foreign languages, one is aware of intonation contours which are phonetically very different from those of English or other familiar languages. To what extent these differences reflect fundamental differences in the way in which intonation is used can only be known after thorough studies have been made.

A distinction must be made between SENTENCE INTONATION (of the type discussed here), and LEXICAL PITCH, or TONE; some languages use tones in the same way that English uses stress, i.e., in such languages the same sequence of segmental phonemes can have different meanings depending on the tone. In Thai, for example, the phoneme sequence /naa/ can have five possible meanings depending on the tone, as follows:

naa	(middle tone)	'field'
(nɔ́ɔj) nàa	(low tone)	'custard apple'
nâa	(falling tone)	'face'
náa	(high tone)	'mother's younger brother/sister'
nǎa	(rising tone)	'to be thick'

NOTES

5.5. Thai: Haas 1964

SUGGESTED SUPPLEMENTARY READING

Juncture: Trager and Smith 1951
Stress: Chomsky, Halle, and Lukoff 1956
Intonation: Pike 1945, Bloch and Trager 1942

FOLLOW-UP

1 Define: juncture, microjuncture, macrojuncture, stress, pitch (intonation), phonological word, emphatic stress, compound stress.

2 Distinguish: segmental—suprasegmental; (sentence) intonation—(lexical) tone.

3 The same string of segmental phonemes can have different meanings, if the pattern of suprasegmental phonemes is changed. See how many different meanings can be conveyed by varying the location of stresses and pauses, and the intonation contours, in the following sentences. How many of these different messages can be distinguished using the transcription system proposed in this chapter?

a. Please give it to me /pliz gɪvɪt tumi/

b. All right, I'll do it /ɔrayt ayl duɪt/

c. Yes /yɛs/

d. No /no/

e. See you later /siyə letər/

f. Hello (on telephone or in person) /hɛlo/ or /həlo/

g. What do you mean /wədəyə min/ or /wət duyə min/

h. Are you coming /aryə kəmiŋ/ or /ar yu kəmiŋ/

Chapter 6

PHONOLOGICAL THEORY

6.1 DISTINCTIVE FEATURES

The description of English phonemes given in Chapter 3 represents an approach to phonological description which was developed in the United States over twenty years ago, and which is still used by many linguists. It is well adapted to the solution of practical problems of transcription and the development of new writing systems for hitherto unwritten languages. In fact, this method was developed in large part as a response to just these needs. More recently, however, a rather different approach has come increasingly into use for purposes of formal linguistic description: known as the DISTINCTIVE FEATURE approach, this method of phonological description was in fact derived from earlier work of the so-called "Prague school" of linguistics. According to this system the phoneme, instead of being regarded as a fundamental unit of linguistic structure, would be considered a secondary unit, since it can be broken down further into more fundamental features (also sometimes known as PHONOLOGICAL COMPONENTS). For example, the English phoneme /t/ is distinguished by its voicelessness from /d/ (and from other voiced consonants such as / n z l r /); by its apicalness, it is distinguished from labials such as / p b /, palatals such as / c j š /, and velars such as / k g /; its stopness distinguishes it from nasals, fricatives, laterals, vowels, etc. Thus each of these features is more than a phonetic quality of /t/—each is a distinctive feature of the English phonological system, and therefore one of the basic units of English structure.

The essential characteristic of distinctive features is their distinctiveness. Physical measurements of sounds on a sound spectrograph (see 4.7) show that there is a good deal of variation, and phonemes which are phonetically close may actually overlap in terms of their absolute phonetic properties, without losing their distinctiveness. For example, the French phonemes /e/ and /ɛ/ (as in *thé* /te/ 'tea', *taie* /tɛ/ 'pillow-case') differ in tongue height and tension. A large number of measurements of these two phonemes, taken from different speakers and in different phonological environments, from speech at different speeds and with varying degrees of excitement, etc., shows a considerable overlap, but under any given set of conditions the two phonemes stay distinct. Thus it is not the absolute phonetic characterization of the phonemes and their allophones that is important, but the fact that they are consistently differentiated. Further, it is this distinctiveness that unites the various instances (allophones) of the phoneme, and makes it possible to consider them the same: for example, though the allophones of English /t/ range from retroflex to dental and from aspirated to unaspirated to flapped, they are all united by the presence of the three features mentioned, and at the same time distinguished from the allophones of all other phonemes. A more striking example is English /h/, which can be either voiced or voiceless, and which can have a great variety of tongue positions since it usually anticipates the quality of its following vowel; in spite of these variations, all allophones of /h/ are distinguished from other segments by the features [−vocalic], [−consonantal], [+continuant] (see 6.2 for the explanations of these features).

Where the earlier phonological theory has been concerned extensively with problems which relate to transcription, the modern theory has added other requirements, mainly (1) that the phonological description of a language should be as efficient as possible; (2) that it should be closely integrated with other parts of the grammatical description (see Ch. 13); and (3) that it should incorporate as far as possible those features which are characteristic of all languages (see 6.2). Though, in contrast to traditional phonology (see 3.8), modern phonological theory has not yet produced any significant practical applications, many linguists consider it of great importance in the development of a unified theory of linguistic structure.

An example of the use of the distinctive feature approach can be seen in the summary chart of consonant phonemes in 3.4. In that chart, one (or more) distinctive feature(s) is shared by the phonemes of each row and of each column: from top to bottom, the rows can be labeled (1) voiceless stops,

(2) voiced stops, (3) nasals, (4 and 6) voiceless fricatives, (5 and 7) voiced fricatives, (8) semi-vowels or frictionless continuants, (9) lateral; the columns are, from left to right, (*a*) labial, (*b*) apical, (*c*) lamino–palatal, (*d*) back (velar–pharyngeal).

This diagram may be compared with Figure 6-4, a distinctive feature representation of English consonants which is more in accord with current practice, and which incorporates two important innovations: the use of BINARY and UNIVERSAL features. Binary features are those which have only two values, of which one can be regarded as the absence of the other, such as voiced vs. voiceless or stop vs. continuant; they are opposed to features like the traditional "point of articulation" which can have three, four, or even more values in a language. Binary features appear to be both more efficient in representing distinctions, and more convenient in formulating phonological rules (6.3), and these reasons have been sufficient to persuade many linguists to adopt them—the inconclusive debate on their psychological reality notwithstanding.

Figure 6-1 shows the application of the binary principle to the Hindi-Urdu vowel system: each of the five features, $\pm$ front, $\pm$ back, $\pm$ high, $\pm$ low, and $\pm$ tense divides the total vowel system into two parts. The traditional intermediate values, mid and central, are replaced respectively by the combinations $\begin{bmatrix} -\text{high} \\ -\text{low} \end{bmatrix}$ and $\begin{bmatrix} -\text{front} \\ -\text{back} \end{bmatrix}$. The same facts are shown in a different way in Figure 6-2, which gives the DISTINCTIVE FEATURE MATRIX

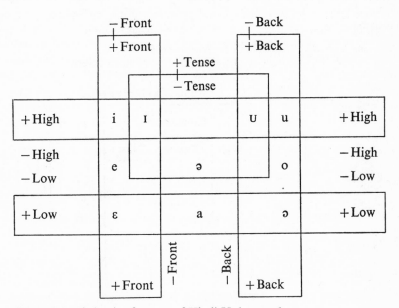

Figure 6-1. Distinctive features of Hindi-Urdu vowels

	i	ɪ	u	ʊ	e	ɛ	ə	a	o	ɔ
High	+	+	+	+	−	−	−	−	−	−
Low	−	−	−	−	−	+	−	+	−	+
Back	−	−	+	+	−	−	−	−	+	+
Front	+	+	−	−	+	+	−	−	−	−
Tense	+	−	+	−	+	+	−	+	+	+

Figure 6-2. Distinctive feature matrices for Hindi-Urdu vowels.

(i.e., the list of feature values) for each vowel. The combination of positive and negative values is different for each phoneme; in fact, this is a necessary condition for the workability of the distinctive feature method of describing a phonological system.

6.2 TOWARD A UNIVERSAL SET OF DISTINCTIVE FEATURES

The discovery that most phonological systems can be described with no more than about a dozen distinctive features has led to a further important development: an attempt to find a universal set of features which will account for all the phonological distinctions found in the world's languages. The features listed below, adapted from Chomsky and Halle 1968, are the result of several reformulations, and should perhaps still be regarded as tentative. Nevertheless, they give some indication of the progress made in this direction. (Only the most commonly-occurring features are mentioned here.)

The first four features to be discussed have been referred to as MAJOR

Major class features

	Vowel	Consonant			Liquid	Glide
		Stop	Fricative	Nasal		
1. Vocalic	+	−	−	−	+	−
2. Consonantal	−	+	+	+	+	−
3. Sonorant	+	−	−	+	+	+
4. Continuant	+	−	+	−	+	+

Figure 6-3. Major phonological classes distinguished by four major class features.

CLASS FEATURES, since they serve to differentiate six major classes of sounds, as indicated in Figure 6-3. The first two features provide a division into four major categories: VOWELS (+vocalic, −consonantal), CONSONANTS (−vocalic, +consonantal), LIQUIDS such as [r] or [l] (+vocalic, +consonantal), and GLIDES such as [h] or [y] (−vocalic, −consonantal).

1   VOCALIC VS. NON-VOCALIC: vocalic sounds include all normal vowels, whether voiced or unvoiced. Sounds which have a greater degree of closure than the high vowels [i] or [u], or which are characterized by interruption or friction, are non-vocalic (this includes glides like [y] and [w] as well as all stops, fricatives, nasals, laterals, and trills).

2   CONSONANTAL VS. NON-CONSONANTAL: consonantal sounds are characterized by closure (as in stops, nasals, or laterals) or by any impedance of the air-stream sufficient to cause audible friction (as in fricatives). Sounds without stoppage or audible friction, such as vowels or the semi-vowels [y w], are non-consonantal.

3   SONORANT VS. NON-SONORANT (OBSTRUENT): sonorants are defined as sounds which allow "spontaneous voicing". Practically speaking, this includes sounds which can be sung without interruption or excessive friction (i.e., all vowels, liquids, glides, and nasal consonants).

4   CONTINUANT VS. NON-CONTINUANT (OCCLUSIVE): continuant sounds include all sounds with an uninterrupted air-stream through the oral passage, i.e., all vowels, glides, fricatives, and laterals. Non-continuant sounds involve checking of the oral air-stream, even if only momentary (as in stops and affricates), and even if the nasal passage is open (as in nasal consonants).

As shown in Figure 6-3, the first two features divide the phonemes of English into vowels (see ch. 3), consonants (including / p t c k b d j g f θ s š v ð z ž m n ŋ /), liquids (/ r l /), and glides (/ y w h /). Vocalic sounds include all vowels plus / r l /; all others are non-vocalic. Consonantal sounds include all consonants as well as / r l /.

The next two features apply to constrictions traditionally described in terms of "point of articulation"; these features have the advantage of being more general, and therefore applicable in a wider range of languages, than any more specific set of distinctions that has been proposed. The following four categories of sounds are differentiated by means of these two features: LABIALS (−coronal, +anterior), DENTALS (+coronal, +anterior), PALATO-ALVEOLARS (+coronal, −anterior), and all sounds produced further back in the mouth (−coronal, −anterior).

5   CORONAL VS. NON-CORONAL: coronal sounds are produced by raising the blade of the tongue from its neutral position; this includes all the

apical and laminal sounds shown in Figure 4-2. Thus, English / t d c j θ ð s z š ž n r l y / are coronal, and / p b k g f v m ŋ w h / are non-coronal.

6 ANTERIOR VS. NON-ANTERIOR: anterior sounds involve an obstruction in the forward part of the mouth, that is any point further forward than the palato–alveolar region where the obstruction for English /š/ is formed. Anterior sounds include all those traditionally described as LABIALS, DENTALS, and ALVEOLARS. English / p b t d c j f v θ ð s z m n r l y w / are anterior, while / k g š ž ŋ h / are non-anterior.

The following five features refer primarily to consonants:

7 VOICED VS. VOICELESS: voiced sounds are accompanied by vibration of the vocal cords.

8 NASAL VS. NON-NASAL: nasal sounds are produced with an open nasal passage.

9 STRIDENT VS. NON-STRIDENT (consonantal sounds only): acoustically, strident sounds are characterized by friction noise. In English, only / f v s z š ž / are strident phonemes.

10 DISTRIBUTED VS. NON-DISTRIBUTED: this feature refers to the extent of contact involved in constrictions such as apical or labial; distributed sounds are those which involve a larger area of contact, as in the case of lamino–palatal sounds which involve a spreading of the tongue over the palate. It has been suggested that this feature can account for the distinction traditionally termed dental vs. retroflex in Hindi-Urdu consonants (see Figure 6-5).

11 ASPIRATED VS. UNASPIRATED: aspirated sounds are followed by a release of air (see 4.4).

The above eleven features are sufficient to differentiate all of the consonants (in the sense used above, i.e., sounds which are −vocalic and +consonantal) of English (Figure 6-4), as well as most of those in the other languages described in the appendix to Chapter 4. The stops of Hindi-Urdu are illustrated in Figure 6-5. The following features relate primarily to vowels (as well as other +vocalic sounds) and are illustrated in Figure 6-6 (p. 76).

12 HIGH VS. NON-HIGH: high sounds involve raising the body of the tongue above the "neutral" position (approximately that of *e* in English *bed*).

13 LOW VS. NON-LOW: low sounds involve lowering the body of the tongue below the "neutral" position.

14 BACK VS. NON-BACK: back sounds involve retraction of the tongue away from the "neutral" position. Apart from back vowels such as English /u o/, the feature [+back] appears in the plain or velarized consonants

	p	t	c	k	b	d	j	g	f	θ	s	š	v	ð	z	ž	m	n	ŋ	y	w	l	r	h
1. Vocalic	−	−	−	−	−	−	−	−	−	−	−	−	−	−	−	−	−	−	−	−	−	+	+	−
2. Consonantal	+	+	+	+	+	+	+	+	+	+	+	+	+	+	+	+	+	+	+	−	−	+	+	−
3. Sonorant	−	−	−	−	−	−	−	−	−	−	−	−	−	−	−	−	+	+	+	+	+	+	+	+
4. Continuant	−	−	−	−	−	−	−	−	+	+	+	+	+	+	+	+	−	−	−	+	+	+	+	+
5. Coronal	−	+	+	−	−	+	+	−	−	+	+	+	−	+	+	+	−	+	−	−	−	+	+	−
6. Anterior	+	+	−	−	+	+	−	−	+	+	+	−	+	+	+	−	+	+	−	−	−	+	−	−
7. Voiced	−	−	−	−	+	+	+	+	−	−	−	−	+	+	+	+	+	+	+	+	+	+	+	−
8. Nasal	−	−	−	−	−	−	−	−	−	−	−	−	−	−	−	−	+	+	+	−	−	−	−	−
9. Strident	−	−	+	−	−	−	+	−	+	−	+	+	+	−	+	+	−	−	−	−	−	−	−	−
12. High	−	−	+	+	−	−	+	+	−	−	−	+	−	−	−	+	−	−	+	+	+	−	−	−
13. Low	−	−	−	−	−	−	−	−	−	−	−	−	−	−	−	−	−	−	−	−	−	−	−	+
14. Back	−	−	−	+	−	−	−	+	−	−	−	−	−	−	−	−	−	−	+	−	+	−	−	−

Figure 6-4. Distinctive features of English consonants and semi-vowels.

of Russian, whereas those Russian sounds termed "palatalized" are [−back] (see Ch. 4, appendix).

15 ROUNDED VS. UNROUNDED: rounded sounds have partial lip closure.

16 TENSE VS. NON-TENSE (lax): tense sounds involve greater overall muscular effort.

	p	t	ṭ	c	k	kʰ	g	gʰ
coronal	−	+	+	+	−	−	−	−
anterior	+	+	+	−	−	−	−	−
distributed		+	−					
aspirated	−	−	−	−	−	+	−	+
voiced	−	−	−	−	−	−	+	+

Figure 6-5. Distinctive features of Hindi-Urdu stops showing five points of articulation and four manners of articulation. The feature *distributed* is relevant only to apical consonants (i.e., those which are +coronal and +anterior).

	i	u	e	o	æ	a	I	U	ɛ	ɔ	ə	ɨ
high	+	+	−	−	−	−	+	+	−	−	−	+
back	−	+	−	+	−	+	−	+	−	+	+	+
low	−	−	−	−	+	+	−	−	−	−	−	−
rounded	−	+	−	+	−	−	−	+	−	+	−	−
tense	+	+	+	+	+	+	−	−	−	−	−	−

Figure 6-6. Distinctive features of English vowels. (This figure includes only those features required for distinguishing vowels from each other; all vowels are, in addition, +vocalic and −consonantal.)

6.3 PHONOLOGICAL RULES

In 3.6, a phonetic rule was given which can be schematically represented as: $/x/ = $ [y], [z],... (with specification of the phonological environments in which [y], [z], etc. appear), and which has the meaning: "The phoneme $/x/$ has allophones [y], [z], etc., appearing in such-and-such environments". Such rules are designed to specify the allophones of each phoneme according to the phonological environment. The type of phonological rule to be discussed here reflects the assumptions and methods of contemporary descriptive linguistics which are discussed in Chapters 9–13 (and therefore may make more sense after those chapters have been read). Briefly, phonological rules in this approach are conceived of as MAPPING one set of representations onto another (i.e., converting from one to the other). The input to the phonological rules consists of the distinctive feature matrices of all phonemes in any sequence in which they may occur in speech; the output of the rules is (ideally) the complete phonetic specification of all the sounds of the language in all combinations which occur. The phonological rules, then, form a set of rules which mediate between the SYSTEMATIC PHONEMIC LEVEL (at which all distinctive feature information is specified) and the SYSTEMATIC PHONETIC LEVEL (at which all phonetic information is specified). Since the same original sound may be subject to several different rules, as will be seen from the following examples, the output of individual rules is often somewhere between the two levels; it is only after *all* the rules have been applied to a particular utterance that we can say that we have reached the systematic phonetic level. The examples given in 12.5 provide further illustrations of phonological rules.

The basic format for the phonological rules under discussion here can be represented generally as:

$$\begin{bmatrix} \pm x \\ (\pm y) \\ \dots \end{bmatrix} \rightarrow z/A\underline{\quad\quad}B$$

—which will be interpreted to mean: "a sound specified as $[\pm x]$ (with possible additional specification as $[\pm y]$, etc.) is given the (further) specification z, in the environment A$\underline{\quad\quad}$B, i.e., preceded by A and followed by B". (The preceding and following environments are given only when necessary; z may be a component or a series of components, a phonetic symbol, or some other phonetic specification.)

Figure 6-7 gives several examples of rules applying to English consonants

$$(a) \quad \begin{bmatrix} -\text{voiced} \\ -\text{continuant} \end{bmatrix} \rightarrow [+\text{aspirated}] \ / [-\text{strident}] \underline{\quad} [+\text{stress}]$$

$$(b) \quad \begin{bmatrix} -\text{continuant} \\ +\text{coronal} \\ +\text{anterior} \end{bmatrix} \rightarrow \text{retroflex} \quad / \begin{bmatrix} +\text{vocalic} \\ +\text{consonantal} \\ -\text{anterior} \end{bmatrix} \underline{\quad}$$

$$(c) \quad \begin{bmatrix} -\text{continuant} \\ +\text{coronal} \\ +\text{anterior} \end{bmatrix} \rightarrow \text{apico–dental} \ / \begin{bmatrix} -\text{vocalic} \\ +\text{consonantal} \\ +\text{continuant} \\ -\text{strident} \end{bmatrix} \underline{\quad}$$

Figure 6-7. Some phonological rules affecting English consonants.

which were discussed in Chapters 3 and 4: rule (*a*) here applies to voiceless stops (/ p t c k /), and specifies that they are aspirated when followed by a stressed vowel, except when preceded by a spirant; rule (*b*) indicates that apical stops (/ t d n /) have a retroflex articulation after /r/, and rule (*c*) specifies that the same consonants have an apico–dental articulation after /θ/ or /ð/. These rules illustrate the way in which different features can be combined to refer to particular groups of phonemes. Another point that emerges from these rules is that it is more efficient to include the variations of several phonemes in a single rule (such as rule (*a*) here, which includes all voiceless stops) than to describe each phoneme singly as in 3.6.

The phonological rules of a language constitute an ORDERED SET, since the output of some rules provides the input to others. For example, English phonology must contain a rule to account for the "reduction" of the last vowel in such words as *courage, human, pompous, solemn* from their "full" values in *courageous, humanity, pomposity,* and *solemnity*. This stress reduction rule must be followed by a rule which specifies the phonetic form of the reduced vowel ([ə], [ɪ], etc.) according to the phonological environment. This sequence is necessary because these reduced vowels are subject to the same environmental effects as vowels from other sources: thus, the phonetic treatment of the unstressed vowels will normally be the same in *courage, cabbage, college, porridge,* etc. (generally more fronted than the vowels of *solemn, column,* etc., or of *human, common, seven, salmon,* etc.).

NOTES

6.2. Distinctive features: Chomsky and Halle 1968

SUGGESTED SUPPLEMENTARY READING

General: Chomsky and Halle 1968
Phonological rules: Halle 1962
Earlier work on distinctive features: Jakobson, Fant, and Halle 1952

FOLLOW-UP

1   Define: distinctive feature, phonological component, distinctive feature matrix, major class features, phonological rule.

2   Distinguish: vocalic—non-vocalic;   consonantal—non-consonantal; systematic phonetic level—systematic phonemic level.

3   Question for discussion: how do the goals and methods of modern phonological theory differ from those of traditional phonemics?

Chapter 7

OTHER TYPES OF SIGNALS

7.1 PARALANGUAGE

Using the transcription system described above in Chapters 3 and 5, consisting of consonants, vowels, stresses, junctures, and intonation contours, it is possible to represent certain rather inhibited types of English: we might, for example, give a fairly accurate rendition of the speech of a person reading aloud from a technical article which has no particular emotional significance for him, or that of a very amateur actor reciting a poem. But for any normal uses of conversational English, the system presented above would be woefully inadequate to represent the wealth of linguistic signals that pass between speaker and hearer. It will not be possible here to do more than suggest some of the other types of signals which are commonly used, because they have not yet been adequately studied for any language. As yet, only a beginning has been made.

The term given to these phonological aspects of language, which are beyond formal linguistic analysis, is PARALANGUAGE. There are several reasons why the study of these PARALINGUISTIC signals needs to be set apart from the other aspects of linguistic phonology. Apart from the fact that paralinguistic mechanisms have not been given standard representations in any traditional writing system, and that they have not been sufficiently studied by linguists, they are not on the whole amenable to the same type of description used for the more normal phonological elements. Many paralinguistic effects involve CONTINUOUS VARIATION, as opposed to the DISCRETE DIFFERENCES which characterize phonemic contrasts.

Differences in pitch and loudness, for example, have been discussed in Chapter 5, as they relate to the establishment of a stress phoneme and intonation contours. Now it is obvious that a speaker's voice may vary considerably in pitch, beyond anything that can be described with the intonation contours of Chapter 5. How much of this can we represent, if we stick to our original criterion of representing only those differences which are significant to speakers? We know that a person can produce many different degrees of pitch, and presumably can react differentially to these also. How can we determine the limit? Since it is impossible to divide the pitch range into discrete phonemic units, linguists have considered this type of variation in absolute pitch (as well as loudness, speed, etc.) to constitute a separate kind of variation. Such differences would not be amenable to the pair test used in establishing phonemic contrasts (see 2.3). Even in cases where the pair test is applicable, it may not be easy to determine whether a particular difference is significant.

The discussion of pitch and loudness in Chapter 5 involved only relative measurements, as opposed to absolute measurements on a scale of wavelengths or decibels. Absolute measurements of such variables as pitch and loudness have not been considered relevant in talking of suprasegmentals, since the only need to talk of measurement was in terms of the relative measurement of one syllable as compared to its neighbors. A male voice and a female voice may be in different absolute pitches, and yet use the same intonation contours. Pitch and loudness can, however, be used in other ways; for example, a person's voice may make a sudden JUMP in loudness, or may show an unusually wide range of pitch. Also a person's voice may be unusually high or low, loud or soft, in comparison with his normal voice, or in comparison with the voices of others with whom he is talking. The same is true for speed of utterance: an excited person is likely to talk faster than normal, a depressed person may speak very slowly.

All of these variables will affect the hearer's perception or understanding of the message, though it might be more normal to say that they affect the hearer's interpretation of the speaker's attitude or state of mind. These are all therefore linguistically significant, or at least potentially so. Such effects stand somewhere in between phonemes and gestures: they use mechanisms similar to phonemes, that is, they use the same parts of the vocal tract, but they involve non-discrete ranges, since it is impossible to attach a distinct phonemic value to every audible change in pitch or loudness. They are to some extent like gestures and other visual effects; for example, a loud voice may produce approximately the same effect as a red face or a belligerent stance.

One further reason why paralinguistic effects have not been studied adequately is that most of us take them largely for granted, since they are part of the background phenomena of our own culture. Thus many of us, laymen as well as linguists, are not aware of the extent to which even these phenomena are culturally conditioned. If we think about it at all, we would probably think that it is perfectly natural that an excited person should talk rapidly, and that an angry person raise his voice. But the more we learn of other cultures, especially those very different from our own, the less universal some of these "natural" reactions turn out to be.

Because of this type of difference it is possible for a person studying a new language or a new culture to miss some of the cues. One example of this was observed in a class of students learning Panjabi, in which one of the tones, a high falling tone, is similar to a very emphatic intonation in English. Students who were being given some words with high tone to practice were puzzled as to why their teacher seemed angry; they had interpreted the high falling tone as meaning the same as it would in their native language. In English, this extra-high and extra-loud stress has been recognized by some linguists as a distinct phoneme, which can be represented by /″/, as in /áy dónt wắnə ít may párıj./ *I don't WANT to eat my porridge!* Apart from up-and-down modifications of pitch, it is quite common to find WIDENING and NARROWING OF RANGE, as in the following cases:

If you dón't wắnt it, dón't eắt it!

[___ —— ‾‾ - ⁄‾ ‾_]

If you dón't wánt it, dón't eát it.

[_____ ‾‾‾ ___ ‾_]

(The first of these might be spoken by a mother, in a state of extreme exasperation, to a child who has decided to throw his spinach on the wall in protest. The second sentence would be perhaps more typical of the gruff speech of a stern father.)

Variations in pitch, loudness, and speed are extremely common, and play a variety of communicative roles in many languages. Another set of variations, known as VOCAL QUALIFIERS, can be produced by various phenomena in the throat and larynx; like the effects described above, these may be also produced simultaneously with sequences of normal phonemes. Various types of WHISPER, for example, can be produced by tensing the vocal cords, and letting the air pass through the narrowed aperture; in this case, the sound is produced by local air friction rather than vibration. A MURMURED

VOICE can be produced by letting the vocal cords vibrate in a very relaxed way with a characteristic breathiness; this is similar to the voiced *h* mentioned in chapter 4, and is sometimes known as TELEPHONE VOICE in Western culture when used by a female. In some languages (for example Gujarati, an Indo-Aryan language of India), murmured vowels are phonemically distinct from normal vowels. A very slow vibration of the vocal cords, with audible individual vibrations, is known as CREAKY VOICE; in our culture this is often associated with extreme fatigue, depression, or indifference, while in certain languages of Southeast Asia it is a phonemic feature.

Other modifications can be produced by tensing the throat muscles above the glottis: a "hard" or METALLIC VOICE effect can be produced in this way, and the effect popularly known as NASALIZATION (as in the movie voice of Bugs Bunny) is produced by a similar mechanism. The opposite effect, produced by relaxing the muscles of the wall of the throat, is sometimes known as FOGHORN VOICE. DRAWLED and CLIPPED VOICE involve not only changes in speed of utterance, but also extra laxness or tension in the throat muscles. Tension in the throat, along with spasmodic glottal closure, yields the phenomenon known as BREAKING VOICE, usually indicative of extreme emotional stress (though any good actor can produce this effect when called upon).

Apart from the phenomena mentioned above, animated speech in any language is punctuated by a variety of special sound effects. These are clearly distinct from other signals which use standard phonemes, and in most cases they make use of phonetic devices which cannot freely combine with "normal" speech. One difficulty about discussing these things in print is that some of them do not have traditional written representations, or even commonly accepted names. Those which can be named include: WHISTLE, LAUGH, GIGGLE, HICCUP, GASP, BELCH, GRUNT, SCREAM, GROAN, SOB, WAIL, CRY, SING, HISS, GULP, SIGH, COUGH, CLEARING ONE'S THROAT, DRAWING IN ONE'S BREATH, etc.

Some sound effects have conventional representations in English spelling, but on the whole these have very little to do with actual pronunciation; for this reason, many of them have given rise to spelling pronunciations. For example, a foreigner who only knew how to read normal English would have a hard time guessing at the actual phonetic value of some of the following noises:

Normal spelling	*Pronunciation*
ugh, ech, yech	[ɪx], [ɪːx]
woo-woo ("wolf whistle")	

Normal spelling	*Pronunciation*
ow, oooh	[uːː], [əuːː], [ɯː], etc. (usually with tensed throat muscles, often with clenched teeth)
blah, bleah	[blæːː] (often with tongue stuck out)
tsk-tsk, tch-tch	(clicks—see 4.4.)
uh, unh (a grunt)	[ʔə̃ː]
aaaaagh	[æːːː] (with extreme tension in glottis and throat)
pooh, pfaugh, pshaw	(represent various things, mostly involving labial friction)

These conventional spellings are very much in the same category as the written representations of animal cries (cluck-cluck, moo, oink-oink, bow-wow, meow, snort, etc.) and other sound effects (bang, boom, crash, thud, crack, splash, etc.). Many of us learn for example to produce acceptable imitations of a dog's bark, an automobile horn, or the like, but again we have no adequate ways of representing such sounds.

7.2 SPEECH AND NON-SPEECH SIGNALS IN THE CONTEXT OF COMMUNICATION ACTS

In face-to-face communication, all perceptible signals potentially have a part to play, and non-speech signals often have a crucial effect on the interpretation of speech signals, or on the way in which particular parts of them are emphasized. Within the broad field of communication study, there are two sub-fields which have been particularly concerned with non-speech communicative acts: KINESICS (the study of the visual aspects of non-verbal communication, including gesture, facial expression, body posture, etc.), and PROXEMICS (the study of the communicative use of space).

Though these fields have not received anything like the attention that has been given to the formal study of speech signals, enough work has been done to show that these are structured signalling systems which have their EMIC (culturally patterned and significant) and ETIC (discriminable but not significant) aspects. Furthermore, all of these signalling subsystems differ significantly from one culture to another, just as phonemic and grammatical systems do. In fact, it has been pointed out that failure to understand non-speech signals can lead to serious misunderstandings (especially in international or intercultural communication), even where there is no deficiency in understanding the linguistic signal. Thus there is potential practical value in the study of non-speech signalling systems, as an accompaniment to language study, or even independently of it. Training in kinesiology is also of value for psychologists and others involved in observation and interviewing. Trained kinesiologists are often able to guess fairly accurately at the gestures and movements used by unseen persons, e.g., when listening to a taped interview or a telephone conversation; the most useful observations, however, involve cases where the speech and non-speech (or paralinguistic) signals are INCONGRUENT (the technical term used here is META-INCONGRUENT)—since these provide valuable clues to the speaker's emotional state, which he/she may be trying (consciously or unconsciously) to conceal.

Study of the structure of communication acts indicates that they are generally divisible into three interrelated phases: an initiating or ADUMBRATIVE phase, the message itself, and a terminal or transitional phase. The adumbrative phase sets the stage, as it were, for the message: it establishes the participants and their relationship to each other, identifies the initiator of the communication, and foreshadows in various ways the type of transaction which is about to take place. When two acquaintances approach each other on the street, for example, various signals may be transmitted before they reach comfortable talking distance; these signals (such as facial expressions, arm movements, changes in gait) can indicate for example whether the communication will be a perfunctory greeting, the exchange of some important information, or a friendly chitchat.

In a telephone conversation, the adumbrative phase includes the greeting (which establishes that both ends of the wire are occupied, that the correct number has been obtained, and identifies the speakers), and the introduction of the subject to be discussed, along with any pertinent background information. At a formal meeting, the adumbrative phase includes also spatial relations such as seating arrangements and distances between participants. The less the parties concerned know about each other in advance, the more elaborate the preparations are likely to be, and the more important they will be in influencing the participants' expectations concerning the content of the forthcoming messages, and perhaps the outcome of the transaction as well.

Study of terminal or transitional phases is even less developed than that of adumbration. Presumably, the terminal phase is less crucial in its effect on the message, except when it is also part of the adumbrative phase of the next message. Clearly, a thorough understanding of human communication requires the recognition that all the signalling sub-systems mentioned here are capable of operating simultaneously with others, with the result that communication often proceeds on two or more levels at once. And since the sequential expectations in each subset of signals differ from one culture to another, it is clear that the overall study of these communicative subsystems is important both for theoretical and practical reasons. (See 18.1 for further discussion.)

NOTES

7.1. Paralanguage: Trager 1958
7.2. Kinesics: Birdwhistell (in Gumperz and Hymes 1972)
Proxemics: Hall 1968
Adumbration: Hall (in Gumperz and Hymes 1964)

SUGGESTED SUPPLEMENTARY READING

Paralanguage: Trager 1958; Pittenger, Hockett, Danehy 1960 (psychiatric, linguistic, and paralinguistic analysis of a psychiatric interview)
Kinesics: Birdwhistell (in Gumperz and Hymes 1972)
Proxemics: Hall 1959, 1968
Non-linguistic or special signalling systems: articles by Cowan, Ferguson, Herzog (in Hymes 1964); Ruesch and Kees 1956; Stern 1957

FOLLOW-UP

1   Define: paralanguage, vocal qualifiers, kinesics, proxemics.

2   Distinguish: continuous variation—discrete differences, emic–etic.

3   The importance of paralanguage and associated systems (gestures, etc.) as accompaniments to language is often underestimated. Here are some ways of attempting to understand the communicative importance of these auxiliary signalling systems:

  a. At the end of Chapter 5 (FOLLOW-UP no. 3), a number of utterances were given which could be said in different ways (i.e., with different patterns of stress, pitch, and juncture). When you say these sentences, you will probably find that you automatically produce certain intonations. What happens if you try to use the facial expressions and gestures which go with one version of a sentence, with a different version instead? Alternatively, what happens if you try to say all the different versions with no gestures or facial expression? (These experiments are most instructive if done in teams of two or more.)

  b. Choose a short dramatic passage (not more than a sentence or two) from a play, movie, novel, etc., and write out in as much detail as possible the way in which you would act it out. Transcribe the material, giving segmental and suprasegmental phonemes, then add descriptions of voice quality, vocal qualifiers, facial expressions, gestures, movements. (For an illustration of this type of thing, see Pittenger, Hockett, and Danehy 1960.)

c. The above constitutes an ETIC description, if it describes the physical details of all actions accompanying the speech act. In order to arrive at an EMIC description, it is necessary to know which details are implied by others, which are in free variation, etc. For example, it might be true that a frown in your culture is regarded as the same emic event as long as the brow is furrowed, regardless of the conformation of the mouth. Or it might be that these are partially independent. How would you go about determining the answer to such questions, in order to produce an emic description? (For some suggestions, see Birdwhistell 1960.)

d. Young children, before they learn to produce linguistic utterances, are able to convey a great deal of information with paralanguage, and those who are familiar with a particular child can often communicate with it quite well. If you have a chance to observe a child at this stage of development, try to describe its communication system, in terms of the different messages it conveys and the means by which they are conveyed.

e. If you have an opportunity to observe members of different cultures (or different ethnic groups in your own culture) communicating with each other, try to describe the differences you notice in paralinguistic features, gestures, facial expressions, movements, use of distance, etc. Can you describe the meanings of specific features you observe? Can you describe specific differences between your system and others (e.g., differences in the meaning of the "same" gesture, or different ways of conveying the same message)?

f. Describe some of the possible meanings of the following signals in your own culture: a handshake, a wink, shaking the head (rotating the head on the neck to left and right alternately), nodding the head (down-and-up movement, facing forward), waggling the head (top of the head moves from side to side), "thumbs up" (arm extended in front, fingers closed in a fist, thumb pointing up). List some other gestures with their meanings.

Chapter 8
SPEECH AND WRITING

8.1 WRITING SYSTEMS

The system for representing English phonemes presented in Chapter 3 differs in many respects from ordinary English spelling. The phonemic transcription is designed of course to avoid some of the inconsistencies of traditional spelling systems, but the reader of this book may nevertheless not be convinced that the advantages are all on the side of the phonemic transcription. In fact, a comparison of the two shows that the traditional system has many useful features which cannot be incorporated in a strict phonemic representation as defined in Chapter 3. This chapter will be concerned with examining some of the relationships between speech and writing, and discussing some of the reasons why a strict phonemic representation is not always the most useful one.

The writing systems most familiar in western society are ALPHABETIC systems, which means that (in spite of many exceptions and inconsistencies) they are constructed on the principle that a character in the script represents a phonemic segment. This can be seen clearly if we compare such systems with those which use a separate symbol for each distinct syllable, such as the

Sumerian cuneiform system used for many languages of the ancient Near East. Such systems are known as SYLLABIC systems. Syllabic and alphabetic systems can be classed together as PHONETIC SYSTEMS, in that they represent pronunciation; they are thus opposed to LOGOGRAPHIC systems, which represent words or meanings and have no direct connection with pronunciation. In the American Indian sign languages which represented an interval of a day by a sign for the sun, and an interval of a month by a sign for the moon, there was no connection with the pronunciation of the words for 'sun' or 'moon' (or 'day' or 'month'). Such systems have the advantage that one sequence of symbols carries the same meaning to people speaking entirely different languages, even though the phonetic form in each language might be completely different. The traditional Chinese writing system makes extensive use of logographic representation, and has the advantage of serving as a link among the many varieties of modern Chinese, some of which are mutually unintelligible in their spoken forms.

Though European languages use alphabetic systems, the system of numerical and mathematical notation which they all use is actually logographic, since written expressions like $7 + 4$, 8×2, $4/5$, $\sqrt{-2}$, etc. stand for sequences of *meanings*, which are the same regardless of how the messages are pronounced: 8×2 means the same whether we read it as *eight times two*, or *huit fois deux*, or *achtmal zwei*, or any other way. Even within a single language, such symbols represent meanings independently of how they are pronounced: thus the symbol *2* alone represents English /tu/, but in *20*, *2nd*, and *1/2* it stands for /twen/, /sekən/, and /hæf/ respectively. (If the same principle were extended, we could get *1ce*, *2ce*, *3ce* for *once, twice, thrice*; *1le*, *2le*, *3le* for *single, double, triple*; *1ary*, *2ary* for *primary, secondary*; *2cycle* for *bicycle*; *3plets* for *triplets*, etc.)

The different types of writing systems appear to have developed by a progressive process of analysis into smaller and smaller items. The earliest graphic messages were probably more or less "natural" pictures of events such as battles, or unique configurations of marks representing individuals' names, for identification of property, etc. Gradually, as certain signs came to stand by convention for certain meanings, usually with increased stylization of the signs themselves, it became possible to combine them more freely so as to produce a greater and greater variety of messages (such as the ones just mentioned).

When such a system is used by speakers of the same language (or closely related languages), particular signs ultimately come to represent not only particular meanings, but the actual sounds of the words which convey those meanings. The stage is then set for a major breakthrough, involving the principle of PHONETICIZATION (also known as the REBUS METHOD of representation). An example of this can be seen in the use of a stylized representation of an arrow in the Sumerian system to represent both the word *ti* 'arrow' and the homonymous word *ti* 'life'. By this method, the 'meaning' of the symbol becomes transferred from the idea "arrow" to the phonemic sequence *ti*, and can represent it whenever it occurs. (This would be comparable to using logographic symbols like *1* and *2* to represent the syllables /wən/, /tu/, etc., as in : *I want this 1, Who 1 the game? They 8 2 much B 4 dinner.*)

Once this principle was extended to cover all the syllables in a language, it produced a very satisfactory writing system. The change from a SYLLABARY or SYLLABIC writing system to a full-fledged ALPHABET is a smaller step than the original shift from logographic to phonetic representation. Even those systems which are basically logographic, such as the Chinese system, make use of syllabic or other phonetic signs to supplement the basic system. (A fascinating description of the development and functioning of writing systems can be found in Gelb 1963.)

8.2 REDUNDANCY

Native speakers of a language can manage quite well with writing systems which are far from accurate. Thus, the requirements for a system to be used for natives need not be as strict as those we have proposed in Chapter 3. For example, anyone who knows English well will have no difficulty in reading aloud a sentence like *I read a lot of books*, because the context will normally tell him whether to pronounce *read* to rhyme with *reed* or with *red*. This is possible in general because of the presence of a great deal of REDUNDANCY, or superfluous information, in normal language; in the present case, we could say that the spoken form of the above sentence contains a REDUNDANT indication of the tense of the verb *read*, since we already know from context whether the speaker is referring to a habitual activity or to some past series of events.

The presence of redundancy in the auditory channel makes it possible for us to understand a conversation over the telephone even with a bad connection, or in a crowded cafeteria. If one does not know a language well, it is much more difficult to understand in such situations, even though the native may be unaware of any disturbance. The elimination of some of this redundancy in the written language occasions no great loss of clarity for the native. This can be illustrated by the following sentence, which most literate English speakers can read with no great trouble:

xxrlxnxs, rxxlrxxds, xnd bxs lxnxs txxk xmxrgxncy mxxsxrxs lxst nxght tx mxxt thx drxstxc dxsrxptxxn xf trxnspxrtxtxxn bx thx strxkx schxdxlxd fxr txdxy xgxxnst fxvx mxjxr xxrlxnxs.

(In this sentence, the letter *x* has been substituted for the symbols *a e i o u*.)

Some writing systems have been devised which exploit this feature of redundancy, and make it possible to write faster by eliminating certain distinctions: shorthand systems work this way, for example. The above sentence shows how easy it is to read English even when most of the vowel contrasts are not marked, as long as the consonants are retained. The Urdu writing system, which employes a variety of the Arabic script, commonly omits most of the signs representing the short vowels / ɪ ə ʊ /; at the same time, it uses a single symbol for the vowels / i e ɛ / and the semi-vowel /y/, and another symbol for the vowels / u o ɔ / and the semi-vowel /w/. Most of these different contrasts *can* be indicated (by diacritical marks) in Urdu script, but in actual practice most handwritten documents, and many printed ones, omit them.

Such a system is more efficient for the writer, since it allows more rapid composition than a strictly phonemic one. Practiced writers of Urdu are able to write their language almost as fast as a shorthand stenographer writes English. The loss to the reader, if he is a native, does not appear to be particularly significant, since those differences not indicated can be recovered from the context. The difference between the words /ʊs/ 'that' and /ɪs/ 'this' would not, for example, appear in normal Urdu writing; this will not interfere seriously with communication, because the context will ordinarily tell the reader which one to choose—and when it does not tell him, then there is probably no significant difference anyhow.

8.3 DIAPHONEMIC FEATURES

If someone wished to impose a phonemic writing system on all English-speaking school children, which of the spellings of *Tuesday* would he insist on: /túzdi/, /túzde/, /tyúzdi/, or /tyúzde/? Would he write *barn* as /báhn/ to please the New Englander and the Southerner, or as /bárn/ to suit the majority of Americans? Should *schedule* be written /skéjuəl/, in American style, or /šédyuːl/, as in the Queen's English? If pronunciation is standardized then everyone would write the same, but this raises very difficult questions about the choice of a standard variety.

Alternatively, everyone could write the way he pronounces. This, however, creates difficulties for the reader, who would be considerably slowed down by having to deal with unfamiliar forms. For this reason, most writing systems have only a single form for each word (though there are occasional variants, such as *connection–connexion*, *gray–grey*, and some languages allow more variation than English does). This means that, if the same writing system is to serve a number of different dialects in an adequate way, it must incorporate DIAPHONEMIC features—i.e., ways of writing that can be pronounced according to different rules in different dialects. Spellings like *Tuesday* and *new* are diaphonemic in this way, since they can be read either with or without a /y/ following the first consonant, depending on the dialect.

If *lute* and *loot* were both written in the same way, this would not be appropriate for those varieties of English which distinguish them (e.g., RP /lyuːt/ vs. /luːt/). Similarly, the writings *du* and *tu* in such words as *graduate*, *educate*, *situation*, *spatula*, represent /j/ and /c/ in most U.S. dialects, but /dy/ and /ty/ in RP. Spellings with *r* in pre-consonantal position, as in *beard*, *bared*, *bard*, *board*, cause no great trouble for speakers of "*r*-less" dialects, since the written *r* can be converted into a lengthening of the vowel or a following /ə/ (depending on the dialect and the phonological circumstances) by fairly systematic rules; thus speakers of these dialects have no trouble pronouncing new words containing *r*.

Though most Americans have the same vowel /æ/ in words like *bath* and *pass* as they do in *man* and *hat*, speakers of standard British have /a/ in these words, as in *calm* and *father*. Similarly, the sound written with *o* in *hot*, *on*, *bother* is for many Americans the same phoneme /a/ which occurs in *far*, *Kahn*, *father*—though for standard British speakers it is the same as the vowel /ɔ/, which occurs lengthened in such words as *bought* /bɔːt/, *lawn* /lɔːn/, *northern* /nɔːðən/. Since, however, there are general rules by which one can predict the correct reading in each kind of English, speakers of both varieties are able to give the "correct" pronunciation for most words they encounter in print, even if they are unfamiliar. Thus, in spite of apparent inconsistencies within each "dialect", the traditional system works better than it might be expected to, and for this reason linguists may well hesitate to tamper with it.

8.4   MORPHOPHONEMIC FEATURES

In certain cases, the imposition of strict phonemic spelling would disturb some of the regularities which appear in the traditional spelling systems. In the following pairs of words, the second member differs from the first only by the addition of *-ity* in normal spelling, whereas in the phonemic form other differences also appear:

stupid /stúpɪd/	*stupidity* /stɪpídɪti/
solid /sálɪd/	*solidity* /sɪlídɪti/
human /(h)yúmɪn/	*humanity* /(h)yɪmǽnɪti/

legal /lígɪl/	*legality* /lɪgǽlɪti/
prior /práyər/	priority /prayɔ́rɪti/

(There is some variation in the pronunciation of the forms in the righthand column; some speakers have /u/ or /yu/ instead of /ɪ/ in the first syllable of *stupidity*, *humanity*, /i/ in the first syllable of *legality*, etc.)

Since there are regular rules underlying the vowel changes illustrated here, English speakers have very little trouble knowing how to read these forms. These rules, which speakers know without necessarily having learned them consciously, are as follows: (1) words ending in the suffix *-ity* /ɪti/ are always accented on the syllable preceding the suffix; (2) unaccented vowels are reduced to /ɪ/ or /ə/, or are lost completely (depending on the position in the word and on the dialect). Since these rules exist, it would be possible to replace the strict phonemic spellings in the left column above with the following modified phonemic spellings, which will produce the correct pronunciations of the forms in the second column when the suffix /ɪti/ is added and the above two rules are applied:

stupid /stúpɪd/, Br. /styúpɪd/
solid /sálɪd/, Br. /sɔ́lɪd/
human /(h)yúmæn/
legal /lígæl/
prior /práyər/

Such spellings as these are known as MORPHOPHONEMIC spellings; their implications are discussed in detail in Chapter 12.

Many traditional writing systems contain features of this kind, not necessarily by design, but often as a result of conservatism. When SOUND CHANGE (see 21.2) produces differences in different forms of the same word, the standard spelling often fails to change, thus sacrificing some of its earlier phonemic accuracy, but continuing to show the relationships among different forms. A familiar example to students of French involves the "silent" *s* in such examples as the following:

"silent" *s*	*s* = /z/
les fruits /lefrɥi/ 'the fruits"	les arbres /lezarbr/ 'the trees'
mes frères /mefrɛr/ 'my brothers'	mes amis /mezami/ 'my friends'
Regarde-les! /rəgardle/ 'Look at them!'	Regarde les autres! /rəgard lezotr/ 'Look at the others!'

The rule is that final *s* is "silent" when followed by a consonant or by a pause, but is pronounced /z/ when followed by a vowel or by one of the three semi-vowels (cf. *les yeux* /lezyö/ 'the eyes', *les oiseaux* /lezwazo/ 'the birds', *les huitres* /lezµitr/ 'the oysters'). In German and Russian, all voiced stops such as / b d g / become voiceless at the ends of words, so that for example German *Kalb* 'calf', *Eid* 'oath', *Tag* 'day' are pronounced /kalp/, /ait/, /taːk/, but in their plural forms they retain the voiced stops: *Kälbe* /kelbe/, *Eide* /aide/, *Tage* /taːge/. In both these languages, the standard spelling takes no notice of the alternation. Another obvious example of this is the English "possessive '*s*": speakers of English are often unaware (and have no need to be aware) that the uniform writing '*s* represents /s/ in *Pat's* or *Mac's*, /z/ in *John's* or *Bill's*, and /ɪz/ in *Liz's* or *George's*. (These examples are discussed further in 12.1.)

8.5 SOME PROBLEMS

In English and numerous other languages, there are many distinctions observed in normal spelling which have no phonemic correspondence: we are taught, for example, to distinguish in spelling such words as *read–reed*, *loan–lone*, *by–buy*, *bore–boar*, *bear–bare*, *pair–pear*, *beach–beech*, *steel–steal*, *ore–oar*, *site–cite–sight*, etc., even though we do not distinguish them in pronunciation. Such distinctions are perhaps useful in that they supply some additional redundancy to compensate for that which is lost as a result of other defects in the writing system.

In many cases, the differences have a historical basis, i.e., the difference in spelling indicates that there was originally a difference in pronunciation. In some cases the spelling also provides information about the origin of words; for example, the *gh* in *sight* indicates Anglo-Saxon origin, whereas the *c* of *cite* is a mark of French origin. Many scholars have resisted spelling reform for this reason, since they consider it convenient to have this type of record of the history of words, as well as a visual way of distinguishing homonyms. One might raise the question whether this historical information, which is of little value to the common man, is worth retaining in the face of the intellectual effort needed to teach the average child how to spell. (In some cases, the presence of orthographic devices such as the apostrophe which distinguishes *dogs* (plural) from *dog's* (possessive), and the capital letters which distinguish *Turkey* from *turkey* and *Smith* from *smith*, may serve a useful function.) Other languages are also subject to this type of problem. Urdu has five different characters which represent the phoneme /z/; the reason is that in words of Arabic origin, certain differences which are phonemic in Arabic are indicated in Urdu writing, even though Urdu speakers do not pronounce the distinctions.

The following list shows some of the duplications of spelling used in writing certain English consonant phonemes:

Phoneme	Spelling
c	*ch*ew, ca*tch*, *c*ello
k	*c*at, *k*in, si*ck*, so*cc*er, *q*uiet, li*qu*or, *ch*orus
j	*j*aw, *g*in, lo*dge*
m	*m*eet, su*mm*er, la*mb*, hy*mn*
n	*n*et, *gn*u, *kn*ow, *pn*eumonia, di*nn*er
f	*f*in, *ph*one, ga*ff*, enou*gh*
s	*s*in, ki*ss*, de*c*eive, a*s*certain, a*x* (*x* = /ks/), Kat*z*
š	*sh*in, addi*ti*on, so*ci*al, *s*ure, *sch*napps
ž	vi*si*on, gla*zi*er, gara*ge*, ca*s*ual
y	*y*ou, v*i*ew, c*u*te, f*e*w, b*eau*ty, f*j*ord
w	*w*in, q*u*een, g*u*ava, Zo*u*ave

On the whole, the consonant situation is not bad compared to the vowels. Following are most of the spellings used for the various vowels and diphthongs of English in stressed position:

Phoneme	Spelling
i	b*e*, s*ee*, f*ie*ld, mach*i*ne, b*ea*m, rec*ei*ve, p*eo*ple, k*ey*, C*ae*sar, qu*ay*, prett*y*, br*ea*the, p*i*zza (13)
ɪ	f*i*t, pr*e*tty, s*ie*ve, w*o*men, g*ui*ld, b*u*sy, m*y*th, (cr*ee*k) (8)
e	f*a*te, st*a*tion, b*ai*t, s*ay*, br*ea*k, th*ey*, r*ei*n, g*au*ge, n*eigh*bor, str*aigh*t (10)
ε	g*e*t, br*ea*d, *a*ny, h*ei*fer, s*ai*d, s*ay*s, b*u*ry, fr*ie*nd, g*ue*st, G*eo*ffrey (10)
æ	b*a*t, l*au*gh, c*a*lf, pl*ai*d, h*a*ve (5)
ə	b*u*t, bl*oo*d, s*o*n, c*o*me, c*ou*ple, d*oe*s, w*o*rd, b*i*rd, h*e*rd, h*ea*rd, sh*a*rd (11)
a	f*a*r, l*o*ck, Sh*a*h, c*a*lm, s*e*rgeant, h*ea*rt, g*ua*rd, su*a*ve (8)
ʊ	b*oo*k, f*u*ll, w*o*lf, c*ou*ld (4)
u	t*oo*, l*u*te, tr*ue*, n*ew*, thr*ou*gh, can*oe*, m*o*ve, s*ou*p, fr*ui*t, man*eu*vre, w*o*mb, tw*o*, S*au*lt, S*iou*x (14)
ɔ	s*aw*, f*o*r, c*ou*rt, *a*ll, f*au*lt, br*oa*d, t*au*ght, br*ou*ght, w*a*lk (9)
o	g*o*, n*o*te, g*oa*t, d*oe*, s*ou*l, r*ow*, s*ew*, b*eau*, th*ou*gh (9)
ay	b*y*, w*i*ne, l*ie*, h*igh*, *ai*sle, h*eigh*t, g*ey*ser, *I*, b*uy*, *eye*, l*ye*, l*ei*tmotiv (12)
aw	*ou*t, n*ow*, b*ou*gh, F*au*st (4)
oy	b*oi*l, b*oy*, Fr*eu*d (3)

An examination of these lists shows that there are few letters or combinations of letters that do not have more than one reading. Various historical factors are responsible for this, of which the main ones are: (1) the loss of certain earlier contrasts, such as those represented by *ee* in *see* and *ea* in *sea*, *ie* in *lie* and *igh* in *high*, without any changes in the spelling; (2) sound changes such as those which resulted in the present values of the vowels in words such as *fate, mete, kite, wrote, cute* (followed by consonant plus "silent *e*") as compared with their values in *fat, met, kit, rot, cut*; (3) the importation of foreign words from various sources without adaptation of spelling, such as: *cologne, machine, attaché, schnapps, Mauser, sauerkraut, señorita, chihuahua, caballero, pizza, dolce, Veldt, philosophy, myth, xenon, isthmus.*

8.6   SOME SOLUTIONS

From time to time one hears proposals of spelling reform for English, but they are generally not taken seriously—and when one sees the kinds of reforms that have occasionally been proposed, one can understand this. It is of course at the initial reading stage that most trouble is encountered, and it is possible that a reformed spelling would possibly be worth the effort of children and teachers to learn our present system. Until the present, however, no linguists have taken this matter seriously enough to realistically examine the possible alternatives.

An attempt to alleviate the problem at the early learning stage resulted in the Initial Teaching Alphabet (ITA), which was tried on a large scale in Britain in 1963–64. The ITA follows by and large the phonemic principle, but the representations are designed so as to provide an easy transition to conventional spelling. Thus, for example, children would initially learn to read *ie* as /ay/ in such words as *bie* (= *by* or *buy*), *lien* (= *line*), *niet* (= *night*), *fiev* (= *five*). Phonemes which are not distinguished in ordinary spelling have different but similar representations in ITA. Thus, cases of /z/ which are represented by *s* in normal spelling have a special symbol ƨ in ITA (e.g., *boyƨ* = *boys*, *houƨeƨ* = *houses*, etc.). Once the student has mastered the principle of graphic representation, it is possible to introduce him in a gradual way to the massive irregularities of normal English spelling.

Any attempt to reform a spelling system should first take stock of those features which are functional, such as diaphonemic and morphophonemic writings, and try to retain these as much as possible. Apart from this, the main problems will involve finding some sort of balance between the traditional system and one which is approximately phonemic.

Figure 8-1 indicates some possible solutions for English vowels. Under the heading Modified Spellings, the spellings in Column I are arrived at by taking the most common representations of each sound and then eliminating conflicts. Those in Column II go farther toward making the writing congruent

Phoneme (see Ch. 3)	Example (normal spelling)	Modified spellings (I)	(II)	(III)*
ɪ	bit	i	i	i
i	beat	ee	ie	iː
ɛ	bet	e	e	e
e	bait	{ ay (final) / ai (non-final)	ey	eː
æ	bat	a	æ	æ
ʌ	but	u (/ər/ = er)	ə	ə
a	pa	ah	a	a
ʊ	foot	oo	u	u
u	boot	ue	ue	uː
ɔ	bought	au	o	o
o	boat	oa	ow	oː
ay	bite	{ y (final) / ie (non-final)	ay	ay
aw	bout	ow	au	aw
oy	point	oi	oy	oy
ɪ, ə (unstressed)		e	ə	ə

Figure 8-1. Some possible modified spellings for English vowels.

* Vowel symbols in column III are used in transcribing English examples in the following chapters.

with pronunciation, by using similar representations for the pairs /ɪ i /, /ɛ e /, / ʊ u /, and / ɔ o /. Column III presents a system, similar to Column II, which will be used (mainly for typographical reasons) in transcribing English examples in the following chapters.

On the whole, consonants are less troublesome than vowels; the only ones which cause trouble are / c ŋ θ ð š ž /. Retaining the traditional combinations *ch ng th sh* for / c ŋ θ š /, one might propose the parallel representations *dh* (for /ð/) and *zh* (for /ž/). The following examples illustrate these proposals.

Standard Spelling:
Airlines, railroads, and bus lines took emergency measures last night to meet the drastic disruption of transportation threatened by the strike scheduled for today against five major airlines.

Modification I:
Airliens, railroads, and bus liens took emerjensee mezhers last niet tue meet dhe drastik disrupshen ov transportaishen thretnd by dhe striek skejueld for teday egenst fiev maijer airliens.

Modification II:
Erlayns, reylrowds, ænd bəs layns tuk əmərjənsi mezhərs læst nayt tue miet dhə dræstik disrəpshən əv trænsporteyshən thretnd bay dhə strayk skejuəld for təday əgenst fayv meyjər erlayns.

Modification III (revised phonemic transcription system):
/érlaynz↑, ré:lro:dz↑, ænd bə́s+lyánz—, túk imə́rjənsi: mezherz lǽst náyt—, tu: mí:t dhədrǽstik disrə́pshən əv trænsporté:shən—, thrétnd bay dhəstráyk skéjuəld for tədé:—, əgénst fáyv mé:jər érlaynz↓./

British (RP):
/éəlaynz↑, ré:lro:dz↑, ænd bə́s+láynz—, tuk imə́:jənsi: mézhəz lást náyt—tu: mí:t dhədrástik disrə́pshən əv transpəté:shən, thrétnd bay dhəstráyk shédyu:ld foə tudé:—, əgé:nst fáyv mé:jə(r) éəlaynz↓./

SUGGESTED SUPPLEMENTARY READING

Writing systems: Gelb 1963
English spelling: E. Trager 1957
History of English spelling: Strang 1970

FOLLOW-UP

1   Define: alphabetic writing, syllabic writing, redundancy, diaphonemic feature, morphophonemic feature.

2   Distinguish: phonetic writing system—logographic writing system.

3   The last section of this chapter introduced a revised phonemic transcription system (exemplified in modification III of the sample sentence), which will be used throughout the rest of this book to cite English examples in phonemic form. The advantage of this system over the one previously proposed is that it requires fewer special symbols. The following exercises are suggested in order to help you familiarize yourself with this new system:

   a. Convert the words given at the end of Chapter 3 (FOLLOW-UP nos. 3 and 4) into the new transcription, and check them against the following list: bæt, pic, drənk, ble:m, laj, shu:z, mæth, sed, ay, celo:, indayt, yat, be:kt, jəj, bo:, e:t, əv, of, næt, dho:, go:st, hæf, yoːk, shud, muːv, stoːv, ləv, kwayər, sam, mər, ko(ə)r, siːn, kweshcən/kwescən, ic, eː(t)th, mith; biːt, teːk, streːt, tok, laws, luk, foːn, red, riːd, eːt, sayt, weːt, miːt, cek, strec, brij, noː, saw, haws, hawz, noyziː, bosiː, skaw(ə)r, suːt, kræk.

b. Convert the following words in the new transcription into ordinary English spelling: /bot, boːt, sut, suːt, kyuːt, pen, peːn, pæn, ric, riːc, ifekt, ifektiv, foːniːm, foːniːmik, kalij, kəlazh, kəlayd, kəlizhən, klinik, kiniːziks, mes + kit, məskiːt, kəloːn, koːlən, kaləniː, məshiːnəriː, mishəneriː, prins, bənænəz, forid/farid, thing, rædhər, tar, tawər, tayər, tuːr, toːr, tiːr, teːr, meriː, mæriː, meəriː, inglish/. (The pronunciation is that used in those areas of the United States which lack any particular regional color. See the end of Chapter 25 for the normal spellings of these words.)

PART II

FORM AND FUNCTION

Chapter 9

THE STUDY OF
GRAMMATICAL STRUCTURE

9.1 INTRODUCTION

In Part I we examined the properties of linguistic channels which make it possible for one individual to transmit messages to another. Communication, of course, requires a channel. But there must be something else: the sender and the receiver of the message must share a set of conventions or rules which enable them to encode and decode messages in their language. Parts II and III will focus on the nature and form of such rules.

When we say that people who speak the same language share a set of rules, we mean that linguistic behavior is organized and has a structure which follows rules. The job of the linguist is to study the linguistic structure of a language and to attempt to formulate these rules. In studying phonology, we found that what at first appears to be a confused jumble of sounds is actually a pattern of sounds, that can be accounted for by a few basic phonemic entities or distinctive features. Phonemes and distinctive features are abstract entities which are posited by the linguist. They cannot be directly observed in what people say or write; rather, they represent the underlying elements that a linguist posits in order to explain the observed data (i.e., people's linguistic behavior).

The phonemic transcription of a sentence is its PHONOLOGICAL REPRE-SENTATION. A complete description of a sentence would also include its GRAMMATICAL REPRESENTATION and its SEMANTIC REPRESENTATION. The primary motivation for presenting the phonological description of a language before its grammatical and semantic description is that the sounds of a language are immediately available for observation and analysis. It is convenient to first study how the sounds of a language combine into larger units of language structure.

Semantic representations, which will be discussed in Part III, are designed to show what information is conveyed by each part of a sentence. In order to do this, of course, we need to be able to identify what we mean by a "part of a sentence." Grammatical representations identify the formal parts which are capable of being associated with meanings: the MORPHEMES (Ch. 11), WORDS (11.3), and the ARRANGEMENTS in which they occur (Ch. 10).

For someone who wants to learn a language, or who has some other practical motivation for looking into the nature of language, all this may sound unduly technical or irrelevant. Such a person wants to know how particular messages can be conveyed in a specific language. But a linguist, whose interest is not necessarily limited to a particular language, also wants to know what GENERAL PROPERTIES of language allow it to serve as a com-munication system, and in what ways different languages are similar or dissimilar.

Even if we restrict ourselves to the first need, it is still a large task to describe a language adequately. For one thing, the number of possible sentences in any language is potentially infinite. It has often been pointed out that it is possible to produce sentences which have probably never been heard or uttered before, but which are completely understandable. For example:

> I know that you know that he knows that the property which he inherited from our granduncle is in dispute.
> Seven percent of the new 10-millimeter plastic valves were defective, and had to be returned to the factory.
> I don't know the man who took the spoon that Horace left on the table that was lying upside down in the upstairs hallway of the building that burned down last night.

If it is at all possible to write rules which account for such sentences, these rules must be very general and abstract, since it is obviously impossible to list all the possible sentences in a language. Moreover, every language may impose restrictions on sentence structure which do not exist in other languages. There are, for example, general rules which govern the ORDER of elements in particular languages, and these differ from one language to another.

Suppose, for example, a beginning student of Hindi-Urdu is given a bilingual dictionary and instructed to translate the sentence *He is not here.* The dictionary will tell him that *he* should be translated as /vo/, *is* as /hɛ/, *not* as /nəhĩ/, and *here* as /yəhã/. With no further information, he might be expected to use English word order and produce the sentence /vo hɛ nəhĩ yəhã/ (assuming that he can pronounce it properly). A Hindi-Urdu speaker would understand the sentence, but it would sound strange to him. The normal Hindi-Urdu version would be /vo yəhã nəhĩ hɛ/ (though there are other possible orders, if the speaker wants to express particular emphasis).

But even if the student is given the correct form of that sentence, he is still not in a position to translate any other sentence. Suppose he is given the sentence *He went home*, and again following English word order renders it as /vo gəya ghər/ (having found out that /gəya/ means 'he-went', and /ghər/ means 'house' or 'home'). Again a native speaker would understand the sentence, but correct it to /vo ghər gəya/.

At this point, rather than continue with this trial-and-error method, he might be given some general rules which would help him translate as many different sentences as possible. In a rather informal way, we might formulate the following rules for word order in Hindi-Urdu:

1   the subject of a sentence (/vo/ in the above examples) is usually the first word;
2   the verb (/hɛ/ and /gəya/ in the above examples) is normally the last word in a sentence;
3   all the other words come between the subject and the verb; if /nəhĩ/ 'not' is present, it is the last word before the verb.

Though greatly oversimplified, these rules would guide the beginning student in forming such new sentences as:

   a. vo yəhã hɛ
      he here is
      'He is here'.
   b. vo ghər nəhĩ gəya
      he home not went
      'He did not go home'.
   c. vo aj nəhĩ gəya
      he today not went
      'He did not go today'.
   d. vo kəhã gəya
      he where went
      'Where did he go?' (= 'He went where?')

e. vo phəl laya
   he fruit brought
   'He brought fruit'.
f. mɛ̃ phəl laya
   I fruit brought
   'I brought fruit'. etc.

A point has to be made about the different needs of someone learning a language, and someone describing it. It is entirely possible that a language teacher would prefer to expose a student to sentences such as these, before giving any explicit rule. He might even ask the student to deduce the rule from the examples. Some teachers even avoid talking about rules at all, preferring to expose students to large amounts of material in a new language so that they "learn" the rules unconsciously, rather than from the teacher.

These however are questions of teaching techniques. However a teacher may decide to teach, the linguist must describe the language as explicitly and as exhaustively as he can. Even the teacher who does not mention rules may need to use a description of the language which gives explicit rules. It will help him design sentences which will best show the students how the language operates. Even the teacher instructing students in his native language may not know certain rules, if he has not seen a linguistic description of his language. Thus the descriptive linguist's task is more general than the language teacher's.

Students of foreign languages will be familiar with rules like those given for Hindi-Urdu word order. But there are many assumptions hidden in such rules. For example, rules of this type commonly use terms like *subject* and *verb* without defining them, since it is assumed that these can be generally defined for all languages. It is also often assumed that these definitions are known to students. In fact both these assumptions are wrong. Without going into detail here, let us simply point out that some languages are different enough from our own so that often the expected rules and categories do not apply. This can be illustrated by errors that foreign learners of a language make. Here are some specimens:

1 It didn't enough.   (It wasn't enough.)
2 I will ready soon.   (I will be ready soon.)
3 He is very thief.   (He is a big thief.)
4 He is coward   (He is a coward.)
5 (Q: How do you like the spaghetti?)
   A: They're very good.   (It's very good.)
6 We stayed Buffalo.   (We stayed in Buffalo.)
7 I slept the other bed.   (I slept in the other bed.)
8 He came yesterday to school.   (He came to school yesterday.)

All of these sentences are aberrant, but easily understood, at least in the appropriate contexts.

In order to correct sentences 1–2, a grammar of English must state that *enough* and *ready* belong to a class of forms (traditionally called ADJECTIVES) which can occur in such contexts as *It is* _____, *He is* _____, *It will be* _____, *He was* _____, *She was* _____, etc. (with a form of *be*, or one of a very small class of words such as *get* or *become*—as in *He got ready*). *Enough* and *ready* are used in sentences 1–2 as though they were verbs (such as *suffice* in *It didn't suffice*, or *come* in *I will come soon*). To those who know English, it may seem obvious that *enough* and *ready* are adjectives and not verbs, but since it is not obvious to others, it is necessary to provide this information explicitly.

The above statement shows in rough form the two types of information that must be given for such cases: (1) the GRAMMATICAL CATEGORIES to which each form belongs, such as *enough* = adjective, *suffice* = verb (this is usually done in existing dictionaries, though with some differences which will be discussed below); and (2) grammatical rules describing the FUNCTIONS of (members of) each grammatical category. It is not sufficient to give someone only the first type of information, and then expect his intuition to tell him how verbs, adjectives, and so forth should be used.

It is important to remember that the two kinds of information are so closely linked that one can determine the grammatical category of a form only when one knows its function in a sentence. Sentences 3–4 above illustrate this point further: it is not reasonable to expect everyone to know that *thief* and *coward* are nouns in English, and therefore require a preceding article (*a(n)* or *the*). In many other languages, words which refer to similar concepts are actually adjectives (cf. *honest, dishonest, crooked, fair, brave, afraid*, etc.).

Sentence 5 illustrates the need to specify that there is a class of nouns in English which do not normally form plurals. The usual term for this is MASS NOUN (including *spaghetti, wheat, water, air*), as opposed to COUNT NOUN (such as *vegetable, house, man*), which form plurals more readily, and require the plural form when preceded by words like *these* or *those*. The arbitrariness of this feature of English can be seen when we notice for example that *noodle* is a count noun, whereas *spaghetti* is a mass noun, *rice* and *wheat* are mass nouns whereas *oats* is a count noun, etc.

Language students often have difficulty using grammatical terms such as these, partly because these terms are taught so imprecisely in elementary school English classes. But students also misunderstand the purpose of these terms. A linguist has to establish grammatical categories and give them names because only then can he write rules that work. He must find the proper categories that make his rules valid. He can use major categories like noun, verb, adjective, etc. for many languages (though they do not exactly correspond from one language to another). But he always has to establish subcategories for particular rules.

Sentences 6–7 above illustrate a sub-class of verbs such as *stay, sleep, go, come, remain* (usually known as INTRANSITIVE VERBS), which do not occur in sentences that have a noun immediately following the verb as in sentences 6–7. Another sub-class includes verbs like *see, visit, pass, like, prefer, know* (known as TRANSITIVE VERBS), which are usually followed by a noun (as in *We saw Buffalo* and *I prefer the other bed*).

Sentence 8 illustrates a need for even smaller sub-categories, since the rule must determine where different categories of adverb phrases occur. For example, in a sentence like *I went from school to the park*, an ADVERB PHRASE OF ORIGIN (*from school*) may intervene between the VERB OF MOTION (like *go*) and the ADVERB PHRASE OF DESTINATION (*to the park*); but in a sentence like *I went home yesterday*, the ADVERB PHRASE OF TIME (*yesterday*) follows the adverb of destination (*home*).

These examples not only show the need for EXPLICITNESS in a descriptive grammar, but also make it clear why it must be EXHAUSTIVE. The ideal descriptive grammar of English must allow anyone who uses it, no matter what his native language, to find in it rules that direct him to construct any conceivable correct sentence in English. Another way of saying this is that a complete descriptive grammar would make it possible for someone who spoke no English to recognize any incorrect English sentence, because it would provide rules for forming all possible correct English sentences. If the rules did not describe any particular sentence, then it would be judged incorrect.

In this way such a grammar would be very different, say, from a manual of English for speakers of Persian, which would concentrate on the types of mistakes commonly made by Persians, but would ignore those features of English which are similar to Persian. A complete descriptive grammar of English could serve as a source book for any and all such manuals, be they for speakers of Persian, Malay, Eskimo, or Spanish. This is of course an immense task, which has not yet been accomplished for any language. It is not even certain that with our present techniques such a task can be accomplished. Nevertheless, it seems a worthwhile goal to aim for.

All of the rules discussed so far in this chapter are GRAMMATICAL RULES. Such rules are clearly distinct from PHONOLOGICAL RULES, which tell how forms are pronounced, and from SEMANTIC RULES, which tell what they mean. In the case of the hypothetical student of Hindi-Urdu mentioned above, even if we assume that he knows how the individual words are pronounced and has some idea of their meanings, he will still need a grammatical rule to help him get them in the right order and to understand the order of words in sentences he reads and hears. The examples of foreign English given above illustrate violations of grammatical rules only—since there is nothing peculiar about the meanings of the messages, and even if such sentences were pronounced badly, they could still be understood.

Examples of this type indicate that grammar and semantics are to some extent independent, even though a complete description of a language must include both. One way of describing the difference between grammar and semantics is to say that grammar answers the question: "Which sentences are correct?" (or WELL-FORMED, to use a term borrowed from logic), and semantics answers the questions: "How are meanings organized into forms and sentences?" and "How are messages interpreted or understood?" One may argue that the last question involves much more than the description of linguistic forms and their organization into sentences. For instance, it is now generally agreed that linguistic structure and socio–cultural structure are intimately connected (see Ch. 18).

This distinction between grammar and semantics does not, however, neatly divide the domain of descriptive linguistics into two distinct parts, since the question "How are meanings organized?" actually implicates the whole process of producing messages, even down to the pronunciation. On the other hand, some linguists believe that once the question "Which sentences are correct?" has been answered, nothing further can be said about a language. Often, the distinction between grammar and semantics reflects primarily the approach a linguist has to linguistic description, i.e., where he puts the greatest emphasis. In this book, the question of describing well-formed sentences in formal terms is approached first. In Part III we will look at things from the other end, i.e., from the point of view of meaning.

It should also be made clear that grammar is not directly related to "common sense", or truth, or logic. Most lies are perfectly grammatical, and even certain types of nonsense (such as *He lost the money I forgot to give him*) do not violate any known rules of grammar. Such sentences may even be translatable (e.g., French: *Il a perdu l'argent que j'avais oublié de lui donner*), which indicates that, whatever is wrong with them, it is not strictly linguistic.

On the other hand, it is possible to construct sentences in a mechanical way which seem to have certain properties of real sentences, and yet it is hard to imagine any real-life context in which they could be used; the following were constructed by picking words from a dictionary at random:

The drama denatured the humble badminton.
The biography chart facilitated the confiture.
Arthritis delighted the purport.
The capacitor entailed the burgess.

Such examples teach us that a sentence can be superficially "correct" without having any foundation, so to speak; that is, they are semantically aberrant since they fail to communicate anything. Such judgments must be tempered with some caution, however, since gifted writers are capable of stringing together words in unusual ways in order to produce new and esthetically pleasing effects. An extreme example of this is Lewis Carroll's *Jabberwocky* ("'Twas brillig, and the slithy toves Did gyre and gimble in the wabe, All mimsy were the borogroves, And the momeraths outgrabe...").

The goals of descriptive grammar are often described in terms of accounting for the ability of native speakers to manipulate their language. A native speaker can produce sentences in his language which he has neither heard nor uttered before, and which are correctly understood and interpreted by other speakers. Likewise, he is able to correctly understand and interpret sentences produced by other speakers. The description of a language must in some way explain this ability of the native speaker. This ability, or knowledge about well-formed sentences that native speakers have is, of course, LATENT knowledge, since few speakers of any language can describe the structure of the sentences they produce and hear. The linguist's task is to discover the rules that underlie the speakers' usage. In order to do this the linguist needs to observe the linguistic behavior of people, and collect an adequate sample of the sentences of the language, which he then analyses.

9.2   GRAMMATICAL ARRANGEMENTS

All languages use two different devices to convey differences between messages. Two sentences may be different from each other either because (*a*) they have different elements, or because (*b*) the elements are in different arrangements. (Of course two sentences may be different in both these respects, i.e., different elements and different arrangements.) The following sets of sentences contain the same elements, but differ in meaning because of differences in arrangement:

9   *a.* Slowly he entered the room and sat down.
    b. He entered the room slowly and sat down.
    c. He entered the room and sat down slowly.
10 *a.* This is a watch pocket.
    b. This is a pocket watch.

In some cases, differences in arrangement seem to make very little difference in meaning, as in the following sets of sentences:

11 *a.* Here they are.
    b They are here.
12 *a.* John ran away.
    b. Away ran John.

13 *a.* Sometimes we go to the movies.
     b We sometimes go to the movies.
     c. We go to the movies sometimes.
14 *a.* I saw him, but I didn't see her.
     b. Him I saw, but her I didn't see.

In sentences 11–14, different arrangements convey differences in emphasis, which is different from the type of distinctions illustrated in sentences 9–10.

In other cases sentences which are made up of different parts have in some sense the same arrangement, as illustrated by the following pairs:

15 *a.* John drinks milk.
     b. Bill eats spinach.
16 *a.* Jack and Jill ran up the hill.
     b. The union leaders and their bodyguards entered through a side door.
17 *a.* I saw Bill playing tennis.
     b. The investigators observed several of the officials accepting bribes.

In such cases, the relationships among the parts of the sentences seem to be in some way the same for each pair, even though the two sentences may not share a single part. Thus, in 15*a–b*, *John* is related to *drinks* in the same way that *Bill* is related to *eats*; *drinks* is related to *milk* in the first sentence as *eats* is related to *spinach* in the second. In 16*a–b* the following parts correspond: (1) *Jack–The union leaders*, (2) *and–and*, (3) *Jill–their bodyguards*, (4) *ran–entered*, (5) *up–through*, (6) *the hill–a side door*.

When we talk about arrangements of elements, we do not mean only the sequential order of elements. Arrangements have to do with the relationships between the various parts of a sentence. For instance, in 16*a*, the relationship between the elements *Jack* and *Jill* is different from the relationship between *Jack and Jill* and the rest of the sentence. When two sentences are said to have the same arrangement (as in 16*a–b* above), it means that the relationship between the parts in the two sentences is identical. Another way to describe the similarity between parts of two sentences is to say that the corresponding parts have the same FUNCTION.

Sometimes the same sequence can result from different arrangements, giving rise to GRAMMATICAL AMBIGUITY. The sentence *He is a funny man* is ambiguous because it contains an ambiguous word, *funny* (= 'laughable' or 'strange'). The sentence *He entered the room and sat down slowly* is ambiguous because of its arrangement; it can mean either of the following:

18 He entered the room slowly, and sat down slowly.
19 He entered the room, and slowly sat down.

Here the question is: what part of the sentence do we consider *slowly* to belong to? Does it go with the whole sentence (which would give the first reading above), or does it just go with the second part (following *and*)? Here are some more examples of grammatical ambiguity:

20 He invited all his old friends and relations.
21 I saw a man eating (man-eating) fish.

In sentence 20, *old friends and relations* could mean either *old friends and old relations*, or *relations* (of unspecified age) *and old friends*; here it is a question of whether *old* is taken as going only with *friends*, or with both *friends and relations*. In the next sentence, *man eating fish* can mean either a man engaged in the activity of eating fish, or a kind of fish (which eats men): in the first interpretation, it would be grammatically parallel to *man eating spinach* or *boy throwing stones*, and in the second reading it would be equivalent to *fast-swimming fish* or *spinach-eating man*. (In the written form, of course, we distinguish these two constructions by the use of the hyphen.)

There is a partial parallel to grammatical structure in our system of numerals. If we equate the numbers *1 2 3 4 5 6 7 8 9 0* with sentence elements, then we can say for example that while *10* and *20* differ in content, *12* and *21* differ only in arrangement; *2* is the same wherever it occurs, but its position in a sequence will dictate whether it refers to units, tens, hundreds, etc. Thus, in the numeral system, arrangement can signal differences independently of content. The parallel is not perfect, of course, since the numeral system is much simpler than a real language. The ways in which real words vary in meaning, for example, is much more complex, and the possibilities for different arrangements are much greater.

There is, however, one property of mathematical language which is quite parallel to the property of language illustrated by examples like *old friends and relations*, and which may serve to clarify the way such cases work. The mathematical expressions $(2 \times 4) + 3$ and $2 \times (4 + 3)$ contain the same elements in the same order. But they have different meanings because they have different bracketing. Either could be read as *two times four plus three*, which would be ambiguous unless we introduce a comma intonation to mark the location of the brackets, thus: *two times four, plus three* versus *two, times four plus three*.

Borrowing this mathematical use of brackets, we could write the two different readings of *old friends and relations* as (*old*) (*friends and relations*) vs. (*old friends*) (*and*) (*relations*), or in a more general way as (adjective) (noun and noun) vs. (adjective noun) (*and*) (noun). Similarly, *He entered the room and sat down slowly* is either (*He entered the room and sat down*) (*slowly*), or (*He*) (*entered the room*) (*and*) (*sat down slowly*); *man eating fish* is either (*man*) (*eating fish*), parallel to (*boy*) (*throwing stones*), or (*man-eating*) (*fish*), parallel to (*fast-swimming*) (*fish*).

Since these ambiguities result from different possible grammatical arrangements, the grammatical description must account for them, in the sense that there must be as many grammatical representations of each of these sentences as there are readings. The different bracketings shown here are one way of indicating these differences. Others will be presented in the next chapter.

SUGGESTED SUPPLEMENTARY READING

English grammar: Jespersen 1905, 1964, Kruisinga 1925 (traditional treatments); Fries 1952, Trager and Smith 1951 (structuralist approach)

FOLLOW-UP

1 Define: function.

2 How are grammatical categories defined?

3 Why must a grammatical description be explicit? Why must it be exhaustive?

Chapter 10

GRAMMATICAL DESCRIPTION

10.1 FORM CLASSES AND GRAMMATICAL RULES

In 9.2 the phrase *old friends and relations* was shown to have two different readings which could be represented by different bracketings, viz., (*old*) (*friends and relations*) vs. (*old friends*) (*and*) (*relations*). In each case what we have done is divide the expression according to the relationships among the parts. In the first bracketing, the phrase is analyzed as consisting of two main parts: (1) *old*, (2) *friends and relations*. The second bracketing reflects an analysis into three main parts: (1) *old friends* (2) *and*, (3) *relations*. These parts, into which the larger construction is analyzed, are known as its IM-MEDIATE CONSTITUENTS (or ICs).

The fact that the smaller sequences can be further subdivided is not of immediate relevance to the larger construction; thus, the relationship between *old* and (*friends and relations*) is the same as that between *old* and *man* in the expression *old man*; similarly, the relationships between (*old friends*) and (*relations*) are parallel to those obtaining in a simpler expression such as (*cats*) (*and*) (*dogs*).

The value of immediate constituents in grammatical analysis is not only

I	saw	Bill	playing	tennis.
The investigators	observed	several of the officials	accepting	bribes.
1	2	3	4	5

Figure 10-1.

that they provide a way of representing certain kinds of grammatical ambiguities, but also because they allow us to reduce sentences of varying complexity to the same basic parts. This can be illustrated graphically with respect to one of the pairs of sentences of 9.2 (Figure 10-1). From the point of view of the second sentence in the figure, the expression *several of the officials* is an indivisible part of the sentence which has a function identical to that of the single word *Bill* in the first sentence. One could even imagine a much longer and more complex expression in position 3, such as *three of the top officials, who had been exonerated by a previous investigating committee.* Such examples, which can be multiplied ad infinitum, show that the key to the discovery of immediate constituents is SUBSTITUTABILITY in a given context. Those sequences which can replace each other in the same GRAMMATICAL ENVIRONMENT, such as *Bill* and *several of the officials*, share a grammatical role. By virtue of this, they are said to belong to the same FORM CLASS.

In order to illustrate these points in more detail, we will write a grammatical description of a small sample of English below. The sample is representative, and therefore the grammatical description that results could ultimately be expanded and modified to account for complexities of English not included in the sample. We could start with any sentence in the language, substitute one element after another, and ultimately the grammar that we would end up with would be more or less the same, no matter which sentence we started with.

The following sentence will do for a start: John likes Mary. Making the simplest possible substitutions, we find that words like *Tom, Dick, Harry, Lucy, Jane, Nancy*, etc. can be substituted for *John* or *Mary*; *loves, knows admires, respects, trusts* and the like can replace *likes*. Thus far, then, the sample can be said to show only two form-classes: *John, Tom, Mary, Lucy,* etc. belong to one class, and *likes, loves,* etc. belong to another.

A sentence may be formed by taking one member of the first set, followed by a member of the second set, followed by a member of the first set. This statement can be represented in its essentials by the following more formal description:

1 *a* Sentence = 1 + 2 + 1
   b 1 = *John, Tom, Dick, Harry,*
        Mary, Lucy, Jane, Nancy

    c 2 = *likes, loves, knows, admires,*
        respects, trusts

This description contains two form classes, 1 and 2, and a single grammatical construction, 1 + 2 + 1. The grammatical statement so far stands for $8 \times 6 \times 8 = 384$ sentences, and is, in effect, a shorthand way of listing all of those sentences.

Though the description is very limited, it has one property required of a linguistic description, namely that it permits us to recognize whether a sentence is *well-formed* by purely FORMAL CRITERIA. Those sentences which conform to the description (such as *Tom admires Harry, Lucy trusts Jane, Dick knows Dick*) are well-formed sentences, since they are all cases of 1 + 2 + 1. Those which do not conform (such as **John loves admires*[1] or **Jane Harry loves*) are not well-formed.

Of course, many good sentences are also excluded by this description, and must ultimately be added. Adding them involves different kinds of modifications of the grammar. The simplest modification is to add items to the existing form-classes. If, for example, we add the two items *Ralph* and *Betty* to class 1, and the four items *believes, hates, dislikes,* and *distrusts* to class 2, we will find that the description now accounts for $10 \times 10 \times 10 = 1,000$ sentences. Thus, a small addition to the size of the description considerably increases its POWER (in the sense of the number of sentences it accounts for). This is an important demonstration of the validity of the form class in descriptive grammar.

The power of a grammatical description can be increased further by making use of form classes of greater complexity. Suppose we wish to include the following sentences in our sample:

    Mary knows the grocer.
    Jane loves a doctor.

Since *the grocer* and *a doctor* can substitute for members of class 1 (*John, Mary,* etc.), these expressions can be considered members of the same form class. At this point, it will be more convenient to use some traditional grammatical labels to designate form classes. The label *Nprop* (for proper noun) will be used for the class that includes *John, Mary,* etc., and the label *Ncom* (for common noun) will be used for nouns such as *grocer* and *doctor*;

---

[1] The asterisk is often used to indicate sentences which are not well-formed (either with respect to a particular grammatical description, or to generally accepted ideas of correctness). In this book the asterisk will be used only when it is not clear from context that a sentence is not well-formed.

the labels *Art*, *Adef*, and *Aind* will stand for article, definite article, and indefinite article respectively. The revised sample can be described by amending rule 1*b* to read as follows:

2   1 = Nprop, Art + Ncom
  Art = Adef, Aind
  Adef = *the*, Aind = *a*; Nprop = *John, Tom, Dick,*...;
  Ncom = *grocer, doctor, man, woman, boy, girl,*...

By using this type of device, we take advantage of the fact that class 1 can consist of members of different degrees of complexity.

The power of this class must be further increased, if we wish to add sentences like the following:

Mary knows the old grocer.
The young doctor loves Jane.
Bill mistrusts the new man.

These can be accommodated by amending the first line of rule 2 to read as follows:

3   1 = Nprop, Art (+ Adj) + Ncom

and by adding the rule: Adj = *old, young, new*. (The parentheses indicate that Adj is an optional constituent.) This immediately leads us to consider other sentences containing adjectives, such as:

The doctor is old.
Jane is young.
The boy is new.

These could be included by amending rule 1*a* to read as follows:

4   Sentence = 1 + 2 + 1, 1 + *is* + Adj

(where the comma means "or", as in rules 1*b* and 1*c*).

Ultimately, as more and more sentences are included, this rule will have to be revised much more drastically. Eventually, a very common type of sentence such as the following will have to be included:

John left.
The doctor arrived.

The boy slept.
The girl stayed.

The following version of the grammatical description will accommodate these two new sets of sentences. (Again, it will be useful to effect another revision in our symbolization of classes. Other things being equal, it is not important what label is given to a grammatical category, as long as the label is formally defined. On the other hand, certain labels are in common use and might as well be used. Accordingly, we will use NP (for noun phrase) for the new version of the old class 1, and VP (verb phrase) for the other major sentence constituent; Vtrans denotes transitive verbs, and Vintr denotes intransitive verbs.)

5   *a* Sentence = NP + VP
     b VP = *is* + Adj, Vintr, Vtrans + NP
     c NP = Nprop, Art (+ Adj) + Ncom
     d Art = Adef, Aind
     e Nprop = *John, Tom, Dick*...; Ncom = *grocer, doctor, man*...
     f Adj = *old, young, new*
     g Vintr = *left, arrived, slept, stayed*
     h Vtrans = *likes, loves, knows*...
     i Adef = *the*
     j Aind = *a*

10.2   GRAMMATICAL REPRESENTATIONS

On the basis of such a description, it is possible to construct a grammatical representation of any sentence in the sample by means of a purely mechanical procedure. Thus, for example, given the sentence *Jane likes the old man*, the structure shown in 6 can be assigned to it. In this diagram, items are joined by equals signs according to the rules given in 5. The brackets show the immediate constituent structure: Sentence is divided into the two IC's NP and VP; VP is divided into Vtrans and NP; this second NP is further divided into Art, Adj, and Ncom. The ULTIMATE CONSTITUENTS are those at the

6
$$\text{Sentence} = \begin{cases} \text{NP} = \text{Nprop} = \textit{Jane} \\ \text{VP} = \begin{cases} \text{Vtrans} = \textit{likes} \\ \text{NP} = \begin{cases} \text{Art} = \text{Adef} = \textit{the} \\ \text{Adj} = \textit{old} \\ \text{Ncom} = \textit{man} \end{cases} \end{cases} \end{cases}$$

extreme right, which are not further subdivided by the grammar (though in 10.4, it will turn out to be necessary to divide the form *likes* into *like* and *-s*). Large form classes such as NP and VP are termed MAJOR CON-STITUENTS.

The grammatical relationships shown in 6 could also be shown by the method of bracketing mentioned in 9.2, as follows:

Sentence = NP (= Nprop (= *Jane*)) + VP (= Vtrans (= *likes*) + NP (= Art (= Adef (= *the*)) + Adj (= *old*) + Ncom (= man)))

When a sentence is represented in this way, the set of brackets following a grammatical label encloses the part referred to by that label. Thus the set of brackets which relate to the first NP includes the first (left-hand) bracket, and the second right-hand bracket after *Jane*; the set of brackets which relate to VP are the first bracket after VP and the last bracket after *man*; the brackets relating to the second NP are the one immediately following it and the second one after *man*; etc. Such a labelled bracket diagram conveys the same information as 6, though the latter has the advantage of representing the relationships more clearly. Diagram 7 is still another way of representing the same information.

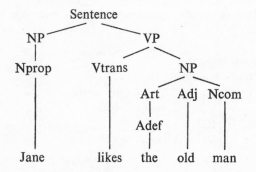

Diagrams 6 and 7 illustrate the phenomenon known as HIERARCHICAL STRUCTURE of grammatical constituents. In diagram 7, for example, we observe that the left-most NP is an immediate constituent (IC), with the VP, of the sentence, while the right-most NP is an IC of VP which itself is an IC of Sentence. The notion of hierarchical structure is crucial in the case of sentences that may be interpreted in more than one way: for instance, the sentence *He invited all his old friends and relations* (9.2) will have two different hierarchical structure diagrams with different grammatical relationships between its ICs, corresponding to the two different meanings.

10.3 INCLUSION AND RECURSIVENESS

The student will probably have noticed that diagram 6 contains two instances of NP: this is the result of rules 5*a* and 5*b*, which make it possible for an NP to be a constituent of a VP as well as a sentence constituent. This property of INCLUSION, which permits a constituent to function on more than one level, can be illustrated more strikingly by sentences such as the following:

> Jane knows the man who left.
> Tom likes the girl who loves Bill.
> John trusts the doctor who is old.

In the first of these sentences, *left* is simultaneously a VP and part of a VP (viz., *knows the man who left*)—or at least it could be described that way, even though this is not possible according to the description given in 5. This modification can be accomplished by intercalating rule 8 between 5*a* and 5*b*, and adding rule 9:

8   NP = NP + Rel + VP
9   Rel = *who*

With this change, the structure of the sentence *Jane knows the man who left* can be diagrammed as in 10.

10

$$
\text{Sentence} = \begin{cases} \text{NP} = \text{Nprop} = \textit{Jane} \\ \text{VP} = \begin{cases} \text{Vtrans} = \textit{knows} \\ \text{NP} = \begin{cases} \text{NP} = \begin{cases} \text{Art} = \text{Adef} = \textit{the} \\ \text{Ncom} = \textit{man} \end{cases} \\ \text{Rel} = \textit{who} \\ \text{VP} = \text{Vintr} = \textit{left} \end{cases} \end{cases} \end{cases}
$$

The inclusion of such a rule increases the power of the description more than may appear at first glance, since in addition to sentences like those just mentioned, the grammar will now also account for much longer sentences like *John loves the girl who likes the man who knows the old grocer who mistrusts the boy who slept*. Such a sentence may be a rather unlikely one in English, but it is at least understandable, and many other similar sentences are possible.

The importance of mentioning such a sentence in this context is that it shows how a rather small grammar can account for a very large number of possible well-formed sentences (since there is no limit on the number and combinations of VP's which can be included in such a sentence). This illustrates a property which has been referred to as the RECURSIVE PROPERTY of language, and rule 8 just given illustrates one of the ways in which this property can be accounted for in a grammar.

10.4 CONTEXT-FREE AND CONTEXT-SENSITIVE RULES

The rules in 5 make no allowance for sentences with plural nouns, such as:

> Bill knows the boys.
> Nancy trusts the doctors.

The easiest way to include these would be to substitute Ncom(–Plur) for Ncom in rule 5c, giving the following revised rule:

11 NP = Nprop, Art (+ Adj) + Ncom(–Plur)

This would indicate that Ncom can be optionally followed by the plural ending; this would permit sentences like those just mentioned. On the other hand, such a formulation would also allow sentences like *Bill knows a boys* and *Nancy trusts a doctors*, while disallowing such perfectly good sentences as *Nancy trusts doctors* and *Bill likes girls*. It happens that in English, most common nouns can be preceded by the definite or indefinite article in the singular form, and by the definite article or no article in the plural. Thus, whereas *Bill likes the girls* is the plural equivalent of *Bill likes the girl*, the plural equivalent of *Bill likes a girl* is *Bill likes girls*.

This statement can be incorporated in the grammar by a new type of rule, given below as 12e. (The following replaces rules 5a–d. Note that rule 5c has been replaced by rule 11, which appears here as rule 12c.)

12 *a* Sentence = NP + VP
  b VP = *is* + Adj, Vintr, Vtrans + NP
  c NP = Nprop, Art (+ Adj) + Ncom(–Plur)
  d Art = Adef, Aind
  e Aind = ∅ in the context: _____ Ncom–Plur;
    = *a(n)* elsewhere

(The symbol ∅ ("ZERO") in this rule is simply a way of noting that Aind is not represented by any phonological segment in this context.) This rule would allow the sentence *Bill likes girls* to be represented as in 13.

13
$$\text{Sentence} = \begin{cases} \text{NP} = \text{Nprop} = \textit{Bill} \\ \text{VP} = \begin{cases} \text{Vtrans} = \textit{likes} \\ \text{NP} = \begin{cases} \text{Art} = \text{Aind} = \emptyset \\ \text{Ncom–Plur} = \textit{girl-s} \end{cases} \end{cases} \end{cases}$$

This type of rule is different from any of the other rules, since in order to apply it one must know the context of Aind, i.e., one must know whether it is followed in the sentence by a plural or singular noun. Such rules are known as CONTEXT-SENSITIVE rules, as opposed to previous rules which are CONTEXT-FREE. A context-free rule applies regardless of context; that is, whenever the symbol on the left of the equals sign appears in a grammatical representation, the symbol(s) on the right can replace it. According to 12c, which is a context-free rule, a Noun Phrase may take the form Nprop, Art + Ncom, Art + Adj + Ncom, Art + Ncom–Plur, etc., regardless of the surrounding grammatical environment. The advantage of a rule like 12e is that it avoids repetition. The same facts about the distribution of articles could be stated in a context-free formulation, but more repetition would be necessary. For example, we might have the following instead of 12c–d:

NP = Nprop, Adef (+ Adj) + Ncom(–Plur), Aind (+ Adj) + Ncom, (Adj) + Ncom–Plur

Apart from being longer, such a formulation obscures certain general structural facts about the language. Another way of stating the facts of 12c–d would be the following, which involves considerable rewriting of 12c, but is equally adequate to describe the situation.

14 *a* NP = Art (+ Adj) + N(–Plur)
    b N = Nprop, Ncom
    c Art = $\emptyset$ in the context: _____ (+ Adj) + Nprop;
           = Aind, Adef in the context: _____ (+ Adj) + Ncom
    d Aind = $\emptyset$ in the context: _____ (+ Adj) + Ncom–Plur

Rule 14a ignores the distinction between Nprop and Ncom, and uses the symbol N for all nouns. This distinction is ordered by 14c, a context-sensitive rule.

If rules 12c–d or 14 are incorporated in the grammar, this will not only allow sentences like *Bill likes girls*, but also *Girls likes Bill* and *The doctors knows Jane*. In order to eliminate such sentences, and to account for the agreement between the first NP and the verb, we need to recognize that forms like *knows* and *likes* have two parts (*know-s*, *like-s*), and that the second part occurs only when preceded by a singular noun. This can be stated as follows:

15 *a* V = v-Ending
    b Ending = -*s* in the context: N + v- _____
           = $\emptyset$ in the context: N–Plur + v- _____

The first of these rules states that a verb (V) consists of a verb stem (*v*) and an ending; the second (context-sensitive) rule gives the form of the ending in two different grammatical environments. Rules of the type of 15*b* can be stated even more economically, as follows:

16 E = -*s* / N + v- _____ ; $\emptyset$

This is to be read: 'Ending occurs in the form -*s* in the context following noun plus verb stem; otherwise (i.e., in all other contexts) it occurs as zero'. In such rules, the form listed without a specific context, in this case $\emptyset$, is the one which occurs in all contexts that are not specified. From now on, this format will be used for all rules of this type. (See also the phonological rules in 6.3.)

By slightly revising rule 16, it will also account for verbs with the past ending such as *trusted, liked, arrived*:

17 *a* E = S, -*ed*
    b S = -*s* / N + v- _____ ; $\emptyset$

An additional rule of a slightly different type is needed to account for the forms *is, are, was, were*; this is shown in 24*b–c* below.

According to the present form of the grammar, the structure of the sentence *The boys trust John* is as in 18.

18

$$
\text{Sentence} = \begin{cases} \text{NP} = \begin{cases} \text{Art} = \text{Adef} = the \\ \text{Ncom} = boy \\ \text{Plur} = \text{-}s \end{cases} \\ \\ \text{VP} = \begin{cases} \text{Vtrans} = \begin{cases} v = trust \\ \text{E} = \text{S} = \emptyset \end{cases} \\ \text{NP} = \text{Nprop} = John \end{cases} \end{cases}
$$

10.5 NOTATIONAL DEVICES

The various conventions used in the rules presented here are for the most part in common use. Occasionally it becomes necessary to improvise, if the situation seems to demand a type of notation not previously used. There are no absolute rules in this, though it is usually advisable to stick to what is conventional where at all possible, since by improvising too much we might run the risk of missing certain generalizations which are statable within the usual conventions.

One common device used in rules has not yet been illustrated. Suppose the sample includes sentences like the following:

John is a doctor.
Bill is the man.
A grocer is a man.

These sentences have the shape NP + *is* + NP, and could easily be included in rule 5*b* by simply adding *is* + NP as a possible type of VP. In the long run, however, this type of treatment would lead to repetition, since this rule already includes *is* + Adj.

Two possible ways of noting this are given below:

19 *a* VP = *is* + Pred, Vintr, Vtrans + NP
   b Pred = Adj, NP
20 VP = *is* + $\begin{bmatrix} \text{Adj} \\ \text{NP} \end{bmatrix}$, Vintr, Vtrans + NP

Rule 19 introduces a new category symbol, Pred, with the members Adj and NP. Rule 20 uses the alternative convention of enclosing the categories Adj and NP one over the other inside square brackets, to indicate that either one is possible at that point. There is very little to choose between these two in this situation, whereas in other situations one may turn out to be more complex than the other.

The same device can be used in order to include sentences containing adverbs, such as the following:

John trusts Bill completely.
Jane knows the man well.
Bill arrived late.
Tom slept soundly.

The adverbs *completely*, *well*, etc. can be included in one of the two ways. They could be brought in by introducing the symbol Adv in the first rule of the grammar, giving it the form Sentence = NP + VP(+ Adv). Alternatively, the Adv could be incorporated into the rule for formation of verb phrases, in which case 22*c* would result. Again, a possible alternative is to set up another category, as shown in 21 by the symbol Vexp (for verbal expression):

21 VP = *is* + ..., Vexp (+ Adv)
Vexp = Vintr, Vtrans + NP

The choice in such cases is mainly dictated by clarity. Whenever possible, we shall avoid setting up new categories.

10.6 RECAPITULATION OF RULES

The grammatical rules presented so far, with all revisions, are recapitulated below in a single set of statements. They are divided into three parts, for reasons commented on below.

22 *a* Sentence = NP + VP
b NP = NP + Rel + VP
c
$$VP = \left[\begin{array}{l} be\text{-E} + \left[\begin{array}{l} \text{Adj} \\ \text{NP} \end{array} \right] \\ \left[\begin{array}{l} \text{Vintr} \\ \text{Vtrans + NP} \end{array} \right] (+ \text{Adv}) \end{array} \right]$$
d V = v-E
e NP = Art (+ Adj) + N(–Plur)
f X = X_1 + Conj + X_2

23 *a* Rel = *who*
b E = S, *-ed*
c Adj = *old, young, new,...*
d Vintr = *leave, arrive, sleep, stay,...*
e Vtrans = *like, love, know, admire, respect, trust,...*
f Adv = *completely, well, late, soundly,...*
g N = Nprop, Ncom
h Nprop = *John, Tom, Dick, Mary, Lucy, Jane,...*
i Ncom = *grocer, doctor, man, woman, boy, girl,...*
j Art = ∅ / _____ (+ Adj) + Nprop; Aind, Adef
k Aind = ∅ / _____ (+ Adj) + Ncom–Plur; *a*
l Adef = *the*
m Plur = *-s*

24 *a* S = *-s* / N + v- _____; ∅
b be-*s* = *is*; be-∅ = *are*
c be-*ed* = *were* / N–Plur _____; *was*
d leave-*ed* = *left*; sleep-*ed* = *slept*; know-*ed* = *knew*

e *man-s* = *men*; *woman-s* = *women*
f *a* = *an* | _____ Vowel

The rules of 22 can be called simply GRAMMATICAL RULES or CONSTITUENT STRUCTURE RULES. They all have a basic form which can be represented schematically as X = Y + Z (+ W...), with the meaning that tl.e form-class X is composed of the constituents Y and Z (and optionally W, etc.). More complex rules, such as 22c and 22e, are simply condensations of a number of related statements of this same basic form; 22c, for example, is a notationally condensed form of the following set of statements:

VP = *be*-E + Adj
VP = *be*-E + NP
VP = Vintr (+ Adv)
VP = Vtrans + NP (+ Adv)

These rules use two types of CONCATENATION SYMBOLS: the plus (+), and the hyphen (-) or dash (−), which indicate grammatical bounds of two sorts (roughly corresponding with open and close juncture respectively, but not always). Note that rule 22b is different from the other rules here, in that it is an OPTIONAL RULE; i.e., it can be ignored without an incorrect sentence resulting.

The rules of 23 have a different basic format, namely X = Y, Z,.... These rules, which we could tentatively call CATEGORY RULES, carry the meaning that the category X consists of the members Y, Z, etc. (All the members of each category must of course be listed, if the grammar is to be maximally explicit.) Some categories, such as Rel (23a) and Plur (23m), contain only one member. This group of rules, as well as those in 24, include both context-free and context-sensitive rules.

The rules in 24 differ from both preceding groups in that the symbols on the right of the equal signs are the actual forms of words, some of which (such as *men*, *knew*) cannot be predicted according to the regular rules which produce such forms as *likes* or *trusted* or *boys*. Rules of this type are discussed in detail in Chapter 12. In some cases, these rules will produce different representations than those presented previously, since such rules as 24b–e have two constituents on the left and only one on the right. These could be represented as in 25, for example, which could represent the VP of *John left*.

25

$$VP = Vintr = \left\{ \begin{array}{l} v = leave \\ \\ E = \text{-}ed \end{array} \right\} = left$$

10.7 FUNCTIONS

Terms like *subject, predicate, object, modifier* are used to describe the roles or functions of particular words or phrases in sentences. They differ from the names of constituent categories used here, such as *noun phrase, verb phrase,* etc. This can be easily seen in a sentence like *John knows the man,* in which both *John* and *the man* are NPs, but *John* is the subject of the sentence, whereas *the man* is the object of the verb *likes.* On the basis of the type of grammatical description presented above, it is possible to give a purely formal definition of such functions. For example, the subject of a sentence can be defined as the first NP occurring to the right of the symbol *Sentence* (in the representation of a well-formed sentence). Thus, *John* is the subject of 26; *the man* is not, since it is not the first NP. It is also possible to define the subject noun of a sentence (also known as the simple subject) as the first N to the right of the Subject NP (again, and always, with the proviso: "in the representation of a well-formed sentence"). Thus, the subject noun of 26 is *John.* Similarly,

26

$$\text{Sentence} = \begin{cases} \text{NP} = \begin{cases} \text{Art} = \emptyset \\ \text{N} = \text{Nprop} = \textit{John} \end{cases} \\ \text{VP} = \begin{cases} \text{Vtrans} = \begin{cases} \text{v} = \textit{know} \\ \text{E} = \text{S} = \textit{-s} \end{cases} \\ \text{NP} = \begin{cases} \text{Art} = & \text{Adef} = \textit{the} \\ & \text{Adj} = \textit{old} \\ \text{N} \ = \text{Ncom} = \textit{man} \end{cases} \end{cases} \end{cases}$$

the object of a verb is the NP which follows any Vtrans; the object noun (or simple object) is the first N to the right of this NP in a grammatical representation. The main verb of a sentence is the first case of *be,* Vintr, or Vtrans which occurs to the right of VP. Thus, the object of the verb in 26 is *the old man,* and the object noun or simple object is *man;* the main verb is *knows.*

Two other terms used to designate grammatical roles are MODIFIER and HEAD. In an expression like *the old man,* the adjective *old* is said to be a modifier, and the noun *man* is called the head. Similarly, in *John arrived late, late* could be called a modifier of the head *arrived.* The simplest way of characterizing such modifiers in formal terms is to say that, when a constituent contains an optional member and an obligatory member, the optional member (when it occurs) is the modifier and the obligatory member is the head. Thus in the construction Adj + N, the Adj is classed as a modifier because it is optional, and the N is the head. (In this case, articles will have to be called modifiers also, since although they are not optional, there are cases where they are represented by zero.) Similarly, the constituent Adv is optional with either Vintr or Vtrans + NP, and is therefore a modifier. While this definition is very different from the traditional one, it happens that it fits all the important cases which are usually classed as modifiers.

NOTE

The descriptive model used in this chapter can, in a general sense, be called a GENERATIVE model. A generative description is one which assigns a grammatical representation or PHRASE-MARKER (see 13.2) to any well-formed sentence, on a purely mechanical basis. The generative model was not traditionally part of the structuralist approach to linguistic description, but is used here to make clear the transition between the structuralist approach and later approaches, which are taken up in Chapters 13 and 17. (See the Preface for a discussion of the sequence of presentation.)

SUGGESTED SUPPLEMENTARY READING

Immediate constituent analysis: Bloomfield 1933, pp. 161ff; Wells 1947
Generative grammar: Koutsoudas 1966, sections 1.1–1.4
Other approaches: Lamb 1966

FOLLOW-UP

1 Define: immediate constituents (ICs), substitutability, grammatical environment, form class, ultimate constituents, major constituents, recursiveness, constituent structure rules, category rules, subject, predicate, object, modifier, head, grammatical ambiguity.

2 Distinguish: context-free rules—context-sensitive rules, optional rules—obligatory rules.

3 If you have understood the presentation of grammatical rules in this chapter, you are in a position to try a similar exercise using material from another language. The following materials from Hindi-Urdu are offered for this purpose. (Suggestion: start with the sentences in *a*, and

write tentative rules to account for them. Then proceed to *b*, and revise
the rules as necessary. Continue in this manner as far as you can go. If
necessary, return to this exercise after you have finished reading Part II
of the book.)

a. vo kɔn hɛ   Who is that, who is he/she?
    ye kɔn hɛ   Who is this, who is he/she?
    vo ram hɛ   That's Ram.
    ye sita hɛ   This is Sita.
    vo ram nəhĩ hɛ   That's not Ram.
    ye kɪtab hɛ   This is a/the book.
    vo phəl hɛ   That is a/the fruit.
    vo phəl nəhĩ hɛ   That is not (a/the) fruit.
    ram kɔn hɛ   Who is Ram?
    phəl kɪtab nəhĩ hɛ A/the fruit is not a/the book.

b. ram mera dost hɛ   Ram is my friend.
    vo əccha phəl hɛ   That is a good fruit.
    sita meri bəhɪn hɛ   Sita is my sister.
    ye mera dost nəhĩ hɛ   He (this person) is not my friend.
    ye mera ghər hɛ   This is my house.
    mera ghər nəya hɛ   My house is new.
    ye nəya ghər hɛ   This is a new house.
    vo nəyi kɪtab nəhĩ hɛ That is not a new book.

c. mera dost kəhã hɛ   Where is my friend?
    vo vəhã hɛ   He's there.
    vo yəhã nəhĩ hɛ   He's not here.
    tera ghər kəhã hɛ   Where is your house?
    vo dɪlli mẽ hɛ   It's in Delhi.
    mera ghər kanpur mẽ nəhĩ hɛ My house is not in Kanpur.
    dɪlli nəya šəhər hɛ   Delhi is a new city.

d. vo phəl laya   He brought fruit.
    mẽ phəl nəhĩ laya   I didn't bring (any) fruit.
    vo aj kɪtab nəhĩ laya   He didn't bring a/the/any book
                              today.

    mẽ kəl kɪtab laya   I brought a book yesterday.
    vo aj dɪlli mẽ hɛ   He/she is in Delhi today.
    vo aj ghər mẽ nəhĩ hɛ   He/she is not at home today.

e. vo gəya   He went (left).
    vo nəhĩ gəya   He didn't go.
    vo kəl gəya   He went yesterday.
    vo kəl aya   He came yesterday.
    vo kəl nəhĩ gəya   He didn't go yesterday.
    vo kəl dɪlli gəya   He went to Delhi yesterday.
    mẽ aj ghər nəhĩ gəya I didn't go home today.

Chapter 11

ULTIMATE CONSTITUENTS: WORDS AND MORPHEMES

11.1 MORPHEMES

When we calculate the length of a page of type, or a telegram, we count in "words." Thus, the following sentences contain respectively six, three, four, and four words:

1 Put these books on the shelf.
2 I'm coming too.
3 Didn't you see him?
4 His stupidity is unbelievable.

According to our traditional notions *these, coming, books, stupidity* and *unbelievable* are words. We may be somewhat less certain about *I'm* and *didn't*. Normally we would say that anything which is represented by a continuous sequence of letters without a space is a single word. But it has already been pointed out that these ORTHOGRAPHIC WORDS do not correspond completely to phonological words, as defined in 5.2. In addition, if we look at examples such as the following, we can see that the placing of spaces is often somewhat arbitrary: *bedroom, bathroom, guest room, rest room; racehorse, sawhorse, quarter-horse, hobby horse; penthouse, greenhouse, summer house, guest house; landlord, land tax; snowman, he-man, top man; dogfood, dog biscuit; undersecretary, vice-president, assistant manager; outlaw, in-law; granduncle, great uncle; stepbrother, half-brother, blood brother; daylight, sunlight, stoplight, traffic light, street light.*)

Note that *book* and *books* are both words, as are *stupid* and *stupidity*; the same goes for *believe, believable,* and *unbelievable.* But *book* is only part of a word in sentence 1, and *stupid* and *believe* are only parts of words in sentence 4. The -*s* of *books* is also part of a word, but is never a whole word. The same is true of the *un-* of *unbelievable*, the -*ity* of *stupidity*, and the -*ing* of *coming.* We may not be entirely sure whether the -*able* of *unbelievable* is the same as the word *able.* The *n't* of *didn't* and the '*m* of *I'm* are not words, but are clearly related to the words *not* and *am.*

Traditional grammar provides a number of labels, such as PREFIX (e.g., *un-*) and SUFFIX (e.g., -*ing*, -*s*, -*able*), to denote parts of words that have identifiable grammatical functions. But there is no traditional term for the larger category which includes items like *un-* and -*ing* which are never full words, as well as items like *book* or *stupid* which function either as full words or as parts of words. The term MORPHEME has been created to fill this need. From the viewpoint of the type of description envisaged in the preceding chapter, morphemes are the ULTIMATE CONSTITUENTS of grammar. That is, they are the smallest segments of the language which must be recognized as distinct entities in order to write correct rules.

Each morpheme in a language has a grammatical function and one or more phonemic shapes (known as ALLOMORPHS or ALTERNANTS); for example, the suffix -*ity* (as in *solemnity, formality*) has the function of converting adjectives (*solemn, formal*) into nouns. The grammatical function of a morpheme is given by the grammatical rules: thus, the grammatical function of the plural morpheme is given by rule 22*e* in 10.6. The function of the noun *boy* is given by rules 22*e*, 23*g*, and 23*i*. The phonemic shapes of morphemes, where there is more than one different shape, are given in rules like 23*a–f* in 10.6, which are known as MORPHOPHONEMIC RULES.

11.2 IDENTIFYING MORPHEMES

How can one identify the morphemes of a language? Let us look first at a clear case, viz., English *book.* First of all, we observe that the same sequence of phonemes /buk/ occurs, with the same or similar meaning, in a number of different sentences (such as *This is my book, Don't read that book*). This makes it possible to isolate it from other morphemes which may be contiguous to it, such as the plural morpheme in sentence (1) above, or the morpheme *-ish* in *He is rather bookish*, the morpheme *store* in *He went to the bookstore*, etc. Furthermore, the sequence /buk/ cannot be divided into smaller sequences which are related to it; it is thus unlike the word *unbelievable*, which can be divided into /ən/ *un-* (compare *untrue*), /biliːv/ *believe*, and /ibl/ *-able* (compare *passable*), all of which are related to the composite form *unbelievable*. In addition, *book* belongs to a well-established grammatical category, common noun (Ncom), and therefore shares the grammatical behavior of the other words in that class. For those cases which are clearly established as morphemes, then, three types of criteria emerge: phonological, grammatical, and semantic. Where these criteria are all in agreement, there is no problem about identifying morphemes. But as it happens, these criteria are often in conflict with each other.

A word like *shelf* in the sentence *Put these books on the shelf* would seem to be parallel to *book* in all respects, and a foreigner investigating English would suspect nothing until he discovered that the expected plural form *shelfs* does not occur. Instead, we have *shelves* /shelvz/. In such a case we must recognize /shelf/ and /shelv/ as different forms of the same morpheme, and state a rule that /shelv/ occurs before the plural morpheme and /shelf/ elsewhere. The alternative would be to say that there is a morpheme /shelf/ which has no plural, and another morpheme /shelv/ which has no singular. This would obviously be inefficient. We can consider these allomorphs of the same morpheme because we can give rules stating the exact circumstances in which each occurs. Thus, the reasoning behind this is very much the same as the principle by which the allophones of a phoneme are established (see Ch. 3). There is a very obvious grammatical motivation for considering the different allomorphs of a morpheme to belong to the same grammatical unit, namely that without this type of identification, certain grammatical generalizations are impossible. For example, a rule like 24c in 10.6, which states that the past of *be* is *were* before a plural noun, would be impossible if we could not use the symbol *Plur* (or some other single symbol) to stand for all the different allomorphs of the plural morpheme.

We cannot always segment forms so that we can state exactly how to represent each morpheme. What do we do, for example, with the words *knew* and *men* in the sentence *John knew the men*? From the point of view of meaning, *knew* is just as much past as *trusted*, and *men* is just as much plural as *boys*. In such cases, we simply have to accept the fact that what consists of a sequence of two units on the level of grammatical representation (i.e., *know* + *-ed*, *man* + Plur) appears as a single indivisible shape or MORPH in its phonological representation. This is the effect of rules 24d–e in 10.6.

Some cases of this type involve ZERO ALLOMORPHS of a morpheme. For example, the plural morpheme is represented by ∅ after *sheep* in a sentence like *He sold three sheep.* Similarly, the past morpheme is represented by $\emptyset$ in a sentence like *I put it there yesterday* or *He hurt his foot.* Such cases as these call for rules of the form $X = \emptyset \,/\, \ldots$, e.g., Plural $= \emptyset \,/\,$ *sheep, fish, deer,* etc. _____.

In other cases, the identification of morphemes is often considerably more complex. English has a (much-debated) set of words which includes such groups as *deceive, deduce, deposit, detract, detain, demote,* etc. (sharing a common initial element *de-*), *transpose, impose, repose, compose, propose, dispose,* etc. (all ending in *-pose*). Many other combinations exist which can be made up of the elements illustrated here, as well as additional elements such as: *ex-* (exceed), *per-* (permit), *sub-* (submit), *pre-* (predict), *con-* (conceive), *-tort* (distort), *-sign* (consign), *-clude* (conclude), *-cede* (concede), *-pend* (impend), *-gress* (digress), *-mit* (permit), etc. We might try accounting for these cases by introducing rules of the following form:

$$v = P - S$$
$$P = ex, per, sub, \ldots$$
$$S = pose, tort, pel, \ldots$$

This would account for sentences like *The man detained John, Tom deceived the boys,* etc. There are, however, two very serious objections. First, not all combinations of P and S are well-formed: e.g., there is no *subgress, transpel, interpend, disclude,* etc. Second, there is no way to guess, on the basis of either the first or the second element, about the grammatical behavior of those which do occur: *expend* is Vtrans, whereas *impend* is Vintr; *concede* is Vtrans, while *recede* is Vintr; etc. Furthermore, there are other grammatical differences of types not yet mentioned: for example, *contends* cannot substitute for *intends* in *John intends to go;* *permits* cannot replace *pertains* in *This pertains to John;* etc.

Thus in this case, the description of these forms does not seem to be in any way simplified by considering them to consist of two morphemes. In other words, there is no grammatical basis for the division. Semantically speaking, it is possible to see certain common features of meaning in some of these forms: e.g., *gress* seems to mean something like "go" in *progress* and *regress.* (Note that there are similar initial elements such as the *re-* of *regain, retake, redo, remake, repaint,* or the *pre-* of *pretreat, precook, prefabricate, pre-assemble,* which have clearly definable meanings—"again" and "before" in these two cases. These are different from the other cases discussed here.) Apparently, then, since these words are difficult both semantically and grammatically, they should perhaps be listed as single-morpheme verbs in the grammatical description of English.

If we treat these cases like this, however, we omit important information from the description. If, for example, we fail to note that there is a morpheme

-ceive /siːv/, we will have no convenient way of describing the fact that all forms ending in this morpheme have the allomorph /sep/ in certain circumstances (e.g., *deception, receptive*). The same applies to forms ending in *-duce* (*productive, reduction*), *-cede* (*recessive, procession*), *-pel* (*repulsive, compulsion*), etc. What this amounts to is simply that the morphological boundary in a word such as *receive* is irrelevant to a description of its meaning or its grammatical usage, but is quite relevant to a description of its pronunciation.

The word *have* in the following sentences illustrates a similar point:

> Where *have* you been?
> I *have* ten dollars.
> I *have* to go.

These three cases involve different meanings and different grammar. In fact, they appear to have little to do with each other except in phonemic form. (In many of the world's languages, these three examples of *have* would be translated by three unrelated words.) The first *have*, an example of an auxiliary verb, requires that the following verb be in the past participial form (*have known, had come*, etc.). The second case, a Vtrans, can be replaced by such transitive verbs as *own, need, like*. The third *have* behaves grammatically like *want, ought*, and is always followed by *to*. In a complete grammar of English, these three instances of *have* would need to be accounted for in three different places. On the other hand, all three conform to certain morphophonemic rules: for example, all three have the allomorph /hæ/, as in *has* and *had*. We can say, then, that there are three morphemes *have* (on the basis of their grammatical behavior, as well as their meaning), all of which share the same allomorphs (/hæv/ and /hæ/). (The fact that all three are historically the same is not relevant to the description of the language as it is today.)

Figure 11-1 is an attempt to depict various kinds of relationships between

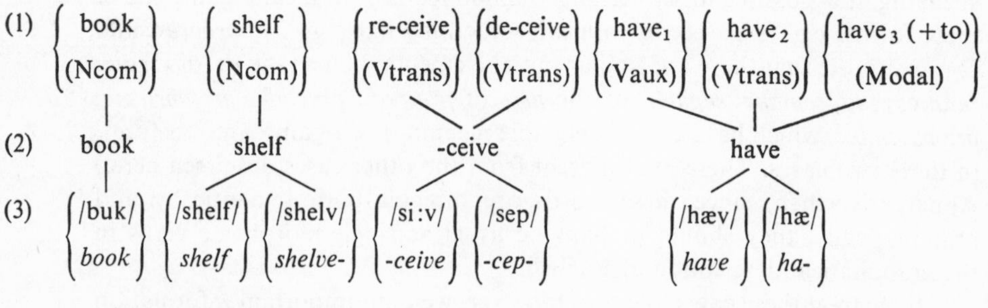

Figure 11-1.

morphemes and their allomorphs which have been discussed here. This situation can only be described in terms of three different *levels* (denoted by numbers in the diagram), corresponding to three different types of rules. The first line represents morphemes, with their grammatical designations, to which grammatical rules (i.e., constituent structure rules) apply. The second level represents MORPHS, i.e., those elements to which morphophonemic rules (see Ch. 12) apply. The third level represents allomorphs, which are actually strings of phonemes (or graphemes) which, when expressed in terms of distinctive features, are subject to phonological rules such as those discussed in 6.3.

11.3 WORDS

Though the morpheme may be a useful unit of linguistic description, much discussion of language uses the term WORD. Often the term is used without any formal definition, on the assumption that everyone knows what it means, and that we can all agree on such questions as the number of words in a sentence. Whether or not this is true from a practical point of view, a strict linguistic definition of the term has proved very elusive.

An early attempt proposed the definition MINIMAL FREE FORM. If a free form is any sequence of (one or more) morphemes which can constitute an utterance by itself—such as *Come on!, No, Hiya Charlie!*, etc.—then a minimal free form would be any such form which cannot be analyzed further —such as *No, Hello*, etc. Many morphemes which we would regard as words, however (such as *and, is, have, can, will, the, of, my, for*), would fail this test, since they do not occur as whole utterances except in artificial circumstances.

On the other hand, such morphemes as these are clearly distinct from BOUND FORMS such as *-ly* in *Come quickly*, or *-er* in *Take the bigger one*. Such morphemes are grammatically dependent on the forms to which they are attached (*quick* and *big*, in these cases), which is not true of such cases as *and, is*, etc. On this basis, it has been proposed to define a word in purely grammatical terms as any sequence of morphemes which never crosses IC boundaries (see 10.1). According to this definition, *bigger, indescribable*, and *reclassify* would be words since they function as immediate constituents in the same way as single-morpheme members of the same classes (such as *big, sad*, or *examine*). On the other hand, since the immediate constituents of *indescribable* are *in-* and *describable*, there can never be such a word as **indescribe* (since it would cross constituent boundaries).

There are some cases where phonological and grammatical criteria fail to give the same answers. In such cases we have to say that there are no clear-cut word boundaries. For example, it is customary to regard *Chicago's* in the following sentence as a single word: Bill took the man from Chicago's coat. In order to introduce such a sentence into a grammar of the type described in Chapter 10, it would be necessary to introduce a rule of the following type:

Adj = NP-Possessive
Possessive = *'s*

This would permit the phrase *the man from Chicago's coat* to be interpreted as: Art + Adj + N = NP.

(This is only one possible way to introduce such an expression into the grammar. The other way would be to add a rule like NP = NP-Possessive + NP, so that *the man from Chicago's* would be interpreted as NP-Possessive. Either of these solutions would also require the addition of rules which would interpret *the man from Chicago* as an NP, a possibility not envisaged in Chapter 10. It would also be necessary to formulate a rule for the elimination of one of the articles, since otherwise these rules would lead us to expect either **the the man from Chicago's coat*, or **the man from Chicago's the coat*. This type of rule is treated in Chapter 13.)

Whichever solution is used here, we end up with a sequence (*the*) *man from Chicago's*, whose ICs are *the man from Chicago* and *'s*. Thus, from the point of view of the grammatical structure of the sentence, the possessive *'s* is attached to the whole preceding noun phrase. It is thus entitled, on grammatical grounds, to be considered a word. Phonologically, of course, it is bound to the preceding morpheme, and thus cannot be considered any more a word than the plural suffix is.

The following example from Marathi, involving the bound form /t/ 'in', is similar:

vaḍa 'house'	vaḍyat 'in a/the house'
ha vaḍa 'this house'	hya vaḍyat 'in this house'
nəva vaḍa 'new house'	nəvya vaḍyat 'in a/the new house'
ha nəva vaḍa 'this new house'	hya nəvya vaḍyat 'in this new house'

As these examples show, where the form /t/ occurs, all words in the preceding NP (demonstrative, adjective, and noun) change their ending /a/ to /ya/. This special form, known as an OBLIQUE form, is required by a following postposition or suffix. For this reason, it makes sense to regard the /t/ as being added to the whole NP, just like the English possessive *'s*.

These last few examples may serve to point out the need for examining the criteria by which a notion like "word" is defined, in order that one may be aware of the imprecise way in which such terms are often used, as well as the fact that some categories which we often consider to be universally applicable are not entirely so.

SUGGESTED SUPPLEMENTARY READING

Nida 1949

FOLLOW-UP

1 Define: ultimate constituents, morpheme, allomorph, morph, zero allomorph, minimal free form, bound form.

2 Distinguish: orthographic word—phonological word (see Chapter 5)—grammatical word.

3 Following are some exercises in morphemic analysis. In each case, the task is to identify the morphemes and formulate rules for their combinations. In order to illustrate how this is to be done, we present the following sample analysis of some Spanish nouns:

a. Instructions: Analyze the forms *muchacha, muchacho, hijo,* etc.

Data: La muchacha está enferma. The girl is sick.
El muchacho está cansado. The boy is tired.
Los muchachos estan cansados. The boys are tired.
Sus hijas son ricas. His/her daughters are rich.

Su hijo es rico. His/her son is rich.
Su hija es rica. His/her son is rich.

Analysis: muchach-a 'girl' hij-a 'daughter'
(muchach-a-s 'girls') hij-a-s 'daughters'
muchach-o 'boy' hij-o 'son'
muchach-o-s 'boys' (hij-o-s 'sons')

(The words in parentheses did not actually occur in the sample, but are inferred from the other words.)

Rules: Noun = Stem—Gender—(Plural)
Stem = hij-, muchach-,...
Gender = -a (feminine), -o (masculine)
Plural = -s

    b. Instructions: analyze the verb forms in the following Hindi-Urdu sentences, and give the rule for the formation of the future forms.

Data:	vo aj aega	He will come today.
	vo kəl jaegi	She will go tomorrow.
	ram kəb ləṭega	When will Ram return?
	mɛ̃ jəldi ləṭũga	I (masc.) will return soon.
	mɛ̃ kəl apse mɪlũgi	I (fem.) will meet you tomorrow.

    c. Analyze the following verbal forms from Swazi (South Africa), and give the rules for the order of affixation (from Ziervogel 1952):

  *Bona 'see' (imperative)
    Bonani 'see' (imperative plural)
    kuBona 'to see'
    kuBaBona 'to see them'
    kusaBona 'to continue to see'
    kusaBaBona 'to continue to see them'
    ngiBona 'I see'
    siBona 'we see'
    uBona 'you (sing.) see'
    niBona 'you (pl.) see'
    ngisaBona 'I am still seeing'
    ngisaBaBona 'I am still seeing them'
  *The /B/ represents an implosive consonant in these examples.

Chapter 12

REPRESENTING MORPHEMES

12.1 MORPHOPHONEMIC WRITINGS

The morphophonemic spellings mentioned in 8.4 have presumably been retained in use for the sake of the effort they save. If we had to write *s* for the plural in words like *cats* and *hats*, and *z* in *dogs* and *hogs*, it would not only involve a great deal of redundancy, but would also tie the written word unnecessarily to the spoken word, thus slowing down the performance of reading and writing. The same would be true in French if the "silent" *s* were not allowed, and one had to write *lé dame* for 'the ladies' and *les autre* for 'the others'.

The argument applies with even more force in cases where a large number of distinct morphemes are involved: e.g., it would involve a lot of unnecessary effort if all German morphemes ending in voiced stops (such as *Kalb, Eid, Tag*) had to be written with / p t k / before juncture, and with / b d g / otherwise. In descriptive linguistics, the purpose of morphophonemic rules is to eliminate as far as possible such redundancies in the representations of morphemes; in a sense, the work of linguists is an attempt to formalize and extend the type of rules which exist in traditional writing systems such as these.

The simplest type of morphophonemic rule is illustrated by the following, which accounts for the alternations between voiced and voiceless stops at the ends of words in German:

1   voiced stop → voiceless stop / _____#

("Voiced stop changes to voiceless stop when followed by juncture.") Such a rule is a very powerful one, in that it covers a large number of cases in a very simple statement. Traditionally, alternations which can be described by such rules are called AUTOMATIC ALTERNATIONS, since the rules apply without exception to a particular sound or sequence of sounds whenever it occurs.

The majority of alternations are not so simple, however, and thus it is often necessary to use special MORPHOPHONEMIC WRITINGS to simplify the forms of rules. For example, the rule relating to French "silent" *s* (see 8.4) could be stated tentatively as follows:

2   z → ∅ / _____ C

("/z/ is rendered as zero when followed by a consonant.") There are two problems with this rule: the first is that there are cases of /z/ which are always pronounced, regardless of what follows: cf., *treize dames* /trɛzdam/ 'thirteen ladies', *treize hommes* /trɛzɔm/ 'thirteen men', *la chaise de Jean* /lašɛzdežã/ 'John's chair', etc.

There is, however, another alternative for handling this situation, which will appear more efficient when we note that there are many other consonants which are "silent" under similar conditions, as in the following examples:

"silent" consonant	not "silent"
froid /frwa/ 'cold' (Masc.)	*froideur* /frwadœr/ 'coldness', *froide* /frwad/ 'cold' (Fem.)
art /ar/ 'art'	*artiste* /artist/ 'artist'
arrêt /arɛ/ 'stopping place'	*arrêter* /arete/ 'to stop'
argent /aržã/ 'silver'	*argenterie* /aržãtəri/ 'silverware'
plomb /plõ/ 'lead'	*plombier* /plõbye/ 'plumber'

These examples show that there must be a general rule that consonants are "silent" except when followed by a vowel or semi-vowel. To mark those which are never silent, it will probably be most efficient to adopt the device used in standard French spelling, namely the "mute *e*" (*e muet*) written at the ends of such words as *treize, chaise, froide*. Thus, we could represent the "mute *e*" by /ə/ (since /e/ is used to represent the vowel of *été* /ete/), and write the above examples as follows: (dez daməz/ *des dames*, /des ɔməz/ *des hommes*, /trɛzə daməz/ *treize dames*, /trɛzə ɔməz/ *treize hommes*, /frwad/ *froid* (Masc.), /frwadə/ (Fem.), /art/ *art*, /art-istə/ *artiste*, etc. Note that this would have the advantage (as the normal French spelling does) of having the same basic written forms for morphemes such as *froid(e)* 'cold', *plat(e)* 'flat', etc., which have a "silent" consonant only in the masculine form.

In order to supply the correct phonemic forms on the basis of morphophonemic writings like those just given, the following rules would now be needed:

3 $C (\neq k f l r) \rightarrow \emptyset /$ _____ $\begin{bmatrix} -\text{vocalic} \\ +\text{consonantal} \end{bmatrix}$ (see 6.2)

4 $\vartheta \rightarrow \emptyset /$ _____ #

In rule 3, C stands for any consonant. (The chief consonants which escape this rule are / k f l r /, as in *avec* /avɛk/ 'with', *œuf* /œf/ 'egg', *bal* /bal/ 'ball' (dance), *bar* /bar/ 'bar'.) Note that these two rules are ordered: i.e., the second must be applied after the first. The first rule, when applied to the writing /frwad/, gives the form /frwa/; the second rule, when applied to /frwadə/, gives the phonemic form /frwad/. If the two rules are applied in reverse order to the writing /frwadə/, the result would be /frwadə/ $\rightarrow$ /frwad/ $\rightarrow$ /frwa/, which would be an incorrect result.

By using morphophonemic writings of the type just mentioned, it becomes possible to treat many alternations in the same way as those which are completely automatic. This is accomplished by finding a BASIC FORM for each morpheme, from which the actually occurring forms are derived by the rules. This means, in effect, that the sequences written are to some extent fictitious: /trɛzə daməz/, /frwadə/, etc. are not actually occurring phoneme sequences in modern French. On the other hand, some of these writings appear to represent earlier stages of the language, and thus the morphophonemic rules reflect linguistic changes. As it turns out, ordered morphophonemic rules tend to recapitulate historical changes to some extent. Where the history of a language is unknown, one can of course only guess at it, but even in such a case, it is likely that the approach used here would produce a set of rules which reflect historical changes.

In some cases, the choice of a basic form is not as obvious as in the examples just mentioned. For example, the three allomorphs of the possessive morpheme in English appear in the following environments:

(a) /s/ after /p, t, k, f, th/: *Phillip's, Nat's, Mack's, Cliff's, Beth's*;

(b) /əz/ after /ch j s z sh zh/: *Fitch's, judge's, Bess's, Liz's, Josh's*;

(c) /z/ elsewhere (i.e., after all voiced sounds other than /j z zh/): *ma's, boy's, girl's, Ed's, Sue's*, etc.

It is possible to write rules in such a way as to derive these three alternants from any one of them as a starting point; thus rule 5 starts with /z/ as the basic form, whereas rule 6 starts with /əz/:

5   z → əz /ch, j, s, z, sh, zh _____; → s/ p, t, k, f, th _____
6   (*a*) əz → z/ C (≠ ch, j, s, z, sh, zh) _____
      (*b*) z → s/ p, t, k, f, th _____

The solution to this problem involves a number of considerations which are discussed in 12.5. According to the approach suggested there, the preferred base form is neither of the above possibilities.

12.2 OTHER TYPES OF ALTERNATIONS

Some morphophonemic alternations are not amenable to description by the means mentioned above. This is most obvious in cases of UNIQUE ALTERNATIONS such as *go–went* (originally different verbs, cf. *to wend one's way*), *be–am–is–are–was–were*, French *va* 'goes'–*aller* 'to go' (also from different verbs), *person–people, child–children*, etc. Where two distinct forms have converged into one, as in *go–went*, this is known as SUPPLETION; *go* and *went* are known as SUPPLETIVE ALLOMORPHS. The reason that these cases are different from those above is that the rules which describe them must mention specific morphemes, rather than general phonological environments (such as before a vowel, in unstressed position, before /i/, after /p, t, k/, etc.) as in the above cases. The type of rules required for such cases will be discussed in 12.5 A–B.

12.3 STYLE VARIATION

The term STYLE is used to refer to dimensions of variation which depend on the social situation. This type of variation is quite widespread in the world's languages, and can involve any aspect of language structure. Style variations are perhaps most noticeable in phonology, though vocabulary and syntactic rules are also involved. The following examples show some common types of variation in educated American English; the versions on the right are more informal, intimate, and relaxed than those on the left:

    What are you doing?   Whatcha doin'?
    Do you want a cup of coffee?   Ya wanna cuppa coffee?

I don't want to.   I don' wanna.
What is this?   Whatsis?
It's all right.   'Tsawright.

On the whole, it seems that this type of variation can best be described by treating the formal variants as basic forms, and deriving the informal ones from them by morphophonemic rules of various types.

SANDHI rules involve special ways in which words or morphemes combine morphophonemically. This can be exemplified by such changes as SIMPLI-FICATION of consonant clusters (e.g., /síksth stríːt/ → /sík stríːt/ *Sixth Street*, /bést sélər/ → /bés sélər/ *best seller*, /klóːdhz/ → /klóːz/ *clothes*) or the ASSIMILATION of a consonant to the point of articulation of an adjacent consonant (e.g., /díd yu/ → /díjə/ *did you*, /gát yu/ → /gácə /*got you*, /fóːn búːth/ → /fóːm búːth/ *phone booth*, /rúːt bíːr/ → /rúːp bíːr/ *root beer*, /réːn kóːt/ → /réːng kóːt/ *rain coat*, /swís cíːz/ → /swísh cíːz/ *Swiss cheese*). The LOSS of certain phonemes, such as unstressed vowels, is characteristic of informal speech in various languages (e.g., /kəlǽps/ → /klǽps/ *collapse*, /səpóːz/ → /spóːz/ *suppose*, /bilóng/ → /blóng/ *belong*, etc.).

Changes like these are often of the automatic type, but there are also those variations which affect only single morphemes or small groups of them. Examples of this type in U.S. English are /práliː/ for *probably*, /sə́mpm/ for *something*, the loss of /h/ in pronouns (e.g., /wér íziː/ *Where is 'e?*, /wə́tsiz néːm/ *What's 'is name?*, /gívər dhís/ *Give 'er this*), the loss of /dh/ in *this* and *that* (e.g., /wətsís/ *What's this?*, /izǽt ól/ *Is that all?*), and the loss of /v/ in *of* (as in /kə́pəkófiː/ *cup o' coffee*). There are also cases where individual morphemes are completely lost, as for example the words *are* and *do* in the first two sentences above. (The social implications of such alternations are discussed in Chapter 19.)

12.4 ENGLISH VERBS

English verb morphology is an example of a highly irregular group of forms, showing alternations which are intermediate between unique and automatic. Apart from a small number of anomalous verbs (*be, have, do* are the main ones), the irregular verbs of English show the four patterns of alternation displayed in the following table. Column 2 shows the past form; column 3 gives the past participle form (as in *He has come, He had driven*); the form in column 1 is used in all other cases.

As the letters to the right indicate, class A has the same stem allomorph in all cases; class B has one allomorph in the past, and the other in the other two positions; class C has the same allomorph in the past and past participle,

	1	2	3	
A	hit	hit	hit	(X–X–X)
B	come	came	come	(X–Y–X)
C	feed	fed	fed	(X–Y–Y)
D	sing	sang	sung	(X–Y–Z)

and the other in the other positions; class D has three allomorphs, one in each column. These classes can be referred to as STEM ALTERNATION CLASSES. There is another set of classes, known as SUFFIX ALTERNATION CLASSES. whose membership cuts across classes A–D. These are shown in Figure 12-1. The endings for each of these classes are shown at the right. Note that class 1 has the regular endings, as found in a regular verb such as *play* or *love*, whereas class 2 has /t/ in places where we would expect /d/ according to the regular rule.

	1	2	3	
1	fli: / *flee*	fle-d / *fle-d*	fle-d / *fle-d*	(d–d)
2	bring / *bring*	bro-t / *brough-t*	bro-t / *brough-t*	(t–t)
3	chu:z / *choose*	cho:z-∅ / *chose-∅*	cho:z-ən / *chose-n*	(∅–ən)
4	fi:d / *feed*	fed-∅ / *fed-∅*	fed-∅ / *fed-∅*	(∅–∅)

Figure 12-1. English verbs: suffix alternation classes.

A notation for describing the peculiarities of irregular verbs can be devised on the basis of classes A–D and their intersections with classes 1–4. The following list shows examples of the different combinations which occur, with the suggested notation (the missing combinations are: B1, B2, D1, D2):

A1: All regular verbs (i.e., all those not marked as belonging to one of the following classes)
A2: bərn-2 (*burn*)
A3: bi:t-3/4 (*beat*)
A4: hit-4 (*hit*)
B3: blo:/blu:-B3 (*blow/blew*)
B4: kəm/kem-B4 (*come/came*)
C1: fli:/fle-C (*flee/fled*)
C2: bring/bro-C2 (*bring/brought*)
C3: chu:z/cho:z-C3 (*choose/chose*)
C4: dig/dəg-C4 (*dig/dug*)
D3: drayv/dro:v/driv-D3 (*drive/drove/driv-en*)
D4: swim/swæm/swəm-D4 (*swim/swam/swum*)

Note that there are cases, such as /biːt-3/4/, where there is a choice of class for a verb (in this case, the choice is between *beat* and *beaten* as a past participle).

12.5 SOME MORPHOPHONEMIC RULES OF ENGLISH

When a linguist attempts to write rules to account for any moderately complex morphophonemic situation, he finds that any decision he makes will implicate a large number of forms beyond those he is primarily focusing on. This can be illustrated by considering how one might write a series of ordered rules to account for English plural forms. The purpose of such a description is to make it possible to derive actually occurring phonemic forms from all possible cases of the sequence Noun-Plur which could occur in grammatical representations. (This is actually a rather large subject, which can only be partially treated here, but even this partial treatment will serve to indicate the complexity of descriptive strategy involved.)

A. "Irregular" forms

Plurals like *children, oxen, teeth, mice, sheep, men*, etc. represent the oldest group of English plural forms, which survive from a time when the system of plural formation was similar to that of modern German (cf. *Kind* 'child', plur. *Kinder*; *Maus* 'mouse' plur. *Mäuse* /móize/). In a descriptive grammar of English, these forms could be described by such special rules as:

7   *a* chayld–Plur → children
    b tuːth–Plur → tiːth
    c maws–Plur → mays
    d shiːp–Plur → shiːp
    e mæn–Plur → men
       etc.

B. Learned plurals

Plural forms like *media, theses, alumni*, whose method of formation comes from Latin or Greek, require rules similar to those just mentioned—for example:

8 *a* míːdiːəm–Plur → miːdiːə
      b thíːsis–Plur   → thiːsiːz
      etc.

(In contemporary spoken language, many of these plural forms are replaced by regularized forms such as *mediums* or *medias, thesises, alumnuses,* etc.)

C. "Regular" plurals

The vast majority of English plural forms have the alternants /s/, /z/, and /əz/ in the same distribution as that given for the possessive morpheme in 12.1. For reasons which will become apparent, all of these plural forms can be derived from the following starting point:

9   Plur → s

D. Noun-stem alternations

Apart from the plural suffix and the possessive, there are three other forms which show the alternation /s/–/z/–/əz/ under the same phonological conditions; these are: (1) the "third person singular" ending in verbs (as in *cuts, sees, changes*); (2) the contracted form of *is* (as in *Jack's here*); (3) the contracted form of *has* (as in *Mary's gone out*). While these endings are all subject to the same conditions, there are changes in nouns followed by the plural suffix which do not occur in the other cases, e.g., the plural of *wife* is *wives* /wayvz/, but the possessive (singular) is *wife's* /wayfs/.

The method of ordered rules provides a way of handling this case, since it is possible to order the rules so that some apply only to the plural forms, and some apply to both the plural and the other forms. First, it will be helpful to see how the question of *wife–wives* (as well as other similar cases like *shelf, knife, loaf, leaf,* etc.) can be handled. It will not do, for example, to propose a simple rule like the following:

   f → v / ———— s

This would not be suitable, since there are many words ending in /f/ (such as *belief, reef, staff, laugh, fife*) which do not change in the plural. It is equally impossible to make the rule operate in the opposite direction and derive the singular forms in /f/ from the plural forms with /v/, since there are numerous other words which have /v/ in both singular and plural (e.g., *cove, dove, hive, stove, groove*).

In such a case, the forms with the /f/–/v/ alternation must have some difference in their base forms as compared with the other two groups of words which do not show the alternation. Considering the probabilities of history as well as the most likely direction of changes in general, a reasonable solution would be to add a hypothetical final vowel in the base forms of *shelf* etc. (writing them as /shelfə/, /wayfə/, /loːfə/, /liːfə/, etc.), and derive the alternants by the following rules:

10   ə → ∅ / _____ #   ("/ə/ is rendered as zero before juncture")
    a f → v / _____ V   ("/f/ changes to /v/ before a vowel")
    b ə → ∅ / v _____ s   ("/ə/ is rendered as zero between /v/ and /s/")
    c s → z / v _____   ("/s/ changes to /z/ after /v/")

These rules, applied in the order given, would produce the following changes in the words under consideration here:

Base forms:	wayfə	wayfəs	hayvə	hayvəs	fayf	fayfs
	↓		↓			
Rule 10:	wayf	,,	hayv	,,	,,	,,
		↓				
Rule 10(*a*):	,,	wayvəs	,,	,,	,,	,,
		↓		↓		
Rule 10(*b*):	,,	wayvs	,,	hayvs	,,	,,
		↓		↓		
Rule 10(*c*):	,,	wayvz	,,	hayvz	,,	,,
	wife	*wives*	*hive*	*hives*	*fife*	*fifes*

Such a procedure is not as arbitrary as it may seem. For one thing, voicing of consonants between vowels is very common, and in fact rule 10(*a*) applies not only to /f/, but also to several nouns ending in /th/ (e.g., *mouths*, *baths*) as well as /s/ (*houses*). Accordingly, this rule can now be reformulated as follows:

11 f th s → v dh z / V _____ V

Similarly, rule 10(*b*) is also capable of being more general, since it can apply to the /t/–/d/–/əd/ alternation of the past tense morpheme (as in *looked* /luk-t/, *raised* /reːz-d/, *aided* /eːd-əd/), if it is reformulated as rule 15 below. But first, it will be noted that rules 10(*b–c*), with slight modifications, will derive all the regular alternants of the five forms with /s/–/z/–/əz/ mentioned above, if /əs/ is taken as their basic form. It is necessary therefore to introduce these forms at this point by a rule of the following type:

12 his, hæ-s, i-s (unstressed) → -əs.

(The possessive form is introduced here as /his/, which is its archaic form—as in *John his book*, cf., dialectal German (*dem*) *Hans sein Buch*. The 'third singular" ending of verbs is not introduced by this rule, but would be introduced in the same way as the plural suffix; see A–C above.)

The rules presented so far, omitting 10(*a–c*), would produce sequences like /wayf-əs/ 'wife's' and /wayvəs-əs/ 'wives'' (possessive plural). Since the possessive plural is always homonymous with the simple plural whenever the plural suffix is present in the form /s/ (or any of its derivatives), the following rule may be introduced at this point:

13   -əs-əs → -əs

This rule would reduce /wayv-əs-əs/ to /wayv-əs/, but would not for example make any change in /mays-əs/ 'mice's' or /men-əs/ 'men's' (which would be changed to /maysəz/ and /menz/ by the next two rules).

The following two rules now apply to all cases of the sequence /əs/, of whatever origin:

14 $\text{ə} \rightarrow \emptyset \; / \begin{cases} C\,(\neq \text{c j s z sh zh}) \underline{\quad\quad} \text{s} \\ C\,(\neq \text{t d}) \underline{\quad\quad} \text{d} \end{cases}$

("/ə/ disappears between /C_____s or C_____d, except for the consonants listed." As noted above, this rule also applies to the past morpheme.)

15 $\begin{matrix} \text{s} \rightarrow \text{z} \\ \text{t} \rightarrow \text{d} \end{matrix} \; / \; \begin{cases} \text{voiced consonant} \\ /\text{ə}/ \end{cases} \underline{\quad\quad} \#$

("/s/ changes to /z/, and /t/ changes to /d/, after a voiced consonant or /ə/.")

The following derivations can now be given to show the operation of rules 9–15:

Base forms:	wayfəs	wayfəs his	wayfə his	wayfə is
			↓	↓
Rule 10:	,,	,,	wayf his	wayf is
	↓	↓		
Rule 11:	wayvəs	wayvəs his	,,	,,
		↓	↓	↓
Rule 12:	,,	wayvəs-əs	wayf-əs	wayf-əs
		↓		
Rule 13:	,,	wayvəs	,,	,,
	↓	↓	↓	↓
Rule 14:	wayvs	wayvs	wayfs	wayfs
	↓	↓	↓	↓
Rule 15:	/wayvz/	/wayvz/	/wayfs/	/wayfs/
	(*wives*)	(*wives'*)	(*wife's*)	(*wife is*)

These rules appear to raise a problem with respect to words ending in /ə/ (like *data* /deːtə/, *Rosa* /roːzə/, *sofa* /soːfə/), or in /əs/ (like *focus* /foːkəs/, *circus* /sərkəs/): the former would lose their /ə/ by rule 10, and the latter by rule 14, if their base forms are as given here. In this case, it will make sense to give the base forms with other vowels than /ə/ (viz., /deːta/, /roːza/, /soːfa/, /foːkus/, /sərkus/) in keeping with the original values of the vowels—as indicated by their standard spelling. The following rules would then account for the actual forms /deːtə/, /sərkəs/, etc.:

16 ə → i
17 V (unaccented) → ə

By rule 16, /roːzəz/ would change to /roːziz/, whereas *Rosa's* /roːzaz/ would change to /roːzəz/ by rule 17. In fact, we find that such pairs of words as these (cf., also *house's* vs. *Hausa's*) are distinguished by some speakers, especially of an older generation. When additional data of this kind appears, it often serves to support a tentative rule. For those who do not make the above distinction, rule 16 can be said to operate a second time after rule 17; alternatively, one could say that the order of the two rules is reversed.

FOLLOW-UP

1 Define: morphophonemic writing, automatic alternation, unique alternation, suppletion, basic form, style allomorphs, sandhi, simplification, assimilation, stem alternation class, suffix alternation class.

2 Collect as many examples of English plural forms as you can, and try to classify them as automatic or non-automatic, unique or non-unique. Do the same for some other language that you know.

3 Residents of Edinburgh often pronounce the place name as /ebmbərə/, though the dictionary pronunciation of the word is /edinbərə/. Can you account for the differences? Can you think of other similar examples?

4 Give some additional examples to show that morphophonemic rules have to be ordered.

5 The following examples illustrate allomorphs in alternation. Identify the relevant allomorphs, state the type of alternation involved (automatic or non-automatic, unique or non-unique), and give a rule to account for the alternation. The first example illustrates the procedure to be followed.

a. Instructions: Identify the prefix allomorphs in the following Latin words:

colligo 'bring together' (lego 'bring')
committo 'unite' (mitto 'send')
compono 'put together' (pono 'put')
condūco 'lead together' (dūco 'lead')
contingo 'touch' (tango 'touch')
confirmo 'confirm' (firmus 'firm')
conjectus 'a throwing together' (jactus 'thrown')
illectus 'unread' (lectus 'chosen')
immemor 'forgetful' (memor 'mindful')
impūrus 'impure' (pūrus 'pure')
indignus 'unworthy' (dignus 'worthy')
intactus 'untouched' (tactus 'touched')
infectus 'unworked' (factus 'done')
injustē 'unjustly' (justē 'justly')

Solution: the alternation is non-unique, and (as far as the data here goes) automatic. The following rule accounts for the data given here:

$$n\text{-} \rightarrow 1 / \underline{\hspace{1cm}} \text{-l, m} / \underline{\hspace{1cm}} \text{labial}$$

b. Refer to FOLLOW-UP 3*b* in Chapter 11. On the basis of the data given there, plus the following data, write rules for the variation in verb stems and tense suffixes (past and future) for Hindi-Urdu:

vo kəl aya	He came yesterday.
mɛ̃ kəl ayi	I (fem.) came yesterday.
vo kəb ləṭa	When did he return?
vo ramse kəb mɪli	When did she meet Ram?
mɛ̃ phəl laũga	I (masc.) will bring (the) fruit.
vo phəl layi	She brought (the) fruit.

c. Refer to FOLLOW-UP 3*c* in Chapter 11. On the basis of the data given there, plus the following data, write rules to account for the negative forms in Swazi:

ungaBoni 'don't see' (imperative)
ningaBoni 'don't see' (imperative plural)
kungaBoni 'not to see'
kungaBaBoni 'not to see them'
kungasaBoni 'not to see any more'
kungasaBaBoni 'not to see them any more'
kangiBoni 'I don't see'
kasiBoni 'we don't see'
kauBoni 'you (sing.) don't see'

kaniBoni 'you (pl.) don't see'
kangisaBoni 'I don't see any more'
kangisaBaBoni 'I don't see them any more'

6 Analyse the following English words into their constituent morphs, and give an example of each morpheme in another environment.

Illustration- *synchronic*: morphs *syn-*, *chron-*, *-ic*; examples in other environments: *syn*tax, *chron*ology, geograph*ic*.
Data: irredeemable, resolute, substitution, condemnation, circumlocutory, singer, hostess, analyst, analysis, dermatology, philosophy, terrific, scandalous, jealousy, ambidextrous, polysyllabic, transitory, mathematics, companion, sympathetic, abstention, container, compensation, ninety, fifteen, twelve, carriage, acknowledge, autumnal, cantankerous, sorely, splendid, novitiate, contumacious, paternalistic.

Chapter 13

TRANSFORMATIONAL GRAMMAR

13.1 INTRODUCTION

In chapter 10 we presented a sample description of a specimen of English, to show some of the relationships between grammatical rules and features of sentences in a particular language. That description was arrived at within a descriptive model which has come to be known as the IC or IMMEDIATE CONSTITUENT MODEL. The IC model accounts for some of the basic and crucial relationships that parts of sentences have with each other and with the sentence. However, being able to cut up a sentence into its constituent elements does not necessarily give us all the information we need about it. There are several facts about natural language which the IC model is not able to explain adequately. In order to understand some of its short-comings, we have to turn to a theory of grammar which has been called the TRANSFORMATIONAL-GENERATIVE (or TG) theory. This chapter deals with this theory and the insights it has brought to theoretical and descriptive linguistics.

13.2 INADEQUACIES OF THE IC MODEL

Before we go on to look at the transformational generative theory, let us examine some of the ways in which the IC model fails to account for certain facts. To return to our earlier example (9.2): *He invited all his old friends and relations*, we noticed that this sentence can be analyzed in two different ways to give us two different constituent structures or PHRASE-MARKERS. As we pointed out in Chapter 10.2, IC provides a formal representation of grammatical ambiguity by assigning two or more constituent structures to a single sequence of morphemes. It is important to note that the multiplicity of meaning in such sentences cannot be ascribed to the individual meaning of morphemes (ultimate constituents), or to their linear order.

However, in many instances where more than one meaning is possible, the IC model does not provide multiple constituent structures. Take for example the sentences:

1 *a.* This actor reads well.
   b. This poet reads well.
   c. This book reads well.

IC analysis would assign a single constituent structure to each of the sentences of 1. It is obvious that sentence 1*b* can be interpreted in two ways: as in 1*a*, where the poet does the reading, or as in 1*c*, where it is the work of the poet that is read. In such cases of STRUCTURAL HOMONYMY, IC analysis is found inadequate.

Secondly, in a sentence like

2 John (and) Dick and Henry are room-mates.

IC analysis can assign one of the many possible bracketings to the co-ordinated nouns *John (and) Dick and Henry*, all of which would be arbitrary. The possibilities would be: [John (and)] [Dick and Henry]; [John (and) Dick] [and Henry]; and [John] and [Dick] and [Henry]. In such cases, then, IC analysis is inadequate.

Thirdly, in English and many other languages there are instances of DISCONTINUOUS CONSTITUENTS, as in:

3 Did John polish the table?

Here *John* separates *Did* and *polish the table*, which belong together. IC analysis cannot explain such discontinuity of constituents. Furthermore, the

IC model has no machinery to show that sentence 3 is, in some way, related to sentence 4:

4   John polished the table.

Fourthly, IC analysis fails to account for the fact that sentences 5 and 6 are understood by native speakers of English to mean the same thing:

5   John killed Mary.
6   Mary was killed by John.

IC analysis would assign different phrase-markers to the two sentences, without revealing the relationship between them. In sentence 5 *John* would be considered subject, while in 6 *Mary* would be labelled subject. This failure of the model to reveal the relationship between ACTIVE (5) and PASSIVE (6) sentences is also reflected in its failure to bring out the relationship between other sentence types, such as AFFIRMATIVE and NEGATIVE, DECLARATIVE and IMPERATIVE, SIMPLE and COMPLEX.

Convinced of the inadequacy of the IC model, in 1957 Noam Chomsky proposed a new theory of linguistic description which has come to be called TRANSFORMATIONAL-GENERATIVE (TG for short) THEORY. Since 1957 a considerable amount of research in linguistics has been within this theory, and although there have been significant changes over the past fifteen years, some of Chomsky's basic assumptions have remained unchallenged; indeed, they have been further strengthened by many research findings.

As noted in the Preface to this book, we can distinguish three phases in the development of TG theory. The first is the phase initiated by Chomsky's *Syntactic Structures* in 1957. This phase is discussed in 13.3–13.8. The second phase, which was initiated by Chomsky's *Aspects of the Theory of Syntax* in 1964, is discussed in 13.9–13.12. The most recent developments are discussed under the heading of semantics-oriented descriptions in Chapter 17.

13.3   ASSUMPTIONS OF THE TG THEORY

The TG grammar assumes that, since a child is able to "learn" his language within a relatively short period (between ages one to five) without any formal training—and, in fact, by actually listening to incomplete and ungrammatical sentences uttered by older people (including his parents)—the ability to learn a language can be assumed to be a product of an INNATE CAPACITY that a human being is endowed with. This fact makes a human being unique among animals. Exposure to a specific language merely activates this innate capacity of the human child. Once the child has acquired the 'grammar' of his language, he is able to GENERATE and to understand an unlimited number of NOVEL SENTENCES. Also, since a child is able to learn any NATURAL LANGUAGE that he is exposed to, it is assumed that all natural languages follow similar principles of sentence construction. Apparent differences in languages are considered to be a result of language-specific rules which operate on a UNIVERSAL GRAMMAR which is common to all languages, and which accounts for the CREATIVE PROPERTY of language and the regularities in language.

Related to this are the notions of COMPETENCE and PERFORMANCE. The child's knowledge of the grammar of his language is his competence, which he shares with all the other speakers of that language. Performance has to do with what a speaker actually speaks, which is often conditioned by extra-linguistic factors like inattention, memory limitation and wrong application of the knowledge of the grammar of the language. In this view, a linguist is primarily concerned with studying competence.

Competence has to do with the speaker's knowledge of a set of finite rules which combine, or are applied recursively to generate, an infinite number of sentences. A theory of grammar that attempts to describe competence must capture these rules which the native speaker is able to manipulate. This can best be done by first providing a description that shows how sentences and parts of sentences are related, rather than by first describing units of sound and then showing how these combine into higher linguistic units. Study of syntax reveals how sentences that have similar UNDERLYING STRUCTURE (or DEEP STRUCTURE) may have dissimilar SUPERFICIAL or SURFACE STRUCTURES, e.g., sentences 5 and 6 above, and vice versa (e.g., sentences 1a–c above).

An adequate theory of grammar must also account for the way in which a speaker-hearer is able to distinguish between GRAMMATICAL and UNGRAMMATICAL sentences. In other words, a theory which attempts to explain the human child's ability to speak his language, must also explain how a native speaker is able to interpret correctly the sentences that he hears, and how he is able to distinguish between grammatical and ungrammatical sentences. Consequently, knowledge of one's language lies not only in being able to produce sentences that are novel (those that have not been heard before by the speaker), but also in the speaker's ability to correctly interpret novel sentences, and to recognize sentences that violate the rules of his language and are, therefore, ungrammatical.

The TG theory is an attempt towards fulfilling the above goals of a linguistic theory. It rejects outright the earlier insistence of STRUCTURAL LINGUISTICS on a step-by-step classification of a corpus of data and setting up a mechanical procedure for discovering linguistic structure at each level (i.e., phonology, morphology and syntax).

It would be in order to point out here than when TG theory claims that an adequate theory of linguistic description must duplicate the grammar that a native speaker intuitively learns, it in no way claims that the rules that a linguist formulates are actually the rules that a native speaker uses. It merely claims that the fact of competence shared by the speaker and hearer must be formulated in rules that are general, generative and simple.

13.4 PHRASE-STRUCTURE RULES AND TRANSFORMATIONAL RULES

The innate capacity of the human being to learn a language can be regarded as a mechanism that enables him to discover certain rules of sentence formulation in his language. Once the learner has discovered these rules, he can use them to create or generate new sentences. The rules are finite but the sentences that the organism can generate are (potentially) infinite. In this sense the grammar that a native speaker has in his mind is GENERATIVE. A theory of language description must also reflect this generative property of language.

A human being is able to abstract from his language a finite number of KERNEL SENTENCES, or BASIC SENTENCE PATTERNS, which he can combine or TRANSFORM in various ways. The rules that he uses to transform the kernel sentences into other sentences are formulated by the linguist as TRANSFORMATIONAL RULES. A transformational-generative grammar, then, is a grammar that has two kinds of rules: (1) generative (which generate the basic sentences) and (2) transformational (which operate on the basic sentences, to yield derived or transformed sentences). Both kinds of rules, as we shall see below, are presented as formulas. Formulaic presentation is purely a device for concise statement; it does not claim that the human mental processes actually operate in terms of such formulas.

The rules that have to do with the generative part of a TG grammar are called PHRASE STRUCTURE (or PS) rules, which are a type of REWRITE RULES; for instance, $S \rightarrow NP + VP$ is a phrase structure rule, where the arrow ($\rightarrow$) means: rewrite S as NP + VP. It will be recalled that rules 21–23 of 10.6 above were of a similar type, but used the equals sign in place of the arrow. However, there is a crucial difference between the grammar outlined in Chapter 10 and TG grammar. In TG grammar only the basic or kernel sentences are described in terms of PS rules, while in the structural model (i.e., IC analysis) *all* sentences are described in terms of phrase structure. For instance, rule 21*b* of 10.6 cannot be a PS rule in a TG grammar, since it does not produce a kernel structure.

In fact, the term *phrase structure* is used in the TG theory in a restricted specialized sense. In a wider sense, constituent structure grammar may be called phrase structure grammar, in that it assigns constituent structure to sentences. PS rules in a TG grammar carry double information; they reveal both the CONSTITUENT and HIERARCHICAL structures of a sentence. In other words, a phrase-marker that is assigned to a sentence reveals the FUNCTIONAL relationship between parts of sentences—e.g., subject of, object of, etc.—and the grammatical class or category to which a constituent belongs (see 13.5 below).

13.5   COMPONENTS OF A TG GRAMMAR

In its original form, the TG grammar consisted of three components, each consisting of a set of rules. First, the phrase structure rules generate kernel sentences showing grammatical categories and functions. Second, the transformational rules combine kernel sentences in specified ways. Third, the morphophonemic rules convert the SYNTACTIC STRINGS into PHONOLOGICAL STRINGS.

The PHRASE STRUCTURE COMPONENT consists of PS rules. For instance, the following PS rules will generate certain types of English sentences:

Symbols:

(I)	$S \rightarrow NP + VP$	S = Sentence
(II)	$VP \rightarrow Verb + NP$	NP = Noun Phrase
(III)	$NP \rightarrow D + N$	VP = Verb Phrase
(IV)	$Verb \rightarrow Aux + V$	Verb = Verb Structure
(V)	$Aux \rightarrow T$	D = Determiner
(VI)	$D \rightarrow the$	N = Noun
(VII)	$N \rightarrow \begin{Bmatrix} boy, apple, \\ tables \ldots \end{Bmatrix}$	Aux = Auxiliary
(VIII)	$V \rightarrow \begin{Bmatrix} eat, polish, \\ \ldots \end{Bmatrix}$	V = Verb T = Tense

The above rules by no means represent the total PS component of a grammar of English, but they will suffice at this point to introduce the various theoretical implications of TG grammar. Rules I–V are PS rules in a strict sense, while rules VI–VIII are LEXICAL SUBSTITUTION RULES. The curly braces { } in rules VII–VIII indicate CLASSES of morphemes; the class in rule VI has only one term (*the*), while classes in rules VII and VIII have a large number of terms (morphemes or FORMATIVES) as their members. The dots (...) in the two rules indicate OPEN SETS, while the absence of dots in rule VI indicates a CLOSED SET. Rules V and VI are partial rules. For the present we will assume that in English, *Aux* can be rewritten only as *T(ense)*, and further, that T can only be past tense (the reason for this will become clear in 13.6 below). Similarly, rule VI assumes that *D(eterminer)* in English can only be rewritten as *the*. The above rules will generate English sentences like 7 and 8, and several more; the number of sentences that can be generated by these rules will be indefinitely large once we add more nouns and verbs to the lists in rules VII and VIII.

7   The boy ate the apple.
8   The boy polished the table.

Notice that our present rules will not generate a sentence like *The boy eats the apple* (see 13.6 below).

The step-by-step application of rules for sentence 7 will give us the following DERIVATION of the sentence:

S
NP + VP   (Rule I)
NP + Verb + NP   (Rule II)
D + N + Verb + D + N   (Rule III)
D + N + Aux + V + D + N   (Rule IV)
D + N + T + V + D + N   (Rule V)
the + N + T + V + the + N   (Rule VI)
the + boy + T + V + the + apple   (Rule VII)
the + boy + T + eat + the + apple   (Rule VIII)

Sentence 7 can also be represented by a TREE DIAGRAM (Figure 13-1). Notice that while the tree diagram shows the constituent structure for sentence 7, it does not tell us about the order in which the PS rules have been applied. The tree diagram, however, does reveal the functional relationship of constituents. For instance, an NP that is DOMINATED directly by S (i.e., derived directly

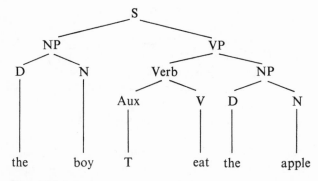

Figure 13-1.

from S by a PS-rule) is the subject of S, while the NP dominated by VP is the object; the VP dominated by S is the *predicate* of S (compare 10.7). The information contained in the derivation and the tree diagram can also be represented by LABELLED BRACKETING: S [NP [D [the] + N [boy]] + VP [Verb [Aux [T] + V [eat]] + NP [D [the] + N [apple]]]].

The last line in the derivation of sentence 7 is called the TERMINAL STRING; all the other lines being PRE-TERMINAL STRINGS. It is important to note that the terminal string is not a kernel sentence; it is a KERNEL STRING which is the result of the PS component. Rules of the other two components must apply to it before it can become pronounceable, when it will become a kernel sentence. Of course, it can become a derived or transformed sentence if certain transformational rules apply to it (see below).

13.6 CONTEXT-FREE AND CONTEXT-SENSITIVE RULES

The PS rules given above will generate sentences like 7 and 8, but not those like 9–12:

9 The boy eats the apple.
10 The boys eat the apple.
11 The boy eats the apples.
12 The boys eat the apples.

We can either reformulate some of the existing rules, or else add more rules, to incorporate sentences 9–12 in our grammar. For instance:

(III) (*a*) NP → $\begin{Bmatrix} \text{NP Sing} \\ \text{NP Plur} \end{Bmatrix}$ *Symbols:*

     (*b*) NP Sing → D + N + ∅   Sing = Singular

     (*c*) NP Plur → D + N + s   Plur = Plural

The revised rules IIIa–c will take care of *boys* and *apples* in sentences 9–12. However, in order to generate verb forms *eat* and *eats* we will have to make more than one change in our rules. Rule V must be revised as follows:

(V) (*a*) Aux → $\begin{Bmatrix} \text{Pres} \\ \text{Past} \end{Bmatrix}$ *Symbols:*
                 Pres = present

Rule V*a* will now enable us to generate sentences 10 and 12; but in order to generate sentences 9 and 11 we would need to write a rule like V*b*:

(V) (b) Pres $\rightarrow \begin{Bmatrix} \text{s/ NP Sing Subject} \\ \emptyset\text{/ NP Plur Subject} \end{Bmatrix}$

Rule V*b* is a CONTEXT-SENSITIVE RULE, while the other rules are CONTEXT-FREE RULES (compare 10.4).

13.7 THE TRANSFORMATIONAL COMPONENT

Let us now look at the transformational component. Every kernel string which is a terminal string in the derivation of a sentence has to undergo certain OBLIGATORY TRANSFORMATIONS. For instance, the terminal string for sentence 7 would require the AFFIX TRANSFORMATION (T–Aff) which would permute the constituents *Past + eat*.

the + boy + *Past + eat* + the + apple ⇒
the + boy + *eat + Past* + the + *apple*

One might argue that since *Past + eat* have to be permuted, it would be more satisfying to rewrite *Verb* as *V + Aux* rather than *Aux + V* in the first place (see PS rule IV above). However, the motivation for writing *Verb* → *Aux + V* in a grammar of English is provided by a number of OPTIONAL TRANSFORMATIONS which may be applied to a kernel string.

For example, sentence 7 can be transformed into a question:

the + boy + *Past* + eat + the + apple ⇒
Past + the + boy + eat + the + apple

The QUESTION TRANSFORMATION in English requires the *Aux* (here *Past*) to be moved to a position before the subject NP. To the string resulting from the question transformation, we need to apply another obligatory transformation *T–do*, which attaches the empty morpheme *do* before *Past*:

do + Past + the + boy + eat + the + apple
(did   the   boy   eat   the   apple?)

It will therefore be necessary to revise rule V again as follows:

(V) (a) Aux → Tense + (Modal) + (have + en) + (be + ing)

(b) Tense → $\begin{Bmatrix} \text{Pres} \\ \text{Past} \end{Bmatrix}$

(c) Modal → {can, may, shall, will, must}

This rule, together with T–Aff, will produce the following derivation of the sequence *could have eaten* (as in *Who could have eaten that cake?*):

	Aux	+ V	
Tense + Modal	+ have + en + V		(Rule V*a*)
Past + Modal	+ have + en + V		(Rule V*b*)
Past + can	+ have + en + V		(Rule V*c*)
Past + can	+ have + en + eat		(Rule VIII)
⇒	can–Past + have + eat-en		(T–Aff)

As this example shows, T–Aff has the effect of permuting any affix (*Past, Pres, en,* or *ing*) and a following verb stem (*Modal, have, be,* or *V*).

The QUESTION TRANSFORMATION moves *Tense* + $\begin{Bmatrix} Modal \\ have \\ be \end{Bmatrix}$ to the position preceding the subject NP. For example:

13 (*a*) The boy *can* eat the apple. ⇒
    (*b*) *Can* the boy eat the apple?
14 (*a*) The boy *will* eat the apple ⇒
    (*b*) *Will* the boy eat the apple?

The question transformation in English provides part of the motivation for writing *Aux* before *V* in a grammar of English. Other optional transformations also require the *Aux* to appear before *V*. For example, the NEGATIVE TRANSFORMATION (*T–Neg*) in English requires the negative morpheme to be inserted after *Tense* + $\begin{Bmatrix} Modal \\ have \\ be \end{Bmatrix}$, as in:

15 (*a*) The boy *will* eat the apple.
    (*b*) The boy *will not* eat the apple.
16 (*a*) The boy *has* eaten the apple.
    (*b*) The boy *has not* eaten the apple.
17 (*a*) The boy *is* eating the apple.
    (*b*) The boy *is not* eating the apple.

If PS-rule IV had rewritten *Verb* as *V* + *Aux*, we would have had to write additional rules to shift the *Aux* to a position before *Neg* + *V* in a negative sentence in English.

A transformational rule is different from a PS-rule in that it operates on a P-marker and not on a category symbol. A transformational rule has two parts to it: STRUCTURAL DESCRIPTION (SD)—the constituent structure P-marker of the input string—and STRUCTURAL CHANGE (SC)—the change needed to derive the constituent structure P-marker of the transformed string. Transformational rules can apply only to strings that can be analyzed in terms of the structural description of the particular T-rule. For example, the PASSIVE TRANSFORMATION in English will have the following shape:

$$\text{SD: } NP_1\text{-Aux-V} + NP_2$$
$$\text{SC: } X_1\text{-}X_2\text{-}X_3\text{-}X_4 \Rightarrow X_4\text{-}X_2 + be + en\text{-}X_3\text{-}by + X_1$$

The passive transformation involves three operations: (1) Subject and object NP switch positions; (2) *by* is prefixed to the original subject NP in its new position; (3) *be* + *en* is inserted between the *Aux* and *V*. To take an example:

John will have polished the table
NP_1 – Aux – V – NP_2 $\Rightarrow$
The table will have been polished by John.
NP_2 – Aux + be + en – V + by – NP_1

The negative transformation (T–Neg) in English would have something like the following shape:

$$\text{SD: } NP\text{-Tense} \left(+ \left\{ \begin{matrix} M \\ have \\ be \end{matrix} \right\} \right) \text{-Z} \qquad \begin{matrix} \text{Symbols:} \\ M = \text{Modal} \\ Z = \text{any constituent} \end{matrix}$$
$$\text{SC: } X_1\text{-}X_2\text{-}X_3 \Rightarrow X_1\text{-}X_2 + not\text{-}X_3$$

(The symbol Z in the SD is termed a PLACE HOLDER: it represents any constituent occurring at that point, which is not crucial in the application of the rule.) Sentences 18 (*a–d*) and 19 (*a–d*) below illustrate the application of T–Neg:

18 (*a*) John should wait.   (NP–Past + M–Z)
     (*b*) John had waited   (NP–Past + *have*–Z)
     (*c*) John was waiting   (NP–Past + *be*–Z)
     (*d*) John waited.   (NP–Past–Z)
19 (*a*) John should not wait.   (NP–Past + M + *not*–Z)
     (*b*) John had not waited.   (NP–Past + *have* + *not*–Z)
     (*c*) John was not waiting   (NP–Past + *be* + *not*–Z)
     (*d*) John did not wait.   (NP–Past + *not*–Z)

Note that the obligatory T–do applies in 19*d* after T–Neg, producing NP–*do* + Past + *not*–Z.

The QUESTION TRANSFORMATION (T–q) would apply after the negative transformation, and would have something like the following shape:

$$\text{SD: NP--Tense} \left(+ \begin{Bmatrix} \text{M} \\ \textit{have} \\ \textit{be} \end{Bmatrix} \right) (+ \textit{not})\text{--Z}$$
$$\text{SC: } X_1\text{--}X_2\text{--}X_3 \Rightarrow X_2\text{--}X_1\text{--}X_3$$

The AFFIX TRANSFORMATION (T–Aff) can be formulated as follows:

$$\text{SD: X--}\begin{Bmatrix} \text{Tense} \\ \textit{-ing} \\ \textit{-en} \end{Bmatrix}\text{--}\begin{Bmatrix} \text{V} \\ \textit{have} \\ \textit{be} \end{Bmatrix}\text{--Y}$$
$$\text{SC: } X_1\text{--}X_2\text{--}X_3\text{--}X_4 \Rightarrow X_1\text{--}X_3\text{--}X_2\#\text{--}X_4$$

(where $\#$ = WORD BOUNDARY). The DO-TRANSFORMATION is as follows:

$$\text{SD: } \#\begin{Bmatrix} \text{Tense} \\ \textit{-ing} \\ \textit{-en} \end{Bmatrix}$$
$$\text{SC: } X_1\text{--}X_2 \Rightarrow X_1\text{--}\textit{do} + X_2$$

That is, this transformational rule inserts the verb stem *do* before any affix left unattached after the operation of T–Aff.

The operation of T–Neg, T–q, and T–do can be illustrated by the following derivation:

the + boy + Past + eat + the + apple
T–Neg: the + boy + Past + *not* + eat + ...
T–q: *Past + not* + the + boy + eat + ...
T–do: *do-Past* + not + the + boy + eat + ... (= Didn't the boy eat the apple?)

The following derivation illustrates the operation of T–Neg, T–q, and T–Aff:

the + boy + Pres + have + en + eat + the + apple
T–Neg: the + boy + Pres + have + *not* + en + eat ...
T–q: *Pres + have + not* + the + boy + en + eat ...
T–Aff: *have–Pres* + not + the + boy + *eat-en* ... (= Hasn't the boy eaten the apple?)

Transformations such as the passive, question, negative etc. in English apply to a single P-marker and are called SINGULARY (or SINGLE-BASED) transformations. Transformations that EMBED one string into another are called GENERALIZED (or DOUBLE-BASED) transformations. An example of the latter type would be a RELATIVE CLAUSE TRANSFORMATION, where a CONSTITUENT STRING is embedded into a MATRIX STRING, as in:

20   Matrix: The boys ran away
      Constituent: The boys stole the apples
      Result: The boys who stole the apples ran away.

The transformational rule can be represented informally as follows:

$$\text{SD: NP}_1\text{–Aux}_1\text{–Y } \#\#\# \text{ NP}_2\text{–Aux}_2\text{–Z}$$
$$X_1 \quad X_2 \quad X_3 \quad X_4 \quad X_5 \quad X_6$$
$$\text{SC: } X_1 \text{ –who–} X_5 \text{ –} X_6\text{–} X_2 \text{ –} X_3$$
$$\text{NP–who–Aux}_2\text{–Z –Aux}_1\text{–Y}$$

(### = sentence boundary)

The relevant phrase-markers for the sentences of 20 would be:

Matrix: D + N + Past + V + D + N
Constituent: D + N + Past + V + Adv
Result: D + N + *who* + Past + V + D + N + Past + V + Adv

Generalized or double-based transformations are of two types, EMBEDDING and CONJOINING. Roughly, the results of these two types give us the traditional distinction of COMPLEX and COMPOUND sentences respectively. Sentence 20 is an example of an embedding transformation, where the constituent sentence is subordinated to the matrix sentence. A conjoining transformation does not subordinate one sentence to another; rather, the two conjoined constituents retain their sentential identity and are linked by a coordinating conjunction (such as *but, and, or*), as in the following sentences:

22   (*a*) John went home *and* Mary went to work.
      (*b*) Mary wants tea *but* John wants coffee.

13.8 THE MORPHOPHONEMIC COMPONENT

The morphophonemic component of a TG grammar (see 13.5) contains rules which convert the TERMINAL SYMBOLS in a P-marker into phonological sequences. Thus, there must be rules to convert terminal sequences like *eat* + *Past* (sentence 7), *can* + *Past* (13.7), and *do* + *Past* (sentence 19*d*) into the phonological sequences /eːt/ (or /et/, depending on the dialect), /kud/, and /did/. The types of rules needed in the morphophonemic component are illustrated in 12.5.

13.9 REVISIONS OF TG THEORY: DEEP STRUCTURE AND SURFACE STRUCTURE

The brief outline of transformational–generative grammar given above follows closely the system of TG grammar introduced by Noam Chomsky in *Syntactic Structures* (1957). The vast and growing research within the theory since 1957 has modified the theory, although, as we suggested above, the basic assumptions (as described in 13.3) remain the same. A crucial refinement of the original theory has to do with the distinction between DEEP STRUCTURE (corresponding to the meaning of sentences) and SURFACE STRUCTURE (corresponding to the external form of sentences). In the revised theory, transformations are seen as mediating between these two levels of structure, or as mapping one level onto another. As will be pointed out below, this revision has necessitated some changes in the formulations of the transformational rules presented above in 13.7.

The following examples illustrate the motivations behind this revision in the theory:

23 John likes Chinese food, and so does Mary.
24 Richard couldn't tell the truth, because he was afraid to.
25 John bought a new hat.

For each of the above sentences we intuitively understand:

23 (*a*) John likes Chinese food. Mary also likes Chinese food.
24 (*a*) Richard couldn't tell the truth, because he was afraid to tell the truth.
25 (*a*) John bought a hat. The hat is new.

Sentences 23*a*–25*a* represent the meanings of sentences 23–25 more explicitly. More generally, for every sentence there are at least two levels of representation: the *deep structure level*, which corresponds to the meaning of the sentence (i.e., 23*a*–25*a*), and the *surface structure level*, corresponding to the form of the sentence (i.e., 23–25). Deep structure is converted into surface structure through transformations. In other words, deep structure is related directly to meaning or semantics, and surface structure is related to sound. By implication, surface structure is meaningful only by virtue of its deep

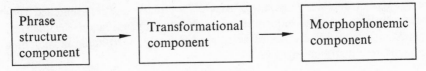

Figure 13-2. Original version of TG theory.

structure, and the deep structure of a sentence is accessible only when converted into surface structure to which phonological rules can apply.

Diagrammatically, the components of grammar in the original system and the revised system would be as in Figures 13-2 and 13-3 respectively. The BASE generates underlying phrase-markers for sentences, to be interpreted by the SEMANTIC COMPONENT which consists of a DICTIONARY and a set of SEMANTIC RULES (see Chapter 17). Once the deep structure of a sentence has been assigned the correct meaning, it goes through specified transformational operations and is converted into surface structure which, although modified, retains the meaning of the deep structure. In the last stage, the surface structure goes through a phonological component which converts it into sound. (Some examples are given in the following sections.)

13.10 FURTHER DEVELOPMENTS

The deep–surface distinction has led to significant revisions of the theory. The earlier distinctions between *optional* and *obligatory transformations*, and between *singulary* and *generalized transformations* (13.7), have been found unnecessary. All transformations now are singulary and obligatory. This has been made possible by writing the symbol S (sentence) on the right hand

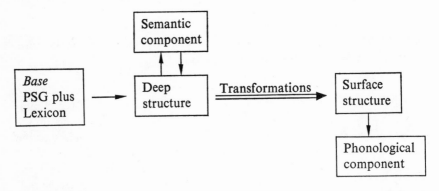

Figure 13-3. Revised version of TG theory.

side of a PS rule (see below). The base can now generate P-markers that have embedded constituent structures in the deep structure strings. Transformations apply to these deep structure P-markers, to produce surface structures P-markers.

For instance, the deep structure of sentence 26 would be as in Figure 13-4.

26 The man who works here knows the boy who stole the apples.

Similarly, the deep structure of an interrogative sentence would be different from its declarative counterpart, in that it would have the constituent *Question* in its deep P-marker; for instance, Figure 13-5 shows the deep structures of sentences 27 and 28:

27 John can fix the car.
28 Can John fix the car?

In the earlier model, the question transformation (13.7) applied to the declarative P-marker (which would imply that the two sentences had identical deep structures). The development in the theory illustrated by Figure 13-5 has resulted from the assumption that transformations do not change meaning —at least, not referential meaning (see Chapter 14). Within the present framework, transformations (like question, negative, passive) are activated to apply to a string by the presence of optional elements in the deep structure; these elements are generated by the base, and motivated by the meaning of the sentence.

One of the basic implications of this development has been the concern

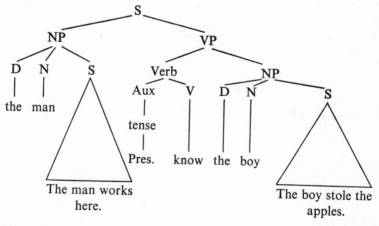

Figure 13-4.

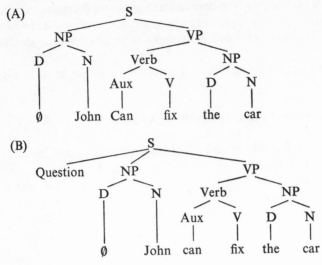

Figure 13-5.

with the order in which transformations may apply, since it is clear that transformational rules are ordered. For example, in English the REFLEXIVIZA-TION TRANSFORMATION applies before the IMPERATIVE transformation, as shown by sentence 29:

29 you bathe you   (Deep structure)
     you bathe yourself   (T–Reflexive)
            bathe yourself   (T–Imperative)

(Since T–Imperative deletes the subject NP, it must apply after T–Reflexive which operates on this same subject NP.) Many questions remain about the matter of ordering of transformational rules, and very few generalizations can be made on this subject at present.

13.11 LEXICAL RULES

Another development in the theory has been the exclusion of lexical sub-stitution rules (see 13.5) from the PS component. A deep structure P-marker, generated by the base, carries only the syntactic information about the constituent structure, and provides the grammatical morphemes (or forma-tives); the lexical elements in a kernel string are represented by DUMMY SYMBOLS which have to be filled in by the LEXICON (an inventory of all the

LEXICAL FORMATIVES in the language). The lexicon specifies, in terms of syntactic and phonological matrices, the SYNTACTIC and PHONOLOGICAL FEATURES of each entry. (The role of lexicon in a TG grammar is discussed in Chapter 17.3.)

13.12 CONCLUSION

The discussion of TG theory presented in this chapter has been intentionally over-simplified, and controversial details have been deliberately kept out of it. Current research will no doubt lead to the modification of much that is accepted at present, and there will probably continue to be substantial disagreements among individuals, even among those who accept the major assumptions of TG theory. For a fuller understanding of the theory, the reader is directed to the suggested readings given at the end of this chapter. We also call the reader's attention to the importance of work in non-generative transformational grammar, particularly that of Zellig Harris, which forms a basic part of the background of modern grammatical theory, but which we have been unable to discuss in detail for lack of space.

SUGGESTED SUPPLEMENTARY READING

Bach 1964; Koutsoudas 1966; Chomsky 1965; Jacobs and Rosenbaum 1970; Bach and Harms 1968; Harris 1952, 1957

FOLLOW-UP

1　Define: phrase-marker, string, terminal string, derivation, lexicon.

2　Distinguish: deep structure—surface structure, competence—performance, phrase structure component—transformational component—morphophonemic component, obligatory transformation—optional transformation, singular transformation—generalized transformation, transformational rule—rewrite rule.

3　Refer to problem no. 3 in the FOLLOW-UP to Chapter 10. Complete that problem if you have not already done so, and then continue with

the data given below, one step at a time (i.e., first *a*, then *b*, then *c*, etc.).
The data given here can best be described with transformational rules.

a. ye ghər mera hɛ   This house is mine.
   ye ghər nəya hɛ   This house is new.
   mera ghər nəya hɛ   My house is new.
   nəya ghər mera hɛ   The new house is mine.
   mera yəhã hɛ.   Mine is here.
   ye nəya ghər mera hɛ   This new house is mine.

b. vo admi kɔn hɛ   Who is that man?
   vo kəl aya hua admi kɔn hɛ   Who is that man who
                                        came yesterday?

   ye ghər mẽ jane vala admi mera bhai hɛ   This man going in the
                                        house is my brother.

   vo kıtab layi hui lərki meri bəhın hɛ   That girl who brought
                                        the book is my sister.

   vo phəl khane vala lərka kɔn hɛ   Who is that boy eating
                                        fruit?

   mera bhai ane vala hɛ   My brother is coming.
   meri bəhın phəl layi hɛ   My sister has brought
                                      (the) fruit.

   meri bəhın phəl layi hui hɛ   My sister has brought
                                      (the) fruit.

c. ram bazar jake phəl laya   Ram went to the bazaar and brought
                               fruit.

   sita phəl lake bebiko degi   Sita will bring fruit and give it to baby.
   vo ramko kıtab deke gəya   He gave the book to Ram and left.

d. ramko jane do   Let Ram go.
   sitako ane do   Let Sita come.
   mẽ ramko kəl jane nəhĩ dũga   I (masc.) won't let Ram go
                                    tomorrow.

   sitako phəl lake bebiko dene do   Let Sita bring fruit and give it to
                                        baby.

4   Derive the following sentences according to the model presented in 13.7:

   Have you seen the movie?
   John won't go.
   You're not listening.
   Wasn't John working?
   Mary hasn't read the book.

PART III

MEANING

Chapter 14

APPROACHES TO
THE STUDY OF MEANING

14.1 LINGUISTICS AND THE STUDY OF MEANING

It would be generally true to say that we do not speak unless we have something to say, and this something is MEANING. In fact, linguistic communication —language—is nothing but meaning converted into sound. This being the case, it might well be argued that it would be more profitable to begin with meaning, and then show how the conversion takes place. Some linguists are, in fact, currently proposing that languages be described in just this way (see 17.6). In this presentation of linguistic principles and methods, the reason for beginning with sound (Part I) and working our way through form (Part II) in order to get to meaning can partly be found in the development of modern linguistics. The other part of the reason is that, while sound is directly observable, meaning can be approached only through form.

Modern linguistics, as it has developed during the last four decades, has emphasized form at the cost of meaning for a number of reasons. In their endeavor to be scientific and objective, modern linguists rejected the speculative and subjective aspects of traditional grammar. The linguist's concern with objectivity compelled him to reject anything that could not be objectively verified, and to direct his energies to what was observable, relegating meaning to a future time when adequate tools for analyzing it would become available. Also, the initial success with which the linguist met in analyzing form without taking meaning into account led him to the false conclusion that it is possible to describe a language without accounting for meaning at all.

In his 1933 book *Language*, Leonard Bloomfield clearly states that while it is desirable to describe meaning, it is impossible to treat it with precision and rigor. Hence, he argues, it would be desirable to limit the scope of linguistics to observable data, leaving out of the scope of the field those aspects of language which were not directly observable or physically measurable. Bloomfield's pronouncements were perhaps taken too literally by later linguists. Consequently, modern linguists continued to ignore meaning, often claiming that it was properly the domain of other fields, such as logic, philosophy, psychology, etc.

14.2 MEANINGS OF "MEANING"

The linguist's reluctance to touch meaning is easily understood when we ask ourselves a simple question like, "What is meaning?" Although everyone understands, in a general sense, the meanings of words and sentences, there is no simple answer to this question. The word *meaning* itself may be used in various different meanings, e.g., *What do you* mean *by staring at me? What does this word* mean? *What does this sudden rise in the water-level* mean? It is clear that the word does not have the same meaning in these different cases. Specialists such as philosophers, logicians and linguists who grapple with these problems have no simple solutions. Some of the ways in which this question has been answered are discussed below.

A. Meaning as the thing named

This theory states that the meaning of a word is the thing it names. The term *thing* in this definition has to be interpreted as referring to objects like *table*, actions like *kill*, states like *know*, qualities like *blue* and abstract notions like *courage*, besides many other "things" which can scarcely be called things. This is a fairly attractive theory, and is one of the oldest. Obviously, many words in a language refer to objects in the physical world, and even to call the color *blue* a thing may have some justification.

However, there are several shortcomings in this theory. First of all, it would be difficult for it to accommodate words like *no, to, but*, or suffixes like *-ed* meaning 'past tense' or *-es* meaning 'plural'. Secondly, no matter how loosely we understand the term *thing*, it would be difficult to include words that have distinct meaning but do not refer to any existing thing, for example *phoenix* or *angel*. Such words surely have meaning which is understood by the speaker-hearer, but the objects they name cannot be identified in the physical world.

B. Meaning as ideas

To overcome the shortcomings of the above theory, this view maintains that the meaning of a word is an *idea* associated with the word in the mind of the speaker-hearer. At a first glance one may find this theory—usually called the MENTALISTIC theory of meaning—attractive, for it accounts for *phoenix* and *angel* which now belong to the mental world of ideas. But once we look closely at ideas we run into problems. If the meaning of a word is an idea in the mind of the speaker, then how does he communicate his meaning to the hearer? Surely ideas are private to the speaker.

The supporters of this theory would argue that ideas in the mind are related to images. This would be tenable for physical objects, for when one says *table* both the speaker and hearer probably have an image of *table* which makes communication possible. But what about words like *courage* or *honesty*? Even more difficult to imagine are images for grammatical notions. Also, even for physical objects one's images may have various qualities that are irrelevant to the communication of meaning. Definitions of ideas in terms of concepts and thoughts are equally unsatisfactory.

C. Meaning as behavior

This, like the mentalistic theory, is a psychological theory of meaning. It is different from the 'ideas' theory in that it locates the meaning of a word not in the mind but in the manner in which the hearer responds to a word when he hears it. This theory of meaning—known as the BEHAVIORAL or causal theory—is based on experiments in learning behavior in lower animals, the findings being extended by analogy to the way humans use verbal symbols. As with other notions of behavioral psychology, this theory suffers from the quite mistaken extension of conclusions based on the behavior of lower animals to human behavior.

Further, in attempting to account for meaning in terms of overt measurable behavior on the part of the hearer, the behavioral theory fails to make a distinction between actual observable behavior and the hearer's disposition to respond to a word. Very frequently, in a communication situation, a hearer either has an option to respond in one of several possible ways to a message, or does not respond in an overt observable manner. In such a situation the theory would have to contend with several meanings for a given word, any one of which may, unpredictably, be responded to by the hearer, or else relate the meaning to the hearer's disposition to respond. However, getting at the latter is at least as difficult as describing 'ideas' in the mind of the speaker-hearer. In effect, then, this theory is no better than the mentalistic theory.

D. Meaning as abstraction

A more recent way of looking at meaning, which incorporates the theory of things named (A above), is the theory of SIGNIFICATION, which holds that the relationship between FORMS (words, morphemes) and their REFERENTS (the "things" they refer to) is an indirect one, mediated by the MEANING. This relationship is depicted in Figure 14-1. This diagram is meant to indicate that the relationship between form and referent is indirect, in that it is mediated by the meaning, which is part of linguistic structure. For example, speakers of English know that a banana is a fruit by virtue of their knowledge of the meaning of the word *fruit*.

This is not as obvious as it may seem, as we can see if we look at an example from another language. The word *pazam* in Tamil (often mistakenly translated as 'fruit') refers to fruits which are eaten without cooking, such as *vaaza-pazam* '(ripe) banana', *maam-pazam* '(ripe) mango', etc. Fruits and vegetables which need cooking before they can be eaten are called *kaa(y)*: e.g., *vaaza-kaa(y)* '(green) banana, plantain', *maan-kaa(y)* '(green) mango', *kattri-kaa(y)* 'eggplant', etc. Thus, the name given to a particular referent (for example, a green mango) depends both on the observable characteristics of the referent (shape, color, hardness, etc.) and on the particular system of meaning (English, Tamil, etc.) which is being used. Thus the name (*pazam, fruit*) does not stand for the referent, since there is no natural or direct link between name and referent. Rather, the name stands for a particular category of referents, or for a particular way of categorizing referents. Meaning, then, is a way of categorizing referents.

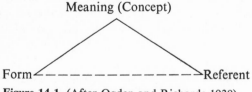

Meaning (Concept)

Form ← — — — — — — — — — → Referent

Figure 14-1. (After Ogden and Richards 1930).

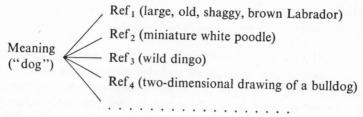

Figure 14-2. Multiple referents.

We often take it for granted that any referents which have the same name are the same in some fundamental sense. This sense of sameness, however, derives at least in part from the fact that the categorization is made for us by the language, and we imbibe the categorization as we learn to use the language. We seldom notice, for example, that a word like *dog* can refer to referents as different as those depicted in Figure 14-2, all of which differ in some detail from each other. In other words, a form can have multiple and varied referents.

Clearly, then, meaning is a kind of abstraction based on the properties shared by a class of things or events. This notion of abstracted properties is not limited to animate beings or material objects such as *elephant* or *banana*, but is also true of abstract notions like *courage*, or actions like *run* (which may refer to various acts of running), or even abstract relations like *in*, *from*, *after*, etc. The relationship between meaning and form is also not necessarily one-to-one. A single form may combine with two or more meanings, thus referring to distinct classes of referents, as shown in Figure 14-3 (see 14.6).

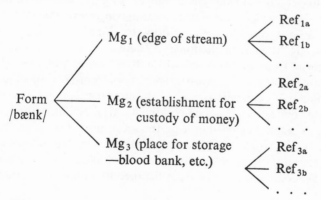

Figure 14-3. Multiple meaning.

14.3 KINDS OF MEANING

Traditional grammar divides meaning into MATERIAL MEANING and FORMAL MEANING. Under material meaning are included the meanings of members of major parts of speech such as nouns, verbs, adjectives and adverbs, for, according to traditional grammar, these refer to concepts which make up the "matter" of discourse. Other parts of speech are meaningful in a different way, in that they combine the major parts of speech to provide the total meaning of discourse (or sentences). In other words, the major parts of speech are thought to provide the matter, while the other parts of speech provide the form. In modern (structural) linguistics a similar distinction is made between LEXICAL MEANING and STRUCTURAL MEANING. Major form classes are said to have lexical meaning which is found in dictionaries; other classes like articles, prepositions, etc. have structural or GRAMMATICAL MEANING.

It is important to note here that while lexical meaning operates at the level of the word, grammatical meaning operates at different levels, e.g., at the morpheme level (the possessive morpheme in English), at the form class level (noun, verb, etc.); or in terms of grammatical function (subject–predicate, verb–object, modifier–head, etc.), grammatical structure (phrase, clause, sentence), sentence type (declarative, interrogative, imperative, etc.), and so on. In a broad sense, it may be argued that linguists who make a distinction between lexical and grammatical meaning are, in fact, making a distinction between linguistic or structural meaning, which operates at various levels, and CONCEPTUAL MEANING. The devices that a language uses to signal grammatical (or linguistic) meaning make up its grammar. It is this meaning that structural linguistics has mainly concentrated on, relegating lexical meaning to the background under the plea that it is not feasible to subject lexical meaning to techniques of analysis developed for grammatical meaning.

One of the levels at which grammatical meaning operates is that of minor form classes like articles, pronouns, prepositions, etc. Members of these form classes are generally listed in a dictionary. There is need, therefore, for distinguishing them from those forms which have lexical meaning. One criterion for distinguishing these GRAMMATICAL ITEMS from LEXICAL ITEMS is in terms of CLOSED and OPEN SETS (see 13.5). In any language, grammatical items are few and constant (in meaning and function); they form closed sets of items usually of small membership, e.g., the set of pronouns, of number (singular vs. plural), of articles, and so on. Lexical items belong to open sets which have indeterminately large membership; new lexical items which are coined to fulfill the communicative needs of the speech community are added to these open sets.

The choice of a term from a set is itself meaningful. In other words, a part of the meaning of a term is its paradigmatic opposition to other terms within a set. For example, a part of the formal meaning of plural number in English is that it is in opposition to singular number, both of which make up a closed set of numbers in English. An example of an open set would be a set of English words like *chair, sofa, settee, ottoman, stool, bench*, etc. Each term in the set carries, in addition to its lexical or conceptual meaning, the meaning of *not* being any of the other terms. The set principle, when applied to lexical items, breaks up the total stock of lexical items into subsets that belong to particular SEMANTIC FIELDS (see 15.5).

It is important to note that with the addition of every new term to the set, all the existing terms undergo a change in their meaning within the set, in that each is now in opposition to an additional item in the set.

14.4 THE LEXICON AND ITS CONTENTS

A monolingual dictionary is a list of lexical items in a language, explicated in that language. Ideally such a list should cover the whole lexicon, i.e., all minimal formal units of the language. However, in practice, most dictionaries fail to include some minimal units, or include some morpheme sequences which are not minimal units. A lexicon should include sequences of two or more morphemes only if their meaning cannot be predicted on the basis of individual morphemes and arrangements. Thus an English lexicon should explain *hot dog, blackbird* (term for several specific varieties of birds), *kick the bucket* (jocular or slang for 'die'), but need not explain *hot day, black hair, eat the apple*, etc.

In other words, the lexicon must include all the information needed to understand sentences, apart from that which is provided by the grammatical description. Sometimes it is not clear whether certain categories of items should be included in the lexicon, e.g., English nominal compounds: sequences like *car seat, vapor trail, garbage can, city dump* are formed by productive processes which can be used by any native speaker of English, and be understood by other native speakers. Obviously we cannot list all such items as lexical units, since new ones are created every day. On the other hand, attempts to describe such compounds as syntactic constructions have not been entirely successful so far.

14.5 IDIOMS

Morpheme sequences such as *blackbird* and *kick the bucket*, which are not semantically transparent, are commonly known as IDIOMS. Semantically, idioms are not analyzable in terms of the individual meaning of morphemes, and must, therefore, be considered single units from a descriptive point of view. The term *idiom* has also been used by grammarians and language teachers to include certain grammatical forms which cannot be translated automatically. For example, the Hindi-Urdu expression /mʊjh-ko malum nəhĩ/ 'I don't know'—literally "to me (it is) not apparent"—is often presented to students as an idiom, though from the point of view of Hindi-Urdu speakers there is no need to single out this expression for special treatment. It conforms to a normal sentence type (sometimes known as the *impersonal construction*), and the meaning of each morpheme is the same in this sentence as in other cases: (mʊjh-ko/ 'to me' as in /mʊjh-ko ləgta hɛ/ 'it seems to me', /malum/ 'apparent' as in /ɛsa malum hua/ 'This became apparent', etc. This expression is peculiar only from the point of view of its English translation, which happens to use a different type of construction. In addition to the ambiguity implied in the term 'idiom', we must distinguish *idiom* from *idiomatic*, which is often used in the sense of a casual or ordinary way of speaking.

14.6   LEXICAL MEANINGS

In traditional grammar, relationships between lexical items are accounted for in terms of SYNONYMY and HOMONYMY. Two different forms that share a meaning are called SYNONYMS, e.g., *buy*: *purchase*, *ill*: *sick* in English (see below). Lexical items which share a phonetic form but are semantically distinct are called HOMONYMS. The English *bank* (14.2) is an instance of homonymy. In cases where there is no orthographic : phonetic correspondence, we may have cases of HOMOGRAPHY, involving distinct phonetic forms which are written identically, e.g., the English *bases*, pronounced (1) /beːsiːz/ (plural of *basis*) and (2) /beːsəz/ (plural of *base*). Forms that are written differently but pronounced identically are instances of HOMOPHONY, e.g., *right*, *write* and *rite* in English are pronounced /rayt/.

Homonymy is not always so clear-cut as in the English word *bank* where there is an obvious gap between the two meanings: 'edge of a stream' and 'establishment for custody of money'. It is often very difficult to decide whether a given phonetic form in its various meanings is one lexical item or a set of homonyms. For example, the word *train* may mean any of the following:

1   part of a robe or skirt trailing on the ground
2   series of railway carriages drawn by an engine

3 body of followers
4 to teach
5 to aim

Train is distinguished from *bank* as an instance of MULTIPLE MEANING where *one* lexical item has a *range* of meanings which can be grouped together. In *bank* there is no single range of meaning that will cover both the meanings. Historically, too, *bank* comes from two distinct sources, while *train* can be related to differentiated meanings of a single original form.

Lexical meaning is further complicated by the possibility of EXTENDED MEANING. Words like *head, mouth, eye*, in addition to their common meanings (parts of the body) may have extended meanings, as in *head* (of an organization), *mouth* (of a bottle) and *eye* (of a needle). Extended meaning (or METAPHORICAL EXTENSION as this is called in traditional grammar) may be regarded as a special case of multiple meaning, and, normally, items like *head, mouth* and *eye* would be listed only once in a dictionary of English. Traditionally, extension of meaning is regarded as GENERALIZING the basic meaning of a form to include new referents which are in some way like the original class of referents; the head of an organization is its most important member, the eye of a needle is shaped like a human eye, etc.

On closer examination, the distinctions between homonymy, multiple meaning and extended meaning prove to be somewhat arbitrary since dictionaries do not agree on which items are homonyms and which involve multiple or extended meanings. Also, when the lexicographer involves historical or textual evidence, his classification may not necessarily match the intuition of the native speaker. Lyons, in his *Introduction to Theoretical Linguistics*, cites the example of *ear*, as human organ, and *ear* referring to parts of cereal plants, which are listed in modern dictionaries as two separate words, since they have, in fact, developed from two different words in Old English: (1) *eare*, (2) *ear*. But it is possible, Lyons argues, that speakers of modern English use these words on the analogy of *head, mouth, eye*, etc. as metaphorical extensions, and the knowledge of historical development of the language does not materially alter the usage.

Returning to synonymy: modern linguists generally assume that there are no complete synonyms in a language, i.e., if two forms are phonemically different, then their meanings are also different. Thus, *buy* and *purchase* are similar in meaning, but differ at least in their level of formality and therefore are not completely interchangeable: that department of an institution which is concerned with acquisition of materials is normally the *Purchasing Department* rather than the *Buying Department*; a wife would rarely ask her husband to *purchase a pound of butter*; etc. Though in some contexts words may appear completely synonymous, there are likely to be differences in other contexts. Thus, in speaking of a person who is mentally deficient (or in expressing one's annoyance at someone who has acted stupidly), the terms *idiot, imbecile,* and *moron* are more or less interchangeable, whereas in a technical sense these refer to three distinguishable levels of mental deficiency, and would not be considered equivalent by a psychiatrist working in a mental institution. When cases of synonyms are looked at carefully, it usually turns out that differences of this type are present. Thus, this assumption of modern linguistics has so far turned out to be justified.

Another traditional semantic relationship is ANTONYMY. Words which oppose each other in meaning are often listed in dictionaries as ANTONYMS. However, the traditional usage lumps together different kinds of antonyms, e.g., EXCLUSIVE opposites like *night–day* (of which one excludes the other), POLAR opposites like *hot–cold* (which exclude each other but leave intermediate areas to be accounted for by other terms like *warm, cool*); pairs like *man–woman, man–boy,* or *husband–wife* (which are opposed to each other by the presence of absence of particular properties like sex or age); pairs like *lend–borrow, buy–sell* which refer to reciprocal activities; and others.

14.7 MEANINGS OF GRAMMATICAL ARRANGEMENTS

Grammatical arrangements are meaningful, and the meaning of a sentence is a combination of the meaning of lexical items and the meaning of grammatical arrangements. If this were not so, there would be no difference of meaning in the two English sentences:

> The cat chased the dog.
> The dog chased the cat.

Traditional grammar has attempted to define these meanings of grammatical arrangements, but the results are not satisfactory because no real attempt has been made to be precise. We are told, for example, that in an NP + VP construction, the NP (or subject) designates the *actor* (person or thing performing an action), and the VP designates the *action* performed. If the VP is of the type: V + NP (i.e., transitive verb with direct object), the second NP denotes the *recipient* of the action. To see how well this description fits the facts, we can look at the following sentences:

	NP	+	*VP(V*	+	*NP)*
1	John		hit		the ball.
2	John		got		a virus.

	NP	+	VP(V	+	NP)
---	----------		-----		-----------
3	John		ignored		the silence.
4	John		heard		a noise.
5	John		likes		this place.
6	This place		suits		John.

Sentence 1 would seem to fit the description all right, since we will all probably agree that in this case *John* performed an action, and that the *ball* was affected by it. In sentence 2 it would seem to be the other way around, and we might have expected *A virus got John* instead. In sentence 3 there does not seem to have been any action at all (at least not on John's part), nor anything to be acted upon. Sentence 4 could probably give rise to a heated debate, depending on whether one views such an event as involving activity or passivity on John's part. Sentences 5 and 6 are particularly difficult, since they both refer to the same situation. Clearly, grammatical meaning needs to be described in a more satisfactory way. Most often, rules for interpreting meaning of grammatical signals are rules of thumb and, therefore, *ad hoc*. (See 17.4–5 for a new approach to this question within contemporary grammatical theory.)

14.8 SOCIAL MEANING

In this chapter, so far, we have discussed some of the traditional attitudes towards meaning, and some of the devices used by traditional grammarians and linguists to account for meaning. The various classifications of meaning mentioned involve linguistic structure, without reference to the social context of linguistic communication. It is a fact of language use, that different people who speak a language may have different meanings for the same word, or different words for the same meaning. These differences may arise from the special experiences of an individual, or they may be differences peculiar to a social group, class or region. Although we will discuss in Chapters 18–20 the implications of the ways in which linguistic and social structures intersect and correlate, some of the basic issues involved in considering linguistic meaning in the social context may be mentioned here.

Individual differences in language use are best explained in terms of CONNOTATION and DENOTATION. Connotation has to do with the associations that a lexical item has for an individual. For example, the word *sea* will arouse a very different chain of associations in the minds of a sailor, a travel agent, a swimmer, a fisherman, a businessman, and so on. Regional differences of meaning or form may be illustrated by the example of *elevator* in American English being equivalent to *lift* in British English.

However, significant differences in meaning can arise out of socio-economic differences between groups of people. At the lexical level one may cite the examples of pairs of words used for the same meaning by different social groups as in: *serviette* vs. *napkin*, *mirror* vs. *looking glass*, *wealthy* vs. *rich*, and so on. In Britain, the second word in each of the above pairs is said to be a marker of the upper classes. But social differences are not only reflected in the choice of words by two or more social groups. Phonology, morphology and syntax have been found to vary in ways which can be systematically correlated with social factors such as socio-economic class, education, age, caste, and so on. (These types of variation are discussed in 18.3 and 19.) Furthermore, differences in the choice of lexical items are often related to the social identity of speakers. For example, the usual word for 'rice (cooked)' in Tamil is *cooru*, but some Brahmins and other high-caste speakers use the word *saadam* (derived from Sanskrit *prasādam* 'offering of food sanctified by the deity') for the rice they eat themselves, reserving *cooru* for that eaten by others.

14.9 MEANING AND COMMUNICATION

As we pointed out in 14.1 above, speaking is a meaningful activity. However, it is customary for speakers of a language to use various conventionalized devices (utterances), not for conveying meaning in the senses discussed so far in this chapter, but for establishing some sort of contact prior to actual meaningful communication (see 7.2). For example, in English expressions like *How do you do?* and *Nice day, isn't it?* are not used for communicating some experience like information, wish, desire, command and so on; nor is the hearer expected to answer by narrating how well or unwell he is, or giving a summary of the current weather report. Such expressions are used in different languages as a means of creating a proper cultural context for linguistic communication. Any account of meaning must account for such devices which the society uses in various communication situations. Properly speaking, this belongs in the study of ethnography of communication (see (18.1).

NOTES

14.1. Linguistics and meaning: Bloomfield 1933, pp. 139–140
       Form, meaning, and referent: Ogden and Richards 1930

14.6. English *ear*: Lyons 1968: 406–407

14.8. Tamil *co:ru-sa:tam*: Ramanujan 1968

SUGGESTED SUPPLEMENTARY READING

Ogden and Richards 1930; Lyons 1963, 1968 (Chs. 9–10); Ullmann 1962; Joos 1964;
Nida 1964*a–b*, 1949; Osgood, Suci, Tannenbaum 1957; Sebeok 1964; Weinreich
1963

FOLLOW-UP

---

1 Define: referent, multiple meaning, idiom, extended meaning, metaphorical extension.

2 Distinguish: lexical meaning—structural meaning; material meaning—
formal meaning; closed sets—open sets; synonym—homonym; connotation—denotation.

3 Explain the differences between the various theories of meaning mentioned in 14.1: meaning as the thing named, meaning as an idea, meaning
as behavior and meaning as an abstraction.

4 Explain why earlier linguists emphasized form at the cost of meaning.

5 Why must the lexicon of English explain the meaning of *hot dog*, but
not of *hot day*?

Chapter 15

MEANING AND CULTURE: SOME SEMANTIC DOMAINS

15.1 SEMANTIC DIFFERENCES AMONG LANGUAGES

Because meaning is the core of communication, it has always been a central part of the study of language and communication systems among anthropologists and others concerned with the social uses of language. The anthropologist's interest in language relates to his interest in cultural behavior, and generally takes into account the total social context of the communication situation: the situations which lead a person to speak, the limitations imposed by the social context as to who can speak, what one is expected to say or not say, etc. (see 18.1). Thus the anthropologist's approach to language goes beyond the formal structure of utterances, and very often leads him to look for correlations between the linguistic form and the patterns of social behavior which are institutionalized in the society.

Anthropological studies of semantics have typically examined particular semantic DOMAINS such as kinship terms, color terms, or sets of terms for classifying natural phenomena such as plants, animals, diseases, meteorological phenomena, supernatural beings (gods, ghosts, etc.). These studies have often concentrated on the *differences* among languages in the semantic distinctions which they recognize, though recently more and more attention has been given to the investigation of universal features (see 16.4). The following sections present some examples of the results of such studies.

The emphasis on semantic differences in the anthropological literature can be contrasted with the "common-sense" attitude toward language differences which may be found among language students (as well as many language teachers) in the United States, who generally seem prepared for differences in pronunciation and in grammatical rules, but still expect that every English word will have a more-or-less exact equivalent in any other language. To a certain extent, this expectation of one-to-one TRANSLATABILITY is justified as far as the usual western European languages are concerned, but when we go beyond this familiar culture area, semantic differences begin to assume much greater importance. Eugene Nida, in a discussion of problems encountered by Bible translators, has discussed several cases of "untranslatable" words or concepts; one of the most striking ones is the difficulty encountered in rendering the word *desert* into the language of the Maya Indians, who are said to be unable to conceive of any place without vegetation except a space cleared for a maize field.

Apart from such inescapable environmental differences, every culture has social institutions which are complex and unique enough that they could only be rendered in the language of other cultures by means of lengthy explanations: such would be the case for English terms like *football* or *Parliament*, and English speakers would be in a similar position with regard to terms referring to rituals, games, etc. of other societies. The same situation arises with regard to terms which summarize a whole experience or attitude which is relevant to members of a particular society. An example is the American adjective *corny* (referring to anything presented in an overly sentimental or theatrical way, in an attempt to appeal to unsophisticated tastes), which is perhaps derived from the speech of touring theatrical troupes, expressing their idea of the type of presentations that appealed to the inhabitants of the "Corn Belt" (the rural Midwest of the United States).

The differences which are of the greatest theoretical interest, and which are perhaps the most likely to cause confusion in translation and language learning, are those involving different classifications of similar phenomena, where speakers of different language have different OBLIGATORY DISTINCTIONS available to them. In French, for example, one cannot refer to one's cousin without specifying his/her sex: one must say either *ma cousine* /makuzin/ (female) or *mon cousin* /mõkuzẽ/ (male). Similarly, one cannot address a single person without making a choice between *tu* 'you' (familiar, cf. older English *thou*) and *vous* 'you' (formal). In English, we *can* make such distinctions by saying *my girl cousin* or *my female cousin* (*my cousin Mary*, of course, requires no specification), by using various forms of address to indicate one's relationship to one's hearer (see 16.2), etc.; but the distinctions are not obligatory in English, since we can avoid them if we wish.

English, on the other hand, has a distinction between *V-ed* (traditionally "past tense") and *have V-en* (traditionally "perfect") which is missing in some other languages, occasionally leading foreign speakers of English to utter sentences like *I have seen him yesterday*, which sound strange to some speakers of English. English speakers must also choose between singular and plural when they use a noun (except for mass nouns like *stuff*), whereas in Chinese it is possible to specify plurality (by using numerals, or terms which translate our *some, many*, etc.) but one is not obliged to do it all the time as we are. Occasionally, the fact that we must distinguish number in English can lead to an awkward expression. For example, cases like 'Any person or persons who enter or enters...' can be expressed much more conveniently in Chinese. On the other hand, an English sentence like 'There are people there' involves some awkwardness in Chinese, since it would require a phrase meaning 'two or more' to capture the exact meaning of the English.

The implication of these differences is that, in any language, the choice of a particular meaning may entail certain other obligatory choices, which may differ from one language to another. Therefore, languages differ not so much in what *can* be said in them, but rather in that some things are relatively *easier* to say in one language than another. (We return to this subject in 16.5)

15.2 PRONOUNS: LINGUISTIC REFLECTIONS OF HUMAN RELATIONSHIPS

The example of French *tu* and *vous* mentioned above is similar to distinctions found in many languages all over the world. Students of these languages may be given textbook rules for using these various terms, but usually it is necessary to "get into the culture" in order to learn which term is expected in various situations. A student in a French-speaking region will find, for example (after a suitable introductory period when a certain degree of familiarity is achieved), that he or she is expected to use *tu* to fellow students of the same sex; that young children are addressed as *tu* regardless of any other differences in status; that older strangers must be addressed as *vous*; etc.

This two-way distinction is capable of indicating three different kinds of relationships, depending whether two individuals both use *tu* to each other, or both use *vous*, or whether one uses *tu* and the other *vous*. In the first case, with mutual use of *tu*, the relationships is both intimate and equal (e.g., members of the same family, friends of the same age, etc.). With mutual *vous*, the relationship is formal and without major inequalities in age or class status. The non-reciprocal use of *tu* and *vous* indicates a relationship with a major inequality, either in age and/or class status. Thus, two distinct dimensions of difference can be factored out of the opposition between these two terms: that of DISTANCE (intimate vs. formal) and that of DEFERENCE (familiar vs. deferent). The use of *vous* gives respect to the addressee but at the same time puts him at a distance, whereas the use of *tu* grants him intimacy but denies respect.

Certain distinctions in English are based on a very similar social pattern. In addressing a person by name, English speakers must make a choice between two high-frequency patterns: the person's first name, or the last name preceded by a title (such as Mr., Miss, Mrs., Dr., Professor, Captain). Studies of this distinction by Roger Brown and his colleagues show that it patterns very much like that between *tu* and *vous*, and similar distinctions in other European languages. The distinction also correlates with other differences in the language: for example, in business concerns where one person (e.g., the boss) addresses another (e.g., a workman or secretary) by first name, but is himself addressed by title and last name, the person addressed formally will also be given formal greetings such as *good morning* or *good afternoon*, to which he or she is free to respond with informal greetings such as *Hi*.

English also expresses further distinctions with several low-frequency patterns. Titles without name (Doctor, Sir, Ma'am, Officer, Your Honor), or double titles (Mr. Chairman, Mr. President), usually indicate extreme formality, though some titles are used in this way when one does not know the name of the person addressed (e.g., Mister, Miss). The use of nicknames or multiple names usually indicates the greatest intimacy. Couples and close friends often have a variety of ways of addressing or referring to each other. For example, a man named John Jones may be known to his close friends as *John, Johnnie, Jack, Joker* (or some other playful name), *Jonesy, Jonas*, etc.

Thus, English contains approximately the same distinctions described above for French, but expresses them in a slightly different way—which makes it a little easier to avoid the distinction when one is not sure which form to use. In English-speaking societies, it is not uncommon for a person to be unsure about what form of address to use, and to seek to avoid it as far as possible; so also in other societies with other distinctions. In urban parts of the Hindi-Urdu area, for example, middle-class people sometimes find themselves in a dilemma when addressing working-class people: the use of the informal /tum/, though perfectly acceptable in the traditional rural situation, may be thought somewhat demeaning nowadays, especially in addressing a person with some education. The formal /ap/, on the other hand, would be inappropriate.

Two devices are used to avoid the choice. One is pronoun deletion, which is in any case quite common in Hindi-Urdu. The other is the use of an infinitive form of the verb in making requests, etc. Thus, in asking an elevator operator or a taxi driver to stop, one can use the infinitive /rokna/ (instead of the informal /roko/, or the formal /rokiye/). A novel solution to this dilemma was suggested in a Marathi short story, in which a young man avoided the choice between formal /tumhi/ and informal /tu/ in addressing a young lady in whom he had a romantic interest, simply by switching to English whenever the occasion arose.

15.3 KINSHIP

Kinship terms constitute one of the most-studied semantic domains. Generally speaking, the study of kinship is an integral part of the study of social structure, which includes marriage and residence patterns as well. Nevertheless, some anthropological linguists have become interested in the structure of kinship systems in their own right, and it is this study which gave rise to the techniques of componential analysis as they are currently applied in semantic study (see 16.2).

One of the simplest methods for diagramming kinship terms is shown in Figure 15-1. This shows part of the English kinship system, including most terms for blood relations (terms for in-laws are not included, nor are terms for step-relations or half-relations such as half-brother). Such diagrams are drawn from the point of view of a hypothetical individual, referred to as EGO (Latin for 'I'). In this case, EGO can be of either sex (though in some kinship systems, such as that of Hindi-Urdu, the sex of EGO affects the choice of terms for certain relatives). Notice that in Figure 15-1, only the mother's relatives (parents, brothers, sisters, etc.) are shown, not the father's. In the case of English, the terms for the equivalent relatives on the father's side would be the same.

This can be contrasted with the Hindi-Urdu situation, which requires a much fuller diagram (divided here into three parts for ease of reading). Hindi-Urdu shows the following additional distinctions: where English uses the terms *uncle* and *aunt* for all brothers or sisters of ego's parents, Hindi-Urdu has five distinct terms: *tau* for FEB (father's elder brother), *caca* for FYB (father's younger brother), *bua* for FZ (father's sister), *mama* for MB (mother's brother), and *mɔsi* for MZ (mother's sister). Similarly where English has only two terms *niece* and *nephew*, Hindi-Urdu distinguishes according to whether one is speaking of a brother's or sister's children; for *grandfather* and *grandmother*, Hindi-Urdu also distinguishes father's parents from mother's parents. Thus, the criterion known as "sex of the linking relative" is a relevant one in the Hindi-Urdu kinship system, though not in the English system. (This is discussed further in 16.1.)

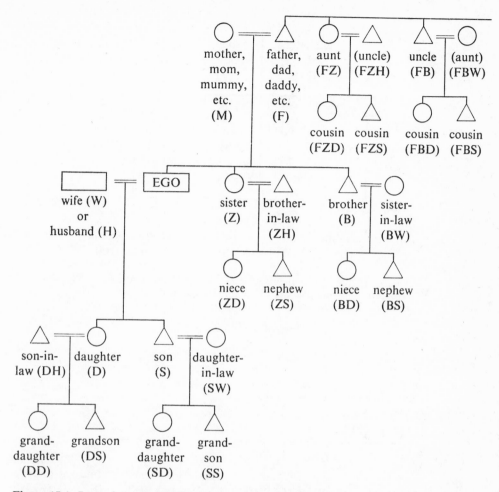

Figure 15-1. Part of the English kinship system. Triangles indicate males; circles indicate females. The vertical line indicates descent, and the horizontal line joins children of the same parents. The equals sign joins marriage partners. Primary kin are symbolized by the single letters M (mother), F (father), B (brother), Z (sister), W (wife), H (husband), D (daughter), S (son); other kin can be designated by combinations of these letters—e.g., SW (son's wife), FB (father's brother), MZS (mother's sister's son), etc. Note: some English speakers call their FZH and FBW 'uncle' and 'aunt' respectively, whereas some do not regard them as relatives.

What is the nature of the relationship between the system of kinship terms and the culture, or (since the kinship system itself is part of the culture) how does it correlate with other kinds of cultural behavior? The attempts to answer this question can be considered to form a whole sub-branch of the study of social structure, and cannot be dealt with here. It is often assumed

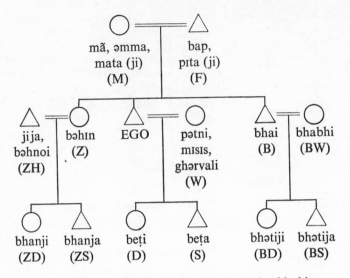

Figure 15-2A. A segment of the Hindu-Urdu kinship structure, showing primary kin of a male ego. (Sex of ego is relevant in determining the choice of certain terms for in-laws.)

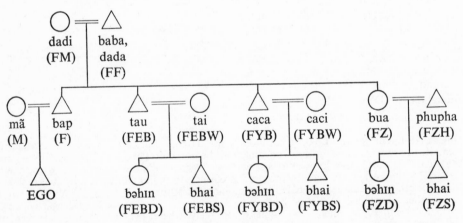

Figure 15-2B. Extension of Figure 15-2A, showing relatives on Ego's father's side.

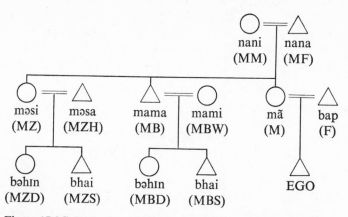

Figure 15-2C. Extension of Figure 15-2A, showing relatives on Ego's mother's side. (Source: Sylvia Vatuk, "A Structural Analysis of the Hindi Kinship Terminology". *Contributions to Indian Sociology* 3.94–115 [1969].)

that, if a distinction is made consistently by people in a society, that distinction must be somehow relevant to them. Often, the reasons for relevance are obvious, but in some cases they must be sought very diligently, and sometimes they can only be guessed at. Generally speaking, it is reasonable to assume that where distinctions such as that between FEB, FYB, MB, etc., or the earlier European distinction between FB (Latin *patruus*) and MB (Latin *avunculus*) exist, that these different categories corresponded to different role expectations. An example of this may be found in the South Indian kinship systems, in which one's parallel cousins (children of one's parents' same-sex siblings, i.e., FBS and FBD, MZS and MZD) are generally called by the same terms as one's own brothers and sisters, but cross cousins (FZS, FZD, MBS, MBD) are called by distinct terms. This is shown in Figure 15-3, which gives part of the kinship system used by lower-caste (i.e., non-Brahmin) Tamil speakers in Tanjore. This distinction would appear to correlate with the fact that the preferred marriage partner in this area for a male is the younger cross cousin (FBD or MZD), whereas marriage with parallel cousins is not permitted. In North India no marriage with a cousin is permitted. Thus in both these cases, the terms for *brother* and *sister* designate individuals whom one cannot marry.

The absence of a particular distinction does not necessarily indicate that there is no difference in behavior or roles. English does not have single terms for older and younger siblings, as Tamil does (though we do occasionally use phrases like *big sister*, *kid brother*), but there are some differences in roles at least for some people—e.g., the older sibling is expected to be protective of the younger. Conversely, the presence of a linguistic distinction does not necessarily indicate a behavioral distinction: English-speaking societies do not differentiate terminologically between male and female

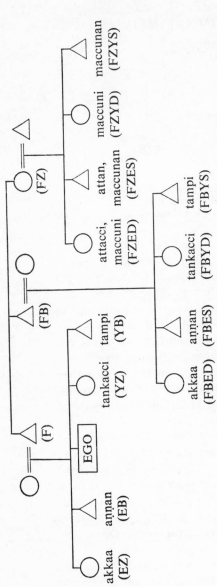

Figure 15-3A. This and the following figure show the terms for Ego's natal kin of the same generation in low-caste Tamil.

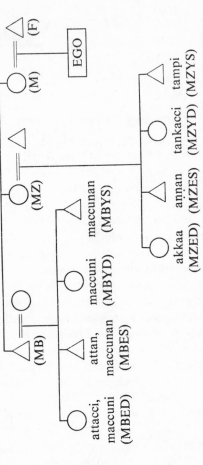

Figure 15-3B. Ego's paternal, same-generation natal kin (low-caste Tamil). The letters E (for elder), Y (for younger) refer to age relative to Ego. (Source: Kathleen Gough, "Brahman Kinship in a Tamil Village". *American Anthropologist* 58, pp. 826–853).

cousins as the French and Germans do, but there do not appear to be (at least at the present time) any differences in roles correlating with this in French or German society. Thus, a thorough understanding of the cultural basis for such distinctions requires not only a deep study of current social structure, but also detailed information about earlier stages of the society.

15.4   COLOR TERMS

In a rainbow, or in the color spectrum produced by passing light through a prism, there is a continuous gradation of colors without natural divisions. Yet, speakers of a language classify this continuous band into discrete segments, and appear to agree by and large on the locations of the division (though one does hear occasional arguments). On the other hand, anthropologists and linguists have reported considerable differences among different languages in their ways of classifying colors. Figures 15-4A–4C provide a rough representation of the systems of color terms in English, Hanunoo (a

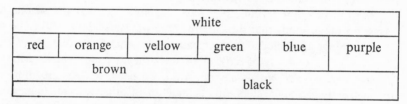

Figure 15-4A. Two-dimensional representation of English basic color terms. The horizontal axis corresponds roughly to the variation in wavelength seen in the color spectrum; the vertical axis represents the light–dark dimension. Note that most dark colors tend to be classed as black, and very light or washed-out colors merge into white. Darkish reds, oranges, and yellows are classed as brown. (Not shown: pink, gray.) A more detailed description is available under *color* in *Webster's International Dictionary* (second and third editions).

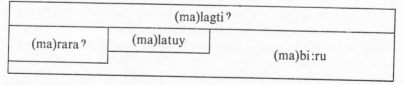

Figure 15-4B. Representation of Hanunoo basic color terms: *mabiːru* includes black, violet, indigo, blue, dark green, dark gray, and other deep shades; *malagtiˀ* = white and very light tints; *mararaˀ* = maroon, red, orange, yellow; *malatuy* = light green, and mixtures of green, yellow, and light brown. (Source: Conklin 1955.)

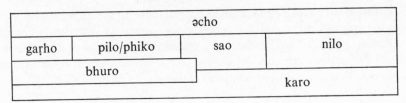

Figure 15-4C. Representation of Sindhi basic color terms.

language of the Philippines), and Sindhi (spoken mainly in northern India and Pakistan).

According to current theories, color distinctions are made at two levels in many languages: the first level consists of an all-inclusive classification into BASIC COLOR TERMS, on which speakers show maximal agreement. Generally, these terms have well-defined FOCAL AREAS, i.e., a limited range of shades which are regarded as typical specimens of the term and on which there is near-universal agreement among speakers. Between the focal areas are regions of greater or less indeterminacy. The second level includes a large number of more specific terms; English second-level terms include, for example, *crimson, scarlet, beige, khaki, salmon, lavender, chartreuse, saffron, indigo, teal, fuchsia,* and many others.

Studies of color terminology have generally ignored the second-level terms, on the grounds that they are in some way secondary—either because their meanings are included in the meanings of other terms (e.g., *scarlet* may be regarded as a variety of *red*), or because they are compound terms (e.g. *Chinese red, powder blue, charcoal gray*), or because they are limited in application (e.g., *blond* refers only to hair) or in other respects (e.g., do not occur in all dialects). Individuals vary considerably in the number of second-level terms they use, and in the consistency with which they use them. Thus, an artist or an interior decorator might have a much larger vocabulary of terms than others. In Hanunoo, Conklin mentions that men are more versatile than women in describing different varieties of reds and grays, whereas women excel in the blue area.

The study of cross-cultural differences in color terms is of considerable interest to anthropologists, psychologists and others, because the differences can be easily tested by presumably objective methods, and because they appear to some to furnish rather powerful evidence for the hypothesis of "cultural relativity"—that the outside world is what we perceive it to be, rather than existing separately from our awareness of it (see 16.5). In this vein, students of this phenomenon have long assumed that the different divisions of the color spectrum represent arbitrary and perhaps haphazard segmentations of reality.

This assumption is now being questioned as a result of a claim made recently by two linguists, Brent Berlin and Paul Kay, that there is a universal inventory of just eleven basic color categories on which all languages base their terminological distinctions, and that these always arise in a given order in the evolution of a language: first, *black* and *white*; second, *red*; third, *green* and *yellow*; fourth, *blue*; fifth, *brown*; sixth, *purple, pink, orange, gray*.

If this claim can be supported convincingly, its implications could well go beyond color terminology; there are difficulties, however. For one thing, it would be necessary to explain how there can be such a uniformity of evolutionary sequence, in spite of tremendous differences in the color patterns of the physical surroundings and the different ways in which colors and colored objects are used in different societies. Another objection concerns the method of investigation used in establishing the color terms: Berlin and Kay followed the usual method of showing a set of color chips to informants and noting their responses. Thus, the study examined color terms without any of their natural cultural or linguistic context, using categories which were created under the stimulus of commercial needs in western countries, rather than familiar items in the informants' culture—or even naturally occurring phenomena like the rainbow. These and other problems will need to be resolved before this theory will be generally accepted.

NOTES

15.2. English pronouns: Brown and Gilman 1960
English terms of address: Brown and Ford 1961
15.4. Hanunóo color terms: Conklin 1955
Universal color distinctions: Berlin and Kay 1969

SUGGESTED SUPPLEMENTARY READING

Pronouns: Brown and Gilman 1960; Friedrich 1966
Kinship: Lounsbury 1956, 1964; Romney and D'Andrade 1964; Wallace and Atkins 1960
Color terms: Berlin and Kay 1969

FOLLOW-UP

1 Comment on the statement: "Anything that can be said in one language can be said in any other."

2   Look up some English words in a good bilingual dictionary (English–French, English–German, etc.). Try to plot the various ways in which words which are said to have the 'same' meaning translate each other. Example:

English   *French*

believe —— croire
think —— penser

(Examples: *Je n'y crois pas* 'I don't believe (in) it'; *Je ne crois pas qu'il viendra* 'I don't think he'll come'; *A quoi pensez-vous?* 'What are you thinking about?')

3   Observe the ways in which you and people around you use terms of personal address or personal reference (names, nicknames, pronouns, titles like *sir*, etc.). Can you discern any system in the ways in which these things are used?

4   Try to plot your own use of kinship terms in the way illustrated in 15.3. Compare with a classmate's usage. What differences do you find? (Alternatively, use the system suggested in 16.2.)

5   Look up *color* in Webster's *International Dictionary* (second or third edition), or in any unabridged dictionary which gives colored illustrations. Observe the arbitrariness of our color divisions. Try to find samples of colors (e.g., in magazines) which illustrate the differences in codability (16.5) of colors; show them to various people, and note the extent of agreement or disagreement in the color terms used.

Chapter 16

MEANING AND CULTURE: ANALYTICAL APPROACHES

16.1 TAXONOMIES AND HIERARCHICAL STRUCTURE

This and the following section present two major principles of semantic analysis developed by cultural anthropologists. Many terms in a language can be said to imply the meanings of other terms. For example, the term *trout* entails the term *fish*, *oak* entails *tree*, *horse* entails *animal*, *table* entails *furniture*, *car* entails *vehicle*, etc. The category of referents named by *trout* belongs to the (superordinate) category named by *fish*, and therefore the meaning of *trout* includes a semantic component of "fishness." The terms for superordinate categories in these cases are sometimes referred to as CLASSIFIERS, since each refers to a whole class of objects or terms.

The meanings of classifiers are, in fact, coterminous with the categories to which they refer. That is, the meaning of *tree* is the whole category which includes *oak*, *pine*, *maple*, *birch*, *ash*, *aspen*, *elm*, *chestnut*, etc. Conversely, the individual terms can be said to contain (or entail) the meaning of the general term *tree*, in addition to their individual meanings which distinguish them from each other. (In fact, many speakers of English probably know that an *aspen* is a tree, and a *haddock* is a fish, even if they cannot tell an aspen from a maple or a haddock from a halibut.)

This semantic relationship between classifier and members of a class is characteristic of many semantic domains in language, especially those dealing with phenomena of the visible world. The relationship implies a hierarchical structure, which can be drawn as in Figure 16-1. Such a set of terms is often referred to as a TAXONOMY. Note that, in such a taxonomy, certain terms (such as *tree* and *pine* in Figure 16-1) are both classifiers and members of categories.

Certain linguistic facts are implied by the hierarchical relationship. In English, for categories like the one illustrated in which all the members are nouns, it will generally be true that the sentence *Y is a(n) X* will be a true and grammatically acceptable sentence, if X is a classifier and Y is a member of the class. It will also be true that X can substitute for a specific Y in certain circumstances; e.g., one might say, *We're having flounder for lunch*, and later, *How do you want the fish: broiled or fried?* These relationships are made use of in establishing the membership of certain semantic domains in a language, including those like kinship and colors discussed above: for example, the set of kinship terms in a language (15.3) includes all those terms which appear in naming people who are referred to generally as *relatives*, *kin*, *kinfolk* or the equivalent; the set of color terms (15.4) includes all words which can be used in answering the question "What color is that?"

Interest in folk taxonomies has become quite strong in recent years, and enough information has been collected on them to indicate that taxonomic structure is probably a universal characteristic of languages. The languages of even the most "primitive" peoples (i.e., those lacking indigenous modern technology and the comforts and neuroses associated with it) show elaborate taxonomies, which are in no way inferior in complexity or rationality to those found in the more "advanced" countries.

The principle of hierarchical classification has been exploited by scientists in such fields as botany, geology and medicine, for creating complex technical taxonomies. The principle was presumably not invented by them, but more

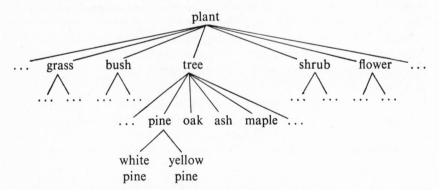

Figure 16-1. Hierarchical structure of part of English plant taxonomy. (Dots imply omissions.)

likely discovered in their natural languages. Technical taxonomies are based on detailed and exhaustive examination of classes of phenomena, and are periodically changed when new phenomena emerge. Thus, *neutrinos* and *viruses* are relatively new categories.

Folk taxonomies, on the other hand, reflect a somewhat more haphazard classification of a limited sub-class of various species. Thus, English plant terminology reflects the experience of English speakers, and (except for those who have lived in different botanical surroundings or have studied botany extensively) has very few terms to deal with tropical vegetation. In fact, with our increasing urban orientation, fewer and fewer people are able to identify the referents of *oak*, *maple*, and the like. Certain distinctions in our system are suitable for the categories we observe around us, for example the distinction between *tree* and *bush* (or *shrub*). Yet we might find it difficult to know how to classify certain plants found in other areas of the world, into one of these categories.

Taxonomic structure is often viewed as one of the most important organizing principles for the description of meaning and of the manner in which the human brain deals with its environment. No doubt this is true, and yet this study is not without problems. Figure 16-2 (which shows an alternative method of diagramming a taxonomic hierarchy) indicates some of these potential difficulties. A general problem with this method of classification is that there often exist overlapping classifications of the same category. For example, *persons* are not only divided into *adults* and *children*, but also into national groups (Americans, Russians, Chinese, ...), racial groups (caucasian, negroid, mongoloid, ...), professional classifications (teacher, butcher, baker, machinist, ...), social and economic groups, and others. In addition to their division into zoological categories, animals are also divisible into such categories as domestic animals vs. wild animals; land, sea and amphibious animals; tropical, arctic and temperate animals; vertebrates and invertebrates; etc.

This means, of course, that the taxonomic structure of a language contains a complexity which cannot be captured in such a simple two-dimensional diagram. Another type of complexity appears with terms like *animal* in Figure 16-2, which functions on two different levels. On the higher

animal/creature/being											
person/human (being)			animal								
adult/ grown-up	child		mammal				bird		fish...		
man	woman	boy	girl	horse	cow	tiger	dog	crow	swan	cod	sole	bass

Figure 16-2. Partial hierarchical diagram of the English category *animal*.

level, it includes all living creatures, whereas on the lower level it excludes human beings. (Cf. the expression *higher animals*, for example.) This is a fairly common pattern in many languages. For example, the English term *cow* is used to refer to both the genus and the female member of it, and similarly for *goose*; Hindi-Urdu *admi* means 'person' in certain cases (e.g., /kɪtne admi a gəe/ 'How many people came?') and 'male person' in others (e.g., /car admi ɔr tin ɔrtẽ/ 'four men and three women')—not unlike English *man*. Such cases are often regarded as involving POLYSEMY or MULTIPLE MEANING, though it is possible to consider words like *cow* as having only a single meaning which is limited in certain contexts: e.g., if one says *three bulls and seventeen cows*, it is clear that *cow* refers only to females, whereas if one says *a herd of cows grazing*, the hearer is free to assume what he likes.

People who know a little linguistics occasionally mention taxonomies found in "primitive" languages which are thought to be different in kind than (and sometimes even inferior to) those found in English or other languages. For example, one variety of Eskimo is reported to have several words for different forms of snow (*aput* 'snow on the ground', *qana* 'falling snow', *piqsirpoq* 'drifting snow', *qimuqsuq* 'a snowdrift'), but no word for 'snow in general'. If this is considered peculiar, then an Eskimo linguist would be entitled to be equally surprised to find that speakers of English are so "primitive" that they have no single word for the stuff they walk on— though they have *land, earth, ground, soil, dirt, mud*, which refer to different aspects of it.

The data now available on this subject point to three general facts: (1) languages differ considerably in the details of categorization, though (2) all languages embody the principle of taxonomic classification, and (3) there is no basis for judging any system to be inferior to any other. Another example of this last point can be seen in Figure 16-3, showing the relations of the words for 'seal' in Barrow Eskimo. The lack of a word for 'seal in general' cannot be taken as evidence for an inability to generalize, since there exist words for more general categories, though not at the precise points where English has them. This can be compared to the lack of non-technical

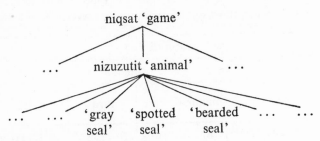

Figure 16-3. Part of the animal taxonomy of Barrow Eskimo. (After Nida 1964, p. 81.)

English words for such categories as *equidae* (horses, asses, zebras), *felidae* (cats, cougars, tigers, lynxes, etc.), or *canidae* (dogs, wolves, jackals, foxes).

16.2 COMPONENTIAL ANALYSIS

SEMANTIC COMPONENTS are recurrent features or properties of meaning which can be abstracted and used for the purpose of describing sets of semantically related terms. They are similar in principle to phonological components (Ch. 6). For example, the set of terms *man, woman, child, dog, bitch, puppy* can be accounted for in terms of the features human, canine, male, female, adult, young. *Man* is human, male, adult; *puppy* is canine, young, etc.

This illustration uses SINGULARY features, each of which has a positive distinctive value in the system. Many descriptions make use of BINARY or two-valued features (see 6.1), which make it possible to describe the same facts with half the number of features, as illustrated below:

	$\pm$ *male*	$\pm$ *human*	$\pm$ *adult*
man	+	+	+
woman	−	+	+
child	$\pm$	+	−
dog	$\pm$	−	$\pm$
bitch	−	−	$\pm$
puppy	$\pm$	−	−

Traditional grammar, with terms like 'first person', 'second person', 'third person', 'singular', 'plural', 'present', 'past', etc., was based on a type of componential analysis. In recent times, this technique has been particularly developed in the treatment of kinship systems (15.3), which are generally describable in terms of a small number of components. Thus, the English system requires the following features to account for all its distinctions:

1   SEX of the relative (e.g., brother vs. sister);
2   GENERATION of the relative with reference to Ego (0 = Ego's generation, +1 = Ego's parents' generation, +2 = Ego's grandparents' generation, −1 = Ego's children's generation, −2 = Ego's grandchildren's generation, etc.);
3   CONSANGUINEAL or blood relation, vs. AFFINAL relation or relation by marriage;
4   among blood relations, LINEAL or vertical relationships are distinguished

from non-lineal (e.g., father and son are in lineal relationship, but not uncle and nephew);

5   among non-lineal relations, a distinction can be made between degrees of COLLATERALITY, based on the smallest number of generations separating two kinsmen from their common ancestor: thus, brothers are first-degree collaterals, but first cousins are second-degree.

The following table illustrates the features of some English kin terms (x = feature irrelevant):

	Sex (± *male*)	Generation	Type (± *blood*)	± *lineal*	Degree of Collaterality
brother	+	0	+	−	1
cousin (first)	±	0	+	−	2
aunt	−	+1	±	−	1
great-nephew	+	−2	+	−	1
mother-in-law	−	+1	−	×	×

The Hindi-Urdu system described in 15.3 requires additional features, including (6) sex of the linking relative, which distinguishes for example one's father's sister (/bua/) from one's mother's sister (/məsi/), (7) sex of ego, which distinguishes a man's brother's wife (/bhabhi/) from a woman's (no term), and (8) age of relative in relation to linking relative, which distinguishes father's elder brother (/tau/) from father's younger brother (/caca/).

It is important to note that, even within the same set of terms, some forms are more MARKED semantically than others: for example, *bitch* is marked as +female, but *dog* is UNMARKED for sex. The use of unmarked terms makes it possible to do more work with the same number of terms. Though linguistic purists may encourage us to treat related terms as being equally marked, normal usage often exploits the principle of unmarkedness. For example, the English word *city* can be considered as marked for size (+large), whereas its companion *town* is not marked as −large, though it can be used with that implication when it is opposed to *city*; thus we have cases like *the cities and towns of the eastern seaboard* (equivalent to the somewhat more technical-sounding *metropolitan centers*), as well as cases which use *town* in the more general meaning, such as: *As the troops moved closer to the town, people began evacuating the city* (from the *New York Times*, Dec. 14, 1971).

Some types of EXTENDED MEANING (see 14.6) can be accounted for in terms of the SUPPRESSION of one or more semantic components. Figure 15-2 shows the Hindi-Urdu terms /bhai/ and /bəhɪn/ used for cousins, as well as for 'brother' and 'sister'. Strictly speaking, the terms refer to ego's direct siblings, but are extended to include all same-generation kin. In such a case, we can say that the component specifying degree of relationship (first-degree collateral) is suppressed. A further extension to more distant relations, or to other people of approximately Ego's age, could possibly be described in terms of the suppression of all components except those relating to sex and generation. (Because of the existence of these extended meanings, it is common to hear such expressions as /əsli bhai/ 'real brother' used to indicate that a term is being used in its strict sense.)

The traditional lexicographer's approach to such cases is to regard each meaning as separate, and to treat a word like /bhai/ as polysemous. Thus, Webster's Third International lists seven different meanings for *brother* (1—biological brother; 2—kinsman or member of the same clan; 3—coreligionist; etc.). In such a treatment, the links between the different meanings are left implicit. The componential approach suggested here makes these links more explicit in some cases, but there are others that cannot be handled adequately by this approach either. For example, if /bhai/ is used in the meaning 'mate' or 'match' (e.g., /tum canəkyə ke bhai ho/ 'You are a match for Chanakya'), it is difficult to see how this can be described in terms of components. Thus, componential analysis appears to account for only part of the meaning, particularly that part which is involved in contrasts with other terms in a set. It sees the meaning of a word in atomistic, rather than holistic terms, and thus cannot necessarily account for the totality of semantic potential inherent in a word.

If one examines the features of kinship systems mentioned above, which are claimed to be applicable to all kinship systems, it is clear that this universal applicablity is achieved at a cost. These components do not necessarily capture that which is most relevant to the structure of individual languages. English, for example, might be described more adequately by making use of such features as ±*nuclear* (member of the nuclear family—i.e., either Ego's parents and siblings, or Ego's spouse and children), or ±*extended-nuclear* (including all terms which differentiate sex except those beginning with *great-*). But these features would not be particularly relevant for many other languages.

This problem relates to a more general debate currently going on in semantic theory as to the UNIVERSALITY of semantic components, which was discussed with reference to color terms in 15.4. Though it is generally agreed that, at the present stage of our knowledge, we have not discovered universal components, some workers would at least propose as a goal the description of semantic systems in terms of components that reflect the cognitive structure of the human mind. More work of the type described in 15.4 must be done on many different types of semantic material, before we will know whether such a goal is attainable.

16.3   OVERT AND COVERT CATEGORIES

Those categories of words which are distinguished by a particular formal mark, such as *plural* in English nouns, *past* in English verbs, can be called OVERT categories. Those categories lacking such a mark are often called COVERT categories: for example, many English nouns referring to humans (such as *boy, girl, son, daughter*, or names like *Jack, Jane, Seymour, Phyllis*) carry no distinguishing mark for gender, yet in a discourse where pronouns are used, all these words have a potential link with either *he* or *she*. In other words, such words are covertly marked for gender.

We owe this distinction to Benjamin Lee Whorf, who pointed out that both types of category are common in a variety of languages. He has described, for example, how objects are classified in Navaho both on the basis of animateness, and on the basis of shape. There are two classes of inanimate objects, which we could term approximately 'round objects' and 'long objects' (Navaho does not use any terms to distinguish these two classes). There is no overt affix of any kind to distinguish the names for these two types of objects, nor is there (as in English) any pronominal distinction. Rather, they are marked by the use of certain special verb stems, which vary depending on whether a 'long' or 'round' object is referred to. (Certain important verbs show this variation, though not all verbs are sensitive to this difference.) Whorf terms such a category a CRYPTOTYPE; it is a submerged or subtle distinction in meaning, which is shown by linguistic analysis to be functionally important in grammar.

16.4   ELICITING SEMANTIC DATA

For those semantic domains which have been most thoroughly investigated, methods of eliciting data are most developed. For color terms (15.4), there exist sets of color chips which can be shown to an informant to get him to identify a particular color term. Such information can be supplemented by asking the informant to name the color of particular natural objects. Sometimes one runs across unexpected problems: Conklin found that, although Hanunoo has color terms, it has no word for 'color'. Eliciting of kinship terms may proceed by observing which terms occur in conversation, and may be supplemented by asking direct questions like "What is the term for father's brother's wife?" etc.

In all such cases, observation of normal conversation in normal contexts is necessary in order to get full and reliable data. For example, Frake's study of terms for diseases among the Subanun of Mindanao made extensive use of actual discussions of cases, which provided a richness of data which would probably have been impossible to obtain if he had simply started out with an English list and tried to get translations of them. For pronouns (15.2) and other terms for personal reference, the total social context is necessary if we are to fully understand their implications. Thus, it is essential to know a great deal about the backgrounds of the speakers and their relationship to each other.

Semantic elicitation must also control for the linguistic context; isolated sentences are often not enough to determine the semantic distinctions. For example, the meaning of Hindi-Urdu "past perfect" forms such as /aya tha/ 'had come', /dekha tha/ 'had seen', cannot be described adequately on the basis of isolated sentences, since these forms are often used to introduce a narrative of a past event, whereas the continuation of the narrative often goes on in the "simple past" (/aya/, /dekha/). This difference would not appear clearly without extended context.

With rather subtle distinctions of this type, explicit questioning of informants about the meaning is usually of little help. In many cases, though, some explicit questioning is needed, because we cannot expect all the necessary data to appear in spontaneous conversation. Thus, a linguist may question informants about the acceptability of a sentence or usage (e.g., "Would you ever call this person *bhai*?"), or one may ask for explicit definitions ("What does *mama* mean?") or paraphrases ("Is there any other way to say this?") of terms which have been used. When such responses are offered spontaneously, they are particularly valuable.

Another device, discussed by Bendix, is the use of SEMANTIC TESTS which check the semantic relations between various sentences: for example, in investigating the meaning of English *lose*, one might ask informants to evaluate (or to attempt to interpret) sentences like *He lost his watch, but he has it* or *He's lost his watch, but he knows where it is*. This method allows the linguist to test specific hypotheses about the IMPLICATIONS of the forms being tested: the hypothesis that *lose* implies 'not having' leads to the prediction that informants will reject the first of these sentences, or will at least find it difficult to interpret; the hypothesis that *lose* implies 'not knowing location' leads to a similar prediction with regard to the second sentence, in most of its interpretations.

16.5 LINGUISTIC RELATIVITY: THE "WHORF HYPOTHESIS"

The notion that differences between languages correlate with different "ways of thinking" or different "world views" was formulated most explicitly by

Benjamin Lee Whorf. Whorf noted the obligatory nature of semantic and grammatical categories in languages (see 15.1), and the background character or many distinctions: we take for granted such distinctions as singular–plural, past–present, etc., until we are confronted by linguistic systems which are differently constructed. Believing that the obligatory distinctions present in one's mother tongue direct one's attention to particular features of situations, to the exclusion of others which do not happen to be codified by the linguistic structure, Whorf proposed the hypothesis that

> ...the background linguistic system (in other words, the grammar) of each language is not merely a reproducing instrument for voicing ideas but rather is itself the shaper of ideas. ... We dissect nature along lines laid down by our native languages.
>
> (Carroll 1956, pp. 212–13)

One of the examples most often cited in support of this point, variation in color terminology, has been discussed in 15.4. The examples provided by Whorf himself include specific cases of paired descriptions of events, which show the same structure in one language but are very different in another. For example, he notes that in Shawnee the sentences translating English 'I pull the branch aside' and 'I have an extra toe on my foot' have the same basic grammatical structure, built around a stem element meaning 'forked shape'. Whorf assumed, without additional evidence, that these two events were intrinsically related from the viewpoint of a Shawnee observer.

Later critics have seized on this as the weakest part of his argument, since we have no basis for assuming *a priori* that the similarity of the sentences is more than superficial. Whorf's argument would suggest, for example, that English speakers cannot distinguish between ownership, possession and kinship relations because they use the verb *have* to refer to all three (He has money, He has his brother's hat, He has two sisters), or that Hindi-Urdu speakers are unlikely to distinguish between present and past time because the same word /kəl/ refers to 'yesterday' and 'tomorrow', another word /pərsõ/ refers to 'the day before yesterday' and 'the day after tomorrow', etc. (Actually, Hindi-Urdu speakers have no more trouble with time than Marathi speakers who have distinct words for these. In Hindi-Urdu, /vo kəl aega/ 'he *kal* will-come' and /vo kəl aya tha/ 'he *kal* come was' are clearly specified by their verb endings as referring to 'tomorrow' and 'yesterday' respectively.)

Many of Whorf's critics have pointed out that the correlation between linguistic form and cognition or behavior should be treated as a hypothesis to be checked, rather than a proven fact. Thus, given the fact that in Marathi the verbs for 'find' and 'remember' require the "impersonal" construction (which is typically used for verbs indicating involuntary actions like 'know', 'feel', 'think', which cannot normally be imperativized), whereas the verbs for 'lose' and 'forget' occur in the more usual subject-verb constructions, one might hypothesize that Marathi speakers regard the latter actions to be more voluntary than the former. Such a hypothesis would predict that Marathi speakers and speakers of other languages without this distinction would react in different ways to sentences like *I lost it intentionally, I found it intentionally*, etc. (see 16.4). Very few attempts have been made to investigate such correlations.

One of the clearest pieces of evidence we have relates to color terms, and indicates that a person's ability to remember a color specimen correlates to the CODABILITY of the word for it (i.e., its accessibility in terms of frequency, morphemic simplicity and closeness to the focal area) in the speaker's language (see 15.4). Though this evidence supports the notion of linguistic relativity with regard to color terms, it provides no basis for generalizing to other areas of the lexicon which do not involve the same kind of continuous variation.

Many workers in this area would accept a weaker version of Whorf's idea, which one might formulate as follows. Each language provides certain ready-made categories, and speakers tend to find it convenient to think in terms of these categories, at least in the routine aspects of their lives. It is always possible however for innovative individuals to create new categories, and thus make it possible for themselves and others to reflect on the old categories and transcend them.

Perhaps the principle problem with Whorf's formulation is that it insists on regarding the linguistic structure as the primary causal factor which determines other differences. We can easily find cases where this position is not defensible, however. If, for example, people in different societies have different reactions when they hear such words as *father, mother, king* or *socialism*, can this be accounted for purely in terms of semantic structure? Or do we need to take into account the different kinds of experience that people in these societies have had with fathers, kings, commissars and the like?

Cases involving differences in marriage rules and incest taboos are perhaps more striking in this respect. We noted above (15.3) that kin classifications sometimes correlate with marriage rules, e.g., that terms for *brother* and *sister* are sometimes extended to include all those individuals with whom marriage or sexual union is not permitted. Generally people have strong moral feelings about their own incest rules, and when they find that some other society permits sexual unions which their own society treats as incestuous, they are likely to regard such people as "immoral," "barbarous," "bestial," or the like.

In such cases, must we necessarily regard the difference in linguistic structure as the *primary cause* of the differences in people's ways of thinking about incest? It would seem to make more sense to regard such attitudes as derived from people's total experience—of which language is only a part. This experience includes childhood socialization, in which one observes adult behavior, is told stories which inculcate cultural norms and values, and learns to behave differently with different people. Looked at from this point of view, the structure of kinship terms can be seen to summarize and symbolize people's cultural experience, rather than causing it. The same can probably be said, by and large, of many of the phenomena presented as evidence of the Whorf hypothesis. Language does not exist in a vacuum.

16.6   GENERAL SEMANTICS: "THE WORD IS NOT THE THING"

The field known as GENERAL SEMANTICS can be considered to deal with linguistic PATHOLOGIES resulting from misunderstandings of the relationship between words and things. It has been pointed out that the relationship between words like *house* or *dog* and their referents (specific instances of houses and dogs) is essentially different from that between words like *intelligence*, *freedom*, *pride*, *patriotism* and their referents.

The main difference between these two groups of terms is that, in the former case, we can agree by and large on the diagnostic indications or observable attributes which determine whether something is a dog or not, whereas there is no comparable agreement on the diagnostic indications of patriotism or patriotic behavior, for example. Some might find it a sufficient indication of patriotism that a person has a flag pasted on his car window. Others might feel that this is a somewhat superficial and perhaps even irrelevant indication. Some might say that patriotism now is the same as patriotism during the American Revolution; that our efforts should be bent on watching for and repulsing foreign invaders, and checking intrusions on our "sovereignty." Would we agree, for example, that it would be patriotic to board a foreign vessel in an American port and toss its cargo into the ocean? It is hard to find much agreement on such questions.

Or consider *intelligence*, one of our highest cultural values. Though many of our so-called "intelligence" tests have been revealed as mainly testing conformity with certain kinds of conventional upper-middle-class verbal behavior, still we persist in regarding the results of all such tests as though they measured some innate characteristic of individuals. It might be possible to obtain a substantial concensus of opinion about what intelligence is, i.e., what the referent of the word *intelligence* is. We might try starting with Webster's Third International, which defines it as "the faculty of understanding," or we might suggest something slightly more sophisticated, such as "the individual's capacity to make use of information." But even assuming that people are willing to agree on some such definition, the agreement will be meaningless unless we can agree on how to recognize or to measure it. A problem arises only when we forget that abstract words like *intelligence* and concrete terms like *dog* are related to their referents in fundamentally different ways.

On the other hand, it is often convenient to ignore this difference between abstractions and concrete terms. For example, if a politician is able to defend a particular policy in terms of its supposedly beneficial effects on such abstract entities as 'the economy' or 'the unity of the party', he may feel justified in ignoring the fact that the policy he proposes inflicts some very concrete ills on particular human beings. Other examples of the use of linguistic labels to justify official policy are not hard to find in the current scene. Though the unity or disunity of Vietnam is still a debatable point, the United States government justifies its treatment of North and South Vietnam as distinct political entities by using distinct labels. When a belligerent act takes place against a country friendly to us, we are likely to label it as an *invasion*, or at least an *incursion*; when we do it to someone else, our government feels entitled to call it a *police action*. (A similar example is the phrase *job action*, used as a substitute for *strike*, especially in cases where strikes are illegal.)

One of the most striking of the recent coinages is the verb *brainwash* (said to be a translation of a Chinese term), which has come to have the meaning 'change a person's ideas by overwhelming persuasive techniques' (usually with the implication that the person subjected to this treatment has no responsibility for the outcome). The currency of this term apparently dates from a period when the United States government was extremely embarrassed by reports that some of its members had not behaved in the expected fashion, when subjected to persuasion as prisoners during the Korean War.

These examples, which can be easily multiplied, illustrate an important pathological process known as REIFICATION. Where there is a name, there must be a thing (e.g., 'intelligence'). Where there are two different names, there must be two different things (e.g., 'job action' ≠ 'strike', 'malnutrition' ≠ 'starvation'). The opposite process is GENERALIZATION: two referents that have the same name are assumed to be the same in important respects. No doubt many of us have noticed instances of this, as when the behavior of a few individuals is used as a basis for condemning an entire group of people. PERSONIFICATION occurs when complex entities are treated as individuals. For example, 'Country X is Country Y's staunch ally'; 'It's bad for the country'; 'The party is against it'; etc. The dangers of such loose talk are obvious, but such examples are heard every day.

These cases are not to be regarded as defects of a particular language, but rather the products of a general hazard inherent in the use of abstract terms. The general semanticists would suggest that we need to educate ourselves to be aware of such potential word traps, and be prepared to analyze our own and others' statements in order to detect any of these defects.

NOTES

16.3. Overt and covert categories: Carroll 1956, pp. 87–101, or Whorf 1945
16.4. Semantic tests: Bendix 1966
16.5. The "Whorf hypothesis": Hoijer 1954, pp. 92–126
16.6. General semantics: Hayakawa 1952

SUGGESTED SUPPLEMENTARY READING

Semantic analysis: Lamb 1964; Lyons 1963; Bendix 1966
Taxonomic structure: Frake (in Hymes 1964); Conklin 1972
Componential analysis: Goodenough 1956
The "Whorf hypothesis": Carroll 1956; Hoijer 1954
General semantics: Hayakawa 1972; Korzybski 1933; Chase 1938, 1964; Johnson 1946; Lee 1941, 1949

FOLLOW-UP

1   Define: taxonomy, hierarchical structure, classifier, semantic component, (semantically) marked vs. unmarked, linguistic relativity, reification, generalization, personification.

2   Distinguish: overt—covert (categories).

3   Attempt a componential analysis of the following sets of terms:
    a. horse, stallion, mare, colt, filly (look them up in the dictionary if necessary)
    b. chair, sofa, bench, stool, throne, . . . (add others if you wish).
    c. private, corporal, sergeant, lieutenant, captain, major, colonel, general (do you know the names of any major sub-categories which these can be grouped into?).

d. Other possibilities: rooms in a house (living room, bedroom, etc.); clothing, vehicles, cosmetics, academic subjects, parts of a city, etc. Some terms are strongly linked to a particular culture: for example, terms for the rooms in a house are linked to the way in which the rooms are used. (The German *Stube* 'living room' was formerly the room in which there was a *stove*, used for both cooking and heating.) Can you identify other examples of this kind of link between terminology and culture?

Chapter 17

TECHNIQUES OF SEMANTIC DESCRIPTION

17.1 INTRODUCTION

In this chapter we will explore some recent proposals for the description of semantics, particularly within the framework of generative grammars. With the growth in insights regarding syntactic description of language, the linguist has naturally gone on to ask about the way syntax and semantics are related. One single factor that has contributed to this quest is the recognition of two levels of description, i.e., deep and surface structure (13.9). The attempt to plumb the depths of syntactic deep structure has made it necessary for the linguist to draw a line between syntax and semantics. A natural consequence of this questioning has been the tendency in contemporary research to locate the deep structure of sentences in the semantic component of language.

While the anthropologist has made a significant contribution to the study of semantics, his approach has been determined by his primary concern with ethnography. The linguist, on the other hand, has turned to semantics in order to explicate the devices that human language employs for converting meaning into sound. The anthropologist's major tool for describing meaning —viz. componential analysis (16.2)—is being exploited by contemporary linguists in their attempt to uncover the relationship between form and meaning. The contemporary linguist has become aware of the fact that any theory of language that does not account for meaning is inadequate, and that formal structure can be understood only by attempting to discover the semantic distinctions that are manifested in form. This awareness on the part of the linguist has led him to question the validity of theories of language that ignore the semantic aspect of language, or relegate it to the background. As we will see below (17.2), this persistent questioning has led the TG grammarians to modify their theory to incorporate semantics in it. Some linguists have modified the TG theory to the extent of abandoning the distinction between syntactic and semantic components (17.4). Others have proposed new theories of language in which semantics plays the central part (17.6).

A claim that was first made in modern linguistics by TG grammar was that certain characteristics of language are universal. This is quite contrary to the earlier structural belief that languages are unique, and that they have very little in common. The claim for inter-language commonalities in TG grammar, which is syntax-oriented, is made with regard to the syntactic base rules (13.9). This claim of universality of linguistic structure is made even more strongly by linguists who view semantics as central in a theory of language. In fact, semantics-oriented theories tend to forward the argument of universality as a motivation for considering semantics as central. It is difficult to say, at present, to what extent the claim of universal semantic structure is tenable. Not all semanticists are agreed on the nature and extent of inter-language commonalities, and certainly not all linguists agree with this claim.

While the contemporary linguist has exhibited a good deal of boldness in attempting to capture the structure of meaning in his theories, he is fully aware of the dangers of drifting into a kind of semantics that is outside his sphere and enters areas of entology and philosophy. The linguist is concerned with those aspects of meaning which are reflected directly in formal structure, which can be called 'linguistic semantics' (as opposed to 'philosophical semantics').

17.2 RECENT DEVELOPMENTS IN TG GRAMMAR

As we saw in Chapter 13, recent developments in transformational generative theory have resulted in setting up a SEMANTIC COMPONENT. As against the original components—Phrase-Structure, transformational and morpho-phonemic—the current theory, as outlined in Chomsky's *Aspects of the*

Theory of Syntax, has three major components: (1) a syntactic component, (2) a phonological component and (3) a semantic component. The syntactic component is the generative part of the grammar and is, therefore, called the BASE, while the other two components are INTERPRETIVE, i.e., they apply to the output of the base. The base consists of PS rules and the LEXICON. In order to understand the relationship between the PS rules and the lexicon, it would be useful to examine some of the arguments used by the proponents of TG grammar. Let us look at an example in English:

1 *The apple ate the boy.
2   The boy ate the apple.

The PS rules in Chapter 13 will generate both these sentences. If the grammar is to be such that it must leave nothing to the reader's intuition, in other words, if it is to be EXPLICIT in the sense defined in 9.1, then our rules for English must be able to prevent sentence 1 from being generated. Similarly, the grammar should be able to generate sentences 3 and 4 as GRAMMATICAL, and block sentence 5 since it is UNGRAMMATICAL.

3   The tiger may frighten the boy.
4   Truth may frighten the boy.
5 *The boy may frighten truth.

In a strict sense all of these sentences are grammatical, since they are all produced in conformity with the PS rules of the base, and exhibit permissible sequences of major form classes. The trouble with sentences 1 and 5 is that they are either unacceptable (in the sense that there is no natural linguistic context in which they could be expected to occur), or else peculiar (i.e., they require particular types of contexts in order to be meaningful). It is not enough to know that *ate* in 1 and *frighten* in 5 are verbs, or even that they are transitive verbs; it is equally crucial to specify that *eat* requires an animate subject and *frighten* requires an animate object—though these rules may be suspended under certain circumstances, as pointed out below. Once it is recognized that such information is relevant to the description, the question arises whether it is syntactic or semantic. Clearly, if it is semantic, then it should be located in the semantic component. But the semantic component is assigned a purely interpretive role within the theory, i.e., it is seen as operating on the output of the syntactic base component. Consequently, all such information must be provided by the syntactic component for, as we shall see below, this kind of information is essential for correct semantic interpretation.

One way of accomplishing this is to distinguish BRANCHING RULES (such as $S \rightarrow NP + VP$, $VP \rightarrow V + NP$) from SUBCATEGORIZATION RULES, which have the function of specifying the restrictions operating within sentences. The model under discussion here recognizes two types of restrictions: SELECTIONAL RESTRICTIONS (such as the requirement that *frighten* must have an object NP expressed), and subcategorizations. The rule requiring some verbs to occur with a following object could be expressed in the following form:

$$\text{Verb} \rightarrow [\pm \rule{2em}{0.4pt} \text{NP}]$$

(i.e., 'Verb is specified as occurring either with or without a following NP'). That is, some verbs will be specified in the lexicon as $[+ \rule{2em}{0.4pt} \text{NP}]$, and others as $[- \rule{2em}{0.4pt} \text{NP}]$. Those specified as $[+ \rule{2em}{0.4pt} \text{NP}]$, such as *frighten*, can only occur with a following NP, etc.

Subcategorization, which relates to the types of restrictions illustrated in sentences 1–5, can be described by rules of the following type:

N → [+Noun]
[+Noun] → [±Common]
[+Common] → [±Count]
[+Count] → [±Animate]
[+Animate] → [±Human]
etc.

(i.e., 'N is further specified as +Noun, which is further specified as either +Common or −Common; if +Common, it is then further specified as +Count or −Count; etc.'). These rules operate on the P-markers generated by the base component, having the effect of converting class symbols (such as N, Verb) into COMPLEX SYMBOLS, as illustrated in Figure 17-1.

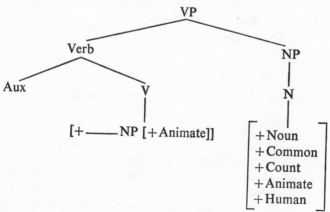

Figure 17-1. Derivation of complex symbols.

The conversion of the PRE-TERMINAL STRINGS resulting from this process (e.g., the last line of 17-1) into terminal strings is accomplished by selecting suitable FORMATIVES from the lexicon, which would consist of an unordered list of entries, each of which consists of a phonological description of a formative and its syntactic features. Thus the entry for *frighten* would include the SYNTACTIC FEATURE [+ _____ NP [+animate]], and the entry for *boy* would contain the information [+Noun, +Common, +Count, +Animate, +Human]. Note that nouns are represented by bundles of syntactic features, whereas verbs are represented by both syntactic and CONTEXTUAL FEATURES. Like phonological components, these features are generally binary (see Ch. 6 and 16.2).

The distinction between subcategorization and selectional restriction is crucial, for semantically deviant sentences such as 1 and 5 can be accounted for by postulating that selectional restrictions may be violated but not subcategorization. For example, the verb *frighten* in 5, which normally requires a [+animate] noun in the object NP, *may* take a [−animate] noun like *truth* (where *truth* may be understood as 'personified'); but it would be impossible in English to have a sentence like

6   *The boy may frighten fatten.

which would violate the selectional rule that says *frighten* requires an object NP (since *fatten* is not an NP). Sentence 6 is as ungrammatical as 7, which would be recognized as such by any native speaker of English:

7   *truth the frighten may boy.

The LEXICON, also known as the lexical sub-component of the base, then, provides the subcategorization of major categories in terms of syntactic features and selectional restrictions; the formatives listed in the lexicon include both LEXICAL FORMATIVES (such as *boy, apple, truth, frighten*) and GRAMMATICAL FORMATIVES (such as Past, Modal, Plural).

17.3 THE SEMANTIC COMPONENT OF A TG GRAMMAR

The syntactic base component in a TG grammar generates deep structure P-markers which specify the grammatical relations that hold between the constituents, each of which terminates in a formative—lexical or grammatical. The lexical formatives are further specified, in terms of syntactic features, for inherent meanings. The output of the base constitutes the input for the SEMANTIC COMPONENT, which interprets the information furnished by the deep structure P-markers and assigns a set of readings to the P-marker. The semantic component consists of two parts, a DICTIONARY, which provides meanings for the lexical formatives, and a finite set of PROJECTION RULES which assign a semantic interpretation to each string of formatives that is generated by the base.

Typically, a dictionary entry shows a full analysis of the meaning of each lexical item in terms of semantic components, with a statement about the relationships among the items. A well-known specimen of a lexical entry in a dictionary is that of the noun *bachelor* in English, suggested in a pioneering article by Katz and Fodor (1963). An entry for this word must include the information provided in Figure 17-2A. Given the lexical item *bachelor* in a deep structure P-marker, the semantic component will assign it one of the four possible readings shown there. The choice of a specific reading is determined by the syntactic information provided by the base: for example, if in a deep P-marker the noun *bachelor* appears with the specification [−Human], then the semantic component can only assign meaning (4) to it. If the noun is marked [+Human], then additional syntactic information will

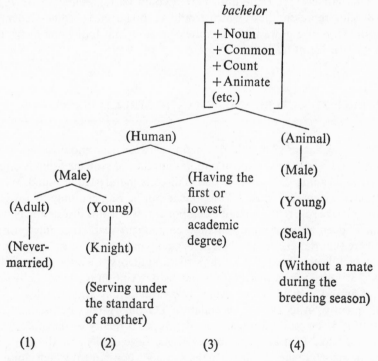

Figure 17-2A. Sample dictionary entry for the word *bachelor*. (After Katz & Fodor 1963 by permission of the authors and Linguistic Society of America.)

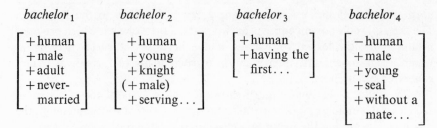

Figure 17-2B. Alternative semantic representation for *bachelor*.

have to be provided before a particular reading can be assigned to it. The projection rules in the semantic component would be formulated so as to resolve potential ambiguities in the same way that a native speaker would be able to resolve them. For example, the projection rules would eliminate reading (2) as a possible reading for *bachelor* in the phrase *the old bachelor*. Projection rules apply first to terminal nodes of a deep P-marker, and then apply successively to the next higher level in the constituent structure until the meaning of the sentence is combined through a process of AMALGAMATION.

Alternatively, the same information could be represented as in Figure 17-2B. This representation, which would be preferred by some students of semantic structure nowadays, separates *bachelor* into four homonyms, each with its own list of features.

17.4 DEEP STRUCTURE AND SEMANTIC STRUCTURE

We noted in Chapter 13 that the distinction between deep and surface structure is motivated by the need to posit a representation of sentences that is directly related to meaning, and another that is directly manifested in sound. We saw above that a central syntactic component can be retained only by assigning an interpretive role to the semantic component. But is this distinction between syntactic deep structure and semantic component real? It is interesting to note here that the distinction between syntax and semantics in TG grammar has, in fact, been inherited from the structural theory. Like the structuralists, in 1957 Chomsky believed that a linguistic description involved the description of an independent syntax which was prior to any semantic description. Consequently, in its earliest formulation TG theory relegated semantics to the future. Later, several researchers developed a theory of semantics which was linked to TG grammar. However, the development of the notion of semantic structure did not displace the syntactic component which continued to be thought of as autonomous and independent. In fact, by 1965 it was firmly believed that for an adequate semantic description it is essential to have a central and generative syntactic component. The effect of the 1965 position was to further underline the distinction between syntactic deep structure and semantic structure.

In the last few years, however, various transformational grammarians have questioned the validity of such a distinction, and have suggested that deep structure and semantic structure may be identical. Specifically, it has been argued that functional relationships like *subject of*, *object of*, can be handled more adequately in terms of semantic structure rather than syntactic structure. Consider the following examples:

8 John broke the window (with the hammer).
9 The hammer broke the window.
10 The window broke.

In these sentences *John*, *the hammer*, and *the window* appear as surface structure subjects. A syntactic deep structure would also assign to constituents the function of subject. A little reflection will show that the three NPs are not the same. *John* in 8 is the 'doer' of the 'action', i.e., *breaking*. In both 8 and 9 *The hammer* is an instrument. In 10 *The window* is what is traditionally called the subject of an intransitive verb. However, neither *The hammer* nor *The window* performs the semantic role of agent, which *John* in 8 does. Clearly, then, surface subjects may be traced to various deep structure relationships.

Such deep relationships have led linguists like Fillmore to propose a semantic deep structure, which comprises a set of CASE RELATIONS between nouns and a verb in a sentence. A sentence is rewritten as Modality + Proposition, where MODALITY accounts for tense, aspect, mood, etc. and PROPOSITION consists of a verb and one or more noun phrases, each of which is associated with the verb in a particular deep 'case' relationship such as *agent, instrument, object, dative, locative* and so on. (The deep structure ordering of cases does not reflect the order of elements in the surface structure.) Transformational rules, which lead from the deep to the surface structure, re-order the constituents in specified ways. Each of the deep cases is realized, typically, as a surface case form or case marker, and the relationship to the verb is indicated through devices like word-order, inflection, or prepositions and postpositions.

It is assumed in this theory, which has come to be known as CASE GRAMMAR or THEORY OF CASE, that in a simple sentence there can be only one occurrence of each of the case relations. Depending on which of the cases occur in a given sentence, the surface order of elements is determined by a set of specified transformational rules. Notions like *subject of* and *object of*, etc. then are seen as purely surface structure relationships which have distinct semantic functions. For example *John*, *The hammer* and *The window* in 8–10 above are surface subjects which perform different semantic functions in relation to the verb *break*. It is possible to set up a type of hierarchy showing what surface functions a deep case may have when it occurs with or without other deep cases. For instance in 8, of the three cases, agent (*John*), instrument (*the hammer*) and object (*the window*), the agent alone can be the surface subject. In 9, which does not have an agent, the instrument (*the hammer*) is realized as surface subject and the deep object (*the window*) is also the surface object. But in 10 where there is only one case, namely the deep object (*the window*), it is realized as the surface subject. These facts may be generalized to say that if there is a deep agent, it takes precedence over other cases as the surface subject. In the absence of an agent, the deep instrument may be realized as a surface subject, and so on. The theory requires that every verb in a language be specified for the cases that may occur with it. Such specification of the CASE-FRAME for the English verb *break* would be:

Break $(+ [\underline{\hspace{1.5cm}} (A) + (I) + 0])$.

This may be interpreted to mean that the verb must obligatorily have a deep object, and it may optionally have a deep instrument or a deep agent or both.

Without going into the details of case grammar, which has been considerably refined and elaborated in the last few years, it may be pointed out that this theory incorporates a bulk of the techniques and devices of the TG grammar. The one crucial difference between the two theories is that while TG theory recognizes an autonomous deep syntactic component, case theory argues that in order to really understand the way in which languages work, one must look at the underlying semantic relationships that surface structure elements overtly or covertly reflect. It is further claimed that only a semantic description will reveal the commonalities between languages, a task which is assigned to the TG base component, but which it fails to fulfill since it operates with notions like subject and predicate which are in fact surface structure phenomena. It is argued, for instance, that if subject is recognized as a surface notion, then the 'subjectless' sentences which are found in some languages would not be surprising, and could easily be accounted for so long as one is able to show the case relationships reflected by such sentences.

The case grammar, like the TG grammar, attempts to reveal the ways in which meaning is converted into sound in human language; but, unlike the TG grammar, it seeks to obviate the need for recognizing an artificial deep syntax as an intermediate level between semantic structure and surface structure.

17.5 SEMANTICS AND PARTS OF SPEECH

The new semantic orientation has led to a critical re-examination of traditional categories like parts of speech. In 17.3 we saw that in a TG grammar verbs are sub-categorized in terms of the nouns with which they co-occur. These rules, strictly speaking, reflect traditional categorizations such as 'transitive', 'intransitive', and so on. If the semantic theory of case is accepted, then we would have to subcategorize verbs in terms of intrinsic semantic features and case-frames. One proposal for semantic categorization of verbs employs terms like *stative* and *non-stative*. For instance,

11 John opened the door.
12 John knows the truth.

In 11 the verb *open* refers to an action performed by John, while in 12 the verb *know* refers to a state (of knowing) which John is in. Such semantic distinctions are captured by subcategorizing verbs as *stative* : *non-stative*. Formal constraints of co-occurrence further strengthen such distinctions. For example:

13 John is opening the door.
14 *John is knowing the truth.

In 13, a non-stative verb like *open* may occur with the progressive marker *-ing*, but a stative verb like *know* in 14 cannot occur with *-ing*.

Moreover, it has been argued that some traditional distinctions, like that between verb and adjective, are not supported by facts of language. In English, for instance, verbs and adjectives seem to show such remarkable similarity of subcategorization that it might be more fruitful to consider the two as sharing such semantic features as the stative : non-stative distinction. For example:

15 Be good.
16 He is being good.
17 *Be handsome.
18 *He is being handsome.
19 Sleep here.
20 He is sleeping here.
21 *Like the movie.
22 *He is liking the movie.

in 15–16 *good* is a non-stative adjective, while *handsome* in 17–18 is a stative adjective. Similarly, *sleep* in 19–20 is non-stative, and *like* in 21–22 is stative. Stative adjectives and verbs cannot be used in imperative sentences in English (17, 21), nor can stative verbs and adjectives take the progressive aspect (*-ing*), as in 18 and 22. Verbs and adjectives in English share features other than the stative: non–stative distinction. For instance:

23 I *like* to sing.
24 I am *able* (*free, eager,* etc.) to sing.
25 He *designs* models.
26 She is *pretty*.

Some verbs (e.g., *like* in 23) and adjectives (e.g., *able* in 24) often take verbal complements (*to sing* in 23–24), while others (as in 25–26) do not. Such examples suggest that the distinction between adjective and verb is based on very superficial aspects of the structure of English. In a deeper sense, adjectives and verbs belong to the same " part of speech," though they behave differently in the surface structure.

Clearly, this re-examination shows that the traditional classification of parts of speech is far from perfect. But, for the present, semantic re-examination is only able to show the defects of the older classification. The solutions it provides are neither complete nor final. This is largely because the techniques of semantic analysis have not yet been sufficiently formalized. Often, semantic notions can only be arrived at through introspection.

17.6 MEANING AND THE STRUCTURE OF LANGUAGE

Even as the transformationalist is taking a second look at the deep structure : semantic component dichotomy, several models of linguistic description that start with the semantic structure of language and work up to the phonological structure have been proposed. Case grammar as proposed by Fillmore (17.4) is one such attempt. A recent model proposed by Chafe has been called Generative-Semantics (GS). The term 'generative' has the connotation we discussed in Chapter 13, and the term 'semantic' distinguishes it from the TG model where the generative component is syntactic.

Unlike the Fillmore model, the GS model has not developed from the earlier syntactic TG model. The GS model assumes that for any system of communication to be effective, there must exist a medium through which a message (a unit of communication) may be transmitted between the sender and the receiver of the message. Obviously, for the medium to be an effective carrier of messages, it must be able to be easily manipulated by the sender of the message and be readily and appropriately interpreted by the receiver of the message. The human communication system—i.e., language—uses sound as the medium through which experience (meaning, including ideas, emotions, thoughts, etc.) is communicated from one individual to another. The actual form that a message takes is called SYMBOL, and the process of converting experience into symbol is termed SYMBOLIZATION. Symbolization in language

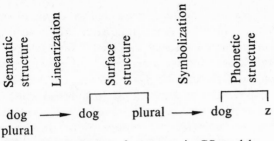

Figure 17-3. Sequence of processes in GS model. (After Chafe 1970.)

is constrained by the medium (i.e., sound) in that it exists on a linear time axis, while experience has no such constraint. On the contrary, experience must be organized on various axes that exist simultaneously. The structuring of experience is seen as SEMANTIC STRUCTURE, which is manifested in a number of relationships like Verb-Agent, Verb-Patient, etc., as depicted in Figure 17-4 below. The conversion of semantic structure into sound is considered to involve two distinct types of processes, known as POST-SEMANTIC and SYMBOLIZATION processes. This whole procedure can be illustrated with a simple example, the English plural noun *dogs*. As depicted in Figure 17-3, the semantic structure must be subjected to a process called LINEARIZATION to give the surface structure dog–Plur in linear order; symbolization rules then provide the phonetic structure.

One of the most powerful arguments for setting up separate semantic and surface structures is the existence of idioms (see 14.5). To illustrate, the word *eye* has, in addition to the meaning 'organ of sight', the meaning 'hole in the end of a sewing needle', The two concepts are distinct in the semantic structure, but are represented by the same form in the surface structure (cf. 14.6). The process of converting a semantic unit into a surface structure form is called LITERALIZATION (another type of post-semantic process). In some cases, literalization involves a conversion to a very different kind of structure: for example, the meaning 'to avoid saying directly what one means' can be literalized in English as *to beat about the bush*. This literalization has the surface form V + Prep + NP, but the parts of this surface representation bear no relation to any particular part of the semantic structure. Notice also that the expression *beat about the bush* is subject to constraints that do not apply in other cases: for example, *the bush* in this expression is invariable, and cannot be changed to *a bush, the bushes, some bushes*, or the like. Thus, expressions like *beat about the bush, drag one's feet, kick over the traces*, and the like can be regarded as single units in the semantic structure which are literalized in particular ways in the surface structure. This seems to be a universal process, since examples of these types can be found in a wide variety of languages.

Semantic structures are conveniently represented as a type of mobile diagrams, as depicted in Figure 17-4. A semantic structure, typically, is a bi-polar configuration of semantic units such as V and N (and some others). The unit V is the central element and the other units exist on semantic axes like AGENT, PATIENT, etc. with the unit V. *Agent, Patient,* etc. are semantic notions which reflect experiential configurations. In a broad sense these notions are comparable to the deep case relationships discussed in 17.4 above. In Figure 17-4A, *the knife* (which manifests N) is related to *sharp* (which manifests V) on the patient axis; in sentence B, *Jack* is related to *laugh* on the agent axis, while in sentence C, *Jack* is on the agent axis and *Jill* is on the patient axis with *see*. A formation rule in English that generates

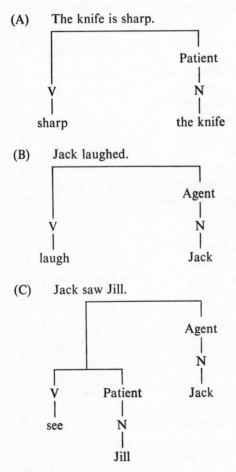

(A)   The knife is sharp.

(B)   Jack laughed.

(C)   Jack saw Jill.

Figure 17-4. Some semantic structures.
(After Chafe 1970.)

sentences like 17-4A could be:

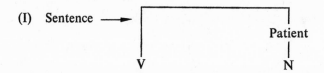

(I) Sentence

V, N, and some other units are called MAJOR SEMANTIC UNITS that participate in semantic structures on various semantic axes. Each major semantic unit, in turn, is composed of a characteristic configuration of MINOR SEMANTIC UNITS which can be SELECTIONAL, LEXICAL, or INFLECTIONAL. For instance, in sentence 17-4A, unit N may be represented by another formation rule (which in fact collapses a number of rules, but that is not of importance here):

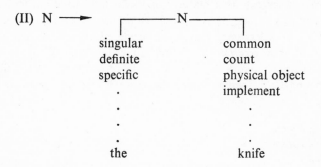

(II) N

Semantic units like *common, count, physical object*, etc. are selectional and are manifested by a lexical unit (noun) like *knife* in sentence 17-4A. Units like *singular, definite*, etc. are inflectional units which are finite in number, and combine with lexical units to yield surface structures like *the knife*. A semantic structure, then, is a configuration of major semantic units that are governed by formation rules.

Post-semantic processes like literalization, linearization, etc. which can be represented as transformation rules, apply in a specified order to semantic structure to yield surface structure. Surface structure is directly converted into underlying phonological structure—a kind of morphophonemic spelling which is converted into phonetic structure by phonological processes which may be represented as phonological rules of the TG grammar type (see Ch. 12). What is significant here is that the GS theory views the V as the central part of a semantic structure, with other semantic units radiating from it. What kind of semantic units may occur with a V, therefore, are determined by the minor semantic features of V. The V in 17-4A is marked for the feature *state*; in sentence (B) it is marked for *action*, and in sentence (C) it is marked $\begin{bmatrix} Action \\ Process \end{bmatrix}$. As in English, the V in any language may be viewed as in Figure

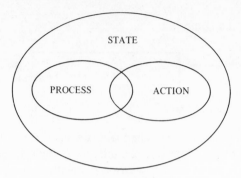

Figure 17-5.

17-5. In English, a *state* V requires a *patient* N, while an *action* V requires an *agent* N. There are several other features of V which we need not go into here. Semantic units like *state, process,* and *action* are called SELECTIONAL UNITS (not unlike the selectional features considered above), which are manifested in lexical verbs like *laugh, kill* and numerous other lexical items. An important process that a V may undergo is DERIVATION. Derivation changes a V with a particular semantic unit into a V with a different semantic unit. For instance:

27   *a.* The rice is *cooked.*
     b. The rice is *cooking.*
     c. Jill *cooked* the rice.

In 27 the same lexical verb *cook* is marked *state* in *a, process* in *b,* and $\begin{bmatrix} action \\ process \end{bmatrix}$ in *c.* It is probably true to say that in every set of such lexical verbs one may be able to determine the basic semantic feature for which the verb is marked.

A semantic model like the GS makes the claim that semantic structure is universal. It is argued that it does not seem unreasonable to believe that human language reflects the similarity of human experience. There is some evidence that the semantic axes on which experience is manifested are not language-specific. Similarly, post-semantic processes like literalization and linearization, as well as the process of derivation in V, are universal, though details vary. Only the beginnings of a general generative-semantic theory have been laid down so far, and it is not possible yet to make definitive statements about what parts of the theory are universally true. The following examples from Panjabi (a language of North India) are given as illustrations of the occurrence of semantic units of the V like *state, process, action,* etc.:

28   kuṛi soṇi e ("girl beautiful is")
     'The girl is beautiful'

29 muṇḍa uṭhɪa ("boy arose")
    'The boy got up'
30 mæ̃ thali pũnji ("I plate wiped")
    'I wiped the plate'

In 28, the "verb" /soṇi e/ is marked *state* and requires a patient (/kuɾi/);
in 29, the verb /uṭhɪa/ is marked *action* and requires an agent (/muṇḍa/);
in 30, the verb /pũnji/ is marked $\begin{bmatrix} action \\ process \end{bmatrix}$, and requires an agent (/mæ̃/)

and a patient (/thali/). Similarly, the process of derivation seems to apply to
V in Panjabi, as the following examples suggest:

31

V	V	V
State	Process	Process/Action
/tej e/	/tej ho rəi e/	/tej kər rəi e/
("sharp is")	("sharp become ing is")	("sharp make ing is")
'is sharp'	'is being sharpened'	'is sharpening'

NOTES

17.2. Complex symbols and their derivation: Chomsky 1965, Ch. 4
17.3. The semantic component: Katz and Fodor 1963
17.4. Case grammar: Fillmore 1968
17.6. Post-semantic processes: Chafe 1970

SUGGESTED SUPPLEMENTARY READING

Fillmore and Langendoen 1971; Chafe 1970

FOLLOW-UP

1 Define, base component (of a grammatical description), selectional
restrictions, complex symbol, contextual feature, post-semantic processes.

2   Distinguish: semantic component (ultimate unit of semantic analysis, 16.2)—semantic component of a grammar (13.9, 17.2); branching rules—subcategorization rules; lexical formatives—grammatical formatives.

3   Explain the role of semantics in modern theories of language description. How is this different from traditional approaches (such as those discussed in Chs. 14–16)?

PART IV

SOCIOLINGUISTICS

Chapter 18

THE STUDY OF LANGUAGE
IN ITS SOCIAL CONTEXT

18.1 INTRODUCTION

The treatment of language illustrated in most of the preceding chapters derives from a combination of various humanistic approaches and interests, including the psychological, logical and mathematical, which focus on language as an *intellectual* activity. In line with these interests, the main concern has been with the individual speaker and his production and interpretation of linguistic utterances. Many of the utterances which have been used as illustrations of linguistic behavior, and from which conclusions have been drawn about linguistic structure, are laboratory phenomena, produced without the normal social context which accompanies speech events, rather than (as is usually the case in real life) in response to a situation in which the speaker is engaged as a participant.

In many cases, the linguist investigating a language had no choice but to use this laboratory approach. This is most obviously true in the case of the native languages of North America, which have been dying out so rapidly that often linguists have had only one or two speakers available to them. Apart from such cases, many linguists would argue that the laboratory approach has been indispensable, that without it we could never have succeeded in isolating the abstract structure of language, and could never have reached our present level of understanding of the workings of language. The distinction between linguistic COMPETENCE and linguistic PERFORMANCE is an attempt to distinguish between the linguist's concern with the abstract structure of language (representing a speaker's competence, or what he is potentially capable of producing or comprehending), as opposed to the speaker's actual behavior (his observable performance) under a variety of situational constraints.

At the same time, an approach to language study which embodies more of the assumptions of social science has been developing, which views language primarily as a *social* activity; this approach has recently crystallized as the field of SOCIOLINGUISTICS, which has goals similar to those described for linguistics but which uses rather different methods of data collection and interpretation. These methods are described below in some detail; first, it is necessary to say something of the broader context in which sociolinguistic work can be placed—i.e., the study of communicative behavior as part of the general study of human social behavior.

The view of language structure reflected in modern linguistic writings presupposes an "ideal speaker-hearer" who possesses (mostly unconsciously) all the rules of his language, and applies them according to certain general principles to produce and interpret utterances. The distinction between competence and performance makes explicit the linguist's recognition that his model of language does not reveal the full variety of an individual's linguistic behavior in different social circumstances, or the variations existing between different groups or different individuals within the same speech community. Linguists have intentionally ignored heterogeneity in language, since their techniques were better suited to deal with homogeneity.

The sociolinguist, on the other hand, assumes heterogeneity at the outset, because of the general observation that linguistic form is very sensitive to variations in the social background of any communication situation. There are few if any societies that do not have obvious constraints on the type of speech which can be used in certain situations. There are various circumstances (for example, those involving religious ceremonies or other rituals) in which only certain participants are allowed to speak at all, and in which there are strict limitations on the form and content of what is said. In English-speaking society, for example, prayers often make use of particular linguistic forms such as *thee* and *thou*, *thou hast*, etc. Only certain individuals are allowed to utter them. There are many occasions in our societies and others when a longish speech may be completely prescribed, so that the speaker has no options at all (e.g., the prayer spoken by the grandmother of a dead baby among the Ashanti, or the prayers spoken at various specified points in western church services).

This broader study of communicative behavior is a sub-field of cultural anthropology known as the ETHNOGRAPHY OF COMMUNICATION. Ethnography in general is concerned with the study of human behavior as it varies from one society to another. Within this context, the study of communication focuses on the communication situation in its total context, asking such questions as: Who are the participants, in terms of their social backgrounds? What is their relationship to each other? What kind of interaction are they involved in? and What effects do these various social factors have on the form of linguistic utterances which occur in the situation? The ethnography of communication is a broader study than linguistics as described above, and while students of this field do not question the validity of the narrower study, some of the results of sociolinguistic work do raise serious questions about the assumptions of linguistics—as will be shown below.

The examples given above show constraints imposed on linguistic behavior by the *type of situation*, and detailed descriptions of such constraints in a society show that they differ a good deal from one society to another. A recent description of the Ashanti includes discussions of the prescribed or proscribed linguistic forms for such things as public announcements (summonses, funerals, legal announcements), prayers (to ghosts, to those who have recently died, to one's ancestors, to gods and spirits); oaths, confessions, greetings, praise, story-telling, etc. All societies have linguistic taboos relating to such subjects as death, menstruation, deformity, poverty, incest or sexual relations in general, which are not allowed to be mentioned in certain circumstances or must be referred to indirectly or by some euphemism. An Ashanti must not mention a pregnant woman's condition to her, on penalty of having to pay a fine if she miscarries. In several parts of India, a wife may not mention her husband's name (and in some more conservative groups, any name or word with similar sounds); she must refer to him as 'he' or 'the children's father' or 'the man of the house' (in some cases, even the expression 'my husband' is not allowed); census-takers and others wishing to know the name of a woman's husband often are obliged to ask a neighbor.

Features of a speaker's *social background* which impose constraints on verbal behavior include the speaker's social class, age, sex, ethnic background, education, profession, urban or rural provenience, linguistic background (monolingual or bilingual), and others. Social class is one of the most important factors in many societies (see 18.3). Differences in speech of the sexes are found in many societies, including Western Europe, though less marked there than in others: morphophonemic differences have been reported for a number of languages (such as Koasati *o:tíl* (women)–*o:tís* (men) 'I am building a fire', *ó:t* (W)–*ó:c* (M) 'he is building a fire'), and lexical differences have been noted in many languages (e.g., Thai *dìchăn* (W)–*phŏm* (M) 'I', *khá/khâ* (W)–*khráb* (M) 'thank you, etc.'). The special features of lexicon among male homosexuals in the United States have been reported in some detail. Age differences are found everywhere: these involve not only the archaic and quaint usage of elderly people (less and less common nowadays in modern urban society), but also certain norms associated with particular age groups, and in some areas particular styles of speech associated with the creation of a "youth culture" distinct from the society as a whole.

A similar phenomenon, BABY TALK, has been described for a number of languages: this is a linguistic subsystem (not identical with child speech) used by adults in talking to babies and young children, and characterized by special intonational features, patterned phonological modifications of normal language (such as reduction of consonant clusters as in English *dink* 'drink', *seepy* 'sleepy'; reduplication, as in English *night(y)-night*, or Marathi *nini* 'sleep', *pipi* 'breast, milk'—cf. *niz-*'sleep', *pi-* 'drink'), and special lexical items (such as English *mommy, daddy, kitty (cat)*).

Some attention has been given to the special vocabularies of professional groups, including musicians, criminals, drug addicts, and the military. Many of these special varieties, especially those of criminals and anti-social elements, homosexuals, and the youth culture, serve implicitly to mark a separate social identity. In cases of criminal groups such as confidence men, the special features of the group speech also serve to conceal the content of conversation from other persons present. (In Maurer's discussion of this, he has noted how surprisingly unaware the confidence man's victim may be of the conversation of those preparing to fleece him.) In such cases, there is a need for a continuing evolution of the in-group variety, as vocabulary items that have been picked up by the society at large need to be replaced in order to keep the in-group speech distinct.

The relationships between speakers account for a great deal of linguistic variation and constraints. Japanese, for example, is famous for the number of distinctions made in its pronominal and verbal systems. But constraints on speech go beyond particular categories like pronouns: they include intonation, vocabulary, morphophonemics, and grammatical rules. Furthermore, the restrictions on verbal behavior affect not only these narrow linguistic categories, but also broader definitions of speech behavior: for example, it is reported that in Burundi, a peasant-farmer is expected to be verbally incompetent in talking to a socially superior person such as a herder, and to show this by stammering, shouting, or making a rhetorical fool of himself— even though, in other circumstances, he may be an elegant and persuasive speaker.

Circumstances and relationships also affect such questions as whether a particular person may begin a conversation with another under certain circumstances, and whether (and by what means) one person may terminate a conversation, or must wait for the other person to do it. Along with all these things, communicative acts of a non-verbal sort must be taken into account as inseparable concomitants of verbal communication: thus, gestures,

facial expressions, stance, distance between speakers, touching and manipulation of objects and persons, are all part of the communication situation, and
thus are both signalling systems in themselves and form part of the context
for verbal signals (see Ch. 7). In some societies, auxiliary signalling systems
also exist, such as the use of "talking" drums in many African societies, or
the famous whistle speech of Mazateco; these systems normally are limited
in the messages they can produce, both mechanically (since they control
fewer distinctions) and socially, and are designed primarily for use where
normal spoken communication does not work.

In general, ethnography of communication embraces all studies of the
correlation between linguistic behavior and other social behavior, either in
individual societies or in a cross-cultural sense. The term SOCIOLINGUISTICS is
sometimes used in this same meaning, though more strictly it refers to a kind
of linguistics which, on the one hand, shares with the ethnography of communication the assumption that the most valuable statements about linguistic
behavior are those which take into account the whole social context of
communicative events, and on the other hand, is concerned primarily with
the (synchronic and diachronic) *linguistic form* of the data. Sociolinguistics
is that branch or variety of linguistics which chooses not to neglect *parole*
in its search for *langue* (see Ch. 1), and which does not give precedence to
competence over performance, but seeks to understand both in relation to
each other.

18.2 REGIONAL VARIATION

We are all familiar with regional variation in some form or other, since
whether we have traveled extensively or not, most of us have encountered
varieties of our native language which differ noticeably from our own.
Those who have traveled widely may have encountered varieties that they
had trouble understanding. We commonly speak of these deviant forms of
speech (i.e., those that differ from our own, or from some variety which we
have been led to regard as "standard") as "dialects," and we refer to speakers
of them as having an "accent" (e.g., a southern accent, a New England
accent). Accents are said to vary in their "strength": someone may be said
to have a "strong" or "thick" southern accent, which may permit us to
guess whether he is from the Upper South or the "Deep South," and whether
he has lived for any great length of time outside of that area.

While it is true that these variations in speech (mostly phonological and
lexical) have a geographical basis, the relationship is more complex than may
appear at first. Suppose a speaker of American English from western New

York State encounters a speaker from eastern Massachusetts; assuming that neither speaker has moved much outside his native speech area and neither's speech has been greatly affected by his education (questionable assumptions nowadays, but perhaps likely to be valid for many comparable situations in other parts of the world), the New York man would notice the following differences between the Massachusetts man's speech and his own (speakers from other parts of the U.S. west of New York would notice most of these same features);

	Eastern Massachusetts	*Western New York*
1.	thirty = /θəːti/, car = /kaː/ (no constricted r sound)	/θərti/, /kar/ (noticeable r constriction)
2.	"intrusive" /r/ in *law and order* /lórənódə/, *the idea is*, etc.	
3.	Words like *door, poor* end in non-syllabic /ə/ instead of /r/: /doə/, /puə/ (but end in /r/ when a vowel follows)	...end in /r/: /do(ə)r/, /pu(ə)r/
4.	Words with *o* like *on, lot, fog* have /o/ rhyming with *lawn, naught, dog*	...have /a/ as in *father, far, calm, want*
5.	Words with *a* like *can't, half, aunt, calf* have the vowel /a/ as in *father, want*	...have the vowel /æ/ as in *ant, man, trash*

The accompanying figures (18-1*A–C*) show the geographical distribution of certain of these features in the northeastern United States. They are mapped in such a way that the overlapping boundaries of dialect features are obvious. This picture of dialect variation (though it represents the state of the language thirty to forty years ago) is typical in several respects. It marks off a particular area (eastern New England) as distinct from neighboring areas, but the boundaries between adjacent "dialect areas" are diffuse rather than sharp. In traveling from western to eastern Massachusetts, for example, the differences would build up gradually. Central Massachusetts could thus be regarded as a broad TRANSITIONAL ZONE between two dialect regions.

The figures do not show variation within each area, such as fluctuations in the speech of individuals, or differences among individuals in the same community. Such variation is, however, present (see 18.3), and is perhaps more marked in the "transitional" areas. The illusion of sharply marked dialect areas relates to the fact that most travel is between large cities, which are usually the centers of FOCAL AREAS (those relatively stable areas separated by transitional zones).

In the longer settled areas, such as western Europe and many parts of Asia, a more complex situation is found, involving regional variation on three (perhaps more) different levels. A study of the Hindi-Urdu speaking

Figure 18-1A. Boundaries of some features of New England speech, showing regional overlapping. In the areas with dots (the whole region east of the dotted line), thirty is pronounced as /θəːtiː/, without /r/-constriction. In the areas with plusses (east of the dashed line), *half* is pronounced as /haːf/. Thus the easternmost areas have /θəːtiː/ and /haːf/, the intermediate area has /θəːtiː/ and /hæf/, and the western area has /θərtiː/ and /hæf/. (Kurath and McDavid 1961, maps 14 and 25)

Figure 18-1B. Overlapping of /r/-constriction in *door* with the "intrusive *r*" (as in *law and order*). The easternmost region (with dots and plusses) says /doə/, /lorənodə/; the intermediate region (with dots, no plusses) says /doə/, /lo + ənodə/; the western region (without marks) says /do(ə)r/, /lo + ənordər/. (Kurath and McDavid 1961, maps 156 and 158)

Figure 18-1C. Overlapping of the /o/-/a/ distinction in two different words (*fog, on*). The easternmost region says /fog/, /on/; the intermediate regions says /fag/, /on/; the west says /fag/, /an/. (Kurath and McDavid 1961, maps 136 and 138)

Maps from H. Kurath and R. I. McDavid, *The Pronunciation of English in the Atlantic States*. Ann Arbor: University of Michigan Press, 1961. Copyright © by The University of Michigan 1961. All rights reserved.

area near Delhi in the 1950's by Gumperz showed clearly the existence of these three levels: (1) village dialects, showing minor phonetic and etymological differences (differences in the pronunciation of particular words), sometimes involving reversals in the status of particular forms in a space of twenty miles or less (e.g., forms regarded as "correct" and used by the more prestigious persons in one village might be regarded as characteristic of low-caste, ignorant, or "old-fashioned" speech in a village only twenty miles away); (2) regional dialects, spoken in the market towns, which avoid the local features and are relatively uniform over a large area (these dialects may differ from each other by more extensive features, such as differences in phonemic distribution or even in the number of phonemes in the total inventory, as well as in lexical differences); (3) the provincial "standard" language, used most widely by the educated elite in the larger metropolitan centers, and native only to long-term residents of the cities. The same pattern is found in Western Europe. Thus, in order to map all these features accurately, separate maps would be necessary to show the three different levels; often, the boundaries in the highest level—the national or provincial "standard" language—are not relevant on the lowest level: for example, literary standard Hindi and Panjabi are the respective official languages of the adjacent Indian states of Haryana and Panjab, but at the level of local village dialect the transition is as gradual across this political boundary as it is at many places within each state. The same is found, or was at least so at a time of lower literacy rates, in parts of western Europe such as the boundary between France and Italy.

An implication of this is that, in areas of this kind, many speakers (particularly those who are most mobile, e.g., traders and, to a lesser extent, farmers who travel often to the various market towns to sell their produce) are "bidialectal" or "multi-dialectal": they learn to function in the regional dialect as well as in their local village dialect. At the next level up, many residents of small and medium-sized towns learn to function both in the regional dialect and (to varying degrees) in the provincial or national "standard." It has been reported from many areas that this type of DIGLOSSIA (see 18.4) is fairly stable, in that speakers who control two varieties do not use the "higher" or more prestigious variety in everyday speech with intimate friends and family, since to do so would be considered pretentious and snobbish.

Regional variation is commonly displayed in the way illustrated by Figure 18-1, with lines known as ISOGLOSSES marking the differences in form. Where BUNDLES OF ISOGLOSSES appear (i.e, when several isoglosses occur in the same place), this marks an important dialect boundary—a relatively sharp transition between dialects. Such boundaries almost always correspond to important social or political boundaries of some kind. Dialect differences have been classified into three basic types: (1) PHONEMIC DIFFERENCES, i.e., differences in phoneme inventory or phonemic distribution which can be stated in terms of phonemic environment—for example, the lack of contrast between /i/ and /e/ before /n/ in *pin-pen*, *tin-ten* in some southern varieties of U.S. English would qualify as a difference in phonemic distribution (these two phonemes contrast in other positions in these varieties), as would the lack of the cluster /hw/ in *which*, *what*; the distinction between (1) *can* and (tin) *can* mentioned above as a characteristic of New York City speech is an example of a difference in phonemic inventory (number of phonemes in the system); (2) ETYMOLOGICAL DIFFERENCES are those which can only be stated in terms of particular words or morphemes—for example, for some speakers (e.g., in eastern New England) words like *log*, *frog*, *bog*, *fog*, rhyme with *dog*, whereas for others, *dog* has /ɔ/ and the others (or some of them) have /a/; this difference can only be stated in terms of the particular words, since the phonological environments are the same; (3) PHONETIC DIFFERENCES are those which affect allophones without having any effect on phonemic differences (for example, the fronting of the first part of the [ou] dipthong in British RP in such words as *no*, *below*, also found in Philadelphia speech).

This classification of course antedates the most modern approach to phonological description, which would distinguish between those changes affecting the underlying forms of individual words (like the *fog–dog* difference) and those involving systematic changes in phonological rules at different levels.

The study of regional variation, under the name DIALECT GEOGRAPHY (French *dialectologie*), can be considered a separate branch of linguistics, which received its original impetus from historical study during the nineteenth century. The most extensive work in dialect geography has been done in western Europe, and materials for linguistic atlases exist for a number of European countries. The extensive materials provided in the *Linguistic Survey of India* of Sir George Grierson (a civil servant in the former British government of India) are extremely rich, though collected without the benefit of modern linguistic training. The *Linguistic Atlas of the Eastern United States*, prepared under the overall direction of Hans Kurath of the University of Michigan, reflects great accuracy and care in the process of collection, which was carried out by a small group of trained linguists; atlas materials for other parts of the United States are currently in preparation.

The linguistic features investigated by dialect geographers include mainly phonological and lexical variants. This is based on the earliest approach to dialect geography, which consisted of circulating lists of words, and asking people to note the words and pronunciation they used for each item. Thus, it is mainly superficial aspects of the language that are investigated, though where the data has been collected systematically and accurately enough, it is possible to say something about phonological structure. The results of this process are a huge collection of minute facts about the forms of words used by speakers, which make possible certain detailed studies of linguistic change (see Chapter 21), and also enable us to make generalizations about the ways in which languages vary in the geographical dimension. The collection of this type of data is extremely time-consuming, and its analysis and presentation even more so, with the result that by the time atlases are published, the situations they depict have often changed considerably.

18.3 SOCIAL AND FUNCTIONAL VARIATION

Geographical variation is the most-studied type of linguistic variation, and perhaps the type best known to the layman. What we are often less aware of is that, within any single region, there are also SOCIAL DIALECTS, i.e., linguistic differences which correlate with the speaker's socio-economic class or stratum in the society. (To be more precise, we can speak of such variation as SUPERPOSED VARIATION or STRATAL VARIATION.) Such variation always involves feelings of "high" and "low" or "good" and "bad" forms of speech, whereas this is not always the case with regional variation; in fact, a person who uses stigmatized forms can often be forgiven if it is known that these are part of "good" speech in his home area (e.g., the educated Southerner who uses such forms as *She ain't* or *She don't*). Though stratal variation has been systematically studied only in a few societies so far, the evidence suggests that it is widespread, at least in complex stratified societies.

It is difficult to separate this type of variation from that known as FUNCTIONAL (CONTEXTUAL, or STYLISTIC) variation, which—though theoretically distinguishable from it—is usually linked to it in a particularly intimate way, as will be shown below. While social variants can be related to the speaker's social class background, functional variation concerns the differences observable in the speech of individuals, as changes occur in the circumstances and situations in which they are speaking. We are all aware that when speaking in public, or in addressing strangers or others with whom we have a formal relationship, we are generally more careful in speaking than in casual talk with family or friends; this affects various aspects of the linguistic structure of what we say. (In fact, some other societies demand much more of this than American society.) The most important variable, then, from the individual's point of view, is the degree of attention he must give to what he is saying; this factor is affected by the type of situation, whether it focuses more attention on the *form* of speech (as in formal, and even more in ritual, situations) or on its content.

The nature of stratal and functional variation, and the intimate relationships between them, can be illustrated by some studies of New York City English by William Labov. The first of these shows the variation in the pronunciation of the phoneme /θ/ *th* (as in *thing, through*), which occurs in three variants for most of the speakers in the sample: the fricative [θ], the affricate [tθ], and the lenis stop [t]. The vertical scale of Figure 18-2 indicates the average *th*-index scores, derived by scoring one point for each instance of the affricate and two points for each instance of the stop, multiplying the result by 100, and then dividing by the total number of occurrences of *th* in the speech sample. (Thus, a person who uses only the fricative [θ] in a particular context would score zero in that context; one who uses equal numbers of the three variants would score 100.)

The horizontal scale represents four contextual styles of speaking: casual speech (A), careful speech (B), reading style (C), and reading word lists (D). (The methods of defining and eliciting these different styles are discussed in 19.1.) The socio-economic classes shown on the diagram as LC (lower class), WC (working class), LMC (lower middle class), and UMC (upper middle class), are defined in terms of an objectively-derived index combining information on occupation, education and family income.

What Figure 18-2 shows, then, is significant in several ways: first, there

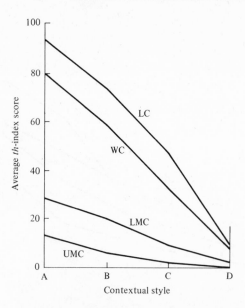

Figure 18-2. Stratification of *th* in New York City. (From Labov 1966 by permission of the author.) (LC = lower class; WC = working class; LMC = lower middle class; UMC = upper middle class)

is a clear correlation between socio-economic index and phonetics, with the higher socio-economic classes closer to the ideal norm of fricative [θ] in all styles. On the other hand, all groups show variation according to style, and of course it is all in the same direction: i.e., deviations from the ideal increase as the style becomes less formal. Thus, an isolated occurrence of an affricate or stop in *thing* or *through* in the speech of a New Yorker would not be sufficient evidence for us to classify him socio-economically, since it is necessary to take into account the overall frequency and the context in which the variants occur. On the other hand, if we are furnished with that information, it is possible to classify a New Yorker according to socio-economic class with a high degree of accuracy; this is so because of the marked stability of indices of this kind. All of these comments apply to phonological variation in general, to the extent that it has been studied. One feature of this figure may be noted which is less general, and that is the clear division between middle-class and other speakers. This may account for the stereotype of uneducated New Yorkers, who are thought to say *tree* for *three*, *tin* for *thin*, etc.

Figure 18-3 depicts, by the same technique, a different phonological variable with somewhat different social implications: this is the frequency of occurrence of a consonantally constricted [r] in final or preconsonantal

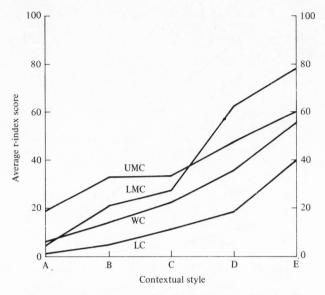

Figure 18-3. Stratification of /r/ in New York City. (From Labov 1966 by permission of the author.)

position (e.g., in such words as *car, guard, door, lord*). It was noted above in 18.2 that the "*r*-less" pronunciation of such words was characteristic of the prestige pronunciation of New York City (as it was, and still is, in other Eastern seaports) in the years before World War II, but now this is changing. The *r*-index scores in Figure 18-3 are simply the percentage of cases where the investigators heard some sort of constricted, consonantal [r], out of all cases where an /r/ could be expected for reasons of spelling or history. (Thus, a score of 100 would mean the speaker used [r] constriction in all such cases.) This figure contains one more contextual style than the preceding one: minimal pairs (E), that is, pairs like *god–guard, sauce–source, bad–bared*, which are homonymous except for the presence of /r/ (when it is used). The pattern of style variation, consistently closer to the ideal norm as the style grows more formal, appears here for all groups as it did in the previous case. There are certain differences, however: first of all, only the upper middle class shows any significant frequency of /r/ in ordinary casual speech, the other three classes huddling together at the bottom of the scale. But in successively more formal styles, the relationship between the upper and lower middle class changes dramatically, and is actually reversed in styles D and E. This "crossover" pattern, in which the upward aspirations of the lower middle class are evident in their closer approximation to the norm than the more secure upper middle class, is characteristic of linguistic variables which are in the process of change. (In this case, the pronunciations with and without /r/ have been present in the society all along, but they are currently undergoing change in their relative "social status.")

The types of variation under consideration in these studies of New York City speech have often been regarded by linguists as "free" variation, i.e., variation which makes no difference and which is not consistently correlated with other linguistic features (such as phonological environment). Some linguists have remarked that, when we say a particular variation is free, that means we do not know how to describe it. Labov's work shows that such variation is not free: it is closely tied to social factors. Such factors then are analogous to environmental factors, such as the quality of a preceding vowel, etc., which linguists invoke as "conditioning" factors to explain allophonic variation. Since the variation, in these and other cases, is continuous rather than discrete, it hardly makes sense to speak in terms of distinct "dialects" or "idiolects;" rather, an individual speaker can be placed statistically at a point between the two extremes of variability (e.g., strong /r/ constriction vs. no /r/ constriction, fricative [θ] vs. stop [t]) on the basis of his class background and the type of situation in which he is speaking; if this principle is accepted, then the same norms apply to all dialects and all idiolects in a region.

Differences between regions may be absolute differences of one of the types described in 18.2, involving constant structural differences (for example, some speakers in the southeastern United States and in England probably never have consonantal [r] in preconsonantal or final position), or else are differences in the statistical probability of a certain variant in a certain style (e.g., speakers from western, central or eastern Massachusetts differ in the frequency with which they use the consonantal [r]).

In addition to these fairly constant and statistically describable differences, there are a number of differences which may be truly free, in the sense that they result from the peculiarities of an individual's history, and are distributed randomly without correlation to regional, social or functional factors. This type of difference can be illustrated by words like the following, which vary in such random patterns that in many cases people of the same immediate family do not agree on all variants: *advertisement* /ǽdvə́rtəzmənt, ǽdvərtáyzmənt/, *amen* /ámén, éːmén/, *Arkansas* /árkənsɔ, arkǽnsəs/, *ballet* /bǽleː, bæléː/, *brooch* /brúːc, bróːc/, *data* /déːtə, dǽtə/, *detail* /díːteːl, ditéːl/, *eczema* /égzəmə, igzíːmə/, *envelope* /énvəloːp, ánvəloːp/, *either* /íːdhər, áydhər/, *economics* /iːkənámiks, ekənámiks/, *forehead* /fóːr+héd, fárəd/ *fungi* /fə́ngay, fə́njay/, *gibberish* /jíbərish, gíbərish/, *inveigle* /invíːgl, invéːgl/, *leisure* /líːzhər, lézhər/, *lingerie* /lánjəreː, lǽnjəriː/, *Muslim* /múzlim, mə́zlim/, *nephew* /néfyuː, névyuː/, *process* (verb) /práses, prásəs, próːses/, *ration* /réːshən, rǽshən/, *puma* /púːmə, pyúːmə/, *status* /stéːtəs, stǽtəs/, *trimester* /tráymestər, traméstər/, *tomato* /təméːto: təméːtə, təmáːtoː/.

Socially, the implications are equally interesting: it is clear, for one thing, that social class affects communication in the same way that geographical separation does, i.e., there is greater similarity in speech among those who are closer to each other (socially or spatially). On the other hand, it is also clear that there is a mutual interdependence and interaction among the different social segments of the society, since by their behavior they tacitly recognize the same norms of speech. In fact, explicit discussions of speech variation with individuals from different social classes in New York City indicates that speakers of all classes show marked agreement on the superiority of a middle-class speaker (tape-recorded) in terms of suitability for jobs, etc. But this is not the whole picture, since there was a different reaction to the same tape-recording when speakers were asked such questions as, "How would you expect this speaker to come out in a street fight?" or "Do you think you would be likely to form a friendship with this person?" In these cases, the reactions of speakers from the lower social groups differed considerably, showing that in these contexts they had a definite negative evaluation of the middle-class speaker.

This result can be taken to indicate that, although in the contexts of education, employment and public affairs the upper-middle-class norm is recognized by all segments of the population, in certain other aspects of life involving human relations, other norms come into play. This may be correlated with the statement made above (18.2) that speakers who have learned to use a dialect more prestigious than their home speech, will still use the home dialect in interacting with their family and friends in their native place, since use of the prestige forms would be interpreted as attempting to rise to a superior social level and create social distance between oneself and one's hearers. In the more "public" contexts mentioned, the elite group (upper middle class) sets the norms; this is made clear by the fact that lower-middle-class speakers "overimitate" this norm in more careful styles of speech. It is also significant that, even in the most casual styles of speech which Labov and his co-workers were able to elicit, the elite speakers are consistently closer to the norm than other groups; this indicates that the elite speaker's ability to set the norm is related to his use of a more controlled type of speech, even in the most informal situations. Elites in many societies (such as the U.S., Europe—including the Communist countries—and India) have a higher level of consciousness of "correctness," and engage in more types of activity which involve conscious use of language such as punning, word games, correcting their children's speech, etc.

An example of social variation from India is illustrated in Figure 18-4, showing the social groups identified by Gumperz in a North Indian village on the basis of phonological differences. This study antedates the work by Labov reported above, and does not include systematic data on differences in contextual style; the data that was collected incidentally, however (e.g., when informants corrected themselves), indicates the same type of relation-

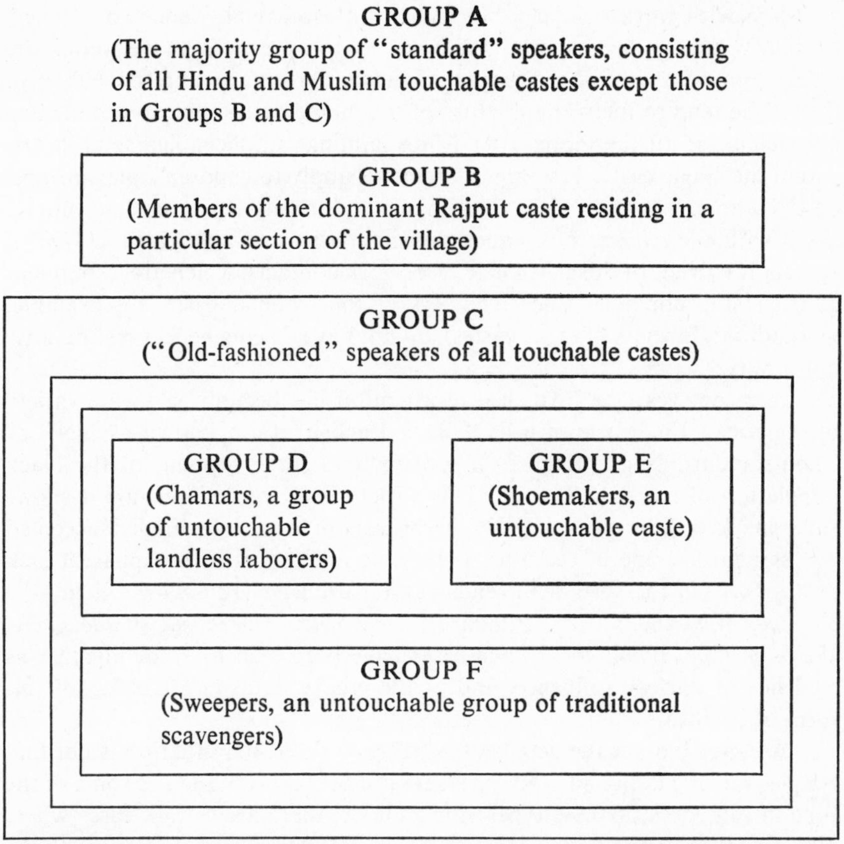

GROUP A

(The majority group of "standard" speakers, consisting of all Hindu and Muslim touchable castes except those in Groups B and C)

GROUP B

(Members of the dominant Rajput caste residing in a particular section of the village)

GROUP C

("Old-fashioned" speakers of all touchable castes)

GROUP D

(Chamars, a group of untouchable landless laborers)

GROUP E

(Shoemakers, an untouchable caste)

GROUP F

(Sweepers, an untouchable group of traditional scavengers)

Figure 18-4. Schematic representation of social groupings defined by phonological (i.e., sociolinguistic) variation in a North Indian village. Each line represents one or more features which distinguishes the group(s) enclosed by the line from those outside it. Groups B–E are all distinct from A, but in different degrees. Group B is distinguished only by a minor phonetic difference in the allophone of the phoneme /ə/ in certain positions. The remaining groups are distinct from A and B because of various etymological differences (variations in the occurrences of phonemes in certain words, mostly in unstressed position), and are distinguished from each other by similar differences. Group F is distinguished from all the others by a difference in phonemic distribution, since F speakers lack the contrasts /aɪ/–/a/, /uɪ/–/u/, and /ɔɪ/–/o/ before consonants (e.g., they have /bal/ for standard /baɪl/ 'ear of corn', etc. (After Gumperz 1958.)

ship between stratal and functional variation as found in the New York study. As the figure shows, it is possible to distinguish six different groups, some of which involve single castes (ranked hereditary groups) while others are based on other social variables. These are clearly social, not geographical groupings, since on the whole, members of the same caste living in different sections of the village speak the same "dialect." The differences also do not correlate with work contacts, but rather with informal friendship contacts (primarily among males, who are freer than women to move about the village and mix with other groups): friendship groups among touchables in the village tend to include a mixture of touchable castes, but do not include untouchables; furthermore, friendships among untouchables tend to be within the single caste. The same statements apply to children's play groups, on the whole. Thus it is clear that linguistic diversity here correlates not so much with the *amount* of contact between individuals, as with the *kind* of contact involved. In this particular case, work contacts, which are as frequent as friendship contacts (since members of the Chamar caste, for example, work for landowners of other castes), do not have an equal effect on linguistic uniformity.

In recent years, a great deal of attention has been given to the variety of American English known as "Black English" (also known as NNE or "non-standard Negro English"), spoken by a large segment of the black population of many U.S. cities. This variety is of interest because it shows some marked differences with those varieties of American English accepted as "standard." One of the most noticeable differences is the apparent lack of any form of the verb *be* in sentences like *He wild, You out the game, We on tape, Who that?* (for "standard" *He's wild, You're out of the game, We're on tape, Who's that?* Such cases have been seen by some linguists as evidence of African influence, and of the creole status (see Ch. 22) of this form of English.

A closer look at the details of NNE shows that the situation is not that simple: for one thing, all NNE speakers use the forms *is* and *are* some of the time in sentences of these types; for another, there are certain cases where NNE speakers never omit a form of *be*, as in the first person (*I'm tired*), the past (*She was likin' me*), the negative (*He ain't here*), the emphatic use (*Allah IS God*), and questions (*Is he dead?*). But the most important fact is that NNE omits these forms only in those cases in which "standard" U.S. English allows contracted forms of the type *he's, you're*. Thus, this feature of NNE, though superficially quite different from the "standard," actually involves only a difference in what generative linguists would call low-level rules; all the elements in the deep structure are identical, and the deletion which occurs in NNE can be described as the elimination of certain phonological sequences which arise as a result of the "standard" contraction rules. This case is similar to the two examples presented at the beginning of this section, in that it requires the assumption of the same basic norms (i.e., the same deep structure), but certain different phonological rules which produce different surface manifestations for speakers of different social groups.

This and other similar cases lead then to an important hypothesis about the social function of such variants: namely, that social differences in surface structure serve as very visible symbols of group identity, emphasizing both intragroup solidarity and intergroup antagonism; whereas the underlying similarity in deep structure assures the continuation of relative ease of communication—serving the function of social, and perhaps more importantly, economic interdependence of groups within the society.

18.4 DIGLOSSIA

In many parts of the world, a person is not considered fully competent in his language until he has learned a distinct formal variety of it, which he can only acquire through years of formal study. Such a situation is known as DIGLOSSIA ("dual speech"). Some well-known examples of diglossia are: Arabic, Swiss German, Haitian Creole/French, Greek, Chinese, and most of the major languages of South Asia (e.g., Bengali, Tamil). In the typical diglossia situation, the formal or "high" variety is used for all writing (except representation of dialogue, and occasionally for folk literature, political cartoons, or the like), and for all formal speaking (university lectures, speeches in parliament, news broadcasts, etc.), while the colloquial or "low" variety is always used for ordinary conversation. Needless to say, the "high" language is considered more prestigious than the "low", and in many cases speakers do not consider the "low" variety to exist, and a person who only knows that variety will be said not to know the language at all (and may even say it of himself).

There is in general a sharp dichotomy between the H ("high") and L ("low") languages in the way in which they are acquired. H is learned in school by the teaching of formal rules and norms, and the reading of exemplary texts (sometimes written hundreds of years ago), while L is learned in the home and in informal interaction with one's peers. In many diglossia situations, H and L are called by different names: e.g., Greek H is *katharévusa*, L is *dhimotikí*; Swiss German H is *Hochdeutsch* or *Hoochtüütsch*, L is *Schweizerdeutsch* or *Schwyzertüütsch*; Tamil H is *sen tamiṛ* or "pure" Tamil, L is *peecu tamiṛ* or "spoken Tamil". In other situations, the L may have no particular name (since it is not considered to be really part of the language), or it may go by a number of regional names. In the Hindi-Urdu area, for example, if one does not speak something close to the "standard" literary form of either Hindi or Urdu, one is said to speak Braj, Avadhi, Hariyanvi or some other "dialect." The situation in this area is complicated by the fact that there are two "high" languages: literary Hindi and literary Urdu, which derive their technical and literary vocabulary from Sanskrit and from Persian-Arabic respectively, and which are written in different scripts and are mutually unintelligible in their extreme forms. Most educated inhabitants of the area learn only one of these, the choice depending on a number of factors (religious, political and regional). The L used by people here will depend primarily on their regional background.

Differences between H and L in linguistic form affect phonology, grammar, and lexicon. Generally speaking, the H phonology has all the phonological distinctions of the L phonology, plus some additional ones. For example, Haitian Creole lacks the /ü/ and /ö/ of French, and substitutes /i/ and /e/ respectively for them, as in /linɛt/ 'eyeglasses' for French *lunettes* (/lünɛt/) and /de/ 'two' for French *dœux* (/dö/). The grammar of H tends to be more complex than that of L, with more irregular morphophonemics, more obligatory categories (such as gender), and in general more exceptions to the exceptions. In lexicon, very often it is necessary to learn large numbers of different words for the "same" meanings, and often the semantic distinctions do not quite match between H and L: e.g., H may make some distinctions not made in L.

For the speaker of English or other western language who finds it difficult to picture such a situation, he may try to imagine what his life would be like if all writing and formal speaking (lectures, public speeches, news broadcasts) were in Shakespearean English, with its distinct vocabulary and grammar. Following are some examples from various languages to illustrate the extent of the differences involved:

	H	*L*	*meaning*
Arabic	hiðā'un	gazma	'shoe'
	ðahaba	rāḥ	'went'
Greek	íkos	spíti	'house'
	éteke	eyénise	'gave birth'
Tamil	avarkaḷ varukiRaarkaḷ	avanka varraanka	'they come'
	raamanuṭaiya viiṭu	raaman viiṭu	'Raman's house'

A number of societies in various parts of the world have diglossia involving distinct languages; such a situation is different from ordinary bilingualism or multilingualism, in that one speaks of diglossia only when it involves a substantial segment of the population, and when the different languages involved are differentiated in terms of the social situations in which they are used. In Paraguay, where widespread bilingualism between Spanish and Guarani (an indigenous language) is found, Rubin found that a majority of people questioned in a rural area reported that they would speak Spanish with a doctor, schoolteacher, person in authority, or well-dressed stranger, and in the streets of a town, whereas they would use Guarani with their family, neighbors, in addressing an unknown barefoot woman, as well as while drinking or telling jokes. Speakers from a town area showed a similar pattern of responses, though with a somewhat greater tendency to use Spanish in close relationships than the rural speakers. Rural speakers were evenly divided on the use of Spanish or Guarani for confession, whereas the majority of speakers in the town reported Spanish for this purpose.

In some areas it is quite reasonable to speak of TRIGLOSSIA, for example in describing the situation in some of the former colonies. In Tanzania, for example, there exist a number of languages used for local intragroup communication, as well as two languages of wider communication: Swahili, the local lingua franca and national language, and English, the main language of higher education, as well as an important language in official and business contexts. A similar situation exists in urban areas of India, where English coexists with Hindi-Urdu and local languages such as Bengali or Marathi. A Tamilian living in Delhi, for example, is likely to use English in professional contexts, Hindi-Urdu with servants and traders, and Tamil with friends and family. Not only the situation, but also the subject matter may determine the choice of language. Professional colleagues or students may chat in their native language over a cup of tea, and abruptly switch into English when the conversation turns to professional or academic matters.

Thus, extensive CODE-SWITCHING is a characteristic of this type of diglossia or triglossia, in which education is imparted in a medium other than the home language. It is also quite common to encounter various degrees of mixing, especially in spontaneous conversation and personal letters. Following are some conversational examples from Tanzania (Swahili in italics):

*wana*lay *wapi* foundation 'where they are laying the foundation'

ile accident *ilitokea alipo*lose control *na aka*overturn and landed in a ditch 'the accident occurred when he lost control....'

A comparable example of switching from India occurs in the following excerpt from a recorded telephone conversation (Tamil in italics):

Yes? *aamaanko* ('yes') —— *yaaru peecuratunko* ('Who is speaking?') —— I am ... speaking, sir —— Good morning, sir —— Oh, yes —— Sure, sure —— *sari* ('all right') —— *enke sar niinka varratu* untimely-*yaa varriinko* ('How is it that you come at such untimely hours, sir?') —— You can always meet me in the office between eight and nine in the morning ... *vere viseesam oṇṇum illinkaḷe*? ('nothing else special?') Thank you.

From the viewpoint of descriptive linguistics, some interest attaches to the structural modifications observable in languages which are used for multilingual communication, particularly where there is extensive switching. Some studies show substantial CONVERGENCE (see 22.3) of the languages in question, at least when used in situations where switching is frequent.

18.5 STATUS SPEECH

In 15.2, we presented examples of differences in speech which depend on the relationship of the speaker to other persons involved in a conversation (those spoken to or about). In many parts of the world, there are speech forms prescribed for certain individuals which reflect their inherited status in the community. In parts of Kerala (southwest India) until recently, low-caste people were expected to use certain special forms for referring to themselves, their dwellings, their kinsmen, and certain intimate activities such as eating, cooking or bathing, thus making it clear that these phenomena were not the same as those involving high-caste people. A low-caste person would refer to himself as *aḍiyan* 'slave' in talking to a high-caste person (in other situations he would use the usual pronoun *ñaan* 'I'), and would use one of a set of prescribed terms for the person addressed (such as *tamburaan* 'protector', *yajamaan* 'lord', etc). He would refer to his own house as *kuppaaḍu* 'refuse place', and the house of other persons depending on their caste (*illam* for a Namboodiri Brahmin house, *mana* for a Namboodiripad house, *maḍham* for the house of an immigrant Brahmin from the Tamil country, and *viiṭu* for others). The low-caste person's food included *kallari* 'stony rice' (*kallu* 'stone') instead of *ari* 'rice' and *veluttadu* 'the white thing' instead of *moru* 'buttermilk'.

NOTES

18.1. Ashanti: Hogan 1971
     Ethnography of communication: Hymes (Introduction in Gumperz and Hymes 1972)
     Men's and women's speech: Haas (in Hymes 1964); Trudgill 1972
     Baby talk: Ferguson 1964
     Confidence men: Maurer 1940
     Homosexuals: Farrell 1972
     Prison argot: Fleischer 1972
     Burundi: Albert 1964
     Non-verbal communication: see notes to Chapter 7
     Competence vs. performance: Chomsky 1965, Chapter 1
18.2. Regional variation: Kurath 1949
     Diglossia: Ferguson 1964
18.3. Superposed and contextual variation: Labov 1964

/th/ and /r/ in New York English: Labov 1964
North Indian village: Gumperz 1958
Variations in "Black English": Labov 1969

18.4. Bilingualism in Paraguay: Rubin 1970
Code-switching: Gumperz (in Lunt 1964)
Creoles: Hall 1966 (see also ch. 22.4)
Tanzania: Abdulaziz-Mkilifi 1972

SUGGESTED SUPPLEMENTARY READING

Language in social context: Hymes 1964, Gumperz and Hymes 1964, 1972; Fishman 1970, sections I–IV

Regional variation: Kurath 1949; Kurath and McDavid 1961; McIntosh 1952; Allen and Underwood 1971

Social variation: Labov 1966, Trudgill 1972

Multilingualism: Fishman 1970, sections V–VI

Diglossia: Ferguson 1964

FOLLOW-UP

1 Define: isogloss, social dialect, superposed variation, functional (contextual/stylistic) variation, diglossia, code-switching, status speech.

2 List some examples from your own experience to illustrate the different kinds of variation discussed in this chapter (regional variation, social variation and functional variation).

Chapter 19

THE SOCIAL STATUS
OF LINGUISTIC VARIANTS

19.1 GRAMMARIANS, CORRECTNESS AND ELITE SPEECH

In a well-known passage in his book *Language* (1933), Leonard Bloomfield discussed the importance of the role of grammarians in the exploitation of the linguistic insecurities of the middle classes in eighteenth and nineteenth-century England. Bloomfield believed that the doctrine of "correctness" arose out of the needs of people, who had risen to relatively high positions in society, to make their speech acceptable in polite society. When called upon to assist in this transformation, the grammarians (mostly recruited from the ranks of Latin teachers) did their best to find rules which would distinguish between acceptable and unacceptable usages. In Bloomfield's words:

> It would not have been possible for "grammarians" to bluff a large part of our speech-community, and they would not have undertaken to do so, if the public had not been ready for the deception. Almost all people, including even most native speakers of a standard language, know that someone else's type of language has a higher prestige.... Snobbery, the performance of acts

which belong to a more privileged group, often takes the shape, therefore, of unnatural speech: the speaker utters forms which are not current among his associates, because he believes (very often, mistakenly) that these forms are favored by some "better" class of speakers. He, of course, falls an easy prey to the authoritarians.

The discussion of social variation in 18.3 above makes it clear that the processes discussed by Bloomfield are still going on: imitation of some features of the speech of more privileged speakers is dramatically demonstrated by the frequency of English /r/ in New York City, for example. The fact that the prestige pattern of one or two generations ago was the opposite (i.e., the non-use of consonantal /r/ in words like *guard, car* was more prestigious in New York), as shown by Figure 18-1, indicates the essential arbitrariness of the prestige variants; in fact, they are subject to constant change, in much the same way that the length of women's skirts or men's hair is subject to shifts of fashion.

While it is easy to see that certain phonological features are arbitrary, and none is inherently "better" than any other, it is worth looking at some of the criteria which have been used over the years by "grammarians" and others to justify their preference for certain forms. In the period discussed by Bloomfield, ideas of what was correct or proper were heavily influenced by Latin grammar. Many of our current taboos, which forbid us to say such things as *It's me* (instead of *It's I*), *None of them are here* (instead of *None of them is here*; cf. Latin *nemo* 'none', singular), or *The majority of them are in favor* (since *majority* is supposed to be the subject of the sentence, therefore requiring a singular verb) result from this preoccupation with the grammatical rules of classical Latin.

In the United States today, this trend is still visible, though the English "experts" periodically bow to the "tyranny of usage," and agree to accept such expressions as *It's me*, or *Who do you trust?* (instead of *Whom*). If there was any suspicion that the forces maintaining these standards of "correctness" were weakening, it must have been dispelled by the furor which arose over the publication of *Webster's Third New International Dictionary of the English Language* in 1961. This work, which based itself on the actual usage in contemporary publications instead of on the prescriptive approach used by the Second Edition of 1936, was denounced furiously in newspaper editorials and magazine articles throughout the country, and numerous editors rejected it entirely, calling it the "renunciation of a public trust," and stating that they would stick to the Second Edition.

What was the fuss all about? The denunciations cited many horrible examples, such as the acceptance of the preposition *like* as a conjunction replacing *as* or *as if* (as in *She acted like she was sick*), the use of *different than* instead of *different from*, the use of *they* (instead of *he*) to refer to antecedent pronouns like *everybody* (*Everybody should bring their own lunch*), or the use of *bi-weekly* to mean 'twice a week' as well as 'once in two weeks' (supposedly the original meaning, cf. *biennial, bi-monthly; semi-weekly, semi-monthly*, etc.).

Occasionally, some attempt was made to justify the "proper" usage in terms of logic or avoidance of ambiguity: e.g., sentences like *She has a nose like a horse*, or *Having eaten our lunch, the steamboat departed* are cited as justifications for imposing certain grammatical restrictions: thus, sentences like the second example here are allowed only when the subject of both clauses is the same. Nobody ever took the trouble to use the criterion of ambiguity in a consistent way; to do so would rule out very many perfectly "proper" sentences such as those mentioned in 9.2 above. In many cases, horrible examples were not provided with specific explanations of their defects; they were simply presented with the idea (expressed or implied) that any person with discrimination should know enough to avoid them.

Now it is clear that educated middle-class speakers do have certain clear preferences about how they express themselves, and that to a certain extent they agree on these preferences. (Some of the obvious differences in usage which come to mind involve different groups within the middle-class stratum, such as young people in the current long hair-drugs-rock music culture.) In fact, if one compares this stratum with others, one difference which is immediately obvious is the extent of awareness of detailed linguistic differences found among middle-class speakers, and their consequent sensitivity to the smallest differences. Among college students, the existence of regional dialect features, and attempts to suppress or accentuate them, are fairly common topics of conversation. It would appear that this awareness of linguistic form is a product of the type of education received by members of this class, but it appears also to be not unrelated to certain political and socio-economic factors of the current scene; this can only be shown briefly here.

Since the arguments used by "grammarians" do not appear to be valid or consistent, it would appear that something else is behind their machinations. The most obvious guess is that these were and are specious attempts to rationalize the irrational: in this case, the arbitrary and inconsistent usage of a particular group, as opposed to the (equally arbitrary and inconsistent) usage of other groups. It is true that even members of the elite were often attacked by prescriptive grammarians for making mistakes. Indeed, the prescriptivists often prescribed one thing and wrote another themselves. But this does not alter the fact that society gave to grammarians the right to legislate and to condemn the usage of a large mass of the population as "incorrect," and that most people accepted this situation. If this peculiar behavior were confined to a small group of academics, it would be unimportant; but actually, the authority of the "grammarians" is enforced by those who control the language of public usage (editors of newspapers, magazines, and publishing houses; news broadcasters and directors of radio and television programs, and their superiors) and public education (school boards, examination boards, officials of state education departments).

Times have changed greatly since the days of lexicographer Noah Webster, whose normative dictionary formed a key part of the system of linguistic domination presided over by the New England "Brahmins" (the wealthy families who owned the northeastern seaports and mills), and propagated by New England schoolmarms who fanned out over the country. New England is no longer considered the home of "correct" American English. But certain aspects of the system appear to be still intact. It still functions to provide "gatekeepers" who keep the "purity" of the language intact, and (even more important) restrict access to public education, the principle key to upward mobility in the society. Over the years since its establishment, this system has functioned as a filter which restricted access to the elite group (and to economic privileges), forcing successive immigrant groups to go through the slow process of acquiring the necessary education and linguistic competence decreed by the system. Gumperz's study (18.3) makes it clear that those segments of the society which are not linked with others by adult friendship groups are linguistically isolated; presumably, the only way this can be overcome is by a gradual inching up on both the educational and social ladders. For those who entered the country as foreign-language speakers, this has been a slow process; for those who are isolated by virtue of their racial or ethnic background (such as Blacks, Mexicans, or Puerto Ricans), it has been an almost insuperable obstacle.

It has been pointed out that, even if Blacks spoke Oxford English, they would still be where they are, and it is difficult to quarrel with this statement. The more important point, however, is that differences in usage can be, and are, used to *legitimize* exploitation in the minds of many people. Groups which do not conform to the linguistic standards established by elite groups are excluded from formal education in many societies (not only the western capitalist countries), and many justifications have been provided by teachers and scholars for this exclusion, in addition to those mentioned above. First of all, the fact that some speakers have a different system from the standard one is regarded as equivalent to their having no system at all, or a defective one. But studies of NNE show that in fact it is subject to the same kinds of rules that other varieties of English are. This includes both variable and invariable rules. Thus, the rule for the deletion of *be* is a variable rule (see 20.2) in NNE, just as the rule for contraction of the copula is a variable in "standard" American English. Some rules are invariable in both varieties: for example, the rule of "negative concord" is invariable for core speakers of NNE, who thus invariably substitute negatives for indefinites in negative sentences (*He don't sit nowhere, He don't like nobody that went to no prep school*).

Many teachers, even including some who sincerely wish to teach their students, are unable to grasp the fact that the students' linguistic system is basically different from their own; the misunderstandings which occur are often ludicrous, and sometimes tragic. One teacher in a New York public school wrote of her problem in getting young black children to produce words rhyming with *old* (which loses its final /d/ in NNE except when followed by a vowel). The children offered /toːl/, /foːl/, /goːl/, which were accepted since the teacher "heard" the words as though they were like her own *told, fold, gold.* When /koːl/ and /boːl/ were offered, the teacher had to ask for clarification: "Do you mean /boːl/ as in 'a bowl of cereal?'" When the child agreed that that was what he meant, the teacher had to reject that response. The children became puzzled; the teacher repeated the word, pronouncing the /d/ distinctly. The children, more and more puzzled, offered other words containing /d/: *did, doll, load.* Eventually the teacher switched to another activity. Numerous teachers have complained that Black speakers cannot learn to use the "third person singular" form of verbs, and even after years of teaching, still write sentences like *She go downtown every week.* Other students, seemingly in response to their teaching, put the *-s* ending in places where it does not belong, producing sentences like *I can goes there.*

Examples like the above, which can be multiplied with ease, indicate some of the problems occurring in education when the difference in linguistic systems is not recognized, and indicate why speakers of deviant dialects are likely to fail examinations, or (in many cases) simply lose interest in school, because what the teacher says just doesn't seem to make sense.

In examinations, a related problem is the confusion between knowledge of the language and knowledge of the majority culture. Thus, a recent English examination for the final year of high school in New York State asked the meaning of "the 8:02" in the following passage:

> The international significance of sliding downhill struck Americans like an avalanche 34 years ago. Until then, snow had been something for wives to shovel out of driveways in the morning so breadwinners could catch the 8:02. Then the winter Olympics of 1932 were held at Lake Placid, New York...

The knowledge that the "8:02" referred to here is a commuter train is more likely to be possessed by a student who belongs to the majority culture, especially if he lives in the suburbs or has friends or relatives who do; thus, such a question automatically discriminates against the inhabitant of a city slum, who is unlikely to have relatives or acquaintances in that social or economic bracket.

Perhaps the most serious trend in this connection is a more recent attempt to interpret non-standard speech as indicating "incoherence" and inability to grasp abstract ideas or to reason consistently. Thus, the absence of a form of the verb *be* (see 18.3) is interpreted as a lack of a grasp of basic logical relations; the occurrence of sentences like *I axed Alvin do he play basketball* (instead of *I asked Alvin whether/if he plays basketball*, with the form of the imbedded sentence appropriate for "indirect speech") are interpreted as showing inability to deal with abstractions. Linguists, knowing that speakers of many languages (such as Russian and Tamil) have sentences without anything corresponding to our *is* in *Who is that?*, would be reluctant to classify the speaker who produces *Who that?* as "incoherent"; knowing that *I axed Alvin do he play basketball* is equivalent in all respects (except social respectability) to the "standard" form, and is produced according to the normal grammatical rules of the speaker who utters it, they are hardly going to accuse him of being unable to grasp abstractions.

Apart from refuting such picayune arguments, it is possible to produce specimens of "Black English" which are as eloquent, as skilful in dealing with abstractions and as rational as anything produced in any other variety of language; conversely, it is not hard to find examples of "standard" speech which are wordy and vague, in spite of having all the markers of "correctness." (Some telling examples can be found in Labov 1970.)

What has been said here should not be taken to imply that the linguistic differences between groups are always so superficial. As pointed out in 18.1, people in different societies are socialized to use and respond to language in different ways. The same is often true of different subgroups within the same society. A number of recent descriptions of verbal behavior among American Blacks, for example, note the prevalence and importance of the verbal activities known as "sounding," "signifying," and "marking." These activities involve displays of verbal virtuosity which are an important part of the Black subculture, and very few, if any, non-Blacks are likely to acquire the skills needed to participate in them.

19.2 RESTRICTED AND ELABORATED CODES

Recent work in England by Basil Bernstein, on the linguistic differences between middle-class and working-class speakers, has shown differences significant enough to be considered different "codes": the RESTRICTED CODE, characterized by relative lack of explicitness and minimal use of linguistic resources, and the ELABORATED CODE, more explicit and more varied in its range of vocabulary and grammatical structures. A number of studies have demonstrated the importance of these differences and have shown that they increase with age. The conclusions reached by Bernstein, Lawton and others need to be taken seriously, even though most work to date has been done in rather controlled situations: classroom discussions, interviews of school-children (involving role-playing, storytelling, responding to verbal and pictorial cues), essay writing, etc. The following specimens of essays illustrate the types of differences which have been observed. They were written by two fifteen-year-old schoolboys, who were given only the subject of the essay ("My Life in Ten Years' Time") and no further instructions (length was also unspecified).

(*Working-Class Fifteen-Year-Old's Essay*)

I hope to be a carpenter just about married and like to live in a modern house and do a ton on the Sidcup by-pass with a motorbike and also drinking in the Local pub.

My hobby will be breeding dogs and spare time running a pet shop. And I will be wearing the latest styles of clothes.

I hope my in ten years time will be a happy life without a worry and I have a good blance behide me. I am going to have a gay and happy life. I am going to work hard to get somewhere in the world.

One thing I will not do in my life is to bring disgrace and unhappiness to my family.

(*Middle-Class Fifteen-Year-Old's Essay—Excerpt*)

As I look around me and see the wonders of modern science and all the fantastic new developments I feel a slight feeling of despondency. This is because I am beginning to wonder who will be in control of the world in ten years time, the machine or man. Already men are being shot round earth in rockets and already machines are being built that will travel faster and faster than the one before. I wonder if the world will be a gigantic nut-house by the time I'm ten years older.... We're doomed. No prayers can save us now, we'll become slaves to great walking monstrosities. Powerless in the hands of something we helped to create. I'm worried about 'my life in ten years time'. (from Lawton 1970, pp. 112–13)

Comparing these two essays we can easily see certain differences. The second essay is more literary, less personal, more concerned with abstractions like "modern science" and "the world." It uses longer sentences, a more extensive vocabulary, and is in all about twice as long as the first essay (this difference in length was typical of the other essays written in this study). The first essay is more direct and personal, more concrete and linguistically more simple and straightforward.

Without making any value judgments, it certainly seems justified to conclude (at least for the segment of British society sampled in this and other studies) that different types of linguistic output, and different ways of using language are related to different patterns of socialization, of language use, attitudes toward language and the like. The learning of an elaborated code appears to be encouraged by middle-class attitudes and values. (A middle-class person may of course use a restricted code in some situations.) It should be made clear, however, that this is not simply a matter of the middle-class person having something that the working-class person lacks. The working-class boy's essay quoted above is more direct, and seems to succeed in giving a picture of its writer as a person. Correspondingly, Bernstein reports that, whereas working-class children may be uncomfortable when asked to deal with abstractions, middle-class children are likely to have difficulties in activities such as role-playing, which involve a more direct and dramatic kind of verbal output.

Though Bernstein's primary concern has been to study the nature of cultural transmission, including the relation between socialization and the use of language, his results have been interpreted (and often misinterpreted) to have implications for the differential educability of members of different social groups. These differences in verbal output have been taken to mean that working-class children are less educable because of their home backgrounds, and that they need special remedial programs in order to fit them into the educational system and enable them to communicate with the middle class. But this argument is based on one unwarranted assumption (which is *not* made by Bernstein himself), namely that the middle-class verbal behavior which is observed in these studies is necessarily superior to the working-class behavior, and therefore must be taught to working-class schoolchildren in order to compensate for their "cultural disadvantages." It has rarely been pointed out that we could also make the opposite assumption: perhaps middle-class children need special training programs to teach them to express themselves directly and concretely so that they can communicate with members of the working class. Perhaps the ability to use abstractions (one of the principal measures of difference between the speech and writing of the two groups) is not an unqualified asset, if there is no compensating ability to relate the abstractions to people's direct needs (see 16.6).

19.3 STANDARD LANGUAGE

If there is no measure by which we can objectively determine the superiority of one linguistic variety over another, then it is clear that the emergence of one variety as the "standard" form is in general a historical accident, which couples that variety with a particular ruling group in a society. On the other hand, the term "standard" implies, both theoretically and in fact, a certain amount of agreement. When the home languages of two groups in a society differ, communication is facilitated if they agree to use a particular variety in intergroup dealings, and any such variety may be called a "standard" form of the language. Looking at various societies which may be said to have some sort of "standard" language, we find considerable variation in the extent of acceptance of the standard, and also in the range of situations in which the standard is used. Acceptance presumably means that people with differing home speech agree to use (to the best of their ability) the prescribed standard form as they perceive it. In the minimal cases, this amounts to a sort of ritual acceptance of the language prescribed for official use: many speakers, even though they may have at best passive control (i.e., comprehension) of the official "standard," will agree that it is the correct, proper or pure form of the language.

This is the situation with many of the languages of South Asia. An anthropologist working in the Hindi-Urdu (see 18.4) area, for example, reports that when one villager was conversing with him in the local dialect, he was scolded by another villager, who said: "Don't use that *dehati bhaṣa* (hick speech), talk *sŭddh* (pure) Hindi." Thereafter, the two men conversed with the foreigner in an approximation of the regional standard (the speech of educated city-dwellers). For those who learn the regional standard at home, the term /šuddh hɪndi/ would refer to a learned, recently concocted, and highly Sanskritized language used only in writing and in radio broadcasts; this is a "standard" for the speech community as a whole only in a very restricted sense, since it plays only a very small part in the lives of most speakers, except for those living in urban areas. Such a case is clearly different from situations where there has been substantial agreement over a long period of time as to what constitutes the standard (or at least enough agreement to allow recognition and elimination of that which is "nonstandard"). This appears to be substantially the case in the United States and Canada, and in Western Europe, though even in these cases the scope of "standard" is restricted to relatively formal usage.

In general, very few people speak "standard" at home or in their most spontaneous moments, since the process of standardization concerns primarily public usage, and most people—however they may talk in public—will, in unguarded moments, lapse into usages that would be unacceptable to their schoolteachers. In any society, people who speak "standard" all or even most of the time are limited to relatively small numbers of urban-based speakers. Therefore, the "standard" is for most people a restricted language, since it is only part of a speaker's communicative repertoire—and, in fact, is likely to lack the full expressive range of spontaneous colloquial speech.

Radio and television announcers in the United States, especially those appearing on national networks, are trained to produce a "colorless" variety of American English which avoids any regional or social dialect features, such as those of New England, the Southeast or the Southwest. This variety, known as "network English," is perhaps the closest thing to a spoken standard in American English. On the other hand, local announcers (such as meteorologists) and character actors (e.g., in cowboy films) often have a noticeable local color in their speech. In northern cities with large black populations, there are stations which are reputed to broadcast in "Black English." A similar phenomenon is noticeable in Britain, where the BBC in response to popular demand has been broadcasting in a variety of regional forms of English for some years now, instead of restricting their output to the traditionally "standard" RP. Clearly, these variants on the air waves have not dethroned the "standard" in countries where such changes have occurred, but their presence indicates that there are activities in which the "standard" does not necessarily reign supreme.

In fact, it actually makes more sense to define the standard in terms of a particular SOCIAL ARENA, since there are different "standards" appropriate for different situations. For Indian villagers carrying on a conversation in their own village, the term "standard" can only mean the village dialect; when they are in the market town, the appropriate form is the regional standard; the literary standard of the cities will become an active standard for them only if they obtain college degrees and write official documents or address public meetings in the cities. Similarly, the southerner in the United States lapses into the regional standard of the south when he visits his home, even though he may have painstakingly removed all traces of this speech while living in the north. And similarly, the most appropriate form of speech for a black-owned radio station which broadcasts soul music to black listeners is "Black English."

This sort of variation is recognized by all who care to observe it, but is not accommodated in our conceptual models of language. Generally questions about the standard language are couched in the form, "What is *the* standard?" —always carrying the implication that there can only be *one* standard valid for everyone in the society all the time (even though we may vary in our degree of loyalty to it). Why must there be *one* standard? Raising the question is difficult, since people seem to take it that "there *has* to be a standard." It is worth questioning, however. It is not entirely clear that the need for uniformity of usage is as valid an argument as it seems to be. Groups who speak different varieties are able to understand each other (when they want to), and repetition tests indicate that conversion from another speaker's usage to one's own takes place immediately and without conscious effort: thus, NNE speakers are able to immediately reproduce such sentences as *Nobody ever sat at any of those desks, anyhow* or *I asked him if he did it* with their own equivalents (*Nobody didn't never sit at none of them desses nohow, I axed him did he do it*).

Thus it is perfectly possible to envisage a society with a variable standard, which each group produces according to his own background. Those who oppose this notion must ask themselves whether their insistence on a single uniform "standard" has any other function than to keep down the speakers of "non-standard" varieties, and to keep them conscious of their inferior position in the society. This question is legitimate, since the maintenance of a rigid "standard" *does* have this function, and furthermore it seems to relate to the pyramidal structure of a stratified society dominated by a single group. It has been suggested that the elite speaker's reaction to very minute linguistic differences, and his tendency to evaluate them, is in some way "natural" or "innate," in the same sense that the ability to acquire and use language is innate. Since simpler societies appear to lack anything corresponding to the difference between "standard" and "non-standard" (though they do not lack linguistic variation, for example between men's and women's speech), the innateness cannot be said to be a characteristic of human speech in general. It may very well be a characteristic of stratified societies, however.

NOTES

19.1. Grammarians and correctness: Bloomfield 1933, pp. 496–499
"Double negative" in NNE: Labov 1972
tole, fole, bole: Shannon 1968
I axed Alvin do he play...: Labov 1972
Signifying and marking: Mitchell-Kiernan 1972
19.2. Restricted and elaborated codes: Bernstein 1972, Lawton 1968

SUGGESTED SUPPLEMENTARY READING

Bernstein 1972; Labov 1969; Lawton 1968; Leonard 1929; Monaco and Zaslow 1972

FOLLOW-UP

1 Explain the difference between a restricted code and an elaborated code. Have you observed differences of the kind discussed in 19.2 in your own experience? What is the social basis of these differences?

2   Look up the terms *standard, standard language,* and/or *standard English* in an unabridged dictionary. How do these definitions correlate with your own understanding of these terms? Ask the same question of others. Do you believe that these definitions refer to actually existing forms of language? How could this belief be tested?

3   It has been suggested that when we react negatively to somebody's linguistic usage, this reflects not our reaction to the usage itself, but negative feeling about the habitual users of such language. (For example, the taboo on *ain't* in the United States may reflect negative feelings toward certain lower-class English and Irish immigrant groups of the nineteenth century.) Often, however, we attempt to justify such reactions on the basis of "logic," "clarity" or the like. Do you know of other cases of usage which is currently considered "incorrect" for the same reasons?

Chapter 20

SOCIOLINGUISTIC METHODS

20.1 DATA COLLECTION

Methods of data collection used by linguists until recently have relied heavily on two basic techniques: the so-called INFORMANT METHOD and INTROSPECTION (the latter used by linguists working on their own native languages). Written sources are also often used, but with the emphasis on spoken language characteristic of modern linguistics, there has been a tendency to prefer those written materials which approximate a spoken style. In the American linguistic tradition, the linguist's professional training includes at least one course in INFORMANT WORK, in which he is trained in the methods of eliciting linguistic data from an individual speaker (known as an informant, i.e., one who provides information). Within this method, there is considerable variation in the extent of control exerted on the informant by the linguist, and the extent of initiative allowed to the informant, but it is common for the linguist to concentrate on data provided by the informant in response to direct questions, often in a CONTROL LANGUAGE (i.e., a language other than the OBJECT LANGUAGE under investigation). Once the linguist develops some proficiency, he can use the object language directly for communication with the informant. It is also possible to work with a monolingual informant *without* a control language, using gestures and other methods of communicating while acquiring a basic command of the language; but this is laborious and time-consuming, and very few linguists would take the trouble to do this if there is a control language available.

Both the informant method and the introspective method (in which the linguist serves as his own informant) are time-saving, inexpensive and more direct in eliciting data than any method which involves observation of normal speaking situations. These methods both suffer however from certain inherent defects, which can become crucial if they are relied on exclusively. In view of the type of variation in contextual styles presented in 18.3, it should be obvious that linguists using these methods would encounter great difficulty in eliciting any but the most formal and careful contextual variants; thus, only a small segment of the total linguistic spectrum is accessible by these methods. More importantly, the material elicited by this method lacks normal context, since it is provided in response to questions like "How do you say X (= an utterance in the control language) in your language?" or "Is Y (an utterance in the object language) acceptable in your language?"

Such questions rely primarily on the informant's INTUITION about what is GRAMMATICAL (i.e., correct) in his language, without the benefit of a surrounding context in which to evaluate it. Though many linguists feel that they can give such judgments consistently, and can trust their informants to do the same, various tests have shown that informants not only differ considerably from each other in what they will accept as "grammatical," but they are not consistent with themselves. In other cases, it has often been found that sentences which were initially rejected by informants were later accepted as perfectly normal when provided with an appropriate context. The unquestioned acceptance of these "intuitive" judgments also begs a very important question: namely, what is the basis of the "intuition?" We cannot rule out the possibility that, when the informant (or the introspective linguist) rejects an utterance as "ungrammatical," he may be applying some very special and unacceptable criteria: he may be saying, in effect, "If I think about it, I won't use (or will hesitate to use) an utterance of this type in front of anyone who might be likely to judge me on the basis of it." This is a far cry from saying, "I would never use this sentence in any context." And there is plenty of evidence to show that informants' statements *about* what they say are not consistent with what they actually say in normal interaction. Regarding the introspections of linguists, we should bear in mind that the person who concerns himself professionally with formal details of language is not only a member of a very small minority, but also one who has developed the awareness of language (with its great potential for social manipulation) to a very high degree; therefore, it would be reasonable to regard the linguist's statements about his own speech with a high degree of suspicion.

Much of the material obtained by the above methods may be of value, but it is difficult to evaluate it unless it can be compared with data from normal speech. Modern sound-recording equipment, especially the latest battery-operated tape recorders, has gone a long way toward overcoming the technical problems involved here. The remaining problems involve the techniques of stimulating spontaneous conversation when informants know they are being recorded, and finding ways to elicit particular words or constructions without disturbing the naturalness of the conversation. Group sessions involving several informants are most likely to produce the desired spontaneity, though group size must be controlled in order to keep noise at a manageable level. Experience has shown that, if the subject of the conversation is of sufficient interest to absorb the attention of the participants, the recorder will be forgotten fairly quickly.

In individual interviews, various methods have been developed by Labov and others for eliciting a variety of different contextual styles: for example, making use of (apparent) interruptions to elicit an informal style, or encouraging the informant to discuss a subject in which he becomes emotionally involved, and therefore less self-conscious. Various CHANNEL CUES (such as changes in speed, pitch, or loudness of speech, changes in breathing, laughter or other signs of emotional reaction) can be used as indications of the spontaneity of the speech.

Techniques for eliciting data on particular questions are still being developed. Phonology does not pose much of a problem, since most phonological entities are frequent enough that they do not depend on subject matter or the like. Problems arise when we wish to get examples of a particular construction or a particular word, without suggesting it to the informant in too obvious a way. For example, one may observe that speakers of NNE say *He don't sit nowhere, I ain't see nobody, They don't live there no more*, where "standard" English uses *He doesn't sit anywhere, I didn't see anybody, They don't live there any more*. The question may arise whether these former speakers ever use the forms *anywhere, anybody*, etc., in such sentences, since the form of the rules for NNE may depend on the linguist's ability to exclude the possibility of the occurrence of such forms. Even though no examples occur in the recorded materials, it is often necessary to check such points, and responses to direct questions on such subjects are likely to be untrustworthy. One possible technique is to simply introduce a question like *Didn't you see anybody* into the conversation in order to see what reaction occurs. If the answer is *No, we didn't see nobody*, this can be taken as evidence against the use of *anybody*.

Alternatively, one may ask the informant to repeat a set of sentences; this device is useful, since it is common for informants to restructure sentences in repetition, as pointed out at the end of Chapter 19. The evidence of such "repetitions" can be extremely useful in investigating differences between the standard and various colloquial forms. In eliciting semantic material, where the linguist wishes to avoid using a particular word, it is often useful to introduce a more general subject: for example, terms for meals (like *supper, dinner, lunch*) may be introduced by asking questions like "What did you eat today?" or "Do you eat anything special on holidays?"

20.2 MODELS FOR THE DESCRIPTION OF LINGUISTIC VARIATION

The implications of the study of sociolinguistic variation for linguistic description are just beginning to be discussed by a few linguists. Since this development is relatively new, only a few significant trends can be pointed out here. It was already mentioned (19.1) that some linguistic variation can be accounted for in terms of VARIABLE RULES; that is, instead of the traditional CATEGORICAL RULES which work whenever the conditions for them are fulfilled, a new type of rule has been proposed which incorporates VARIABLE CONSTRAINTS. As an example, Labov and others have found in studying the deletion of final /t/ and /d/ after a consonant among speakers of NNE in New York and Detroit that, although percentages of deletion varied from group to group, the deletion rule applied in all groups with greater frequency when the next word began with a consonant (e.g., *las' night* for *last night, tol' me* for *told me*) than when it began with a vowel (e.g., *las' April, tol' Andy*); further, the rule applied consistently more often in single morphemes (*las' one, firs' one*) than when the /t/ or /d/ represented the past tense suffix (*lef' me, tol' me*). Some statistics are shown in the following table (after Labov 1970):

PERCENTAGE OF DELETION OF /t, d/ AFTER CONSONANTS IN NNE

	Single-morpheme Clusters		Past-tense Clusters	
	___*Cons*	___*Vow*	___*Cons*	___*Vow*
NYC Middle-class adults	60	28	19	04
NYC LWC adults	89	40	47	32
NYC adolescents	94	62	69	23
Detroit UMC	79	23	49	07
Detroit LWC	97	72	76	34

In order to account for this type of data, Labov has suggested that we can write rules very much like those being written by generative linguists, but incorporating variable constraints which are determined on the basis of the speaker's social background and the formality of the speech situation, in addition to the usual linguistic conditions. Thus, we can learn from a grammar of this type not only that all speakers delete final /t, d/ more often in certain phonological circumstances than in others, but that, furthermore, speakers from certain specific groups have certain stateable norms of deletion in each linguistic environment. The model proposed here, therefore, involves statistical variation along a continuum defined by the application or non-application of a particular rule.

In some cases, a rule will be categorical (applying 100 percent of the time) for all speakers, or for certain groups of speakers; in other cases, non-application of a rule will be categorical for some speakers.

An example of the use of this model in the description of grammatical variation can be found in Labov's treatment of negation in standard U.S. English and NNE; he posits the three following rules:

1	Negative attraction:	Indef	X	Neg			
		1	2	3	$\rightarrow 1 + 3$	2	
2	Negative transport:	Neg	X	Indef			
		1	2	3	$\rightarrow 2$	$1 + 3$	
3	Negative concord:	Neg	X	$\left\{ \begin{matrix} \text{Verb} \\ \text{Indef} \end{matrix} \right\}$			
		1	2	3	$\rightarrow 1$	2	$1 + 3$

Rule 1 is obligatory for all dialects, and provides for sentences of the type *Nobody sits there, Nothing was taken* (assuming these to be derivable transformationally from underlying sequences *Anybody doesn't sit there, Anything wasn't taken*). Rule 2 is an optional rule applying only in formal standard English, and provides for sentences of the type *He sits nowhere, He took nothing* (from underlying *He not Pres sit anywhere, He not Past take anything*). Rule 3 is optional in some dialects, but categorical in NNE, and provides for sentences of the type *He don't sit nowhere, He didn't take nothing*.

A somewhat different type of model has been proposed by students of Creole speech communities (see 22.4), in which there can be said to be variation between a BASILECT (the most highly Creolized variety) and an ACROLECT (that variety most closely approaching international English). It has been pointed out that a number of variable features show, in addition to statistical predictability, certain IMPLICATIONAL RELATIONSHIPS such that, if a speaker is known to have a certain feature X, it can be predicted that he will also have a feature Y. This leads to the notion that the systems of grammatical rules used by different speakers can be RANKED along the continuum between basilect and acrolect.

In analyzing the English-Creole speech community of Guyana, Bickerton found it possible to rank speakers according to their use of *tu* or *fi* (equivalent of English *to*) in sentences like the following (see below for description of the categories involved):

(I)   Jan staat tu/fi wok   'John started to work'
(II)   Jan wan tu/fi mek moni 'John wanted to make money'
(III) Jan kom tu/fi wok   'John came to work'

Apart from two exceptions (see below), those speakers who had *tu* in any of these categories also used *tu* in the preceding ones (e.g., any speaker who had *tu* in sentences of type II also used *tu* in sentences of category I); conversely, those who used *fi* in any type also used *fi* in the following types (e.g., *fi* in type II implied *fi* in type III). These relationships make it possible to rank speakers along the continuum between "pure" acrolect (*tu* in all cases) and "pure" basilect (100 percent use of *fi*), and to predict the possible intermediate combinations such as (I) *tu*–(II) *tu*–(III) *fi*, (I) *tu*–(II) *tu/fi*–(III) *fi*, etc. (the slant line indicating use of both *tu* and *fi* in the same category).

In a study of Jamaican speech, De Camp found a similar type of continuum with respect to certain lexical and phonological items, which made it possible to predict, for example, that the first three sentences below are all normal (for certain speakers in certain contexts), but the fourth one is not:

> The child didn't eat that.
> De pikni no ben nyam dat.
> De pikni didn't eat dat.
> *De child didn't nyam dat.

The reason for this is that, as De Camp puts it, "...*nyam* is a word much farther down the social scale than is *pikni*...Any speaker of sufficient social status and in a sufficiently formal speech situation to say *child* instead of *pikni* would normally not say *nyam*."

On the basis of this type of data, C-J. Bailey has postulated a WAVE MODEL of linguistic structure, which incorporates the notion of waves of change spreading through a speech community in a given order and in particular directions, starting from a particular source (which could be either a geographical region or a social group). With regard to a particular wave, any individual speaker is either changed, unchanged or undergoing change; cases of variation in usage, of course, are symptomatic of individuals or groups which are in the process of change. Thus, in the case of the *tu/fi* variation in Guyana, one could postulate three interlinked changes whose "source" is the elite group in Guyanese society, and which are undergone in the following order by upwardly mobile individuals:

1   *fi* → *tu* with all verbs except inceptives (*staat, bigin*) and desideratives/ perceptuals (*wan, disaid, trai, fuget,* etc.)
2   *fi* → *tu* with desideratives/perceptuals
3   *fi* → *tu* after inceptives

In this case, Bickerton's study showed that the exceptions to the rule—i.e., those anomalous persons who had undergone the changes in other orders—were unusual sociologically as well, in terms of their history of geographical and/or occupational mobility.

The potential value of this approach in Creole studies is clearly very high, but we may question its applicability to speech communities in general. On the other hand, something like the wave model has long been used in historical-comparative linguistics as an explanation of change (see Ch. 23), and this modern adaptation of it seems very promising. Transformationalists have for some time been using the notion of RULE ACQUISITION to explain processes like native language learning, as well as longer-term linguistic changes (see Ch. 21). It is possible that the pursuit of these related theoretical currents may lead to a broadening of the scope of descriptive linguistics, to embrace the linguistic dynamics which reflect intergroup relationships in the society, and perhaps at the same time lead to a reintegration of the diachronic and synchronic approaches to linguistic study. The discovery of this ultimate ideal model of linguistic structure will require many more empirical studies of the type described here. Not only do such studies involve great expenditures of time and money, but there is also likely to be a considerable lapse of time before a definitive picture appears. (Some practical implications of this point are discussed in 25.2.)

NOTES

20.1. Channel cues: Labov 1964
20.2. Variable rules: Labov 1969, 1972
   Negation: Labov 1972
   Implicational relations: Bickerton 1971, De Camp (in Hymes 1971)

SUGGESTED SUPPLEMENTARY READING

Methodology: Labov (In Dingwall 1971)

FOLLOW-UP

1 Define: informant method, introspective method, channel cues, basilect, acrolect.

2 Distinguish: variable rules—categorical rules.

3 The following is suggested as an individual or team project:

    a. Observe the speech of a number of people belonging to different social groups, and/or speaking in different situations. (Different groups include those differentiated by age, race, ethnic background, socioeconomic status, sex, profession, level of education. Different situations might include: informal family or dormitory conversation, formal lecture, semi-formal class discussion, telephone conversation, radio or TV news broadcast or panel discussion, etc.)

    b. Try to note linguistic features which vary between different groups and/or situations. (Linguistic variables may include pronunciation, grammar, vocabulary or combinations of these.)

    c. Forr ⁻late a hypothesis about the way in which the linguistic variation relates to the difference in social situation. (A sample hypothesis might be: people use more contractions like *isn't, don't, can't* in a family conversation than in a formal lecture or discussion.)

    d. Test your hypothesis by observing a sample of speakers in different situations. (If you can use a tape-recorder for this, it will be very helpful. Note, however, that speakers will be somewhat shy of a tape-recorder until they get used to its presence.) Quantify your variables so that you can count the number of instances of a particular variable in each situation. Define your situations or speaker characteristics so that your statements have some precision. (e.g., do not contrast "older people" with "young people," but use specific age limits, even if they are not accurate to the year.)

    e. Write up your project, stating your hypothesis, how it was formed, how it was tested (methods of selecting your sample, methods of observation, quantification of variables), and whether the hypothesis was confirmed or not.

    f. Discuss the implications of your study. What does it mean for communication in your society? If your study showed that particular linguistic variants are correlated with particular social differences, have you any explanation for how this came about?

PART V

HISTORICAL–
COMPARATIVE
LINGUISTICS

Chapter 21

LINGUISTIC CHANGE

21.1 INTRODUCTION

Relations among languages provide some of our most important clues to prehistory. Along with archaeology and physical anthropology, comparative linguistics provides detailed information about earlier movements of peoples and the interrelations among different societies. Linguists began to study linguistic history seriously when they realized that the resemblances in form between the classical language of northern India (Sanskrit) and those of western Europe (Latin and Greek) were too close and too detailed to be attributable to chance. When they investigated further, they found they could reconstruct many features of an extinct and unattested parent language (or PROTO-LANGUAGE) from which these and other languages could be presumed to be derived, as well as some notions of the social structure of its speakers.

The field of historical–comparative linguistics, which traces relationships among languages as they change and diverge from a common original source, was born along with the discovery of the INDO-EUROPEAN family of languages. The same methods were later applied to other language families, including the indigenous languages of North and South America, the Malayo-Polynesian language family of the Pacific and Indian Oceans, a number of language families of Africa and the Middle East, and other families of Europe and Asia (such as Finno-Ugric, Turkic, Sino-Tibetan, and Caucasian). A brief overview of the language families of the world is given in an appendix to Chapter 23.

Central to the methodology of genetic comparison and reconstruction is the assumption that speech communities undergo certain limited types of change, which in some circumstances lead a single original speech community, as it expands or separates, to differentiate itself into separate communities speaking distinct languages. The assumptions about change are amply supported by observation (for example, comparing contemporary languages with older written forms of the same languages) and by comparative reconstruction. The only part of this assumption that cannot be substantiated by data is the part concerning originally uniform speech communities—since we have never observed any. In fact, this assumption was probably based on misconceptions about the nature of contemporary languages and speech communities. Nowadays, thanks to the work of sociolinguists (see Part IV), we have ample evidence of the various kinds of intergroup variation found within the same speech community.

The study of linguistic change is of interest from a number of different points of view, including the following:

1   As a method of history and prehistory, it allows us to trace contacts among groups on the basis of original similarities as well as later influence (22.1). The evidence provided by linguistic similarities is on a par with that provided by archaeology (such as shared techniques of pottery-making or house construction) and physical anthropology (such as blood-group similarities).

2   From the viewpoint of linguistic structure, the study of change shows us ways in which structures are susceptible to change, while at the same time maintaining the essential structural relationships that make communication possible. (Sections 21.2–5 present examples of the most common types of change.)

3   Since there is a rather close relationship between certain language changes and some phenomena observed in studies of language acquisition (e.g., child language and baby talk often reproduce changes which take place historically), some linguists have tried to deal with both in terms of RULE ACQUISITION (i.e., adding rules to the grammar).

4   Since the transmission of language is a social phenomenon, there is also

a sociolinguistic aspect to the study of language change. (This is discussed in 22.5.)

5 The study of language change is also an important component of the PHILOLOGICAL approach to language, which is largely concerned with the interpretation of earlier texts.

The effects of linguistic change are most striking when observed over long periods of time, as the following examples from earlier English will demonstrate. The first selection here is approximately 500 years old, and the second approximately 1000 years old.

> Mastresse, thow be so that I, unaqweyntyd with yow as yet, tak up on me to be thus bold as to wryght on to yow with ought your knowlage and leve, yet, mastress, for syche pore servyse as I now in my mynd owe yow, purposyng, ye not dyspleasyd, duryng my lyff to contenu the same, I beseche yow to pardon my boldness, and not to dysdeyn, but to accepte thys sympyll byll to recommand me to yow in syche wyse as I best can or may imagyn to your most plesure.
>
> (Letter from John Paston to Margery Brews,
> from The Paston Letters, quoted in
> Algeo 1972, p. 189)

> An. DCCCC.XCIIII. Hēr on þisum ēare cōm Ānlāf and Swezen to Lunden-byriz on Nātīvitas Sancte Mārīe mid IIII and hundnizontizum scipum, and hī þā on þā burh festlīce feohtende wǣron.... 'Here in this year came Olaf and Svein to London town on the Nativity of St. Mary with four and ninety ships, and they then the town continuously attacking were....'
>
> (The Anglo-Saxon Chronicle for the year
> 994, quoted in Algeo 1972, p. 135)

The first passage, though sounding somewhat quaint and perhaps difficult to follow in spots, nevertheless appears to be English. The second passage, however, could just as well be in a totally different (though related) language. The order of words (as shown by the order in the translation, which follows that of the original) is different in several places. A number of words are either partially (ēare 'year', hēr 'here', scip 'ship', wǣron 'were', cōm 'came') or completely (byri, byrh 'town', mid 'with', hī 'they', þā 'then, the', festlīce 'continuously', feohtende 'attacking') different in form from their modern equivalents. A grammatical description of the language of the period would provide for differences in grammatical gender, nominal cases (cf. *scipum*, a dative plural form), a complex conjugational system and a radically different phonemic system. Clearly, the difference between the English of that period and what we speak today is comparable with the differences between distinct languages. In the following sections of this chapter, we will discuss the different types of changes involved in such a transformation.

21.2 SOUND CHANGE

Laboratory measurements of speech sounds have shown that even a single individual varies the way he pronounces words. For example, if he pronounces the vowel in *hat* twenty times in succession, spectroscopic measurements will reveal differences in the length, height, and frontness of the vowel. For any particular speaker these variables tend to cluster around a norm, which permits us to assign particular normal or average values for a speaker, or even for a group of speakers. Generally these differences pass unnoticed, but they sometimes differ considerably from one group to another, and such differences account for a great deal of the qualities of different "dialects" of a language.

The change in a group's pronunciation of particular sounds over time is known as PHONETIC DRIFT. Most of the time this does not affect the structure of the language. Thus, a study of the pronunciation of the vowel of *cab*, *cash*, *ham* in New York City speech shows considerable phonetic variation (from lower high front to low mid), though most speakers appear to keep the /æ/ distinct from the neighboring phonemes /e/ and /a/. But if two phonemes drift together so that speakers no longer distinguish them, then the structure is affected. This appears to have happened, for example, in the speech of some areas of the southeastern United States, where the vowels /i/ and /e/ before a word-final /n/ (e.g., in *pin*, *pen*, *tin*, *ten*) are no longer distinct—though they continue to contrast in other environments.

Long-term changes in phonological structure are of three types: MERGER (in which a distinction is lost in some or all environments), SPLIT (involving the emergence of a new phonological contrast), and LOSS (disappearance of a phoneme in one or all of its environments). TOTAL MERGER is relatively rare, but is found for example in the coalescence of the three sibilants of Sanskrit (palatal /š/ as in *šatam* '100', retroflex /ṣ/ as in *ṣaṣṭi* '60', dental /s/ as in *saptaḥ* '7') into a single /s/ in Hindi-Urdu (/sə/ '100', /saṭʰ/ '60', /sat/ '7').

PARTIAL MERGER is much more common, and can be illustrated by the DEVOICING of originally voiced stops at the ends of words in German (also found in Russian and Turkish): cf. *Bad* /báːt/ 'bath', *baden* /báːden/ 'to bathe'; *Kalb* /kálp/ 'calf', plural *kälbe* /kélbe/; *Weg* /vek/ 'way', plural *Wege* /veːge/. The loss of the distinction between /i/ and /e/ in southeastern U.S. is another example of partial merger.

Phonemic SPLIT creates a new phonological distinction. A typical example of this process is the development of a contrast between alveolar and palatal phonemes in the sibilants (s š), voiced affricates (dᶻ dᶼ), and voiceless affricates (tˢ tš) of Marathi. These contrasts were not present in earlier stages of the language, and are not found in the most closely related languages. Nevertheless, it is easy to see how they developed. Each of the above pairs of sounds must have been originally allophones of the same phoneme, with the palatal member occurring before /i/ and /y/ and the alveolar elsewhere (though there may have been fluctuation before a following /e/ vowel). This situation can be seen in the alternations in the right-hand column below.

vaḍa 'manor'	gəla 'throat'	khisa 'pocket'
vaḍe (plural)	gəle	khise/khiše
vaḍyat 'in the manor'	gəlyat 'in one's throat'	khišat 'in one's pocket'

The first two examples (the words for 'manor' and 'throat') indicate that the endings for nouns of this type are /a/ (singular), /e/ (plural), and /yat/ (locative). The form /khišat/ (presumably from /khis-yat/) can be accounted for by a change /sy/ → /šy/ → /š/, which first resulted in allophonic variation, and then (by the loss of /y/) resulted in the originally non-contrastive sounds coming into contrast. The other pairs mentioned above originated in the same way. All splits result, as this one does, from a loss or merger; however, all splits do not create new phonemes. In some cases they merely create new instances of existing phonemes: thus, when Latin intervocalic /s/ changed to /r/ in certain environments (see 21.3), this merely altered the distribution of /s/ and /r/.

Occasionally there occur cases of TOTAL PHONOLOGICAL LOSS, as in the case of Latin /h/ (*homo* 'man', *trahere* 'to draw') which has survived in the Romance languages only in writing (cf. French *homme* /ɔm/, Spanish *hombre* /ómbre/ 'man', Spanish *traer* /traér/ 'to bring'). PARTIAL LOSS, i.e., loss restricted to certain environments, is more common. Examples from English include: the loss of initial /k/ and /g/ before /n/ in *know, knave, knight, gnaw, gnarl*, etc. The loss of English /r/ (in certain dialects) when not followed by a vowel (compare British English *dare* /deːə/–*dared* /deːəd/–*daring* /deːring/, *batter* /bætə/–*battery* /bætri/, etc.). The loss of word-final consonants is very common (cf. the French examples in 12.1), and word-final vowels also are often lost. For example, the final vowels of Sanskrit, which are still attested in the medieval literary languages known as Prakrits, are completely lost in modern Hindi-Urdu and its related languages (e.g., Skt. *agni* 'fire' → Pkt. *aggi* → H-U /ag/; Skt. aṣṭau 'eight' → Pkt. aṭṭha → H-U /aṭh/).

Traditionally, linguists have classified phonological changes in terms of their physical effects (compare 12.3). Some of the common types of changes recognized in this classification are: ASSIMILATION (in which one sound becomes identical with, or more similar to, a neighboring sound—as in the examples just given, Skt. *gn* → Pkt. *gg*, *šr* → *ss*); DISSIMILATION (the opposite process, e.g., the common pronunciation /fébyueri:/ instead of /fébrueri:/ for *February*); METATHESIS (the interchanging of neighboring sounds, as in *irrevelant* for *irrelevant*, or /kɔ́mftərbl/ for /kɔ́mfərtəbl/ *comfortable*); SYNCOPE (the loss of a syllable nucleus, as in /í:vning/ instead of /í:vəning/ for *evening*); HAPLOLOGY (loss of one of two similar adjacent syllables, as in /láybri:/ for *library*); CONTRACTION (the coalescence of a sequence of sounds into a single sound: e.g., the Skt. sequences *-aya-* and *-ava-* are contracted to *-e-* and *-o-* in later languages, as in Skt. *bhavanam* 'being' → H-U /hona/ 'to be', Skt. *nayanam* 'leading' → Marathi /neṇə/ 'to lead'); EPENTHESIS (the insertion of a transitional sound, e.g., the /b/ of Prakrit *tambra* 'copper' ← Skt. *tāmram*); PROTHESIS (adding a sound to the beginning of a word, as in Spanish *escuela* 'school' ← Lat. *schola*, *estar* 'to be' ← Lat. *stare* 'to stand'.

Many of these changes have been explained as producing greater ease of articulation, and this seems to account for cases like assimilation and contraction. But some changes have the opposite effect. For example, Latin voiceless stops between vowels became voiced stops or fricatives in Spanish (e.g., Latin *sapere* 'to know' → Spanish /saber/, *datus* 'given' → /dado/), whereas some voiced stops of early Germanic became voiceless in German. Compare German *t* in *rot* 'red', *trinken* 'drink', *eitel* 'empty' with *d* in English *red*, *drink*, *idle*, where English represents the earlier stage.

21.3 REGULARITY OF SOUND CHANGE

Some of the changes mentioned above are isolated phenomena, for example the change of /r/ to /y/ in *February* or the interchanging of *l* and *v* in *irrelevant*; but many changes are amazingly regular in the sense that, within certain stateable phonological and grammatical conditions, all (or almost all) cases of a particular sound undergo the same change. Without this regularity, it would be impossible to trace the history of particular words with any consistency at all, and thus there would be no field of etymology or of comparative linguistics (see 23.1).

The hypothesis of regular sound change has also sharpened our understanding of how these changes occur. An example of this can be found in the so-called RHOTACISM, the change of intervocalic *s* to *r* in Latin. This change is mentioned by Varro, a Roman grammarian of the first century B.C., and is evidenced by a number of cases which show *s* and *r* in alternation, with *s* apparently the original form. For example, *aes* (nominative) 'copper, bronze', genitive *aer-is*; similarly *flōs* 'flower', genitive *flōr-is*. The verb 'be' has the form *es-* when followed by a consonant, as in *es-se* 'to be', *es-t* 'is', and *er-* before a vowel as in the future form *er-it* 'will be'; etc. There are a number of apparent exceptions to the change *s → r*, such as *nisī* 'except', *nausea* 'seasickness', *rosā* 'rose', *miser* 'unhappy', *causa* 'reason, cause', *cāsus* 'fall', etc.

If we are content to observe that Latin intervocalic *s* changed to *r* some of the time but not all of the time, then we have nothing but a peculiar and unexplained phenomenon. If, on the other hand, the "exceptions" are examined in detail, we see that most of them have alternative explanations: *nausea* and many others are words borrowed from Greek, which did not appear in Latin until after the fourth century B.C.; *causa* and *cāsus* are words which we find written with double *ss* at an earlier period. This *ss* was simplified to single *s* after the change of *s* to *r*, so that this new *s* was not affected by the change; *miser* and *rosā*, and other words with *r* in the next syllable, did not undergo the change (this is sometimes known as PREVENTIVE DISSIMILATION). Finally, words like *nisī* and *dēsinō* 'I cease' were probably recombined from their constituent morphemes (including *sī* 'if', *sinō* 'I put', which had the *s* in initial position). As a result of this investigation, we can state precisely when *s* rhotocized to *r* and the exact condition under which it took place:

> Latin intervocalic *s → r* when there was no *r* in an adjacent syllable. The change was complete by the middle of the fourth century B.C.
>
> (Niedermann 1953, pp. 94–5)

Because so many sound changes are so regular, we now recognize regular sound change as one of the natural phenomena of language. As to *why* it is regular, we are still uncertain (but see 22.1).

21.4 GRAMMATICAL CHANGE

The traditional distinction between phonological and grammatical change depended on a view of language structure which many linguists would now consider obsolete. In the traditional view, sound change is that which involves *only* the physical side of language, and grammatical change is everything else. If we look at change, as most generative linguists do now, in terms of the ways in which the rules of a language are affected, then we can see that sound change affects not only low-level phonological rules (that is, those determining the occurrence of particular phonetic segments in certain environments), but also the more systematic morphophonemic rules (such as those dealing with high-frequency alternations like that between /s/ and /z/ in English plurals, etc.). In addition, the basic underlying shapes of morphemes are affected (e.g., the loss of initial /k/ before /n/ in English changed the basic shapes of morphemes like *knight, knot*).

The changes known as ANALOGIC CHANGES, classed traditionally as a type of grammatical change, have similar effects, among others. Analogic change is so-called because it can be explained as a proportional analogy of the type $X:Y::X_1:Y_1$, or "X_1 is to Y_1 as X is to Y": for example, when a speaker produces the form *growed* (or *knowed*) as a past of *grow* (or *know*), it is assumed that this is done "by analogy" with the more common regular verbs of the type *row:rowed, sow:sowed, tow:towed*, etc. ("*knowed* is to *know* as *rowed* is to *row*".) In languages with both irregular and regular morphological patterns in the same form class, the tendency to regularize the irregular forms is always present, and though many such regularized forms may be regarded as slips of the tongue, baby talk or "substandard" speech, some eventually are adopted by larger numbers of speakers and become part of the language. For example, the regular forms *dived, dreamed, burned* are nowadays considered respectable substitutes for the older *dove, dreamt, burnt*; similarly, Hindi-Urdu /kəra/, /kəri/ 'did' (masc., fem. respectively) are accepted alongside of the older irregular forms /kɪya/, /ki/ as the past forms of /kər/ 'do'. The Hindi-Urdu verbs have for the most part replaced older irregular forms with regularized ones, except for a small number of very high-frequency verbs: thus, the past of /mər/ 'die' is now normally /məra, məri/, and the irregular /mua, mui/ (from Sanskrit *mṛta*) is now found mainly in poetry.

The effect of such changes, as far as the individual words are concerned, is to change the membership of the classes to which morphophonemic rules apply. Thus the morphophonemic rule /o/ → /(y)u/ applies to the past forms of the verbs *know, grow, blow*; if any of these verbs is regularized it is removed from this particular class, and becomes a member of the large class of verbs to which no special rules apply. In other cases, a word may shift from one irregular class to another, or even from a regular to an irregular class: thus, one hears occasional forms like *brung* for *brought* (on the analogy of cases like *sing, sung*); in some cases the new irregular form becomes normal, as with the German word for 'tree', *Baum* /baum/, plural *Bäume* /boime/—in earlier German the plural simply added -*e* without the vowel change. (King 1969, p. 134).

Eventually, of course, some of the less frequent classes may disappear from the grammar entirely: this has almost happened with the English nouns which form the plural in -*n*, once a fairly numerous class including *shoe-shoon, eye-eyen*, but now reduced to *children, oxen*, and *brethren*. The complete loss of a category can be illustrated by the disappearance of the original Indo-European three-way gender distinction in English, though it is retained in German and some other languages (e.g., Gujarati and Marathi in India). In French and several other languages (including Hindi-Urdu), the old neuter gender disappeared, apparently through gradual erosion of individual words which were either lost, replaced or shifted in gender: e.g., Latin *bellum* 'war' was replaced by French *guerre* (fem.), of Germanic origin; L. *librum* 'book' changed to French *livre* (masc.). Thus analogic change, though not always regularizing, is generally in the direction of simplification of surface structure, in that it tends to reduce the number of differences. When new morphophonemic rules and categories are introduced through sound change (see 21.2) or through borrowing (see 22.2), in many cases the irregularities introduced are partially levelled by later analogic change.

In addition to the types of change mentioned above, which affect primarily the outward form of expressions, grammatical changes also affect the number and type of distinctions which can be made in the language. These can be discussed in general under headings similar to those mentioned for phonological changes: merger, split, loss and gain. Some large-scale changes involve various combinations of these.

A clear example of a MORPHOLOGICAL MERGER is the loss of the category of DUAL number in English. In the tenth century, English differentiated the following pronoun forms in the first person:

	Singular	Dual	Plural
Subject	ic(h) 'I'	wit 'we two'	we 'we (three or more)'
Possessive	min 'my/mine'	unker 'of us two'	ure 'of us (three or more)'

The dual forms disappeared during the thirteenth century, and probably were very little used for some time before that, except in the most conservative dialects. Since that time, the plural form has taken over the role of both dual and plural. Therefore, this can be described as a merger of two categories as well as a loss (since the structural distinction between dual and plural is lost).

The term SUPPLETION is given to a type of merger in which two (or more) forms each lose some of their allomorphs so as to coalesce into a single unit with highly irregular alternants. Such is the history of English *go*: *went*, whose past form originally belonged to the now archaic *wend*. Similarly, Hindi-Urdu /tha, thi/ 'was', now functionally the past form of the auxiliary /hona/ 'to be' (/hũ/ 'I am', /hɛ/ 'he/she/it is', /hẽ/ 'they are'), is originally from an entirely different verb (Sanskrit *sthā* 'stand', *tiṣṭhati* 'stands', Prakrit *thia* 'standing, upright').

Large-scale mergers of morphological categories have occurred fairly often as a result, apparently, of sound change. For example, the loss of the inflectional endings of nouns and verbs in English seems to be largely the result of a widespread loss of final syllables. In cases of this type, the loss of category distinctions is often compensated by the development of other devices. For example, the similar loss of noun suffixes in Indo-Aryan languages after the Prakrit period led to the development of a set of postpositions, which functionally replaced the old case endings (just as prepositions have taken over the same functions in modern French and English). In Sanskrit, case endings were used to express such relationships as possessive (*rāmasya* 'of Rama', *grāmasya* 'of the town'), dative (*rāmāya* 'to or for Rama'), ablative (*grāmāt* 'from the town'), instrumental (*rāmena* 'by Rama'), etc. As a result of wholesale loss of final syllables, this set of forms was reduced in modern Marathi to two: a general form without any ending (/ram/ 'Rama', /gav/ 'town, village'), and an "oblique" form (used with a following postposition) ending in /a/: /rama/, /gava/. Relations of the type formerly expressed by the case endings are now conveyed by postpositions, many of them derived from former noun or verb forms: e.g., /rama paši/ 'of Rama' (cf. Sanskrit *rāmasya pārsve* 'at the side of Rama'), /rama ca/ 'belonging to Rama' (cf. Sanskrit *rāmena citaḥ* 'acquired by Rama'), /gava la/ 'to the town' (cf. Sanskrit *grāmāya lagnaḥ* 'attached to the town'), etc.

The opposite of morphological merger is MORPHOLOGICAL SPLIT, which (like phonological split, see 21.2) usually involves the differentiation of two originally non-distinctive variants of a single word or morpheme: for example, *got* and *gotten* (distinguished in U.S. English, though not in standard British), *burned* and *burnt*, *learned* and *learnèd*, *drunk* and *drunken*, *blessed* and *blessèd*, were at one time free variants. *Effect* and *affect*, *capital* and *capitol*, *principle* and *principal*, *past* and *passed*, *ensure* and *insure*, *minute* /minit/ and *minute* /mayn(y)uːt/ were originally variant spellings or pronunciations which became specialized in particular meanings (to the everlasting grief of many generations of schoolchildren, who have had to learn to keep them separate).

When the disappearance of a form coincides with the disappearance of the meaning it denotes, it is appropriate to speak of LOSS. This most commonly occurs in cases of CULTURAL or TECHNOLOGICAL CHANGE, i.e., when certain practices become obsolete and are no longer referred to. For many speakers nowadays, much of the vocabulary referring to sailing ships, their construction and management, is for practical purposes extinct. Thus, terms like *frigate, brigantine, sloop, ketch, yawl, schooner, top-gallant, spanker, poop, dinghy, keelson, futtock*, and *strake* are, for most of us nowadays, mere relics of the romantic past, if we know them at all. The opposite process is of course the creation of new words or phrases, usually to denote technological innovations or new cultural features. Examples of such NEOLOGISMS, or newly-created terms, are: *plastic, blast-off* (of a rocket), *nutrino, lunar module, helicopter, up-tight* (overly tense), *jazz, junky* (a drug addict), *rapping* (a style of talking), etc. Another source of new items is BLENDING of existing items, for example: *terrocious* (= terrific + ferocious), *toffee* (= taffy + coffee), *insinuendo* (= insinuate + innuendo), *skyjacker* (= sky + hijacker).

21.5 SEMANTIC CHANGE

Grammatical changes of the types discussed above (merger, split, loss, neologism, blending) involve changes in the meanings of forms, as well as in grammatical rules and categories. The term SEMANTIC CHANGE, however, has been traditionally reserved for cases where the primary change is in the meaning, without obvious changes in grammatical behavior (except perhaps for detailed distributional differences). The most common types of semantic change, from this point of view, are: NARROWING or RESTRICTION of meaning, WIDENING or EXTENSION of meaning, and SHIFT or TRANSFER of meaning. Extension of meaning can be illustrated by the word *ship*, originally meaning 'seagoing vessel', also used as a verb in the meaning 'transport by ship'. In recent times, it has become possible to talk of *airships* and *space ships*, and nowadays we can "ship" articles by plane, train or truck. A "shipper" may never go near a ship except to take a vacation cruise.

When a term ceases to refer to a whole class of phenomena and only refers to part of that class, we say its meaning has been narrowed or restricted. The term *corn*, which in U.S. English refers only to maize, originally was a more general word for 'grain' and is related to Latin *grānum* 'grain, seed' (cf. German *Korn* 'grain'). A similar narrowing of meaning can be observed in the word /bhat/, the word for 'cooked rice' in several Indo-Aryan languages, from Sanskrit *bhaktam* '(that which is) eaten'.

Semantic transfer or shift involves applying a meaning in a new context. Thus we have the following meanings of the English verb *train* (cf. French *trainer* 'drag'): (1) to draw along, e.g., to drag something along the ground; to draw out, protract; to cause a plant (e.g., ivy) to grow in a certain way; to instruct, teach. The related noun shows a similar sequence of related meanings: trailing part of a skirt or robe; retinue of a royal or important personage; caravan; railroad train; train of powder, etc. In such cases, some of the ultimate meanings appear to have no connection with each other. Can we see any relation between the meaning 'teach, instruct' and the meaning 'railroad train'?

It is possible that transfer and extension are related processes. In any case, it is sometimes impossible to tell exactly how a change takes place. The verb *fix* first meant 'to make firm, to attach firmly' as in *the date is fixed*, *fix the dye*. The shift to the meaning 'repair' (*Daddy, please fix my dolly*) may have taken place in a context in which both meanings were possible (e.g., *fix the wheel* = 'attach the wheel in place' or 'repair the wheel').

The changes known as METAPHORS are similar to shifts, though they involve much more abrupt or dramatic changes in context. To *grasp* an idea is radically different from grasping an object. The similarity between the two is highly subjective. Similarly, when we use the term *soup* to refer to a thick fog, the two objects have little in common as compared with their differences. The essence of metaphor, then, is the emphasizing of marginal or non-essential aspects of meaning. When metaphor is innovative, it can be quite effective. For example, when a sentence like *Do you expect me to drive in this soup?* is uttered for the first time, its novelty may be enhanced by the mental picture of a car struggling through a viscous liquid. On the other hand, when a metaphor becomes fully accepted, it very quickly loses its dramatic force. Thus, expressions like *burn with anger, fall in love, break someone's heart, jump at a chance*, etc., though metaphorical in origin, now seem quite straightforward and undramatic.

NOTES

21.1. Specimens of earlier English: Algeo 1972, pp. 189, 135
21.2. English dual: Strang, pp. 261–263
21.3. Rhotacism in Latin: Niedermann 1953, pp. 94–95
21.4. Rule change: King 1969, Ch. 3

SUGGESTED SUPPLEMENTARY READING

Linguistic change (general): Bloomfield 1933, Ch. 22; Sapir 1921, Chs. 7–8; Hoenigswald 1960

Sound change: Martinet 1955; Bloomfield 1933, Chs. 20–21

Grammatical change: Bloomfield 1933, Chs. 23–24; King 1969

Semantic change: Stern 1931

Change in English: Pyles 1964; Algeo 1972 (workbook to accompany Pyles 1964); Strang 1970

FOLLOW-UP

Define or explain (with examples): merger, split, (phonological) loss, assimilation, dissimilation, metathesis, syncope, haplology, contraction, epenthesis, prothesis, analogic change, morphological merger, suppletion, morphological split, neologism, narrowing (of meaning), widening (of meaning).

Chapter 22

BACKGROUND FACTORS AND MECHANISMS OF LINGUISTIC CHANGE

22.1 INNOVATION AND DIFFUSION; INTERNAL VS. EXTERNAL FACTORS OF CHANGE

Any linguistic change, when viewed in its entirety, appears to be a complex response to a variety of factors. In principle it is possible to distinguish in each change a stage of INNOVATION, in which the change appears as a structural alteration in the usage of some group of speakers, and a stage of DIFFUSION, during which the change continues to be adopted by other speakers until it finally reaches its geographical and/or social limits. Many individual innovations (those we regard as slips, jocular forms, baby talk, etc.) are of course abortive, though some such changes (such as the regularization of the plurals of English *shoes*, *eyes*, or the past of Hindi-Urdu /mər/ 'die'—see 21.4) eventually gain acceptance, perhaps after decades or even centuries of alternation. The past forms of English *dive* (*dived*, *dove*), *dream* (*dreamed*, *dreamt*), etc., are examples of forms which are currently in a state of fluctuation.

Generally speaking, it seems probably that structural changes (such as phonemic split, merger, or loss, morphological merger or split, and changes in syntactic rules) involve fairly lengthy periods of fluctuation on the part of a whole segment of the population (such as the residents of a particular region or city, the members of a particular social group or age-group, etc.), before becoming definitive. The diffusion of a change to other groups (in the case of a complex speech community) will be dictated by the types of social contacts existing between the innovating group and other groups in the society (see 22.5).

Though it is clear that linguistic changes cannot be fully understood without knowledge of the social and physical circumstances in which they take place, linguists have sometimes found it useful to distinguish between the INTERNAL factors thought to be responsible for stimulating certain kinds of structural change, and EXTERNAL factors relating to the social or physical setting. Internal factors, which are presumed to be (at least partially) independent of the environment, and to relate primarily to the interaction between language structure and the speaker-hearer, appear to be of three major types: MECHANICAL (i.e., physiological or articulatory), PSYCHOLOGICAL (perceptual, productive, symbolic), and STRUCTURAL (pertaining to structural pressures within the linguistic system). Among mechanical factors, two very important ones are PHONETIC DRIFT (the tendency for allophones of a phoneme to change phonetically over time, and to vary from one group to another—cf. 18.2–3), and the tendency toward ARTICULATORY SIMPLIFICA-CATION (see discussion and examples in 21.2).

Though these two tendencies account for a lot of changes, there are many instances which escape the principle of simplification, and historical linguists have failed so far to come up with an adequate explanatory theory of phonological change. Certain trends are observable: for example, the tendency for unstressed vowels to be lost, for "unstable" consonants like [h] and [s] to disappear, for consonant clusters to assimilate (see 21.2), for tense vowels to become higher, for nasalized vowels to become lower, etc.

Greenberg has pointed out that the study of synchronic universals can lead to diachronic generalizations. For example, having noted the related facts that (1) all languages have vowels, (2) some languages have no nasal vowels, and (3) no language has more nasal vowels than oral (non-nasal) vowels, it makes sense to regard oral vowels as basic linguistic equipment and to ask the question, under what conditions does a language come to have nasal vowels, and why are they never greater in number than oral vowels? Asking the question in this way leads us to two diachronic generaliza-tions (1) Nasal vowels arise from the loss of an original nasal consonant adjacent to the vowel, after the development of non-distinctive nasalized allophones (e.g., Skt. *grāma* 'village' → *gām* → *gãm* → Hindi-Urdu /gãv/). (2) Merger between nasal vowels is more frequent than between oral vowels. (For instance, in contemporary Parisian French, the nasals /œ̃/ and /ɛ̃/ have merged in all but the most formal speech, whereas the corresponding oral vowels /œ/ (as in *peur* 'fear') and /ɛ/ (as in *père* 'father') are still quite distinct).

The late George K. Zipf, known for his study of frequency in relation to linguistic change, pointed out that the words of highest frequency in a language tend to be short, and that as words increase in frequency (as a result of semantic or grammatical change) they tend to shorten. This no doubt relates to our tendency to shorten the names of people we know well, but it has also been pointed out that this shortening can take place only in contexts where there is a great deal of redundancy (i.e., where there are relatively few possible choices).

In general, the tendency of speakers to simplify must be balanced by the need of hearers to obtain information from the signal, and it has been suggested that the need to maintain an equilibrium between these two opposing forces may account for certain trends in change. Thus, for example, the tendency of speakers to assimilate consonant clusters would be impeded or inhibited by the hearer's need for distinctness. According to this hypothesis, the most frequent consonant clusters in a language would be those which are neither maximally distinct (such as *tm, zk, pl*) nor minimally distinct (such as *tt, nn*). This hypothesis was supported by an examination of Spanish and English by Saporta. However, more study is necessary before this can be accepted as more than a promising possibility.

The possibility of SYMBOLIC factors in linguistic change has been raised by a number of studies. For example, a study by Labov of the speech of Martha's Vineyard (an island off the New England Coast) describes a number of features adopted by new arrivals who are motivated to imitate the speech of old-time residents. These include development of a mid central vowel as the first part of the dipthongs /ai/ and /au/, the use of a constricted /r/, and other variants involving greater oral closure. These variants may have been favored because they are symbolic of the "close-mouthed New Englanders" who are the original residents of the island.

In other cases, the symbolic value may inhibit a change. This appears to have happened in the history of Latin *h* in French, which was lost in most cases (as in *homme* /ɔm/ 'man') but survived in some words as the so-called "*h* aspirée". This functions morphophonemically like a consonant or juncture, in inhibiting the pronunciation of the final consonant of a preceding word: compare *les hommes* /lɛzɔm/, *les hibous* /le ibu/. An examination of the words with "*h* aspirée" shows that some of them (e.g., *halte* 'halt', *hareng* 'herring', *haie* 'hedge') are of Germanic origin, and therefore come by their *h* honestly. Some others, however, can only be explained as "expressive" uses of *h* (e.g., *hibou* 'owl', *hurler* 'yell', *hennir* 'whinny', *hoquet* 'hiccup', as well as exclamations such as *ha, ho, hi, hé, hein*).

A number of linguists have looked to structural pressures within the linguistic system for explanations of change. Perhaps the best-known application of this notion to phonological change is in the work of André Martinet, who invokes a principle of STRUCTURAL INTEGRATION ('intégration structurale') to explain changes like that illustrated below in the vowel systems of the French of Hauteville. It is easy to see that the changed system is more symmetrical than the first, but Martinet cautions against the assumption that a symmetrical system would be more stable than an unsymmetrical one, since other factors are always present. In short, the trend toward structural integration may be regarded as *one* of the factors of linguistic change.

French vowel system (Hauteville)

Earlier system				*Later system*			
i	ü	u		i	ü	u	
e	ẽ	ö	o	e		ö	o
ε	ɛ̃		ɔ̃	ε	ɛ̃		ɔ̃ ə
a	ã				a	ã	

After Martinet 1955, 86–88

Many changes can be regarded as having a COMPENSATORY value, in that they replace distinctions which are lost as a result of other changes. For example, fixed word order, as a device for marking syntactic relationships, developed in most of the modern languages of Europe, as opposed to the older system of "free" order (as in Latin and Greek). This change appears to have the function of compensating for the loss of information contained in the former inflectional endings of nouns. (See also the example of Indo-Aryan postpositions in 21.4.) Some examples of this process in more recent times have been noted by Labov, who points to two varieties of English which have lost final /t/ and /d/ by sound change, but have kept the past tense of verbs distinct by other devices: (1) in Scottish English, which has /æk/ for *act*, /æp/ for *apt*, etc., the past tense has the form /it/, so that the past forms of *lack* and *rap* are /lækit/ and /ræpit/ respectively; (2) in the English Creole of Trinidad and Jamaica (see 22.4), the sign of the past tense has been completely lost for all verbs, but the loss is compensated by the use of *do* to mark the present forms (e.g., *He tell me* = 'He told me', *He do tell me* = 'He tells me').

External factors include the physical and ecological environment, the social matrix of language and influences from other societies. Among the most significant changes which have been observed are those associated with the explosion in technology which has been going on for the past hundred years or so, though it seems likely that earlier technological revolutions (e.g., the change from a hunting-and-gathering economy to sedentary agriculture) may have had similar impact on the languages of the time.

Changes which took place in response to changes in external environment, as groups (such as the Indo-Europeans) moved from place to place, discovered new flora and fauna, and adapted to changed circumstances, must also have been extensive. In these cases, it is difficult to distinguish between the physical environment and contacts with other groups, since many of the changes may have entered as borrowings from other languages (next section). A systematic study of environmental factors in language change is yet to be done. Much more work has been done on the influences of other languages and other societies, and on forces within a society, in shaping the development of language.

22.2 LANGUAGE CONTACT AND BORROWING

Contact between speakers of different languages can hardly take place without producing at least a few cases of linguistic BORROWING, i.e., the transference of lexical items from one language into the other. In some cases the borrowing may be only transitory, and may affect only a few individuals—as, for example, when the crew of a ship spends a few days in a foreign port and picks up a few words of the local language for social and business purposes. In other cases, the borrowed items (called LOANS or LOANWORDS) may become a permanent part of the common speech of every individual—as in the case of words like *animal, because, fruit, mountain,* and *person,* which were introduced into English from French during the Norman occupation of England. In some cases the agent of the borrowing may have only the most superficial knowledge of the source language, as in the case of the boat's crew, or (in many cases) the administrators of colonial powers. In other cases, borrowed forms are transmitted through a large group of bilinguals—as was the case with medieval scholars who wrote in Latin, and over the centuries introduced masses of Latin words into various European languages. The same process took place with Sanskrit in India and in the Buddhist countries of Asia, and with Chinese in Japan and Korea, etc.

The French borrowings mentioned above also illustrate the point that the *range* of borrowed items (in terms of the social or semantic domains affected) correlates generally with the type and extent of contact between the two language groups. In the case of the Normans in England, who were thoroughly integrated into the local society, there is hardly any area of vocabulary that is not affected by French influence. By contrast, the impact of French on the vocabulary of German appears more in the public areas of lexicon (the arts, technology, scholarship, haute cuisine, etc.). Another important social factor is of course the relative PRESTIGE of the two languages (and those who speak them). This difference shows up in the comparison of English with French, which has borrowed relatively little from English until very recently.

The *motivation* for borrowing is the need for terms to denote new concepts or new cultural items. Thus, wine and brick tiles were new items for the Germanic speakers who borrowed the Latin terms *vīnum* and *tegula* (23.1). On the other hand, animals, mountains and fruits were not unknown to English speakers prior to the Norman Conquest, nor were *pork, mutton* and *beef* (cf. modern French *porc* 'pig', *mouton* 'sheep', *bœuf* 'head of cattle'), which were most likely referred to as 'pig meat', etc. In such cases, the reason for borrowing often relates to social prestige, though in the case of words like *animal* and *person*, the new word may also embody a new classification of already-known items (see 16.1).

Apart from introducing new vocabulary items into a language, borrowing may also bring in new phonological and morphological elements. This usually takes place as a cumulative result of many borrowings, and often involves a reinterpretation of features already in the language. For example, borrowings from French, and from Latin through French, with initial *v* (such as *vine, villain, village*) probably helped to create the split of English *f* into two distinct phonemes (note the alternation in *life–live*, etc., and cf. 12.5D). The presence of voiced and voiceless allophones of the original /f/ and the existence of a general voiced-voiceless contrast, must also have been contributory. (Note that Old English in general had no initial /v/, except for some southern dialects in which all initial fricatives were voiced.) The emergence of /zh/ (as in *rouge, garage, illusion, measure*), as distinct from /sh/ (which was original in English, cf. *shoe, bush*), is also directly attributable to French loanwords.

The development in English of productive suffixes (like *-able/-ible* in *capable, possible*) which can be freely combined with elements of Germanic origin (as in *breakable, knowable, teachable, unstoppable*), is due to the presence of many French loans with this suffix, but was no doubt also helped by the prior existence in English of suffixing as a grammatical device. When there is not such a good fit between the borrowing language and the source language, a certain amount of ADAPTATION may take place: for example, English words beginning with clusters like /st/, /sk/ (which do not exist in colloquial Hindi-Urdu) often appear with an initial vowel in Hindi-Urdu. Thus, *school* appears as /ɪskul/, *station* as /ɪsṭešən/, etc. The addition of new lexical items in the language often involves some restructuring of semantics, as the new words interact with the old. For example, when English borrowed French *pork, beef* and *mutton* (used originally in the context of courtly dining), this led ultimately to the creation of a contrast, which had not existed in either language before, between the name of an animal (*pig, cow, sheep*) and the name of the meat taken from it. (In French, it is still necessary to use expressions like *de la viande de porc* 'pig meat' when one wishes to specify clearly the meat rather than the animal).

22.3   CULTURAL CONTACT AND LINGUISTIC CONVERGENCE

In the majority of cases, linguistic borrowing has few profound effects on linguistic structure beyond proliferation of the lexicon. Structural changes of the type mentioned in the preceding paragraph are minimal, and in many cases affect only the usage of individuals in the higher social classes. For example, English speakers who have a distinct phoneme /zh/ in *garage*, *rouge*, or Marathi speakers who have a distinct /æ/ vowel in such words as /tæksi/ 'taxi' or /bæg/ 'bag' (which others pronounce as /tyaksi/, /byag/), are probably mostly upper-middle class.

At the opposite extreme from this type of linguistic influence are certain phenomena lumped together loosely under the heading of CONVERGENCE, which involve the development of structural similarities relatively independent of linguistic borrowing. Convergence in phonology is relatively common, often covering wide and politically disparate geographic areas. The indigenous languages of the Northwest Coast of North America, which represent numerous different linguistic stocks, share many phonetic features.

The countries of South Asia offer another example, which is all the more interesting since it is possible to investigate the earlier historical stages of those languages. One feature which is shared by most of the languages of the area, the retroflex–dental distinction in stops (also nasals, laterals, and spirants, in some cases), is an original Dravidian feature whose appearance in the Indo-Aryan languages follows the classical course of conditioned change. Dentals in certain circumstances became retroflex (e.g., after *r* as in Skt. *mrttikā → mrṭṭikā*), and with the loss of the conditioning environment (e.g., *mrṭṭikā → miṭṭikā*) the retroflex and dental came into contrast. Older literary sources, as well as the modern languages, show very few traces of loanwords from Dravidian, and so there is no possibility of ascribing this change to borrowing. In fact, it appears just like any other phonological change. The only problem is, how did this change happen to take place in Indo-Aryan when it did not take place in the related languages spoken in other parts of the world?

One possibility is to link this type of change with phenomena observable today such as "Irish English", or the English of Anglo-Indians in South Asia, whose native language is English, and who often do not speak the local languages well, but whose phonology is strongly influenced by them. (Such cases are different from foreign "accents" which result from interference of an individual's native language in his second language.) We know that, from a very early period, North Indian villages contained mixed populations consisting of Indo-Aryan and Dravidian speakers. Though they may have remained partly separate from each other, they were required to cooperate and communicate with one another in the interest of agricultural production and economic survival. Thus, while their home languages probably remained distinct (at least in the early period), they had to evolve some means of communicating with each other. This common medium was probably a language which appeared superficially like Indo-Aryan, but introduced many features (phonological, grammatical, and semantic) from the Dravidian and other indigenous languages. In these cases it is common to speak of a SUBSTRATUM language, whose features are carried over when the whole population changes its language at more or less the same time. Such convergence can also take place in areas of stable bilingualism, where there is a good deal of switching between languages (see below).

South Asian languages also provide plentiful examples of grammatical convergence. Although the languages in the area represent three distinct language families, the sharing of such features as word order, postpositions, patterns of verbal affixation and rules for sentence conjunction, make it possible very often to translate longish sentences word-for-word or even morpheme-for-morpheme from one language to another, even when there is little shared vocabulary. The matched sentences from Marathi (Indo-Aryan) and Tamil (Dravidian) given in Figure 22-1 illustrate this point.

Marathi:	t-o	mazh-ya	kəde	ye-un
Tamil:	ava-n	en	kiṭṭe	vant-u
*Gloss:	1-2	of me- 3	near	come-4

Marathi:	mi	t-ikḍe	za-ṇar	nahi
Tamil:	naːn	a-nke	poːh-a	maːṭṭ-en
Gloss:	I	5-place	go -6	not -7

Marathi:	mhəṇ-un	sangit-l-əː
Tamil:	n-u	son-n-aːn
Gloss:	speak-8	say -9-10

Translation: 'He came to me and said, "I will not go there"'

Figure 22-1. Matched sentences in Marathi and Tamil, showing grammatical convergence. (*1: a demonstrative stem, cf. Tamil /aval/ = Marathi /ti/ 'she'; 2: masculine singular ending; 3: Marathi oblique stem required by morphophonemic rules, not present in Tamil; 4: absolutive suffix: M /yeun/ = T /vantu/ 'having come . . .'; 5: demonstrative stem [cf. 1]; 6: Marathi future ending, Tamil infinitive suffix; 7: Tamil personal ending not matched by Marathi in this form [but cf. /tu zaṇar nahi-s/ 'You won't go']; 8: M /mhəṇun/ = T /(en)nu/ 'having said . . .' [cf. 4], used to indicate a direct quote; 9: past suffix; 10: personal ending [agrees with the subject in Tamil, but follows different rule in Marathi].)

Semantic convergence is also widespread. It is found not only in areas like South Asia where it is accompanied by grammatical convergence, but also in such areas as Europe, where (in spite of the existence of several different language families and sub-families, and in spite of diverse grammar and phonology) the intertranslatability from one language to the next is very high. (In fact, this intertranslatability may well have contributed to the naiveté with which some early European linguists were willing to attribute their semantic categories to the whole world.) It appears then that phonology, grammar, semantic structure and lexicon (i.e., the surface shapes of morphemes) are partially independent in the ways in which they respond to language contact.

One of the most extreme forms of convergence has been reported by John Gumperz in the region of contact between Indo-Aryan and Dravidian, where the local languages appear to have converged almost completely in all but lexicon. Their phonological systems are very close, they appear to have substantially the same phrase structure rules and many of the same transformational rules, and almost complete intertranslatability at the morpheme level, but the shapes of morphemes (as in the Marathi-Tamil example above) are mostly different.

22.4 PIDGIN AND CREOLE LANGUAGES

Cases of convergence like those mentioned above all appear to require a long period of cultural contact, and (in some cases at least) involve very close social relationships among the different linguistic groups—even to the point of cultural fusion. The languages known as PIDGINS, which provide some of the most fascinating examples of language contact phenomena, are of a different nature. They appear to be compromise languages used for limited purposes between groups which share no other language, and they generally developed in a very short period of time. They usually show a striking measure of reduction or simplification when compared with "normal" languages. They are a phenomenon of international trade, colonization and military conquest. (The term *pidgin* appears to have been first used with reference to the Pidgin English of the far eastern seaports, probably meaning originally 'business English'.)

Some pidgin languages have remained relatively stable for long periods, while others have died out after a few decades. A number of earlier pidgins have been adopted as the main languages of certain groups, and have developed into full-fledged languages with all the grammatical and lexical elaboration needed for normal human communication. When a pidgin language becomes the first language of some group, it is known as a CREOLE language (from French *créole* 'person of mixed European and colonial backgrounds'). A recent survey of pidgins and creoles by Hancock lists a total of eighty (including a number of extinct ones), mostly in the islands of the Caribbean, various Pacific islands and the coastal areas of Central and South America, Africa, southern Asia and New Guinea.

Cases of known pidgins and creoles range in antiquity from the extinct Sabir (Sabeir), a pidginized form of Provencal which was widely used during the Crusades and in various European ports during the later Middle Ages, to Melanesian Pidgin English, a well-documented English-based pidgin which originated about 100 years ago, grew during and after World War II, and is now in the process of creolization. Some creoles and pidgins have substantial importance in the areas where they are spoken. Haitian Creole French is the native language of over four million Haitians. The various English-based creoles of the Caribbean area (Jamaica, Trinidad, Honduras, Surinam, Guyana, etc.), though not all mutually intelligible, total over one million speakers. In Africa, Sango (a pidginized version of the Nagbandi language) is used extensively in the Central African Republic and neighboring areas, while Swahili has given rise to a number of pidgins in use in East Africa.

The following specimen of Melanesian Pidgin English (New Guinea) may give some idea of the ways in which pidgin languages deviate from their base languages:

> oltagedar mæn meri en i-kam bung. nau papa bilong meri, mama bilong em i-mekim bigfela kaikai tumach. nau mæn i-laik kichim meri, i slipim trifela ring, nau faivfela ring long bilum. em i-kartim i-kam long ples bilong meri ... mæn i-tok "disfela meri em i-samting bilong mi. em i-kartim pikinini, kukim kaikai, plætim taro, wokim oltagedar samting bilong meri"....

> ('All the men and women assemble. Then the woman's parents make a very big feast. Then the man who wishes to take the woman lays three or five rings in a net-bag. He carries them to the woman's village... The man says, "This woman is something of mine. She bears children, cooks food, plants taros, does everything pertaining to women"....')

> (Adapted from Hall 1944)

Since the 1950's, the creolized form of this pidgin (known as Neo-Melanesian) has become the subject of a controversy, with some scholars and officials vigorously supporting it as a lingua franca for the Trust Territory of New Guinea. Others have attacked it as a vulgar and degrading way of speaking which is inadequate for modern communication and serves to perpetuate colonial attitudes. There is no doubt that the language, in a variety of spoken forms, serves an important function in the Territory, though it has some distance to go before it can claim the status of a standardized literary language. There are news broadcasts in it, as well as a newspaper (*Wantok* 'one talk'). The following excerpt from a political education pamphlet illustrates its adaptability to the modern political scene. It also illustrates how easily artificiality can creep into a language which has been used primarily as a spoken medium, when it is first used for literary or official purposes.

> I tru memba i gat diuti o wok long elektoret bilong em. Em i mas toktok bilong ol pipal long dispela elektoret bilong em insait long House of Assembly, long wonem em i sanap bilong ologeta pipal long dispela elektoret, na i mas save gut long ol samting em ol dispela pipal i laikim....

> Official translation: 'Of course an Elected Member has responsibilities to his electorate. He must speak for his electorate in the House, because he represents all the people in that electorate, and he must fully understand what those people want....'

(Wolfers, in Hymes 1971, p. 415)

The following examples, from Jamaican Creole English, illustrate some of the variability that exists in Creole speech communities (see 20.2). This story was originally told in version B below, and then "translated" into versions A (maximally creolized) and C ("standard" Jamaican English, i.e., the usage of educated urbanized Jamaicans):

A Story In Jamaican Creole (from Bailey 1971)

Version A:
Wantaim, wan man en ha wan gyal-pikni nomo.
Im en niem Pini.
Im ena wan priti gyal fi-truu.
Im neba laik fi taak tu eni an eni man.
Im laik a nais buosi man fi taak tu.

...

Version B:
Wans opan a taim die woz a jengklman huu had wan uondli daata.
Har niem woz Pini.
Shi woz a gie an dandi gorl.
Shi didn laik tu taak tu eni an eni man.
Shi laik a gie fain man tu taak tu.

...

Version C:
Once upon a time, there was a gentleman who had an only daughter.
Her name was Peony.
She was a gay and dandy girl.
She didn't like to talk to just any man.
She liked (wanted) a gay, fine man to talk to.

...

Though there is ample data on the historical background of many of the contemporary pidgins and creoles, the processes by which they arose are not yet completely clear. The earliest theory of the development of pidgins, which has been dubbed the 'baby-talk theory' by some, held that pidgins developed as a series of recursive imitations. Speakers of the dominant group (usually Europeans) contemptuously imitated the desperate attempts of other speakers to approximate their language; these imitations were imitated in turn, and so on. This theory, which would lead us to expect *ad hoc* pidgins popping up in any contact situation, fails to explain the great similarities found among pidgins in their grammatical structure, and even their shared vocabulary (including grammatical function words).

Though some of the similarity in structure may be attributed to universal principles of simplification, it can also be shown that independent origin of all pidgins is not tenable. For example, a number of Spanish-based creoles have been shown on lexical evidence to have diverged from a common source, probably a Portuguese pidgin. On the basis of such data, a MONO-GENETIC theory of the origin of pidgin languages has been developed which holds that most or all of the European-based pidgins, and possibly others as well, can be traced back to a single proto-pidgin, which became differentiated in particular places at particular periods by a process of RELEXIFICATION (i.e., total, or nearly total, vocabulary replacement) based on the dominant language of the area. The proto-pidgin may possibly be identified with the extinct Sabir, whose first offspring may have been the Portuguese pidgin which was carried to the Far East in the sixteenth century, replacing Arabic and Malay as trade languages in various ports.

Proponents of this theory point to the fact that pidgins and creoles function commonly as lingua francas among speakers of different languages other than the base language, and that speakers of the latter often have to learn the pidgin from others (as white planters learned the Jamaican creole from slaves in the eighteenth century). The monogenetic theory would imply that the conditions for creation of a pidgin are very special and do not occur very often. Possibly something like the circumstances of the crusades, involving long periods of contact between groups of different backgrounds, is required. They would suggest that transplantation and relexification can occur more easily. Proponents of POLYGENESIS (independent parallel development of pidgins), on the other hand, argue that circumstances like those found in international trade or in the Caribbean slave communities, involving the need for limited communication, are sufficient to explain the present proliferation of pidgins and creoles.

The relation between pidgins and creoles is not as clear as it has been presented by some scholars, such as Robert Hall, who has maintained that all creoles have evolved from pidgins, thus completing a 'life-cycle'. Even in cases of recently developed creoles, it is difficult to trace out the development in detail. In cases of convergence like those mentioned in 22.3, it is not impossible that something like creolization took place, though it is possible to conceive that this happened without any intervening stage of pidginization. Thus there are still significant gaps in our understanding of the process of formation of pidgins and creoles.

22.5 SOCIAL PROCESSES IN LINGUISTIC CHANGE

Internal factors of change such as those mentioned in 22.1 may be sufficient to account for innovations arising in the speech of individuals. They do not provide an explanation for the ways in which changes are diffused from one group to another, nor perhaps even for the initial crystallization of a change within an innovating group. In any speech community which is large or diverse enough so that some speakers have little or no contact with other speakers, some regional and/or social variation can be expected to occur in response to internal factors of change. Gumperz's study of sociolinguistic variation in a North Indian village (18.3, Figure 18-4) indicates the way in which speakers who have close social contact with each other tend to imitate each others' speech. Apparently the same principle applies on a regional basis (18.2).

In such a situation, the majority of speakers belong to groups which are bounded by other groups (regional and/or social) with whom they have limited contact. Variations between adjacent groups are likely to consist mainly of slight allophonic variations, occasional differences in phonemic distribution or phonemic inventory, differences in surface grammar and differences in the shapes of individual lexical items (usually without great differences in semantic structure). These differences do not on the whole interfere with communication at all, though in a traditional society they serve the socially important function of identifying members of different groups and keeping them "in their place," both regionally and socially.

A situation of the type described can be upset by any change which leads members of one group to identify more closely with another group. A village man who travels frequently to a market town may learn some variants of the town speech and use them on return to his village. Individuals living in an urban area may imitate the speech of those belonging to a more privileged class. Persons settling in a new area may imitate the speech of long-term inhabitants. The important part of this process from the point of view of linguistic change is not only the diffusion of linguistic features to other groups, but the different kinds of relationships that can exist between the speech of the imitators and the imitated.

The importance of functional variation (see 18.2) in this process is probably extremely important. Though this type of variation is probably present to some degree in most speech communities, speakers are generally not aware of it and tend to conceptualize linguistic usage (both their own and others') in categorical terms. Thus the middle-class speaker in New York City believes that other people say *dese* and *dose* (instead of *these* and *those*), but excludes his own occasional stop or affricate from awareness. Thus, a speaker who has strong [r] constriction in his own speech, for example, when confronted with a speaker who has constriction varying from weak to none, may reinterpret what he hears as lacking constriction entirely.

In other cases, differences between two systems may lead to misinterpretation of forms. If two vowels are phonetically closer in dialect A than dialect B, a B speaker is likely to merge them in imitating A. The presence of different groups in competing situations may also set forces in motion leading to greater differentiation of the groups, as members of one or the other group attempt (consciously or unconsciously) to emphasize their distinctness. Differentiation may include (*a*) the favoring of non-imitated forms (such as the preference of forms like *I don't want any* over *I don't want none* among educated English speakers); (*b*) the avoidance of imitated forms (such as the movement of an allophone toward an articulation as far as possible from that used by speakers of a stigmatized variety); or (*c*) the replacement of the imitated form (possibly the explanation of the preference of British upper-class speakers for *napkin* over *serviette*, *looking-glass* over *mirror*, etc., mentioned in 14.8).

It is probable that the above processes take place more or less simultaneously within the innovating groups and then in some cases are diffused to other segments of the speech community. In some cases we can observe changes that have continued to diffuse until they reached the limits of a particular political or social boundary (such as the use of negative concord in NNE; see 20.2).

In other cases, the limit of diffusion of a particular change is determined by the presence of some other change. For example, the change /aj/ → /aː/, which spread from Central Yiddish into Southern Ukrainian Yiddish (so that /hajnt/ 'today' → /haːnt/), ended at just that point where a Northern Ukrainian change of /aː/ → /a/ took place (so that /haːnt/ 'hand' → /hant/). It is reasonable to assume in such cases that it was the need to avoid excessive homonymy that prevented the two changes from overlapping in any area. It has been pointed out, on the other hand, that the avoidance of homonymy is not a universal inhibitor of change. This is obvious if we look at languages like French, which has such sets of homonyms as *foi* 'faith'–*foie* 'liver'–*fois* 'time' (all /fwa/), *sceau* 'bucket'–*sot* 'fool'–*saut* 'jump' (all /so/), etc.

Large-scale linguistic changes, such as those involving extensive phonological or morphological mergers with compensating grammatical restructuring, probably are symptomatic of extensive changes in the social structure of the speech community. Since changes in intergroup relationships within the society appear to be one of the primary motivating forces in linguistic change and diffusion, it is possible that many instances of radical change took place in response to large-scale changes in the composition of the speech community as a whole. Though such questions have not yet been sufficiently studied, many cases of extensive change are known to have occurred during periods of great social upheaval. For example, the changes which took place in the transmission of Latin to the indigenous populations of Gaul and Spain are similar in general type (and often in specific detail) to the changes which took place in Indo-Aryan languages in contact with speakers of indigenous languages. The kind of changes which take place in the formation of pidgin languages are also similar, since they involve wholesale loss of phonological and morphological distinctions. Any comprehensive theory of change must take into account the possibility that processes like pidginization and creolization may have been much more common in the past than linguists have generally recognized. The few attempts which have been made to examine linguistic changes in the light of such social factors indicate that this is a very rich field for further research.

NOTES

22.1. Synchronic universals and diachronic generalizations: Greenberg 1963; Frequency and change: Zipf 1965; Frequency of consonant clusters: Saporta 1955; Symmetry of vowel systems: Martinet 1955; Compensatory changes for loss of past affix: Labov 1970, p. 58

22.2. English *f-v*: Strang 1970, p. 233, 288

22.3. Retroflex consonants in Indo-Aryan: Southworth (in Hymes 1971); Grammatical convergence of Dravidian and Indo-Aryan: Gumperz and Wilson (in Hymes 1971)

22.4. Survey of pidgin and creole languages: Hancock (in Hymes 1971); Melanesian Pidgin English: Hall 1943, Wolfers (in Hymes 1971); Jamaican Creole: B. Bailey (in Hymes 1971); Monogenetic and polygenetic theories: De Camp, Introduction (Hymes 1971)

22.5. Yiddish examples from Weinreich, Labov, and Herzog 1968, pp. 153–154

SUGGESTED SUPPLEMENTARY READING

Bloomfield 1933, Chs. 17–27; Weinreich, Labov, and Herzog 1968; Kiparsky (in Dingwall 1971)

Pidgin and creole languages: Hymes 1971
Language contact: Weinreich 1953

FOLLOW-UP

1   Define or explain: articulatory simplification, psychological causes of change, structural pressures for change, symbolic factors in change, linguistic borrowing, phonological adaptation (of loanwords), convergence, substratum language.

2   Distinguish: innovation—diffusion (of a linguistic change); internal—external (causes of change); pidgin—creole (language).

3   What are the different causes of linguistic change? What are the factors which lead to borrowing of words?

4   Can the structure of a language be changed as a result of borrowing?

Chapter 23

COMPARISON
AND RECONSTRUCTION

23.1 GENETIC RELATIONSHIPS

Some languages exhibit enough similarity to each other that the connection between them is obvious without any special knowledge or profound study. Thus, the student of Spanish who knows French will find it relatively easy to learn many words such as *uno, dos, tres* 'one, two, three' (F. *un, deux, trois*); *madre, padre* 'mother, father' (F. *mère, père*); *pobre* 'poor' (*pauvre*), *libro* 'book' (*livre*), etc. In other cases the relationship is more tenuous, though still apparent: *bueno/buena* 'good' (*bon/bonne*), *huevo* 'egg' (*oeuf*), *suerte* 'luck' (*sort* 'fate'), *obra* 'work' (*oeuvre*), etc.

There are still other cases which may not at first glance appear to be related at all, but which can be presumed to be so because they show RE-CURRENT (or SYSTEMATIC) CORRESPONDENCES. Such are, for example, those with initial *h* in Spanish (in writing only), which have French counterparts beginning with *f*: *higado* 'liver' (*foie*), *hija* 'daughter' (*fille*), *hambre* 'hunger' (*faim*), *hecho* 'done' (*fait*), etc. The recurrence of the same correspondence makes it highly improbable that the relationships are due to chance, even in the absence of superficial similarity. In this case we have historical documentation of the change from original *f* to *h* (Latin *fecatus, filia, fames, factus,* etc.).

In the case of languages whose earliest history is not known from written sources, resemblances such as these (whether superficially obvious or not) are primary evidence of earlier contact between the ancestors of contemporary speakers of the languages in question. Thus, if we compare the vocabulary of languages as distant as Hindi-Urdu and English, it is possible to establish evidence of earlier contact on the basis of recurrent correspondences like the following:

English *t* – two	ten	tooth	
Hindi-Urdu *d* – do	dəs	dãt	
English *f* – foot	five	father	
Hindi-Urdu *p* – pɛr	pãc	pɪta	
English *th* – tooth	three	father	
Hindi-Urdu *t* – dãt	tin	pɪta	

On this basis, there is no escaping the conclusion that the ancestors of the speakers of these two languages must have had something to do with each other in pre-historic times. On the other hand, a similar comparison of English and Tamil would yield only one resemblance (*eight*: *eṭṭu*), which is apparently accidental since there are no regular correspondences to support it.

Where it can be shown that resemblances are not due to change, there remain two possible historical explanations. Either the similarities are the result of GENETIC RELATIONSHIP (i.e., the languages being compared were originally forms of the same language, as in the case of French and Spanish), or they are originally distinct languages whose similarities are due to subsequent diffusion of features through contact (borrowing or pidginization-creolization; see 22.1–3). The presence of words like *vaiorin* 'violin', *erekki gita* 'electric guitar', or *tanku* 'tank' in the speech of some Japanese does not lead anyone to conclude that Japanese and English are genetically related. Therefore, in order to substantiate a hypothesis of genetic relationship, one must first exclude the possibility that resemblances are due to borrowing.

The most important kind of evidence for this is the presence of recurrent correspondences in the BASIC VOCABULARY, i.e., that segment of the vocabulary which is least subject to cultural differences. Though there are some controversial questions involved, there is a fair amount of agreement among linguists that words referring to certain universal activities, basic human relationships and common features of the natural world are the least likely of all lexical items to be borrowed. A sample list of 200 such words is given as an appendix to this chapter. Eight of the words on this list (*animal*, *because*, *flower*, *fruit*, *mountain*, *person*, *river*, *vomit*), or 4 percent, are of Latin–French origin, whereas over half of the general vocabulary of English is of French or Latin origin.

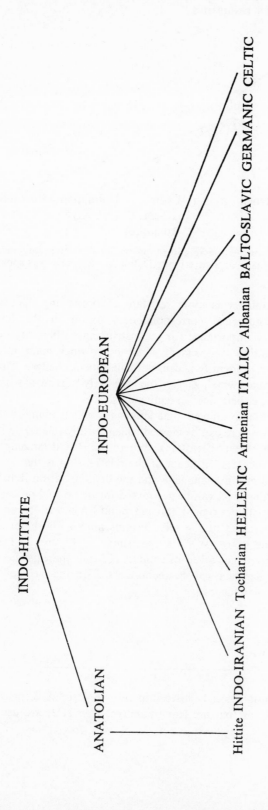

Figure 23-1. Family tree diagram showing the main branches of the Indo-Hittite family (sub-branches are given in capitals).

307

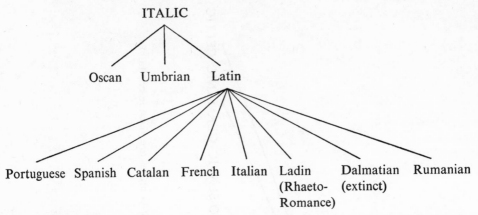

Figure 23-2. Family tree diagram showing the relationships of the Romance languages. (Rhaeto-Romance or Ladin is a language of Switzerland; Dalmatian formerly was spoken in Jugoslavia.)

Since the basic vocabulary is more resistant to borrowing than the general vocabulary, phonological correspondences found in the basic vocabulary are of primary importance for reconstructing earlier stages of the language. This precaution is necessary, since borrowings made at an earlier period may be hard to identify because of subsequent changes. Thus, such words as German *Wein* 'wine', *Ziegel* 'tile' are early borrowings from Latin (*vīnum, tegula*), as are their English equivalents.

Scholars have traditionally agreed that languages which manifest the type of resemblances shown here can be classed as genetically related and as descended from the same PARENT LANGUAGE. Where the parent language is not historically attested, the detailed proof of the relationship is the reconstruction of the presumed original language and the demonstration that the features of the daughter languages can be accounted for by normal processes of historical change from that original starting point. Where this can be done, it is customary to represent the relationships among the languages by means of a FAMILY-TREE DIAGRAM of the type shown in Figures 23-1 and 23-2. In these figures, the names given in capitals indicate the existence of presumed proto-languages, which can be reconstructed on the basis of the features of their daughter-languages.

23.2 RECONSTRUCTION

Linguistic reconstruction is basically history in reverse. It is made possible by the fact that distinctions that are lost by merger (see 21.2) are usually not lost in all environments or in all varieties. Reconstruction within a single variety of a language, known as INTERNAL RECONSTRUCTION, is possible in cases of partial merger: thus, the change $s \rightarrow r$ in Latin can be reconstructed on the basis of alternations like *flōs–flōr-is* (21.3); the change [voiced] → [unvoiced] / _____ (voiced consonants become voiceless in word-final position) in German can be reconstructed from alternations like *Bad–baden* (21.2).

COMPARATIVE RECONSTRUCTION is a very powerful tool because it makes possible the recovery of original contrasts which may have been subject to merger in one language but not in others. For example, the comparison of Latin, Greek and Sanskrit shows that one must reconstruct a merger of the three vowels *e o a* in Sanskrit:

Sanskrit	Latin	Greek	Proto-Indo-European Reconstructed Vowel
*a*sti 'is'	*e*st	ἐστί (*e*stí)	*e[1]
*a*ṣṭau 'eight'	*o*cto	ὀκτώ (*o*któ)	*o
*a*jras 'field'	*a*ger	ἀγρός (*a*grós)	*a

In other cases, the complexity of the changes in the various languages is such that no individual language gives a complete clue to the original situation. Such is the case with the stop consonants of Indo-European, as shown by the following examples:

Sanskrit	Latin	Greek	English	Proto-Phoneme
*p*itar- 'father'	*p*ater	πατήρ (*p*atĕr)	*f*ather	*p
*bh*ar- 'bear'	*f*erō	φέρω (*ph*érō)	*b*ear	*bh (?)
*tr*ayas 'three'	*tr*ēs	τρεῖς (*tr*éis)	*th*ree	*t
*d*aša 'ten'	*d*ecem	δέκα (*d*éka)	*t*en	*d
*dh*ā- 'place'	*f*aciō	θη- (*th*ē-)	*d*o	*dh (?)

In this case, the reconstructed system does not agree with any of the attested languages in inventory and arrangement of distinctive features. Latin shows only four distinct segments (*p, f, t, d*), and Sanskrit actually has a symmetrical system of eight stops (though the voiceless aspirates *th* and *ph* do not appear to reflect the situation in the parent language). Greek and English have the same number of phonemes as the proto-system in these cases, but the arrangement of distinctive features has apparently changed in both.

Such phonological reconstruction makes it possible to infer the approximate forms of many morphemes in the proto-language, and where sufficient

---

[1] The asterisk is used in historical linguistics to indicate reconstructed or inferred forms which are not actually attested.

forms have been retained, some of the morphology and morphophonemics can be reconstructed. Thus, in Indo-European it has been possible to reconstruct a good deal of the noun and verb morphology and to recover certain general morphophonemic processes such as that known as ABLAUT (vowel alternations apparently dependent on the placement of stress). Very little has been done in the way of reconstructing grammatical rules, as noted above. Some attempts have been made to use vocabulary, especially such semantic domains as kinship and words for flora and fauna and features of the physical world, in an attempt to learn something about the nature of the earlier society or to locate it geographically.

In the case of the Indo-European languages, it has been shown that one can get some notion of the structure of the family. It includes common terms for nuclear family members and for a woman's in-laws, but not for a man's in-laws, suggesting a patriarchal and virilocal joint family organization, i.e., one in which a woman became part of her husband's household. Largely by negative evidence (the absence of common reconstructible terms) one can infer the absence of a highly-developed official religion. There was apparently some personification of natural phenomena like the sky and the dawn, and some sort of domestic sacrificial meal can be inferred.

The original Indo-Europeans apparently knew Northern European trees (such as the birch, beech, aspen and oak), animals (dog, cattle, sheep, horse, pig, goat, wolf, bear, fox, eagle, thrush, hare, mouse, snake, salmon, otter, beaver), and insects (fly, hornet, wasp, louse, flea), but not those of India (such as elephant, camel, tiger) or the Mediterranean (donkey, olive, cypress). They knew copper and bronze, but not iron. This evidence has been regarded by some scholars as sufficient to place the home of the original Indo-Europeans in northern Europe (most specifically in the Baltic and North German plains) during the Copper and Bronze Age.

23.3 DATING

The method just described for estimating the time at which a parent language was spoken is only workable in cases where there is substantial evidence of cultural vocabulary available. A more general method, based on percentages of shared vocabulary, is known as GLOTTOCHRONOLOGY. It was pointed out above that the notion of basic vocabulary has been used as a criterion for determining the likelihood of certain features being inherited rather than borrowed. Later examinations of this assumption found out, surprisingly, that the basic vocabulary was not only more stable than the general vocabulary, but that the RATE OF DECAY (i.e., loss) of basic vocabulary items was fairly constant over time for a large number of languages.

Though this examination could only be done on languages which have long periods of recorded history, which necessarily involves mostly the Indo-European family, the amount of variation is surprisingly small. The thirteen languages examined all showed a retention rate (percentage of original vocabulary items retained) ranging between 74.4 percent and 86.4 percent per thousand years, or an average figure of 80.5 percent. Assuming that the rate is constant for all languages at all times is, of course, a big assumption, since there are numerous factors (such as migrations, conquests, creolization) which could affect the rate of change. On the other hand, using this average figure as a basis for computing depths of prehistoric contact between related languages gives us some sort of approximate dating technique, and we have nothing else comparable to it. (Estimating the speed of other types of changes, such as phonological or grammatical changes, is probably much less reliable.) For this reason, lexicostatistics has often been compared with the use of carbon-14 to estimate the time depth of archeological sites.

Given the percentage of vocabulary shared by any pair of languages, it is possible to compute the approximate probable time-depth of their point of common origin, using the assumption of 80.5 percent retention per thousand years. Following are examples of the approximate time depths which would be calculated on this basis:

Percentage of Shared Vocabulary	90%	80%	70%	60%	50%	40%	30%	20%	10%
Approximate Time-Depth in Years	250	500	800	1,100	1,600	2,100	2,800	3,700	5,300

It should be emphasized again that this is a very approximate method, and of course the margin of error is considerably higher at greater time-depths.

23.4   ORIGIN AND EARLY EVOLUTION OF LANGUAGE

If there ever was any hope that comparative reconstruction would provide information about the origin of language, this hope evaporated long ago— along with the hope that work in "primitive" societies would lead to the discovery of some rudimentary form of language. All languages which have been studied or reconstructed, with the exception of pidgins (see 22.4), are fully developed in the sense of having a rich vocabulary, complex phonology and varied syntax. Linguists have made this point repeatedly during the past fifty years. Edward Sapir, for example, wrote in 1921:

> ...we know of no people that is not possessed of a fully developed language. The lowliest South African Bushman speaks in the forms of a rich symbolic system that is in essence perfectly comparable to the speech of the cultivated Frenchman. (1921, p. 22)

Nonetheless, the myth of "primitive languages" keeps popping up repeatedly in scholarly literature and is often propagated by people who should know better but are content to display their ignorance. For a recent (1967) example, we may mention a Professor of English at the University of Michigan who appears to accept without question the report (which he claims to have read "somewhere in popular print") that the Vietnamese peasant has a vocabulary of "only two or three hundred words." (If we stop to think about it, we would realize that even the lowly profession of peasant requires more words than that, just for the purposes of communicating about rice cultivation.)

The search for "primitive" languages in human societies has been unsuccessful, and in the absence of any direct evidence on the origin of language, the best that can be done is to guess at some likely possibilities. The best guesses on the subject have been based on an examination of those non-human communication systems which are most similar to human ones, namely the call systems of the other hominoids, the gibbons and great apes, who are man's closest living relatives. Though we cannot assume that the proto-hominoids (the hypothetical ancestors of the known hominoids) had a call system of the same type that has been observed, say, among gibbons, we have to start with some such assumption or abandon the attempt altogether. This system has a number of the characteristics of human language. It uses the same vocal-auditory channel that human language does, which incorporates the property of TOTAL FEEDBACK (thus, the individual emitting a call is able to hear and monitor his own call, and presumably able to recognize the similarity between another's call and his own). The gibbon call system includes two dozen or so distinct calls, which appear to convey such recognizable messages as: "food available", "danger", etc. Since gibbons and other hominoids move in bands, some of these cries also appear to have the (supplementary?) function of indicating the location of individuals, thus keeping the band together and directing its movement.

Such call systems lack those crucially important features of human language (see 1.6) which we call PRODUCTIVITY, DUAL ORGANIZATION (or duality of patterning), and DISPLACEMENT. The gibbon call system is a CLOSED system, consisting of a certain number of calls, to which new ones cannot be added. In fact, even if new ones are added it would still remain a closed system, unless some mechanism is developed which allows for the creation of new messages. The gibbon's calls are HOLISTIC and unanalyzable lacking the property of dual organization. Each call is totally distinct from all others, and any acoustic resemblances are accidental and unsystematic. Thus, the "danger" call is recognized as soon as enough of it has been produced to make clear that it is not the "hunger" call or some other call. The property of displacement, essential for any sort of cooperative planning or for utilization of previous experience, is also absent from the gibbon call system. Thus it is clear that, if a call system of this type were to develop into human language, it would not only have to increase in size (i.e., number of calls), but would also need to develop new kinds of complexity.

Assuming that the proto-hominoids had a call system like that described for gibbons, how could the additional complexity have developed? Charles Hockett and Robert Ascher, in "The Human Revolution", have sketched how this might have come about as a series of innovations, similar to other types of biological adaptation, which began when the proto-hominoids began to change from being primarily forest-dwelling, tree-climbing vegetarians, toward a mode of life involving bipedal locomotion and hunting, in the savannahs of East Africa. The original impetus for this may have been a climatic change (for which there is geological evidence) which thinned out the forest, making it necessary for some bands of proto-hominoids to survive in open country.

On the whole, the open savannah was a less hospitable place than the tropical forest, since food was less plentiful and there was greater danger from predators. Such adverse circumstances in general would encourage any innovations which led to greater social cooperation. Thus, individuals capable of such innovations, and their descendants, would have a greater chance of survival. The development of upright posture freed the hands for carrying tools, weapons and food. This process in turn freed the mouth (which is needed for carrying when climbing) for other activities.

Certain important biological changes presumably were also taking place during this time, as a result of natural selection. From the point of view of the development of language, the most important were the development of larger, more convoluted brains with their greater storage capacity, and certain changes in the structure of the throat and larynx leading to greater articulatory dexterity. It is difficult to see how these biological changes can have been independent of the development of greater complexity of communication systems. The larger brain has certain biological disadvantages (such as the need for a greater blood supply), and therefore would be disfavored by the natural selection process unless it conferred clear advantages on its owner.

Hockett and Ascher suggest that the closed call system could have given way to an open-ended system only by some process of combining, or blending, two or more of the basic calls. Though this has never been observed among hominoids, it is conceivable that a proto-hominoid confronted by two stimuli would produce a blend of two different calls: say, the "hunger" call and the "danger" call. If such a blend were produced, and understood, often enough to enter the system, it would be more than just a new call. It would introduce a new principle of communication, making the system a potentially PRODUCTIVE one.

However, even if such a system continued to grow by the addition of new calls and the production of combined calls, it would still be limited to those messages which were sufficiently distinct to be discriminable and not too long to be effectively produced and understood. The introduction of DUALITY is the next major step and is comparable to the introduction of the rebus principle in writing systems, replacing picture-writing (see 8.1). How this developed is difficult to picture, but once a productive system was in use, the ability to make increasingly finer phonological distinctions would lead to a more varied and flexible communication system, which would clearly be advantageous for survival purposes.

It is probable that the process we have described happened only once. If so, this leaves us to account for the great diversity of the world's languages and the relatively greater diversity of some areas as compared with others. For example, the indigenous peoples of the Americas appear to have entered through the Bering Straits from Asia beginning about 27,000 years ago. At the present time, there is still no prospect of showing any interrelationships among the majority of these languages or of relating them to known languages of Asia.

It is conceivable that in the period between the appearance of language and the beginning of sedentary agriculture and permanent settlements, when human societies consisted of relatively small bands wandering in search of food and when generations were considerably shorter than today, linguistic change (which is probably as old as language itself) was relatively rapid. The process would have presumably been hastened even more if a group's external environment was undergoing constant change. Thus, when a band separated into two bands originally speaking the same language, it might not have taken more than a few thousand years for all traces of this original relationship to be erased. But as we pointed out before, we have no direct evidence on these questions, and it is possible we never will.

APPENDIX I

List of Words for Lexico–Statistic Dating ("basic vocabulary")

1. all	**3.** animal	**5.** at
2. and	**4.** ashes	**6.** back

7. bad
8. bark (tree)
9. because
10. belly
11. big
12. bird
13. to bite
14. black
15. blood
16. to blow (wind)
17. bone
18. to breathe
19. to burn (intr.)
20. child (young)
21. cloud
22. cold (weather)
23. to come
24. to count
25. to cut
26. day (not night)
27. to die
28. to dig
29. dirty
30. dog
31. to drink
32. dry (substance)
33. dull (knife)
34. dust
35. ear
36. earth (soil)
37. to eat
38. egg
39. eye
40. to fall (drop)
41. far
42. fat (substance)
43. father
44. to fear
45. feather (large)
46. few
47. to fight
48. fire
49. fish

50. five
51. to float
52. to flow
53. flower
54. to fly
55. fog
56. foot
57. four
58. to freeze
59. fruit
60. to give
61. good
62. grass
63. green
64. guts
65. hair
66. hand
67. he
68. head
69. to hear
70. heart
71. heavy
72. here
73. to hit
74. hold (in hand)
75. how
76. to hunt (game)
77. husband
78. I
79. ice
80. if
81. in
82. to kill
83. know (facts)
84. lake
85. to laugh
86. leaf
87. left (hand)
88. leg
89. to lie (on side)
90. to live
91. liver
92. long

93. louse
94. man (male)
95. many
96. meat (flesh)
97. mother
98. mountain
99. mouth
100. name
101. narrow
102. near
103. neck
104. new
105. night
106. nose
107. not
108. old
109. one
110. other
111. person
112. to play
113. to pull
114. to push
115. to rain
116. red
117. right (correct)
118. right (hand)
119. river
120. road
121. root
122. rope
123. rotten (log)
124. rub
125. salt
126. sand
127. to say
128. scratch (itch)
129. sea (ocean)
130. to see
131. seed
132. to sew
133. sharp (knife)
134. short
135. to sing

136. to sit
137. skin (of person)
138. sky
139. to sleep
140. small
141. to smell
    (perceive odor)
142. smoke
143. smooth
144. snake
145. snow
146. some
147. to spit
148. to split
149. to squeeze
150. to stab (or stick)
151. to stand
152. star
153. stick (of wood)
154. stone
155. straight
156. to suck
157. sun

158. to swell
159. to swim
160. tail
161. that
162. there
163. they
164. thick
165. thin
166. to think
167. this
168. thou
169. three
170. to throw
171. to tie
172. tongue
173. tooth (front)
174. tree
175. to turn (veer)
176. two
177. to vomit
178. to walk
179. warm (weather)

180. to wash
181. water
182. we
183. wet
184. what?
185. when?
186. where?
187. white
188. who?
189. wide
190. wife
191. wind (breeze)
192. wing
193. wipe
194. with
    (accompanying)
195. woman
196. woods
197. worm
198. ye
199. year
200. yellow

APPENDIX II

Principal Language Families of the World

AFRO-ASIATIC (also known as HAMITO-SEMITIC) (Africa and the Middle East): SEMITIC (Arabic, Hebrew; various extinct Middle Eastern languages, including Phoenician, Aramaic); Egyptian (extinct); CUSHITIC (fifty or more languages in East Africa); CHAD (West Africa, includes Hausa and over 100 others)

ALGONQUIAN (east coast and Great Lakes region of North America)

ATHAPASKAN (west coast of North America; Apache and Navaho in southwest of U.S.)

CAUCASIAN (Caucasus region; numerous languages of uncertain relationship)

DRAVIDIAN (South India): four major literary languages (Tamil, Telugu, Kannada, Malayalam) and others, including Brahui in Pakistan

FINO-UGRIC (western Europe): Finnish, Estonian, Hungarian

INDO-HITTITE (North America to South Asia, see Figure 23-1): Hittite (extinct); INDO-IRANIAN (IRANIAN: Persian, Pashto; INDIC: Hindi-Urdu, Bengali, Marathi, etc.); Greek; ITALIC (see Figure 23-2); BALTO-SLAVIC (BALTIC: Lithuanian, Lettish; SLAVIC: Russian, Polish, Czech, etc.); GERMANIC: English, German, Dutch, and the Scandinavian languages; CELTIC (Irish, Scots Gaelic)

KHOISAN (Hottentot-Bushman, southern Africa)

MALAYO-POLYNESIAN (Madagascar to Hawaii): Indonesian, Tagalog, Hawaiian, and many others

NIGER-CONGO (includes most of the languages of west and south Africa)

SINO-TIBETAN (China, Tibet, Southeast Asia): Chinese, Thai, Lao, Tibetan, Burmese

NOTES

23.2. Reconstruction of Indo-European lexicon: Thieme (in Hymes 1964)

23.3. Glottochronology: Gudschinsky (in Hymes 1964)

23.4. Language of "primitive" people: Sapir 1921, p. 22; Origin and early evolution of language: Hockett and Ascher 1964; language of the Vietnamese peasant (p. 312): Sheridan Baker, "The New English" (Council for Basic Education, Washington, D.C., 1967)

SUGGESTED SUPPLEMENTARY READING

Reconstruction: Hoenigswald 1950, 1960
Indo-European: Meillet 1937, Buck 1933

FOLLOW-UP

1   Define or explain, with examples where possible: recurrent (systematic) correspondence, genetic relationship, basic vocabulary, parent language, family-tree diagram, internal reconstruction, comparative reconstruction, glottochronology.

2   Write the numbers from one to ten in two related languages you know (preferably in phonemic form). Note the sound correspondences, and

then see if you can find other examples of the same correspondences. (Use the words listed in Appendix I to this chapter.) On the basis of the recurrent correspondences, decide what the probable form of each number was in the parent language. (It might be best to stick to consonants, at least to start with.) Illustration:

English	*German*
/wən/ one	/ain/ ein
/tuː/ two	/tsvai/ zwei

Correspondences: E /n/ – G /n/ (*stone*—G *Stein*)
E /t/ – G /ts/ (*toe*—G *Zehe*)
etc.

Proto-phonemes: /n/ → E /n/, G /n/
/t/ → E /t/, G /ts/
etc.

PART VI

APPLIED LINGUISTICS

Chapter 24

LINGUISTICS
AND LANGUAGE TEACHING

24.1 METHODS

In one sense the term APPLIED LINGUISTICS has a very broad application. It can be used for any area of inquiry where the findings of theoretical or descriptive linguistics may be applied to practical problems. Findings of theoretical linguistics have been fruitfully exploited by sociologists, psychologists, philosophers, anthropologists and demographers, to name a few. But the term applied linguistics is also used in a very specialized and narrow sense, to refer to the application of linguistics to LANGUAGE TEACHING, especially the teaching of a foreign language. In the past three decades or so, many language teachers, depending on the insights of descriptive linguistics, have come to believe that they have made great advances in the teaching of modern languages. Indeed, much of the impetus that linguistics received during and after World War II may be attributed to the involvement of linguistics in language teaching. In a sense, many of the advances made by modern linguistics were motivated by the need for developing effective techniques for teaching modern languages.

Foreign languages have been learned and must surely have been taught from the earliest times. Recently, languages of imperialist governments have been learned by the natives of colonized nations. For example, in British colonies in Asia and Africa, where English was the language of administration, the natives learned English. Whatever the methods of teaching, in recent times English has been taught most extensively to speakers of other languages. During World War II, a number of American linguists were called upon for the first time to teach foreign languages to large numbers of English-speaking people who were later deployed in parts of Europe and Asia. A number of these languages had never been studied by linguists, much less taught to large numbers of foreign learners. In order to teach them, the linguists had to write descriptions of them and devise materials for teaching them. The teaching methods employed at this time, though hardly formalized initially, soon came to be recognized as considerably superior to those used by earlier language teachers.

Before we outline the LINGUISTIC METHOD of teaching, as this method is called, it would be useful to describe briefly two other methods used widely before the influence of linguistics. Indeed, even now the linguistic method is by no means the only method that language teachers use. In a great many language schools in many countries, the older methods are still used, because the language teacher either is unaware of any new methods or has reasons to suspect the efficacy of the linguistic method. A word of caution will be in order here. Below, while describing methods of teaching, we look at each method in isolation. This is not to suggest that in any language teaching situation one method is used exclusively to the exclusion of all other methods. Any language teaching situation normally requires a judicious mixture of various methods and techniques. This is largely true because, while all the language teaching methods discussed below have been used with some degree of success, we do not yet know enough about how people learn a second language. Until we discover how human beings learn a second language and devise a method that best suits a second language learning-teaching situation, language teachers can only use the available methods as each particular learning-teaching situation demands.

One of the oldest methods of language teaching is the GRAMMAR-TRANSLATION METHOD. In this method the language teacher lectures to the learners in their native language on the grammar of the TARGET LANGUAGE (the language being studied). The teacher does not allow a student to use the foreign language and very rarely uses it himself. Typically, a student is required to recite and learn by rote things such as the conjugations of the irregular verbs in the foreign language. He seldom speaks or hears the language, but is expected to know its rules of grammar. He spends a good deal of his time translating sentences in the target language into the native language, with the help of grammatical rules and a dictionary, sometimes without understanding what he translates. Not surprisingly, students taught by this method often acquire a mass of grammatical information about the language, yet cannot speak a word of it.

As a reaction to the grammar-translation method, language teachers used the DIRECT METHOD of language teaching which reached a peak of popularity between the two world wars. In the direct method, the teacher, from the beginning, uses only the target language in class, helping the student to understand the foreign language with the help of gestures and stage props. He does not discuss or explain the grammar of the target language. He aims at *total immersion* of the student in the language. Although the lessons in this method are planned, they generally emphasize the new vocabulary rather than syntax. Unlike the grammar-translation method, the direct method can teach a student to speak and understand the target language, but it can be extremely inflexible and time-consuming.

24.2 THE LINGUISTIC METHOD

While the two methods discussed above are essentially teaching methods, the linguistic method is not so much a teaching method, as a procedure for organizing a language course based on linguistic analysis of the target language. This method has resulted from the practical experience of linguists in language teaching and from recent theoretical advances in linguistics. During World War II, when this method was first used on a large scale, it was popularly termed the MIM-MEM METHOD (MIMICRY–MEMORIZATION), in which a typical lesson consisted primarily of dialogues to be memorized and drills to be repeated after the teacher.

The linguistic method today, although it still emphasizes the mim-mem technique, has come a long way from the wartime language courses. The changes in the method over the last four decades have resulted from the advances made not only in theoretical linguistics but in psychology, particularly in the theory of learning. Linguists today, with the psychologists, have rejected the behaviorist theories of conditioned response (Cf. 13.3). A language student is no longer seen as a parrot memorizing a limited number of grammatical patterns, but is seen as a complex organism who plays an active part in the process of learning. A language course built on the linguistic method reflects the theoretical linguists' findings about the human learner's ability to generalize rules of grammar from the limited language stimulus he is exposed to and his ability to generate and interpret infinite numbers of novel sentences (see Ch. 13). A language course built on this technique today can be divided into five stages known as (1) RECOGNITION, (2) IMITATION, (3) REPETITION, (4) VARIATION and (5) CONTEXTUALIZATION.

The linguistic method, as we said above, uses drills to give the student practice in the patterns (grammatical, lexical and phonological) of the target language. The recognition stage is designed to develop in the language learner the ability to discriminate between two grammatical patterns, words or sounds. For example, an English speaker learning Hindi-Urdu may be given drills to recognize the difference between the following pairs:

1	(a)	vo pərega	'He will fall'
	(b)	vo pər^{h}ega	'He will read'
2	(a)	mɛ̃ roṭi k^{h}ata hũ	'I eat bread'
	(b)	mɛ̃ cavəl k^{h}ata hũ	'I eat rice'
3	(a)	mɛ̃ cavəl k^{h}ata hũ	'I eat rice'
	(b)	mɛ̃ cavəl k^{h}a rəha hũ	'I am eating rice'

In the first pair of sentences the learner must recognize the difference between the sounds /ɾ/ and /ɾ^h/, a distinction unlike any existing in English. In 2(a, b) the learner must recognize the difference between the two words /roṭi/ 'bread' and /cavəl/ 'rice'. And in 3(a, b) he must recognize the difference between two grammatical patterns /k^{h}ata hũ/ '(I) eat' and /k^{h}a rəha hũ/ '(I) am eating'. A recognition drill requires a beginning student to be able to tell only whether two sounds, words or patterns are the same or different. At this stage, the student does not imitate anything, but simply identifies what he hears.

In the imitation stage the student learns to produce in context, and with appropriate gestures, etc., what he has learned to recognize in the first stage. A dialogue or connected discourse is the best context for imitation. In this stage the teacher aims at effortless production, and is not satisfied until the student's response is accurate and spontaneous. Obviously, this stage has to do with the pronunciation of the target language. The earlier belief that it is impossible for an adult learner to speak a foreign language without an 'accent' is untrue. Well-written pronunciation drills, coupled with faithful imitation in context, can take the learner a long way in acquiring a near-native mastery over the pronunciation of the foreign language. However, being able to speak like a native may not always be a desirable goal, because it imposes a severe concomitant obligation on the learner. A native-sounding foreigner is expected by the native speaker to know everything about the language and the associated culture. A foreigner who sounds foreign is easier to forgive for any lapses than a foreigner who sounds native.

The imitation stage leads to the repetition stage, where the student practices the patterns in the target language without having to pay conscious attention to the pronunciation. Imitation and repetition, in fact, go hand in hand. As the sound system of the target language becomes a habit, the student is able to repeat patterns in the target language without conscious effort. A language course could, as many earlier courses did, stop with the repetition stage. At the end of this stage the student is equipped to produce a limited number of utterances in the target language with a near-native accent. He has enough command over the target language to be able to function in a limited number of situations: for example, hiring a taxi, asking for directions, shopping, etc.

If the student, however, wants to be able to use the target language in a real conversational situation, he must be able to operate in novel situations. Stages 4 and 5 are designed to help the student towards this level of control of the target language. In the VARIATION stage, the student is encouraged to generate new sentences in the target language on the basis of his knowledge of the patterns he has learned in the first three stages. Most modern courses employ three kinds of drills for this stage: SUBSTITUTION DRILLS, TRANSFORMA-TION DRILLS and COMBINATORY DRILLS.

Substitution drills require a student to hold a grammatical pattern constant and substitute lexical items in the various slots. For example, a student who has learned sentence 2(a) above may be asked to substitute /kʰana/ 'food', /səbzi/ 'vegetable', /dal/ 'lentils' for the word /roṭi/ 'bread' in the sample sentence. In a substitution drill, the teacher speaks only the sample sentences and gives the cue word to the student who provides the new sentences; for if the teacher repeats the new sentences, it becomes a repetition drill. More sophisticated substitution drills require the student to supply the various concomitant changes that the substitution of a lexical item entails. For example:

4   *a* mɛ̃ roṭi kʰata hũ   'I eat bread'
     b mɛ̃ dal kʰata hũ   'I eat lentils'
     c voh dal kʰata hɛ   'He eats lentils'
     d həm dal kʰate hɛ̃   'We eat lentils'

In 4c /voh/ 'He' requires /kʰata hɛ/ 'eats', and in 4d /həm/ 'We' requires /kʰate hɛ̃/ 'eat'.

In a transformation drill, the principal lexical items remain constant while the pattern changes. For example:

5   *a* mɛ̃ roṭi kʰata hũ   'I eat bread'
     b mɛ̃ne roṭi kʰai   'I ate bread'
     c mɛ̃ roṭi kʰaũga   'I will eat bread'
     d mɛ̃ne roṭi nəhĩ kʰai   'I didn't eat bread'

In a combinatory drill the student is required to combine two or more simple sentences into a complex sentence. For example, sentences 6 and 7 may be given to the student to combine into sentence 8:

6   mɛ̃ gʰər aya   'I came home'
7   mɛ̃ so gəya   'I slept'
8   mɛ̃ gʰər aya ər so gəya   'I came home and slept'

At a later stage the student may be required to combine the two sentences (6 and 7) differently (9):

9 mɛ̃ gʰər akər so gəya   'Having come home I slept'

When using any kind of drill, the language teacher has to be very careful and make absolutely certain his students know what they are expected to do. When the students do not understand what a drill requires of them, they are likely to miss the point of the drill and, indeed, they run the danger of practicing a wrong pattern.

Stage 5, called the CONTEXTUALIZATION stage, provides the student with the contextual information about the patterns he has learned to recognize, imitate, repeat and vary. Here the student learns when a given pattern may be used in a real communication situation; and he learns the semantic and social context in which he can use the utterances he has mastered. In one sense this stage runs parallel with stages 3 and 4, but the student has to master the importance of contextualization. For example, here the beginning student is taught that in Hindi-Urdu the second person plural pronoun /ap/ 'you (plural)' is also used in an honorific sense for second person singular reference. In this stage, too, the student learns to make judgments about the appropriateness of the use of utterances he knows in a given situation. In short, here he learns to respond in the foreign language as a native speaker of that language would, as in the following Hindi-Urdu example:

Teacher: mɛ̃ kya kər rəha hũ?	'What am I doing (now)?'
Student: ap həmɛ̃ hɪndi pəṛʰa rəhe hɛ̃	'You are teaching us Hindi.'
Teacher: mɛ̃ne kəl apko hɪndi pəṛʰai tʰi?	'Did I teach you Hindi yesterday?'
Student: ji nəhĩ, kəl ɪtvar tʰa	'No. Yesterday was Sunday.'

24.3 CONTRASTIVE GRAMMAR

Designing and teaching a language course on linguistic principles involves three discrete and sequenced operations: SELECTION, GRADING and PRESENTATION. The preceding section concentrated on presentation, i.e., the actual teaching of a language course, which is the result of the application of the first two operations.

A human being never really stops learning his native language. While a human child has mastered the basic grammatical (including semantic and phonological) pattern of his language by age six, he continues to learn his language throughout his life by using it in social context and by imitating the innovations that other speakers of the language introduce into the language. (Indeed, every speaker of a language is capable of introducing innovations in his own speech, regardless of whether these are absorbed by the language or not.) The linguist is aware that no realistic foreign language teaching course can aim at teaching the total language. The only effective way of learning the entire language would be through total exposure to the language in its natural setting. Any course that provides formal instruction in a classroom situation must, therefore, aim at teaching only a part of the foreign language.

There is no one unique part of any language that a foreign language course can aim at *ad hoc*. What part of the foreign language should be emphasized in a given course depends on the ultimate use to which the learner is going to put the foreign language. It is not difficult to conceive that the learner may need the language for a very limited or specialized use. For instance, an English-speaking learner may want to learn Russian in order to read technical and scientific journals in Russian, while another may want mainly to understand spoken Russian. The courses for the two learners would be vastly different; the first course would aim at teaching a formal written variety of Russian with a predominantly scientific and technical vocabulary, while the second course would emphasize colloquial spoken Russian with no specialized vocabulary. The two courses would also be different at the levels of syntax and phonology. For instance, the former would have a large number of complex sentence patterns, while the latter would concentrate on simple sentences and phonology with proper emphasis on the role of intonation in spoken Russian.

Whatever the goal of a language course the course designer (here a linguist) has to *select* a definite part of the target language to be included in the course. This first operation, SELECTION, is often made on the basis of REGISTER. Register is a term used in applied linguistics to indicate the uses to which a language is put—informative, occupational, emotive. A particular language course may aim at teaching only one register in the target language. For example the first of our hypothetical courses in Russian would aim at teaching the register of science.

A register, in turn, is analysable into various STYLES, having to do with the formality or otherwise of the situation in which a given register is employed. (Style also reflects the social variation in language use; see Ch. 18.) Broadly speaking, two styles, FORMAL and INFORMAL, may be subsumed under each register.

Many language courses are designed to teach a specific register. For instance, one may have a course in Spanish for businessmen, or scientists, or tourists, and so on. Each register has a typical range of grammatical patterns and lexical items that it employs. For instance, in scientific register it would be unusual to find the first person singular pronoun. Since the selection for a language course is normally based on register, it is obvious that every course will have a typical range of grammatical patterns and lexical items as its teaching goal. For example, a course in English for speakers of Hindi-Urdu which seeks to teach the register of commerce would emphasize grammatical patterns (if any) that are peculiar to the language of business, vocabulary that has to do with commerce, and the format of business letters, contracts, bills, etc. American Peace Corps volunteers, who learn the language of the host country, are usually given specialized courses which relate to their field of work, e.g., agriculture, social medicine, family planning, animal husbandry, small business management, etc.

Once the operation of selection has been carried out, the linguist has an inventory of grammatical patterns, lexical items and phonological patterns that he must incorporate in the language course that he is constructing. At this stage it is essential to know the order in which these various patterns should be introduced in the course. In order to determine this order the linguist performs the second operation, viz. GRADING. Under this operation the linguist's task is to arrange the selected items in an order that will present the least difficulty for the learner and facilitate his learning of the foreign language. For grading the teaching points the linguist has several possibilities open to him. He may decide to introduce the basic grammatical patterns and the most common vocabulary in the earlier lessons, and leave the more complex patterns and specialized vocabulary for the latter part of the course.

By and large the linguist carries out the operation of grading on the basis of principles of CONTRASTIVE ANALYSIS, or contrastive grammar, which involves the contrasting of the grammatical analyses of the two languages— the native language and the target language. By this process the linguist is able to determine the areas where there is divergence between them. Normally, contrastive grammar should be based on descriptive grammars of the two languages. In practice, however, this is rarely done; many such grammars are merely listings of common errors made by the foreign learner, with a rationalization for these errors on the basis of the learner's native language.

Contrastive grammar is a useful tool that a linguist can use in designing a language course. At every level of language organization the linguist can attempt to anticipate the areas of difficulty that the student is likely to encounter. An examination of the sound systems of English and Hindi-Urdu, for example, would reveal that aspirate sounds of Hindi-Urdu (e.g., $/p^h$, b^h, t^h, d^h, c^h, j^h, k^h, g^h,$/$) may be troublesome for the English learner. The linguist, therefore, introduces these sounds in the course at the appropriate stage and provides adequate practice for the acquisition of these sounds in the recognition, imitation, etc. stages.

On the other hand, he allots relatively little time to sounds like /m, n, s/ which are common to both the languages. For instance, in English the present continuous tense is commonly used for future reference, e.g., *John is going to New York tomorrow*, while in Hindi-Urdu the present continuous is very rarely used for future reference. In Hindi-Urdu future time is indicated by future tense, e.g., /mohən kəl dılli jaega/ "Mohan + tomorrow + Delhi + will go". The Hindi-Urdu course would take cognizance of this difference between the two languages and drill the English learner in the use of the future tense in Hindi-Urdu. In an English course for Hindi-Urdu speakers the course would emphasize the distinction between the simple present and present continuous tense, in order to prevent the Hindi-Urdu learner from using the English present continuous tense for present reference other than as in *John is eating his lunch* (*now*). Such judgments can be made at all the levels of language organization, and consequently, the language course concentrates on areas of greatest practical importance from the point of view of the student.

The foregoing would lead one to conclude that a language course need only emphasize the differences between the two languages, while the similar structures are automatically transferred from the native language to the target language. In fact the situation is not so simple. Many linguists and language teachers believe that it is the structures that are similar in the two languages that need greater attention than those that are different. They argue that structures that appear to be similar often have different distributions in the two languages. Not being aware of these subtle differences, the student is likely to transfer the sound, word or pattern in its entirety from his native language to the target language. Those who support this view also argue that it is easier to teach a new sound or pattern than to change the distribution of an old sound or pattern.

Contrastive grammar, which has its supporters and detractors, is an excellent tool for building a language course on sound linguistic principles. However, a contrastive grammar has to be used most cautiously. It can never be used as a device for *predicting* the errors that the foreign learner will make in the target language. For example, by merely comparing the grammar of English and Hindi-Urdu one might be tempted to predict that a Hindi-Urdu speaker will use the typical SOV (Subject–Object–Verb) pattern in English, which has SVO (Subject–Verb–Object) as a typical pattern. As a matter of fact, it has been observed that while Hindi-Urdu speakers make a variety of errors in English, they seldom or never use the SOV pattern for the SVO pattern. We cannot predict because we understand so little about TRANSFER in learning and the level at which transfer, particularly negative transfer (i.e., INTERFERENCE) takes place in a second-language learning situation. Specifically, it is not known whether transfer involves the deep structure or the surface structure of the two languages, or the deep structure of one and surface structure of the other. At best, contrastive grammar can show areas in the target language where the student may find some difficulty.

Apart from its importance in applied linguistics, contrastive grammar has made significant contributions towards our understanding of language universals. It has shown areas of overt and covert similarities between various languages, providing insights into possible similarities among all human languages. For instance, there is some evidence that the deep structure of all languages is similar, and that only the transformational rules are different, thus accounting for surface differences in languages. The exact nature of this universal deep structure can be discovered by comparing different languages. For example, on the basis of such comparison, it is believed that the formal unit *BE* as in *John is tall* is a surface structure element rather than a deep structure element. One is led to such a conclusion because several languages do not have the element BE in their surface structure.

After selection and grading the language course goes through the third operation: PRESENTATION, which has to do with the actual writing of the teaching materials, including the dialogues and the drills, etc., and the presentation of the lesson in the class. We have already discussed in some detail above (24.2) the presentation of lessons in the linguistic method.

24.4 WRITTEN LANGUAGE

So far we have said nothing about the introduction of reading and writing in a foreign language course. It may be inferred from our discussion in 24.2 that a language course is essentially spoken. We have deliberately kept written language out of our earlier discussion, because linguists are sharply divided on its place in a language course. Many believe that written language should be introduced as late as possible, whereas others believe that it should be introduced as early as possible. The stage at which it is introduced must depend on the purpose of the language course and the age of the learner. For instance, in a spoken course, the introduction of writing becomes relatively unimportant. However, in any formal language course, written language would seem to play an important role, especially if the target language has a written tradition. If a foreign learner is able to read and write the foreign language, no matter what the purpose of the course, he is able to operate in the target language independently of the classroom teacher. For practical reasons, therefore, written language should be introduced in a language course at as early a stage as possible.

24.5 TRANSLATION

As a reaction to the old and inefficient grammar-translation method (see 24.1), the modern language teacher has tended to take an extreme position and reject translation altogether. The language teacher's mistrust of translation is easy to defend, for translation can become a dangerous tool if it is not used judiciously. While totally relying on translation will not teach a student to use the language very effectively, the teacher who uses it judiciously can only make his course more useful. As a matter of fact, contrastive grammar implicitly relies on translatability between the two languages. Translation at the level of form, e.g., English Adjective + Noun = Hindi-Urdu Adjective + Noun (as in *fat girl* = /moṭi ləṛki/), forms the basis of selection and grading. Strictly speaking, it is lexical translation that is misused in the grammar-translation method, in that word-for-word translation correspondences are set up in the two languages. A discovery of translation correspondences in the two languages at various levels of language organization can only help the linguist build a more realistic language course.

Also, the importance of translation for testing the achievement of the learner in the target language can hardly be discounted. At advanced levels in language teaching, translation from the target language to the native language and vice versa may be found very useful.

24.6 NATIVE LANGUAGE TEACHING

It is clear from what we have discussed so far in this chapter that linguistics has made a significant contribution in the field of foreign language teaching. Compared with the field of SECOND LANGUAGE teaching, the contribution of linguistics to the field of FIRST LANGUAGE teaching is negligible. Here the linguist has a lot to learn from the researches of modern psychology— especially research in language acquisition. With the linguist and psychologist working together, there is room for hope that in time we will be able to understand the complex mechanism of language acquisition.

The theories of language INNATENESS and the generative capacity of the human child have greatly modified the earlier behaviorist theory of language learning (see 13.3). While the linguist and the psychologist are both convinced of the validity of these new theories, the school teacher often continues to think of language learning as conditioned response. It is true that there is always a gap between a theory and its application to practical problems, but the gap between linguistics and native language teaching has an immediate and direct influence on language instruction.

In most school systems, nearly half the school time is spent on the use of the mother tongue. When the student reads the literary masters in the language, he learns how creative writers have exploited the structure of the language for their purpose. When he is asked to write something himself, the aim is to teach him to manipulate the resources of his language; he learns how to express himself precisely and unambiguously. On a purely linguistic level ambiguity in language can be accounted for in terms of basic patterns and transformations; as also innovative use can be explained in terms of the novel combinations of existing semantic and grammatical features of the language. The traditional exercises in parsing and sentence analysis, no doubt, aimed at making the student aware of the grammatical pattern of his language. Of course, as it happened with traditional grammar, such exercises may become prescriptive and prevent the student from really understanding how the language works.

Another aspect of native language teaching where the linguist can assist the language teacher has to do with social dialects (see 18.3, 19). Social and regional differences in a language that is spoken by a large number of people spread over an extended geographical area is a natural phenomenon. Not only in large societies, but even in urban areas there are always sharp distinctions between the language varieties used by different social classes. In fact, language serves as a mark of both social differentiation and social identification. Often language becomes an awkward index of one's social class. The school teacher often has 'popular' notions of standard and sub-standard language. He is generally intolerant of "sub-standard" dialects and attempts to impose the standard variety on his students.

The role of the linguist in describing the standard language cannot be exaggerated. The linguist can write contrastive grammars of the standard dialect and the non-standard dialects and help the language teacher understand the relationship between the two. For native language teaching a contrastive grammar need only point out where the non-standard dialect is different from the standard dialect. There is, at present, a lot of work being done on the non-standard urban dialects in American cities. The results of this research help provide better structured language courses for speakers of non-standard English in these cities. In a country like India where it is a national policy to achieve universal literacy, and where a large section of the population (especially the older generations) is illiterate, linguistic research helps devise language courses that aim at the adult learner who is learning to read and write his native language. (See 25.2 for some further comments on the linguist's role in educational policy.)

SUGGESTED SUPPLEMENTARY READING

Allen 1964

FOLLOW-UP

1   Define or explain: applied linguistics, linguistic method (of teaching languages), grammar-translation method, direct method, mim-mem method, contrastive analysis, transfer, interference.

2   Discuss the relative merits of the three methods of language teaching described in 24.1. Do you consider any method complete in itself, or do you feel it is necessary to use features of more than one method? (This discussion will be more meaningful if, instead of simply discussing your feelings about the different methods, you try to show with specific examples how one method is likely to be superior to another.)

3   Select a teaching point from a language you know (e.g., the use of the "partitives" *des* and *du*, as opposed to the definite articles *les* and *le/la*, in French; the placement of the verb in German; the use of the subjunctive in Spanish). Prepare a set of drills based on the five teaching stages presented in 24.2. Use as many of the different types of variation drills (substitution, transformation, and combinatory) as the subject matter will allow.

Chapter 25

LANGUAGE PLANNING

25.1 LANGUAGE PROBLEMS

The need for language planning at the government level arises when decisions must be made about the choice of language, or the form of a language, to be used in state education systems, mass media (especially when these are government-run), official meetings, government publications, etc. In most parts of the world where such decisions have needed to be made, the need has arisen out of bilingualism or multilingualism, that is, situations where the same political unit encompasses sizable groups speaking distinct languages. Countries ·or regions with DIGLOSSIA such as Greece, Norway, Denmark or Ottoman Turkey have also seen fit to deal with their language problems at the national government level. But many of the newly-independent countries of the world (such as India, Pakistan, Ceylon, Guinea, Ghana, Kenya, Tanzania, Congo), as well as older countries (such as Belgium, China, Switzerland, Canada, Ethiopia, Mexico, Paraguay) have linguistic "problems" created by the presence of mutually unintelligible forms of speech. In the case of former colonies the language of the former rulers was generally installed as an official language and survives (in varying degrees in different places) as a prestige language. The range of linguistic diversity covers, at one

334

extreme, countries like Canada with a minority group (nineteen percent) of French speakers concentrated in a fairly limited area of the country (Quebec and other eastern provinces); at the other extreme, we find African countries like Ghana with forty-five languages.

The variety of official solutions adopted to deal with these situations is also considerable. Belgium has two official languages, French (spoken by forty-two percent of the population) and Flemish/Dutch (fifty-three percent), and all official documents, notices, etc., must be printed in both languages. The medium of education in schools, on the other hand, is French in the French-speaking southern part of the country, and Dutch in the northern part. Switzerland, with its three official languages (German, French and Italian), has a similar policy, though the minority Italian-speaking group sometimes gets lost sight of. For example, the legally required Italian version of official documents is often omitted. Canada, since confederation 100 years ago, has had two official languages, English and French. The Official Languages Act of 1969 was aimed at ensuring that any citizen can deal with government agencies in either language, even in regions where very little French is spoken. It provides that all districts with ten percent or more of minority-group speakers (French or English) be designated as bilingual districts. In those districts, schools and other government services must be provided in both languages.

India has officially designated "Hindi" as its national language, though English continues to be used extensively at the level of national government, in the courts, and in higher education. Ghana has adopted nine of its forty-five languages as national languages. Two neighboring African states, Kenya and Tanzania, which are both characterized by triglossia involving English, Swahili, and various regional languages (see 18.4), adopted different solutions for various internal political reasons. Tanzania adopted Swahili as its national language, though the displacement of English has been limited mainly to symbolic functions like public notices, stamps and coins, etc. Kenya, on the other hand, has made no official decision about a national language. At least two reasons can be given for this difference. First, Tanzania has a much larger number (102) of distinct ethnic and linguistic groups than Kenya (13), which means that multilingualism in Tanzania is more widespread, with less marked linguistic rivalry among different groups. In addition, in Tanzania Swahili has become linked to the dominant political party, with its socialist policies and anti-imperialist image, whereas such a link has not been possible in Kenya, because of its present economic orientation.

These few examples may indicate that the notion of "one country, one language" is not always feasible or even desirable. Language is so closely associated with cultural and religious identity that, while speakers of different languages will sometimes function together as a political unit, they react very strongly when they suspect that their cultural or linguistic identity is threatened. Throughout the world today linguistic minorities are clamoring for linguistic and cultural identity—the French in Canada, Sindhis in Pakistan, Dravidian speakers in India, the Welsh in Britain, and so on. Socio-culturally speaking, it would seem to be legitimate for these minorities to seek to protect a cultural and linguistic identity which they fear is endangered by the existence of a national language which might eclipse them. Frequently linguistic minorities oppose the national language on purely economic grounds, since they fear that native speakers of the national language would have an edge over others in getting positions in the professions and administration. The resentment of the Dravidian speakers against Hindi as the national language is often interpreted in these terms. While it seems to be in the national interest for a large multilingual country to have a single national language, it would appear to be extremely difficult and dangerous to force on the minorities a language that is not generally acceptable. In this context, such a policy, if insensitively applied, might be regarded as "internal colonialism." Furthermore, it provides an ideal pretext for local politicians to exploit the language issue for their own ends.

Many "language problems" turn out, on closer examination, to be the surface manifestations of socio-economic or political conflicts. Language is often a convenient pretext for trying to win power over a rival group, and there are many ways of making such a course of action appear justifiable. In countries where several languages have a respectable literary tradition, the speakers of each language tend to consider their language superior to the others and the only fit candidate for the status of national language. If groups begin to vie with each other on this basis, their competition may take the form of escalating the classical features of their own languages in an effort to make them appear more "respectable." When this happens, the losers are the uneducated rural people, who find it harder and harder to get an education as the medium of education gets more and more inaccessible to them. Thus, such a situation has the function of maintaining an elite group.

Within one's own group, it is usually possible to mobilize opinion around the language issue by pointing out the beauty or expressiveness of the group language, or its appropriateness and authenticity as a symbol of nationhood. In the case of languages with a literary tradition, its advocates may stress the literary achievements in the language or the length and respectability of its history. Such arguments are, by and large, irrelevant to the issue at hand, though they may be effective for mobilizing support and creating a local power base. (At the same time, they may be effective in isolating the lower classes in neighboring areas from each other.) If members of a particular language group wish to use their own language within their own area for any purpose, this would seem to be sufficient justification for doing so. (Problems may of course arise in terms of the degree of standardization of the language, availability of teachers, textbooks, etc.) When, on the other hand, one group seeks to impose its language on another, then arguments about literary merit or beauty, etc., are equally irrelevant.

An important task for the linguist (or perhaps we should say for the sociolinguist) is to educate both the public and the planners about the different roles of language. In spite of the prevalence of multilingualism in the world, and the existence of multilingual states such as Ghana or Switzerland, many people appear to believe in the "one country, one language" model, at least to the extent of feeling that there should always be a single main national language. Situations like that of Paraguay or Tanzania (see 18.4), in which there is widespread multilingualism with the different languages serving different social functions, are not generally known. It may be that some such solution as this, at least in the short run, is the only feasible alternative in many cases.

Another potentially useful role for the linguist is in demonstrating that historically related languages are greatly similar, rather than completely different as the speakers of these languages often believe. In India, for instance, it would be helpful for people to see how most Indian languages in reality have descended from two or three parent languages. It is also interesting to note here that, in a country with more than one language family, common areal features often develop in time through mutual borrowing of lexicon and grammatical structure. This is true of India, where common linguistic features exist in both the Indo-Aryan family and the Dravidian family of languages (see 22.3). This could possibly foster a feeling of oneness among the speakers of related languages.

In the field of education, the linguist can devise courses for the teaching of the national language and train language teachers in the teaching of native language, second language, and the national language. In a country like India where the national policy is to teach three languages to every school-going child, this is being achieved by setting up language institutes with the help of the government of India.

25.2 THE PRACTICAL ROLE OF THE LINGUIST

It is far from self-evident that the linguist has an important role to play in the formulation of official language policy. In fact, linguists and disciples of linguistics who have assumed this have overlooked several important points. First of all, and obviously enough, the very notion of APPLIED LINGUISTICS implies that we are not dealing with linguistic structure in isolation, but are venturing into real life, where a variety of socio-economic forces exist which push in a number of different directions at the same time. While linguists can provide information about linguistic structure, they are only beginning to understand the various factors (historical background of social groups, political allegiances, socio-economic pressures, etc.) which determine the social *functions* of particular linguistic variants (see 18.3, 19). In fact, linguists have been generally uninterested in such matters until recently. We should not imagine that it is enough to provide descriptions of the various forms of language used in a particular community. Such information is largely irrelevant in influencing language policy decisions, which are made primarily on political grounds.

In general, language policy (like any other official policy) is strongly influenced by group political interests, which in turn are heavily influenced by economic pressures and by the type of economic system existing in the society.

Even when decisions have been made at the official level, this does not mean that the troubles are over. As in the implementation of any official policy, there are likely to be many slips, many delays and many detours. In a discussion of language planning in India, Das Gupta has pointed out how bureaucratic constraints, fiscal limitations and problems of balancing competing priorities have delayed and diluted the implementation of India's national language policies. There is also a genuine question whether government language policy can have any effect at all on the language situation. We do not yet have enough information to measure the impact and direction of specific language policies, since language planning at the official level is too new. It is clear, on the other hand, that (as Joan Rubin has put it in the concluding chapter of her book *Can Language be Planned?*): "Attempts to change language habits may serve to reveal otherwise latent conflicts in other socio-political realms."

When specific instances of conflicts are examined, it becomes clear that rational implementation requires information collected and analyzed by a number of specialists, including not only linguists but also political economists, sociologists and social anthropologists. It is only within the last few years that linguists involved in language surveys and censuses have begun to seriously concern themselves with the definitions of the concepts about which information is needed. If we seek to understand the linguistic situation in any area, particularly the ways in which it affects communication, we cannot simply go about asking people questions like "What language(s) do you know?" We need to have definitions of such concepts as native speaker, language competence and functions of language which are appropriate to the area being studied.

Some linguists appear to feel that such questions as those mentioned here are not their concern, and that it is up to others to apply the findings of linguistic study in practical domains, to the extent that they are applicable. Such a statement is perfectly valid in the sense that linguistic research must be allowed to continue independently of any practical concerns, if it is to be intellectually valid. But for those concerned with applications at all, there are two major flaws in this argument. First and most obviously, no scientific principles can be applied meaningfully without the collaboration of the specialist who has a deep understanding of them.

The other point is less obvious and concerns the attitudes of linguists toward language and its place in society, and the reflections of these attitudes in their work. The quote from Bloomfield at the beginning of Chapter 19 gives an indication of the role of the traditional grammarian in nineteenth-century England, and his remarks can be applied equally to the work of grammarians in other times and places (for example, the grammarians of ancient Greece and Rome). The work of grammarians has been traditionally normative (or prescriptive) and elitist (rationalizing and supporting the status of traditional elites). Modern linguists, especially in the American tradition, have claimed to be free of these vices, but the work of many linguists shows that they still have some distance to go. For example, linguists have generally given lip service to the notion that all forms of a language are equally deserving of study, but many linguists have in recent years shown by their actions that only the educated standard forms (such as they use themselves) are of interest for research. And though linguists have also supported the notion of linguistics as a descriptive rather than a prescriptive field of study (see Chapter 1), many recent articles attest to the survival of the notion that the capricious and irrational usage of particular social groups (or even particular individuals) can have a logical and consistent explanation.

A major problem in this regard is the linguist's notion that he, as a specialist, is uniquely qualified to speak for all users of the language. Actually the truth is close to the reverse of this, since the linguist's concern with language tends to be with its form, whereas those who use the language in the routine of daily life are concerned primarily with its social function. Thus, the only thing that would qualify the linguist to speak for others would be not his own interest and usage, but his ability to observe and report accurately on the usage of the speech community as a whole. Unfortunately, very few linguists have concerned themselves with such matters, though the number appears to be growing with the rise of interest in sociolinguistics.

25.3 CAN LINGUISTICS BE RELEVANT?

As linguists have begun to concern themselves with the sorts of questions discussed here, it has become more and more obvious that there is a need for an integrative field of study which would include linguistics (i.e., the study of language structure), sociolinguistics (the study of language in its social context), and language planning and the implementation of language policy. Such a field would not involve merely the application of principles derived from theoretical studies in practical domains, but would also involve the creation of an overall theoretical framework. It would bring to bear an understanding of linguistic structure and language use on questions of policy-making, and at the same time would make use of information about use and policy in understanding linguistic structure and its evolution.

Such a field would prepare linguists to approach problems of the types discussed in 25.2 and 25.3, by training them to be aware of the various social processes influencing language use, by developing approaches to linguistic study that are more sensitive to these processes, and by making empirical studies to determine the value and applicability of strategies for change. This would involve questioning certain assumptions that are commonly made. For example, the linguist need not assume automatically that the only educational strategy available in linguistically stratified societies is to impose the elite "standard" usage on the whole population. He might consider alternatives such as a pluralistic strategy, which would attempt to give each group passive control over the usage of other groups, or a compromise strategy which would promote a composite standard.

In analyzing linguistic structure, a useful approach might be to make multiple analyses, each one taking the usage of a certain group as its fundamental structure and viewing the usage of other groups from that vantage point. In cases where alternative descriptions of the linguistic data are possible within existing theory, it may be useful to attempt to resolve the indeterminacy by using the different analyses as the basis for different educational strategies. If one strategy turns out to be superior in an empirical test, this could lead not only to a resolution of the particular case, but possibly also to the formulation of generalized guidelines for a whole category of cases.

The need for the linguist's expertise in planning linguistic surveys is becoming well established. It is perhaps not yet recognized, on the other hand, that linguists have any substantial contribution to make in formulating and testing planning strategies. This recognition will come only when linguists have demonstrated its necessity. This task will be made easier to the extent that work in theoretical linguistics reflects facts of language use such as those discussed here.

NOTES

25.1. Turkey: Gallagher (in Rubin and Jernudd 1971); Denmark: Haugen (in Fishman et al 1968); India: Das Gupta and Gumperz (in Fishman et al 1968); Guinea: Armstrong (in Fishman et al 1968); Ethiopia: Bender et al, 1972; Paraguay: Rubin 1968; Congo: Polome (in Fishman et al, 1968); Mexico: Wolf 1959, Ch. 3; Tanzania, Kenya: Whiteley (in Rubin and Jernudd 1971, Fishman et al 1968)

SUGGESTED SUPPLEMENTARY READING

Rubin and Jernudd 1971; Fishman, Ferguson, and Das Gupta 1968

FOLLOW-UP

Suggestions for class discussion:

1 What is the potential for linguistics in solving practical problems like those discussed in this chapter? (Is training in linguistics likely to be useful for those concerned with such problems?)

2 In what other areas is linguistics likely to make practical contributions? (See 16.6, Chapter 19.)

BIBLIOGRAPHY

Abercrombie, David. 1966. Elements of general phonetics. Chicago: Aldine; Edinburgh: Edinburgh University Press.

Abdulaziz-Mkilifi, M. H. 1972. Triglossia and Swahili-English bilingualism in Tanzania. Language in Society 1.197–213.

Agard, Frederick B., and Robert J. Di Pietro. 1965a. The sounds of English and Italian. Contrastive Structure Series. Chicago: University of Chicago Press.

——, and ——. 1965b. The grammatical structures of English and Italian. Contrastive Structure Series. Chicago: University of Chicago Press.

Albert, Ethel M. 1964. "Rhetoric," "logic" and "poetics" in Burundi: culture patterning of speech behavior. In Gumperz and Hymes 1964.

Algeo, John. 1972. Problems in the origins and development of the English language (2nd ed.). New York: Harcourt Brace Jovanovich.

Allen, Harold B. (ed.). 1964. Readings in applied English linguistics (2nd ed.). New York: Appleton-Century-Crofts.

——, **and Gary N. Underwood.** 1971. Readings in American Dialectology. New York: Appleton-Century-Crofts.

Andrew, R. J. 1963. Evolution of facial expression. Science 1963.1034–1041. Also, Bobbs-Merrill Reprint A-256.

Atwood, E. Bagby. 1950. *Grease and Greasy*—a study of geographical variation.

Studies in English (University of Texas), 249–260. Also, Bobbs-Merrill Reprint Language-2.

Bach, Emmon. 1964. An introduction to transformational grammars. New York: Holt, Rinehart & Winston.

———, **and Robert T. Harms** (eds.). 1968. Universals in linguistic theory. New York: Holt, Rinehart & Winston.

Barker, George C. 1947. Social functions of language in a Mexican-American community. Acta Americana 1947.185–202. Also, Bobbs-Merrill Reprint A-5.

Bender, Marvin, L.; R. L. Cooper; and Charles A. Ferguson. 1972. Language in Ethiopia: implications of a survey for sociolinguistic theory and method. Language in Society 1.215–234.

Bendix, Edward Herman. 1966. Componential analysis of general vocabulary: the semantic structure of a set of verbs in English, Hindi and Japanese. Bloomington: Indiana University; The Hague: Mouton.

Berlin, Brent, and Paul Kay. 1969. Basic color terms: their universality and evolution. Berkeley and Los Angeles: University of California Press, (reviewed by Nancy P. Hickerson in IJAL 37.257–275 (1971)).

Bernstein, Basil B. 1958. Some sociological determinants of perception. British Journal of Sociology 9.159–174.

———. 1960. Language and social class. British Journal of Sociology 11.271–276.

———. 1961. Aspects of language and learning in the genesis of the social process. Journal of Child Psychology and Psychiatry 1.313–324. Reprinted in Hymes 1964, 251–260.

———. 1964. Elaborated and restricted codes: their social origins and some consequences. American Anthropologist 66 (No. 6, Part 2). 55–69.

———. 1972. Social class, language and socialization. In Giglioli 1972.

Bickerton, Derek. 1971. Inherent variability and variable rules. Foundations of Language 7.457–492.

Birdwhistell, Ray L. 1960. Kinesics and communication. In Carpenter and McLuhan 1960, 54–64.

———. 1972. A kinesic-linguistic exercise: the cigarette scene. In Gumperz and Hymes 1972, 381–404.

Bloch, Bernard, and George L. Trager. 1942. Outline of linguistic analysis. Baltimore: Waverly Press.

Blom, J. P., and John Gumperz. 1972. Social meaning in linguistic structures: code-switching in Norway. In Gumperz and Hymes 1972, 407–434.

Bloomfield, Leonard. 1927. Literate and illiterate speech. American Speech 2.432–439. Reprinted in Hymes 1964, 391–396.

———. 1933. Language. New York: Holt, Rinehart & Winston.

———. 1942. Outline guide for the practical study of foreign languages. Baltimore: Waverly Press.

Bolinger, Dwight. 1968. Aspects of language. New York: Harcourt, Brace & World.

Bright, William (ed.). 1966. Sociolinguistics: proceedings of the UCLA sociolinguistics conference, 1964. The Hague: Mouton.

Brown, Roger W. 1958. Words and things. Glencoe, Ill.: Free Press.

———. 1970. Psycholinguistics. New York: Free Press.

———, **and Eric H. Lenneberg.** 1954. A study in language and cognition. Journal of Abnormal and Social Psychology 49.454–462. Also, Bobbs-Merrill Reprint P-54.

———, **and Albert Gilman.** 1960. The pronouns of power and solidarity. In Sebeok 1960, 253–276. Also, Bobbs-Merrill Reprint A-274.

———, **and Marguerite Ford.** 1961. Address in American English. Journal of Abnormal and Social Psychology 62.375–385. Reprinted in Hymes 1964, 234–244.

Buck, Carl Darling. 1933. Comparative grammar of Greek and Latin. Chicago: University of Chicago Press.

Carpenter, Edmund, and Marhsall McLuhan (eds.). 1960. Explorations in communication. Boston: Beacon Press.

Carroll, John Bissell. 1953. The study of language: a survey of linguistics and related disciplines in America. Cambridge, Mass.: Harvard University Press.

——— (ed.). 1957. Language, thought and reality: selected writings of Benjamin Lee Whorf. Cambridge, Mass.: Technology Press; New York: Wiley.

Catford, J. C. 1965. A linguistic theory of translation. London: Oxford University Press.

Chafe, Wallace L. 1967*a*. Language as symbolization. Language 43.57–91.

———. 1967*b*. Seneca morphology and dictionary. Washington, D.C.: Smithsonian Press.

———. 1970. Meaning and the structure of language. Chicago: University of Chicago Press.

Chai, Nemia M. 1971. A grammar of Aklan. University of Pennsylvania Ph.D. dissertation.

Chase, Stuart. 1938. The tyranny of words. New York: Harcourt, Brace & World.

———. 1954. The power of words. New York: Harcourt, Brace & World.

Cherry, E. Colin. 1961. On human communication: a review, a survey and a criticism. Science Editions. New York: Wiley; Cambridge, Mass.: Technology Press.

Chomsky, Noam. 1957. Syntactic structures. The Hague: Mouton.

———. 1965. Aspects of the theory of syntax. Cambridge, Mass.: M.I.T. Press.

———. 1972. Language and mind. New York: Harcourt Brace Jovanovich.

———, **and Morris Halle.** 1968. The sound pattern of English. New York: Harper & Row.

———, ———, **and Fred Lukoff.** 1956. On accent and juncture in English. In Halle 1956, 65–80.

Condon, John C., Jr. 1963–65. Bibliography of general semantics. Part I in Etc.: a review of general semantics 20.86–105; Part II in Etc. 20.312–339; Part III in Etc. 21.73–100; Part IV in Etc. 22.59–86.

Conklin, Harold C. 1955. Hanunóo color categories. Southwestern Journal of Anthropology 11.339–344. Reprinted in Hymes 1964, 189–192. Also, Bobbs-Merrill Reprint A-42.

———. 1962. Lexicographical treatment of folk taxonomies. International Journal of American Linguistics 28. In Householder and Saporta 1962, 119–141.

———. 1972. Folk classification: a topically arranged bibliography of contemporary and background references through 1971. New Haven, Conn.: Department of Anthropology, Yale University.

Cowan, George. 1948. Mazateco whistle speech. Language 24.280–286. Reprinted in Hymes 1964, 305–310.

De Saussure, Ferdinand. 1916. Cours de linguistique générale. Paris: Payot. (Translated by Wade Baskin, Course in general linguistics. New York: Philosophical Library, 1958.)

Devereux, George. 1951. Mohave Indian verbal and motor profanity. In Róheim 1951, 99–127.

Dingwall, William Orr (ed.) 1971. A survey of linguistic science. College Park, Md.: University of Maryland Linguistics Program.

Dyen, Isidore. 1956. Language distribution and migration theory. Language 32.611–626.

Ervin-Tripp, Susan. 1964. An analysis of the interaction of language, topic and listener. In Gumperz and Hymes 1964, 86–102.

Farrell, Ronald A. 1972. The argot of the homosexual subculture. Anthropological linguistics 14.97–109.

Ferguson, Charles A. 1959. Diglossia. Word 15.325–340. Reprinted in Hymes 1964, 429–438.

———. 1964. Baby talk in six languages. In Gumperz and Hymes 1964, 103–114.

Fillmore, Charles J. 1968. The case for case. In Bach and Harms 1968, 1–88.

———, and **D. Terence Langendoen** (eds.). 1971. Studies in linguistic semantics. New York: Holt, Rinehart & Winston.

Fischer, John. 1958. Social influences on the choice of a linguistic variant. Word 14.47–56. Reprinted in Hymes 1964, 483–488.

Fishman, Joshua A. 1968. Readings in the sociology of language. The Hague: Mouton.

———; **Charles A. Ferguson; and Jyotirindra Das Gupta.** 1968. Language problems of developing nations. New York: Wiley.

Fleisher, Mark S. 1972. The possible application of ethnosemantics to prison argot. Anthropological Linguistics 14.213–219.

Friedrich, Paul. 1966. Structural implications of Russian pronominal usage. In Bright 1966.

Fodor, Jerry A., and Jerrold J. Katz. 1964. The structure of language. Englewood Cliffs, N.J.: Prentice-Hall.

Frake, Charles O. 1961. The diagnosis of disease among the Subanun of Mindanao. American Anthropologist 63.113–132. Reprinted in Hymes 1964, 192–206.

———. 1962. The ethnographic study of cognitive systems. In Gladwin and Sturtevant 1962, 72–85.

Fries, Charles Carpenter. 1952. The structure of English: an introduction to the construction of English sentences. New York: Harcourt, Brace & World.

Gelb, Ignace J. 1952. A study of writing: the foundations of grammatology. Chicago: University of Chicago Press.

Giglioli, Pier Paolo (ed.). 1972. Language and social context. New York: Penguin Books.

Gladwin, Thomas, and William C. Sturtevant (eds.). 1962. Anthropology and human behavior. Washington, D.C.: Anthropological Society of Washington.

Gleason, H. A., Jr. 1965. Linguistics and English Grammar. New York: Holt, Rinehart & Winston.

Goffman, Erving. 1963. Behavior in public places. Glencoe, Ill.: Free Press.

Goodenough, Ward H. 1956. Componential analysis and the study of meaning. Language 32.195–216. Also, Bobbs-Merrill Reprint A–91.

———. 1957. Cultural anthropology and linguistics. In Paul L. Garvin (ed.). Report of the seventh annual round table meeting on linguistics and language study. (Monograph Series on Languages and Linguistics, No. 9.) Washington, D.C.: Georgetown University Press. Reprinted in Hymes 1964, 36–39. Also, Bobbs-Merrill Reprint Language-29.

Greenberg, Joseph H. 1954. Concerning inferences from linguistic to non-linguistic data. In Hoijer 1954, 3–19. Reprinted in Saporta 1961.

———. 1959. Language and evolution. In Meggers 1959, 61–75. Also, Bobbs-Merrill Reprint A–95.

———. 1961. Some universals of grammar with particular reference to the order of meaningful elements. In Greenberg 1966.

——— (ed.). 1966. Universals of language (2nd ed.). Cambridge, Mass.: M.I.T. Press.

———. 1968. Anthropological linguistics: an introduction. New York: Random House (paperback).

Gudschinsky, Sarah C. 1956. The ABC's of lexicostatistics (glottochronology). Word 12.175–210. Reprinted in Hymes 1964, 612–622. Also, Bobbs-Merrill Reprint A-97.

———. 1967. How to learn an unwritten language. New York: Holt, Rinehart & Winston.

Gumperz. John J. 1958. Dialect differences and social stratification in a North Indian village. American Anthropologist 60.668–682. Also, Bobbs-Merrill Reprint A-98.

———. 1962. Types of linguistic communities. Anthropological Linguistics 4.28–36

———. 1964. Hindi-Punjabi code-switching in Delhi. In Lunt 1964.

———, **and Dell Hymes** (eds.). 1964. The ethnography of communication. American Anthropologist 66 (Part II, No. 6).

———, and ——— (eds.). 1972. Directions in sociolinguistics: the ethnography of communication. New York: Holt, Rinehart & Winston.

Haaᵣ Mary R. 1964. Thai–English Student's Dictionary. Stanford, Cal.: Stanford University Press.

Hall, Edward T. 1955. The anthropology of manners. Scientific American 192.85–89.

———. 1959. The silent language. New York: Doubleday. Fawcett World Library (paperback).

———. 1963. A system for the notation of proxemic behavior. American Anthropologist 65.1003–1026.

———. 1968. Proxemics. Current Anthropology 9.83–108.

Hall, Robert A., Jr. 1943. Melanesian Pidgin English: grammar, texts, vocabulary. Baltimore: Linguistic Society of America and Intensive Language Program of the ACLS.

———. 1950. The reconstruction of Proto-Romance. Language 26.6–27. Reprinted in Joos 1966.

———. 1951. American linguistics 1925–1950. Archivum Linguisticum 3.101–125.

———. 1966. Pidgin and creole languages. Ithaca, N.Y.: Cornell University Press.

Halle, Morris (ed.). 1956. For Roman Jakobson. The Hague: Mouton.

———. 1962. Phonology in generative grammar. Word 18.54–72. Reprinted in Fodor and Katz 1964.

Hamp, Eric P.; Fred W. Householder; and Robert Austerlitz. 1966. Readings in linguistics II. Chicago: University of Chicago Press.

Harris, Marvin. 1971. Culture, man and nature. New York: Crowell.

Harris, Zellig S. 1951. Methods in structural linguistics. Chicago: University of Chicago Press.

———. 1952. Discourse analysis. Language 28.18–23.

———. 1957. Co-occurrence and transformation in linguistic structure. Language 33.283–340. Reprinted in Fodor and Katz 1964. Also, Bobbs-Merrill Reprint Language-38.

Haugen, Einar Ingvald. 1951. Directions in modern linguistics. Language 27.211–222. Also, Bobbs-Merrill Reprint Language-42.

———. 1956. Bilingualism in the Americas: a bibliography and research guide. Alabama: University of Alabama Press.

Hayakawa, S. I. 1952. Semantics. Etc.: a Review of General Semantics 9.243–257. Also, Bobbs-Merrill Reprint Language-43.

———. 1972. Language in thought and action (rev. ed.). New York: Harcourt Brace Jovanovich.

Hefner, Roe-Merrill Secrist. 1949. General phonetics. Madison, Wisc.: University of Wisconsin Press.

Herman, Simon. 1961. Explorations in the social psychology of language choice. Human Relations 14.149–164. Reprinted in Fishman 1968, 492–511.

Herzog, George. 1945. Drum-signaling in a West African tribe. Word 1.217–238. Reprinted in Hymes 1964, 312–323.

Hill, L. A., and J. M. Ure. 1962. English sounds and spellings. London: Oxford University Press.

Hockett, Charles F. 1955. A manual of phonology. Indiana University Publications in Anthropology and Linguistics. Bloomington, Ind.: Department of Anthropology, Indiana University.

———. 1958. A course in modern linguistics. New York: Macmillan.

———. 1960. The origin of speech. Scientific American, September. 3–10.

———, **and Robert Ascher.** 1964. The human revolution. Current Anthropology 5.135–168. Also, Bobbs-Merrill Reprint A-306.

Hoenigswald, Henry M. 1950. The principal step in comparative grammar. Language 26.357–364. Reprinted in Joos 1966, 298–302. Also, Bobbs-Merrill Reprint Language-49.

———. 1960. Language change and linguistic reconstruction. Chicago: University of Chicago Press.

Hogan, Helen Marie. 1971. An ethnography of communication among the Ashanti. Penn-Texas Working Papers in Sociolinguistics (Working Paper No. 1).

Hoijer, Harry (ed.). 1954. Language in culture. (Comparative Studies of Cultures and Civilizations, No. 3; Memoirs of the American Anthropological Association, No. 79.) Chicago: University of Chicago Press.

Householder, Fred W., and Sol Saporta (eds.). 1962. Problems in lexicography. International Journal of American Linguistics 28 (2), Part IV. Bloomington, Ind: Indiana University Research Center in Anthropology, Folklore and Linguistics (Publication 21).

Hymes, Dell (ed.). 1964. Language in culture and society: a reader in linguistics and anthropology. New York: Harper & Row.

———. (see also Gumperz, John J.)

Jacobs, Roderick, and Peter S. Rosenbaum. 1968. Readings in English transformational grammar. Waltham, Mass.: Ginn.

———, **and** ———. 1971. Transformations, style and meaning. Waltham, Mass.: Xerox College Publishing.

Jakobson, Roman; C. Gunnar M. Fant; and Morris Halle. 1952. Preliminaries to speech analysis: the distinctive features and their correlates. Acoustic Laboratory, Massachusetts Institute of Technology, Technical Report 13. Cambridge, Mass.: M.I.T.

Jespersen, Otto. 1956. Growth and structure of the English language (9th ed.). New York: Doubleday. (paperback)

———. 1964. Essentials of English grammar (reprint). Alabama: University of Alabama Press.

Johnson, Wendell. 1946. People in quandaries: the semantics of personal adjustment. New York: Harper and Brothers.

Jones, Daniel. 1956. An outline of English phonetics (8th ed.). Cambridge: Heffer.

Joos, Martin A. 1948. Acoustic phonetics. Baltimore: Waverly Press.

———. 1964. The English verb: form and meanings. Madison, Wisc.: University of Wisconsin Press.

——— (ed.) 1966. Readings in linguistics I (4th ed.). Chicago: University of Chicago Press.

Katz, Jerrold J., and Jerry A. Fodor. 1963. The structure of a semantic theory. Language 39.170–210. Reprinted in Fodor and Katz 1964.

King, Robert D. 1969. Historical linguistics and generative grammar. Englewood Cliffs, N.J.: Prentice-Hall.

Korzybski, Alfred. 1933. Science and sanity: an introduction to non-Aristotelian systems and general semantics. Lancaster, Penn.: Science Press.

Koutsoudas, Andreas. 1966. Writing transformational grammars. New York: McGraw-Hill.

Kruisinga, E. 1925. A handbook of present day English. Utrecht.

Kurath, Hans. 1949. A word geography of the Eastern United States. Ann Arbor, Mich.: University of Michigan Press.

———, and Raven I. McDavid, Jr. 1961. The pronunciation of English in the Atlantic States. Ann Arbor: University of Michigan Press.

LaBarre, Weston. 1947. The cultural basis of emotions and gestures. Journal of Personality 1947.49–68. Also, Bobbs-Merrill Reprint S-157.

Labov, William. 1964. Phonological correlates of social stratification. In Gumperz and Hymes 1964.

———. 1966. The social stratification of English in New York City. Washington, D.C.: Center for Applied Linguistics.

———. 1969a. The logic of non-standard English. Washington, D.C.: Georgetown University School of Languages and Linguistics.

———. 1969b Contraction, deletion and inherent variability of the English copula. Language 45. 715–762.

———. 1970. The study of language in its social context. Studium Generale 23.30–87.

———. 1972. Negative attraction and negative concord in English grammar. Language 48.

Ladefoged, Peter. 1962. Elements of acoustic phonetics. Chicago: University of Chicago Press.

———. 1967. Three areas of experimental phonetics. London: Oxford University Press.

Lamb, Sydney M. 1964. The sememic approach to structural semantics. American Anthropologist 66 (No. 3, Part II). 57–78.

———. 1966. Outline of stratificational grammar. Washington, D.C.: Georgetown University Press.

Lawton, David. 1968. Social class, language and education. London: Routledge & Kegan Paul.

Lee, Dorothy. 1950. Lineal and nonlineal codifications of reality. Psychosomatic Medicine 1950. 89–97. Also, Bobbs-Merrill Reprint S-165.

Lee, Irving J. 1941. Language habits in human affairs: an introduction to general semantics. New York: Harper & Brothers.

————. 1949. The language of wisdom and folly. New York: Harper & Brothers.

Leonard, Sterling Andrus. 1929. The doctrine of correctness in English usage 1700–1800. Madison, Wisc.: University of Wisconsin Press.

Lieberson, Stanley (ed.) 1967. Explorations in sociolinguistics. The Hague: Mouton.

Lounsbury, Floyd G. 1956. A semantic analysis of the Pawnee kinship usage. Language 32.158–194.

————. 1964. The structural analysis of kinship semantics. In Lunt 1964.

Lunt, Horace G. (ed.). 1964. Proceedings of the Ninth International Congress of Linguists. The Hague: Mouton.

Lyons, John. 1963. Structural semantics. Oxford: Basil Blackwell.

————. 1968. Introduction to theoretical linguistics. Cambridge: Cambridge University Press.

Malmberg, Bertil. 1963. Phonetics. New York: Dover Publications.

Mandelbaum, David G. (ed.). 1949. Selected writings of Edward Sapir in language, culture and personality. Berkeley and Los Angeles: University of California Press.

Martinet, Andre. 1955. Economie des changements phonétiques: traité de phonologie diachronique. Bern: Francke.

Maurer, David W. 1940. The con man and his lingo. In David W. Maurer, The big con. Ch. 9, 269–296. Indianapolis: Bobbs-Merrill. Also, Bobbs-Merrill Reprint Language-66.

McIntosh, Angus. 1952. An introduction to a survey of Scottish dialects. Edinburgh: Thomas Nelson.

Meggers, Betty (ed.). 1959. Evolution and anthropology: a centennial appraisal. Washington, D.C.: Anthropological Society of Washington.

Meillet, Antoine. 1937. Introduction à l'étude comparative des langues Indo-Européennes (8th ed.). Paris: Librairie Hachette.

————, **and Marcel Cohen.** 1952. Les langues du monde (rev. ed.). Paris: Centre National de la Recherche Scientifique.

Mitchell-Kiernan, Claudia. 1972. Signifying and marking: two Afro-American speech acts. In Gumperz and Hymes 1972.

Monaco, Joan L., and Elinor L. Zaslow. 1972. Hey, I got sump'n to tell you, an' it cool!: a class for children with severe language disabilities. Rockville, Md.: Montgomery County Public Schools.

Nida, Eugene A. 1945. Linguistics and ethnology in translation problems. Word 1.194–208. Reprinted in Hymes 1964, 90–97.

————. 1949. Morphology, the descriptive analysis of words (2nd ed.). Ann Arbor: University of Michigan Press.

————. 1964. Toward a science of translating. Leiden: E. J. Brill.

———, and Charles R. Taber. 1969. The theory and practice of translation. Leiden: E. J. Brill.

Niedermann, Max. 1953. Précis de phonétique historique du latin. Paris: Librairie C. Klincksieck.

Ogden, C. K., and I. A. Richards. 1930. The meaning of meaning (rev. ed.). New York: Harcourt, Brace & World.

Osgood, Charles E.; George J. Suci; and Percy H. Tannenbaum. 1957. The measurement of meaning. Urbana: University of Illinois Press.

Pickett, Velma Bernice. 1960. The grammatical hierarchy of Isthmus Zapotec. Baltimore: Linguistic Society of America.

Pike, Kenneth Lee. 1943. Phonetics: a critical analysis of phonetic theory and a technic for the practical description of sounds. Ann Arbor: University of Michigan Press.

———. 1945. The intonation of American English. Ann Arbor: University of Michigan Press.

———. 1947. Phonemics: a technique for reducing languages to writing. Ann Arbor: University of Michigan Press.

Pittenger, Robert E.; Charles F. Hockett; and John J. Danehy. 1960. The first five minutes. Ithaca: Paul Martineau.

Pyles, Thomas. 1964. The origins and development of the English language. New York: Harcourt, Brace & World. (See Algeo 1972)

Ramanujan, A. K. 1968. The structure of variation: a study in caste dialects. In Singer and Cohn 1968.

Róheim, Géza (ed.). 1951. Psychoanalysis and the social sciences. New York: International Universities Press.

Romney, A. Kimball, and Roy Goodwin D'Andrade (eds.). 1964a. Transcultural studies in cognition. American Anthropologist 66 (No. 3, Part II).

———, and ———. 1964b. Cognitive aspects of English kin terms. In Romney and D'Andrade 1964a, 146–170.

Rubin, Joan. 1968. Bilingual usage in Paraguay. In Fishman 1968, 512–530.

———, and Björn H. Jernudd (eds.). 1971. Can language be planned? Honolulu: University Press of Hawaii.

Ruesch, Jurgen, and Weldon Kees. 1956. Nonverbal communication: notes on the visual perception of human relations. Berkeley and Los Angeles: University of California Press.

Samarin, William J. 1967. Field linguistics: a guide to linguistic field work. New York: Holt, Rinehart & Winston.

Sapir, Edward. 1921. Language: an introduction to the study of speech. New York: Harcourt, Brace. (Harvest paperback)

Saporta, Sol. 1955. Frequency of consonant clusters. Language 31.25–30.

——— (ed.). 1961. Psycholinguistics. New York: Holt, Rinehart & Winston.

Sebeok, Thomas A. (ed.). 1960. Style in language. New York: Wiley; Cambridge, Mass.: Technology Press.

Sebeok, Thomas A. (ed.). 1964. Approaches to semiotics: cultural anthropology, education, linguistics, psychiatry, psychology. The Hague: Mouton.

Shannon, Gloria. 1968 (February). Bulljive—language teaching in a Harlem school. Urban Review, pp. 5–12.

Singer, Milton, and Bernard S. Cohn (eds.). 1968. Structure and change in Indian society. New York: Wenner-Gren Foundation for Anthropological Research.

Southworth, F. C. 1971. The student's Hindi-Urdu reference manual. Tucson, Ariz.: University of Arizona Press.

Stern, Gustav. 1931. Meaning and change of meaning. Bloomington, Ind.: Indiana University Press.

Stern, Theodore. 1957. Drum and whistle 'languages': an analysis of speech surrogates. American Anthropologist 59.487–506. Also, Bobbs-Merrill Reprint A-215.

Stilman, Galina; Leon Stilman; and William E. Harkins. 1972. Introductory Russian grammar (2nd ed.). Lexington, Mass.: Xerox College Publishing.

Stockwell, Robert P., and J. Donald Bowen. 1965. The sounds of English and Spanish. Contrastive Structure Series. Chicago: University of Chicago Press.

———; ———; **and John W. Martin.** 1965. The grammatical structures of English and Spanish. Contrastive Structure Series. Chicago: University of Chicago Press.

Strang, Barbara M. H. 1970. A history of English. London: Methuen.

Swadesh, Morris. 1959. Linguistics as an instrument of prehistory. Southwestern Journal of Anthropology 15.20–35. Reprinted in Hymes 1964, 575–583. Also, Bobbs-Merrill Reprint A-221.

Trager, Edith Crowell. 1957. The systematics of English spelling. College Composition and Communication 8 (1).26–32. Also, Bobbs-Merrill Reprint Language-89.

Trager, George L. 1958. Paralanguage: a first approximation. Studies in Linguistics 13. 1–12. Reprinted in Hymes 1964, 274–279.

———, **and Henry Lee Smith, Jr.** 1951. An outline of English structure. Baltimore: Waverly Press.

Trudgill, Peter. 1972. Sex, covert prestige and linguistic change in the urban British English of Norwich. Language in Society 1.179–195.

Ullmann, Stephen. 1962. Semantics: an introduction to the science of meaning. Oxford: Blackwell.

Wallace, Anthony F. C., and John Atkins. 1960. The meaning of kinship terms. American Anthropologist 62.58–80. Also, Bobbs-Merrill Reprint A-231.

Weinreich, Uriel. 1953. Languages in contact: findings and problems. New York: Linguistic Circle of New York.

———. 1963. On the semantic structure of language. In Greenberg 1963, 114–171.

———; **William Labov; and Marvin I. Herzog.** 1968. Empirical foundations for a theory of language change. In Directions for Historical Linguistics: A Symposium. Austin, Texas: University of Texas Press.

Wells, Rulon S. 1947*a*. De Saussure's system of linguistics. Word 3.1–31. Also, Bobbs-Merrill Reprint Language-94.

———. 1947*b*. Immediate constituents. Language 23.81–117. Also, Bobbs-Merrill Reprint Language-95.

Whorf, Benjamin Lee. 1938. Some verbal categories of Hopi. Language 14.275–286. Also, Bobbs-Merrill Reprint Language-99.

———. 1945. Grammatical categories. Language 21.1–11. Also, Bobbs-Merrill Reprint Language-98.

———. 1957. Science and linguistics. In Carroll 1957.207–219. Also, Bobbs-Merrill Reprint A-234.

Wolf, Eric. 1959. Sons of the shaking earth. Chicago: University of Chicago Press.

Ziervogel, D. 1952. A grammar of Swazi (siSwati). Johannesburg: Witwatersrand University Press.

Zipf, George K. 1965. The psycho-biology of language: an introduction to dynamic philology. Cambridge, Mass.: M.I.T. Press.

A NOTE ABOUT THE INDEX

The index includes all the technical linguistic terms that appear in SMALL CAPITALS in the text. Where the definition or explanation of the term is not contained on the page or pages given as the first reference, the page number of the main discussion of the term is given in **boldface type.** The authors cited are those discussed in the text, not those mentioned in references.

Index